P9-CMN-625

TEACHER PREP

MERRILL
PRENTICE HALL

Teacher Preparation Classroom

See a demo at
www.prenhall.com/teacherprep/demo

Your Class. Their Careers. Our Future. Will your students be prepared?

We invite you to explore our new, innovative and engaging website and all that it has to offer you, your course, and tomorrow's educators! Preview this site today at www.prenhall.com/teacherprep/demo. Just click on "go" on the login page to begin your exploration.

Organized around the major courses pre-service teachers take, the Teacher Preparation site provides media, student/teacher artifacts, strategies, research articles, and other resources to equip your students with the quality tools needed to excel in their courses and prepare them for their first classroom.

This ultimate online education resource will provide you and your students access to:

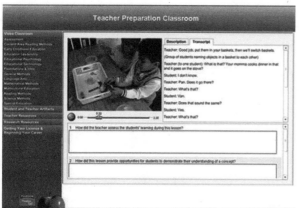

Online Video Library. More than 250 video clips—each tied to a course topic and framed by learning goals and Praxis-type questions—capture real teachers and students working in real classrooms.

Student and Teacher Artifacts. More than 200 student and teacher classroom artifacts—each tied to a course topic and framed by learning goals and application questions—provide a wealth of materials and experiences to help your students observe children's developmental learning.

Lesson Plan Builder. Step-by-step guidelines and lesson plan examples support students as they learn to build high-quality lesson plans.

Articles and Readings. Over 500 articles from ASCD's renowned journal *Educational Leadership*. The site also includes Research Navigator, a searchable database of additional educational journals.

Strategies and Lessons. Over 500 research-supported instructional strategies appropriate for a wide range of grade levels and content areas.

Licensure and Career Tools. Resources devoted to helping your students pass their licensure exam; learn standards, law, and public policies; plan a teaching portfolio; and succeed in their first year of teaching.

How to ORDER *Teacher Prep* for you and your students:

For students to receive a *Teacher Prep* Access Code with this text, instructors **must** provide a special value pack ISBN number on their textbook order form. To receive this special ISBN, please email **Merrill.marketing@pearsoned.com** and provide the following information:
- Name and Affiliation
- Author/Title/Edition of Merrill text

Upon ordering *Teacher Prep* for their students, instructors will be given a lifetime *Teacher Prep* Access Code.

FECTIVE TEACHING IN   1
ISBN:0131738437   5
PO#:10044   1
                             0
                             1

Effective Teaching in Elementary Social Studies

Sixth Edition

Tom V. Savage
Santa Clara University

David G. Armstrong
Late of University of North Carolina, Greensboro

PEARSON
Merrill
Prentice Hall

Upper Saddle River, New Jersey
Columbus, Ohio

Library of Congress Cataloging-in-Publication Data

Savage, Tom V.
  Effective teaching in elementary social studies / Tom V. Savage, David G. Armstrong. —6th ed.
     p. cm.
  Includes bibliographical references and index.
  ISBN 0-13-173843-7 (pbk.)
  1. Social sciences—Study and teaching (Elementary)—United States.   1. Armstrong, David G. II. Title
  LB1584.S34 2008
372.83—dc22

2006039001

Vice President and Executive Publisher: Jeffery W. Johnston
Acquisitions Editor: Meredith D. Fossel
Editorial Assistant: Kathleen S. Burk
Production Editor: Alexandrina Benedicto Wolf
Production Coordination: Thistle Hill Publishing Services, LLC
Design Coordinator: Diane Lorenzo
Photo Coordinator: Lori Whitley
Cover Designer: Aaron Dixon
Cover Image: Corbis
Production Manager: Pamela D. Bennett
Director of Marketing: David Gesell
Marketing Manager: Darcy Betts Prybella
Marketing Coordinator: Brian Mounts

This book was set in Garamond by Carlisle Publishing Services. It was printed and bound by R. R. Donnelley & Sons Company. The cover was printed by R. R. Donnelley & Sons Company.

Copyright © 2008, 2004, 2000, 1996, 1992, 1987 by Pearson Education, Inc., Upper Saddle River, New Jersey 07458.
Pearson Prentice Hall. All rights reserved. Printed in the United States of America. This publication is protected by Copyright and permission should be obtained from the publisher prior to any prohibited reproduction, storage in a retrieval system, or transmission in any form or by any means, electronic, mechanical, photocopying, recording, or likewise. For information regarding permission(s), write to Rights and Permission Department.

Pearson Prentice Hall™ is a trademark of Pearson Education, Inc.
Pearson® is a registered trademark of Pearson plc
Prentice Hall® is a registered trademark of Pearson Education, Inc.
Merrill® is a registered trademark of Pearson Education, Inc.

Pearson Education Ltd.
Pearson Education Singapore, Pte. Ltd.
Pearson Education Canada, Ltd.
Pearson Education–Japan

Pearson Education Australia Pty., Limited
Pearson Education North Asia Ltd.
Pearson Educación de Mexico, S.A. de C.V.
Pearson Education Malaysia, Pte. Ltd.

10 9 8 7 6 5 4 3 2 1
ISBN-13: 978-0-13-173843-0
ISBN-10:   0-13-173843-7

Preface

The challenges to our roles as thoughtful, committed citizens seem to become more difficult with each passing year. New technology has the potential for evil as well as for good. The population seems to be increasingly polarized and progress in solving complex social problems seems painstakingly slow. As a nation, we seem to be more and more isolated in the international community. Reports of atrocities committed under our nation's name call into question some of the values that we consider basic.

In the midst of these challenges, however, we find less and less educational time being devoted to the social studies. Priority has been placed on teaching those subjects that are generally evaluated by high-stakes standardized tests. Therefore, at the very time that more emphasis should be placed on learning our roles as citizens and in seeking solutions to complex political and social problems, students are leaving school with less guidance and less information.

Young people must prepare to be sophisticated, creative, and critical thinking adults who can cope with a changing and challenging world. A sound social studies program has an important role to play in preparing students for the future. Social studies must be more than just the recitation of facts about the past. It must be grounded in reality and focused on helping individuals become active and involved.

It is for these purposes that we have prepared the sixth edition of *Effective Teaching in Elementary Social Studies*. Elementary teachers need to realize that waiting until secondary school to address critical issues is too late. However, we realize that the elementary teacher's role is a complex one. The typical elementary teacher must deal with a number of content areas. Many may not have the background to meet the complex challenges of teaching social studies. Therefore, in this edition we provide an overview of the various social sciences, define a variety of specific teaching methods, provide information relating to the diversity of students in contemporary classrooms, suggest ways of integrating the social studies with other subjects, and provide some concrete methods of assessing student learning.

Users of *Effective Teaching in Elementary Social Studies* have found the text practical, readable, and user friendly. The sixth edition continues this tradition and we hope this valuable tool will help you succeed in teaching this fascinating subject.

Dr. David Armstrong was intensely dedicated to the importance of social studies and made numerous contributions to the field over a career that spanned more than 30 years. For the first time, he was not involved in revising this edition. However, his ideas and his enthusiasm for teaching the social studies continue in this edition. Thank you, David. You are missed.

NEW TO THIS EDITION

This edition has been completely revised. We discuss the importance of teaching to standards in the first chapter. Chapters 2 through 4 focus on the content of the disciplines and we address a few basic questions: What is the nature of each discipline? What are some key concepts and main ideas from each discipline that are useful for elementary and middle school teachers in planning for instruction? What are some examples of classroom applications? Chapter 5 focuses on teaching approaches for knowledge acquisition; Chapter 6 focuses on teaching approaches for knowledge discovery. Several new approaches have been added to each chapter, and we discuss each approach by identifying the instructional sequence for each model. A new section on social skills has been added to Chapter 7. Chapter 10 has been revised with more specific references to backward planning. Chapter 12 has been totally revised to make it more usable to teachers as they determine what students have learned and how to evaluate progress and award grades.

This edition also includes nearly 40 specific Lesson Ideas and Classroom Activities. Some are new to this edition and some are carried over from the fifth edition. The Lesson Ideas also contain references to websites wherein readers can find valuable resources to make their social studies work more interesting and exciting. Numerous suggestions for other lessons also appear throughout the text.

TEXT FEATURES

Each chapter includes the following:

- Chapter Objectives help focus attention on what should be learned as a result of reading the chapter.
- A Graphic Organizer illustrates the relationship between items in the chapter and serves as an advance organizer for the reader.
- Figures help illustrate relationships and extend understanding.
- A summary of Key Ideas help readers review the key elements of the chapter.
- Chapter Reflections prompt readers to extend and deepen their understanding of the content of the chapters.

ORGANIZATION

There is no perfect way of organizing a text's content. Individuals who teach usually have their own preferred way of sequencing the content to suit their lessons. Therefore, we have organized this edition for flexible use. The information in each chapter can be used independently of the content in other chapters.

ACKNOWLEDGMENTS

No work is an independent project. A number of individuals have contributed to the development of this edition. Special thanks go to the credential students at Santa Clara University who have provided insight and critiques of the content. Thanks also go to experienced teachers and social studies educators who have been willing to share ideas and insights. Special thanks go to my wife, Dr. Marsha Savage, who has made numerous suggestions on the use of children's literature and on content reading approaches. Her encouragement and patience are greatly appreciated. I also wish to thank freelance copyeditor Robert L. Marcum for his valuable help with the text. Finally, I would like to thank those who reviewed the previous edition and made useful suggestions to this edition. They are Margaret S. Carter, James Madison University; Paul C. Egeland, Wheaton College; and Thomas B. Goodkind, University of Connecticut.

Brief Contents

Contents

Note: Every effort has been made to provide accurate and current Internet information in this book. However, the Internet and information on it are constantly changing, so it is inevitable that some of the Internet addresses listed in this textbook will change.

Lesson Ideas

Effective Teaching in Elementary Social Studies

ONE

Defining the Social Studies

James P. Blair/Getty Images, Inc. —Photodisc

This chapter will help you to:

- Identify contemporary challenges to the social studies.
- Define *the social studies*.
- Explain the thematic strands that run through the social studies curriculum.
- Define the emphases of (1) *citizenship education,* (2) *global-awareness education,* (3) *history and social science education,* and (4) *reflective thinking and problem-solving education.*

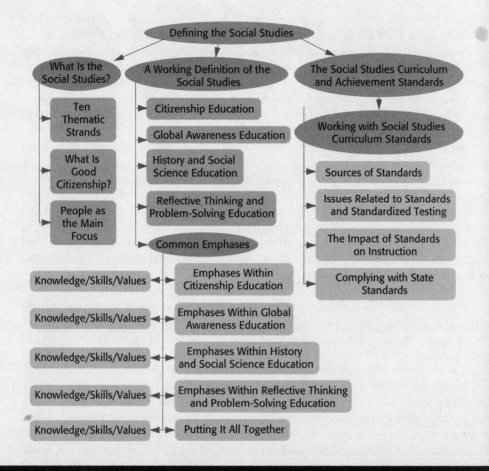

Defining the Social Studies

What Is the Social Studies?
- Ten Thematic Strands
- What Is Good Citizenship?
- People as the Main Focus

A Working Definition of the Social Studies
- Citizenship Education
- Global Awareness Education
- History and Social Science Education
- Reflective Thinking and Problem-Solving Education
- Common Emphases

Knowledge/Skills/Values ↔ Emphases Within Citizenship Education

Knowledge/Skills/Values ↔ Emphases Within Global Awareness Education

Knowledge/Skills/Values ↔ Emphases Within History and Social Science Education

Knowledge/Skills/Values ↔ Emphases Within Reflective Thinking and Problem-Solving Education

Knowledge/Skills/Values ↔ Putting It All Together

The Social Studies Curriculum and Achievement Standards

Working with Social Studies Curriculum Standards
- Sources of Standards
- Issues Related to Standards and Standardized Testing
- The Impact of Standards on Instruction
- Complying with State Standards

- Describe *knowledge*, *skills*, and *values* and explain how they should be included in comprehensive social studies programs.
- State the differences between national and state achievement standards.
- List the positive and negative arguments regarding standards.
- Identify the impact of standards on teaching.

What is the social studies and why should it be taught in elementary and middle schools? Many individuals preparing to teach have a limited understanding of the purposes and the nature of social studies, in part because its curriculum has not been a priority in educational reform movements. The result is that there has been little debate regarding the social studies, and many new teachers enter the field with little more than their recollections of the subject as they encountered it as students.

However, unless you understand why you are teaching a subject and what should be included, you will have difficulty preparing lessons that students find meaningful and motivating. In turn, this will influence your interest and motivation for teaching.

It is our conviction and experience that when the purposes and the nature of social studies are understood, preparing and teaching social studies lessons to elementary and middle school learners can be one of the most interesting parts of the school day. There are numerous opportunities for you to engage your creative and thinking powers and to confront thought-provoking and meaningful issues and questions. When properly conceived, social studies lessons relate to real-life concerns and can easily be extended beyond the four walls of the classroom. Thus, social studies is not just an abstract academic subject, it is focused on life.

You need only to look as far as the headlines of your local newspaper to see that most of the critical issues faced by individuals in the contemporary world are social issues. Social issues are the ones that divide us, that cause us anxiety and call into question some of our most cherished values and beliefs. Complex social issues such as quality of life, war, poverty, prejudice, and social justice raise many difficult questions for which there are few clear answers. As we look at an increasingly divided country where consensus and compromise seems to have been forgotten, we realize that these issues cannot be adequately addressed merely through the application of science and technology. This is why the social studies is important. This is not to say that teaching social studies will cure all social issues. However, it is unlikely that improvements will occur if students do not have an opportunity to study and understand the issues that confront them. Yes, it is important for students to learn basic skills such as reading and mathematics. However, merely learning these skills will not provide individuals with the concepts and understandings they need to apply them to the serious issues we face as citizens.

We certainly agree that much of what has been called *social studies* in the schools has not addressed these big issues. Much of what has been taught under this title has been dull, boring, and of questionable significance. We believe that much of this is related to teacher uncertainty regarding the purposes of social studies and a lack of reflection regarding the relevance of existing social studies programs.

We are convinced that the levels of disinterest some students initially display toward their social studies lessons have little to do with the subject matter itself. Indeed, the focus of social studies should be on people's thoughts, aspirations, hopes, fears, actions, and consequences. What is more interesting than learning about people? The content has tremendous potential for motivating learners. Our purpose in this text is to help you understand the social studies and to develop some exciting approaches to teaching that can help you connect with your students in ways that will be exciting and meaningful for both you and them. We hope that ultimately, you will find social studies to be one of your favorite teaching responsibilities.

FIGURE 1-1 • What Is Your Experience with Social Studies?

Research indicates that teachers allocate more time to those subjects that interest them and that they feel comfortable teaching. As you think about your responsibilities as a teacher, you need to consider your background feelings about every subject you will teach.

Think About These Questions:
1. What do you remember about social studies from your days as a student?
2. What methods were generally used? What methods did you enjoy the most? Which ones did you enjoy the least?
3. What were your experiences in history and the social sciences in college? Did you find the classes engaging or boring? Did you find them meaningful or irrelevant?
4. How have these previous experiences shaped your attitude toward the social studies?
5. If you have negative attitudes toward the social studies, how can you avoid allowing them to influence your professional obligations as a teacher to teach social studies?
6. What could you do to alter any negative attitudes about teaching social studies?

As you continue to work with this text, we invite you to engage in critical reflection regarding the purposes, the curriculum, and the instructional methods of social studies in the elementary and middle schools. As you begin considering these issues, reflect on your own answers to the questions posed in Figure 1-1. This kind of thinking will prompt your continued professional growth.

Teachers in the twenty-first century will be confronting significant challenges that have the potential for changing education as we know it, for good or for ill. Many of these challenges relate to the social studies. A clear understanding of the nature and purposes of the social studies is needed if we are to resolve these challenges in ways conducive to the intellectual growth of future citizens.

What are some of the challenges relating to the social studies that you should be prepared to debate? Although the specific issues vary somewhat from place to place, several are common to most teachers, including the following:

- Pressure to confine social studies content to topics that will be assessed on tests tied to state curriculum standards (Risinger, 2002)
- Perceptions that social studies content is less worthy than that included in other parts of the curriculum
- Occasionally unhappy parents and guardians who say they want you to teach their children to think and question but then complain when their sons and daughters do question and challenge conventional wisdom

- Community standards that support a don't-rock-the-boat orientation while students are constantly confronting controversial issues (Cornbleth, 2002)
- A popular culture that helps shape student attitudes that you may find uninteresting, distasteful, or downright repugnant (Passe, 2002). (You may need to learn something about WWF wrestling, events depicted in television soap operas, and MTV if these offerings affect student attitudes and interests and, hence, provide you an entrée to engage learners in content you think is more important.)

WHAT IS THE SOCIAL STUDIES?

The *social studies* is broadly defined as those parts of the curriculum derived from history and the social science disciplines of geography, economics, political science, sociology, and anthropology. The social studies, in spite of its long history, is still the center of much debate. Understanding a bit of this history can place contemporary debates in perspective.

The term *social studies* was first used in a report in 1916 by the Committee on the Social Studies (U.S. Bureau of Education, 1916). Formerly the Committee on the Social Sciences, this committee consisted of 21 members who represented history, education, and some of the social science disciplines. This was an era when the purposes of education were changing from the education of the few to the education of everyone, from preparation for those who were college bound to the essentials for everyone regardless of their station in life. Compulsory attendance laws were passed that now meant that schools included students from all families, not just the privileged few.

It is clear that the intent of this committee was to make the social studies practical and appealing to all students. The 1916 report presented the social studies as subject matter directly related to the goal of "socially efficient" individuals. This meant that these students would be individuals who were committed to fundamental American values and who would make real contributions to the technical and social development of the nation (National Education Association, 1911). In other words, the broad goal of the social studies was the preparation of students for citizenship. Citizenship continues to be a major emphasis of the social studies.

This definition of the social studies was expanded in later publications. In 1934, Charles Beard, in *A Charter for the Social Studies,* indicated that the development of personal competencies rather than the inculcation of dogma or specialized knowledge should be the major goal of social studies. He stated that this should be accomplished by helping individuals understand, analyze, choose, resolve issues, and act wisely (Beard, 1934).

The social studies continues to reflect many of these earlier influences. However, not everyone agrees with these emphases. Recent proposals for reform have led to increased discussions regarding the purposes and the nature of the social studies. There are those who criticize the term *social studies* as too vague, contending that because of this imprecision, just about anything can fit the label. This, they claim, has resulted in a lack of rigor and accountability. These individuals would prefer to see the term *social studies* replaced with course-specific subject titles such as *history* and the *social sciences.*

On the other hand, supporters of the multidisciplinary approach of the social studies criticize the focus on specific subjects as an artificial fragmentation of knowledge. They assert that the goal of social studies should be to prepare individuals for informed citizenship, not just to be junior historians or social scientists. They advocate a focus on broader topics such as enduring social issues, introducing content from various subjects as needed.

The multidisciplinary approach is generally the dominant one in the elementary grades, with more of an emphasis on courses in the specific disciplines in the secondary schools. This is especially true in the early elementary grades where the curriculum topics tend to focus on home, school, community, and state or region. The fifth grade often indicates a transition, as the topic of study is usually U.S. history. However, a strong emphasis on geography and civics is also included, so it is still a multidisciplinary course.

The National Council for the Social Studies (NCSS) is the leading organization for social studies professionals. In *Expectations of Excellence: Curriculum Standards for Social Studies* (1994), the NCSS Task Force proposes the following definition for the social studies:

> Social Studies is the integrated study of the social sciences and humanities to promote civic competence. . . . The primary purpose of the social studies is to help young people develop the ability to make informed and reasoned decisions for the public good as citizens of a culturally diverse, democratic society in an independent world. (p. 3)

Ten Thematic Strands

Expectations of Excellence (1994) also identifies 10 thematic strands that ought to permeate the social studies curriculum. These strands reflect a multidisciplinary approach to the social studies, cut across history and the social sciences, and are useful in selecting content and as benchmarks against which social studies programs can be measured:

- *Culture*—This theme focuses on the fact that humans create culture as a way of making sense out of their social and physical worlds. The theme has a strong relationship to anthropology.
- *Time, Continuity, and Change*—This theme helps students understand that, although there is some continuity and the past does influence the present, change is inevitable.
- *People, Places, and Environments*—People live in diverse environments. The interaction between people and their environments creates a uniqueness of place. This primarily geographic theme relates to concepts such as location and spatial interaction.
- *Individual, Development, and Identity*—This theme focuses on the importance of individual development and the relationship of individuals to others that inhabit their social world. This theme helps individuals consider how their own identity was formed and how it influences their attitudes and beliefs. This theme is drawn from social psychology, sociology, and anthropology.

- *Individuals, Groups, and Institutions*—Humans are social beings that seek membership in groups. They create social institutions to help them meet needs. Institutions and groups strongly influence their norms, values, and behavioral expectations. This theme is related primarily to sociology.
- *Power, Authority, and Governance*—This theme is central to the development of civic competence. Who has power? How did they get it? How is it used? This theme is drawn primarily from political science and civics.
- *Production, Distribution, and Consumption*—As people deal with the problem of unlimited wants and scarce resources, they must decide what to produce, who gets it, and how. This theme is primarily related to economics.
- *Science, Technology, and Society*—Science and technology exert tremendous influence on culture and on social change. Understanding and predicting the future requires understanding the influence of science and technology. This interdisciplinary theme covers nearly all of the social science disciplines including history, geography, economics, sociology, and anthropology.
- *Global Connections*—Improvements in technology and transportation have increased the interconnectedness of the entire world. Events that happen in one part of the world influence all of us. Students need to understand that decisions made as citizens will have global consequences. This theme also crosses all disciplines.
- *Civic Ideals and Practices*—As stated earlier, this is one of the major responsibilities of the social studies. The purpose of this theme is to emphasize the need to develop civic competence. This theme has a direct relationship to political science, civics, and history.

What Is Good Citizenship?

Although there is general agreement that the social studies should focus on citizenship, there is much less agreement on what this implies. Martorella, Beal, and Bolick (2005) identify two different perspectives regarding the definition of citizenship.

One perspective is what might be termed the "transmission of cultural heritage." Individuals with this perspective define *citizenship* as the inculcation of certain shared values such as a commitment to democracy, respect for authority, and the acceptance of political responsibility. They contend that there is a common core of knowledge that all students should learn. They believe that if all students learn this core, it will be a glue of shared knowledge and values that will hold society together. Individuals holding this perspective generally favor more emphasis on topics such as American history. Multicultural topics are often opposed because they are viewed as detracting from the common core of knowledge and traditional values and thus as divisive.

Almost the opposite of the cultural transmission perspective is the "informed social criticism" perspective. Individuals who hold this perspective view citizenship as helping individuals examine and critique current and past traditions. Their belief is that the improvement of society depends on citizens who are willing to confront injustice and the tensions that accompany a pluralistic society. Emphasis is placed on human dignity and social justice. Advocates of this approach see the content of the

A major purpose of the social studies is to develop an understanding of our heritage and the rights and responsibilities of citizenship.

Irene Springer/PH College

social studies as focused on enduring social issues and investigation of some of those controversial areas that have traditionally been left out of the curriculum. It is not that they oppose a commitment to democracy and an acceptance of responsibility, but that they see these commitments as involving questioning and challenging rather than as simply accepting the status quo.

As might be expected, there is considerable tension between advocates of these two approaches. As a teacher, you will no doubt encounter individuals with both perspectives as you interact with parents, participate in textbook selection, and plan your lessons. You need to know how *you* interpret citizenship in order to defend your actions as a teacher.

People as the Major Focus

Throughout the various definitions of social studies and different philosophical approaches, there is one common focus: people. The social studies is concerned with the study of people both past and present in all their fascinating diversity. History and the social sciences all focus on people. The differences between the various social sciences are basically found in the way they approach this study. History looks at people across time, geography views people and their distribution across space, political science looks at how people have developed systems of governance, economics investigates how people deal with the problem of scarcity, sociology studies how people live in groups, and anthropology considers how people have developed culture. As you might expect, there is considerable overlap among the social sciences.

This focus on people is both a blessing and a curse for the social studies teacher. The blessing is that people are inherently interesting. We can relate to people who lived in the past and to their hopes, joys, and fears. We are also interested in the future. What does the future hold for us and our society? Thus, social studies holds the potential to be extremely relevant and personal.

The curse is that the study of people, and the enormous diversity of people in both the present and the past, involves an overwhelming amount of content. In fact, the content of the social studies can be almost limitless. This brings up important questions: Where do we start? How do we select what to teach? These questions have led to considerable controversy as different individuals have answered them differently.

The following questions can guide you in thinking about where to begin and what to include in your teaching:

- What is human about human beings?
- How do I understand those around me?
- How did we get this way?
- How is the world changing?
- What are the consequences of change?
- Who are we as individuals and as a nation?
- What are the basic values and beliefs that influence our perceptions and guide our decisions?
- What are my responsibilities to others and to the environment around me?
- What do I need to consider when making decisions that may influence the lives of other people?

You may address these broad questions in several ways. For example, you and your students can seek answers through the study of history and the social sciences or through the study of enduring human dilemmas. If you maintain a focus on people and on these important questions, you have excellent possibilities for making social studies an interesting and significant topic to your students.

A WORKING DEFINITION OF THE SOCIAL STUDIES

At this point you may be overwhelmed and confused. The social studies can be so broad and there are so many claims about what should be accomplished that you can easily lose focus and not know how to begin planning for teaching. You need a way of conceptualizing this vast topic in order to develop priorities for your planning and teaching.

As we have sorted through the various definitions of *social studies* we have found it helpful to organize the subject into four basic categories of goals and content: (1) citizenship education, (2) global-awareness education, (3) history and social science education, and (4) reflective thinking and problem-solving education. These categories emphasize promoting citizenship and developing global perspectives through the integration of social sciences and humanities, and encourage you to provide your learners with the tools they need to make reasoned and informed decisions. Note that this categorization does not limit subject matter content to the social sciences. Content drawn from any subject that (1) has a focus on the human experience and (2) will assist your students to become better-informed citizens and decision makers can reasonably appear in your lessons.

The following sections briefly describe each of the four categories to help you move toward an understanding of what you might include in your social studies program.

Citizenship Education

Throughout the history of social studies there has been widespread agreement that citizenship ought to be a major goal. However, as noted earlier, there are different interpretations of what it means to be a "good" citizen. What is involved in teaching *civic competence?* Is the purpose to promote stability through the values and behaviors of the traditional, dominant society? Is it the inculcation of patriotism? Is it unquestioned obedience to the laws of society? Is it acceptance of the status quo? Is it voting in elections? Is it active involvement in public affairs?

Although it can be argued that the entire school curriculum ought to focus on the preparation of the youth for citizenship, the social studies has some unique responsibilities. It is in the social studies where students should encounter those great documents that form the foundation of our nation. It is in the social studies where students should encounter the values and beliefs that shape our view of ourselves and the rest of the world.

Quigley (2003) notes that while subjects such as history, literature, and other subjects are useful in developing citizenship competences, they cannot replace specific attention to civics education. He contends that one of the reasons students are doing poorly on tests relating to citizenship understandings is the lack of systematic and sustained attention to civic education. The social studies should have a strong emphasis on the topic of citizenship and the challenges of living in a pluralistic society.

Although different perspectives exist about the purposes of citizenship education, three common threads run through most of the discussions. First, there is general agreement that young people need to be encouraged to commit to such core American values as democratic decision making (NCSS Task Force on Curriculum Standards for Social Studies, 1994). Second, it is widely acknowledged that citizenship education lessons should encourage students to not merely accept but to also critique actions (Leming, 1989). Third, it is expected that good citizenship education programs will produce young people who will leave school with a predisposition to become actively involved in public affairs.

Risinger (2003) cites research by the Pew Charitable Trust that indicates that young Americans have lost faith in the political system and do not believe it matters which political party is in charge. Not only has this led to a lower percentage of young people voting in national elections, it appears that they also have rejected the broader role of citizen. Risinger cites this as an indication that the schools are failing in meeting one of the central purposes of education, preparing students for the duties of citizenship. He wonders if this estrangement from governmental and civic participation is so pervasive that there is no way to reverse the trend. To address this serious concern, he indicates that attention must be devoted to the role of citizens, beginning in the primary grades.

Is it realistic to expect elementary school learners to deal with difficult public issues and problems? Some research suggests that the answer is "yes." Even quite young students are aware of important social problems (Berman & La Farge, 1993). Young people are much more attuned to "what is really going on" than you might suppose. You need to take advantage of this sensitivity, for example, by teaching lessons that help your students develop competence in areas related to cooperation, compromise, and conflict resolution. Students can learn to approach issues in ways that will make a difference (Berman & La Farge).

Global-Awareness Education

Aspects of your social studies program connected to global-awareness education seek to sensitize your students to perspectives of people in other cultures and other lands. This need, long appreciated by social studies educators, became startlingly clear to all Americans when terrorists struck the World Trade Center in New York City in September 2001. This seminal event dramatically underscored a need for individuals throughout the world to understand the perspectives and motives of people in cultures other than their own.

The "enGauge" project of the North Central Regional Educational Laboratory sees global awareness as one of the critical skills for the twenty-first century (North Central Regional Educational Laboratory, 2005). *Global awareness* is defined as the recognition and understanding of the interrelations among governments, organizations, sociocultural groups, private economic entities, and individuals across the world. Students who are globally aware are defined as having the following characteristics:

- Are knowledgeable about the connectedness of the nations of the world historically, politically, economically, technologically, socially, linguistically, and ecologically.
- Understand that these interconnections can have both positive benefits and negative consequences.
- Understand the role of the United States in international policies and international relations.
- Are able to recognize, analyze, and evaluate major trends in global relations and the interconnections of these trends with both their local and national communities.
- Understand how national cultural differences impact the interpretation of events at the global level.

- Understand the impact of ideology and culture on national decisions about access to and use of technology.
- Participate in the global society by staying current with international news and by participating in the democratic process. (North Central Regional Educational Laboratory, 2005, n.p.)

The increasing interdependence of the world's peoples and the accelerating rate of technological change together make a strong case for the importance of global-awareness education. Educators throughout the world recognize this set of conditions. The United Nations' Children's Fund (UNICEF) has recognized this reality and has supported projects designed to provide guidelines that teachers worldwide can use to include more global-awareness programs in their classroom teaching (Selby et al., 2000).

Global-awareness instruction also provides you with opportunities to take advantage of the diversity you have in your own classroom. Given present demographic trends, it is quite probable you will have some students in your class who were born outside of the United States or whose parents were born outside of the United States. Today more than 10 percent of the total U.S. population is foreign born. This figure represents an increase from 7.9 percent in 1990, and present trends suggest these increases will continue for the foreseeable future. In some metropolitan areas, more than 40 percent of the total population consists of people born outside of the United States (Schmidley, 2001). In short, many learners have direct, personal ties to other countries and other cultures, and these connections can result in high levels of student motivation when your lessons pay positive attention to people and cultures with roots in other lands.

History and Social Science Education

To become effective citizens, your students need a solid knowledge base. Studying social problems and enduring social issues cannot be done productively in a vacuum. History and the social sciences (and other subjects that sometimes provide social studies content) have developed successful methods of investigation about humans and accumulated much information. This content has great potential for enriching lives and improving rational decision making. Applying ideas and concepts drawn from these disciplines can help students understand the variables involved when considering social problems and can suggest alternative solutions.

The academic content of the social studies program is not limited to history and the social sciences. Any subject that deals with human behavior can provide you with good content for your social studies lessons. When you look for lesson content, your purpose should be to find information that can help members of your class better understand their world. You do not want to select content because it is associated with a particular academic subject, such as history or geography, but rather because it may have potential to help your learners learn significant things about the world "as it is" and "as it might be."

The study of social studies brings students into contact with the great accomplishments of human civilization.

UN/DPI Photo

Reflective Thinking and Problem-Solving Education

Citizens in democratic societies need to be good thinkers. When your pupils mature, they will be called on to respond to pressing problems of all kinds. Decisions they make will influence their own lives and those of others in the community, state, and nation. Hence, you should regard development of learners' reflective thinking and problem-solving abilities as among the key purposes of your social studies program. Lessons associated with this focus will help members of your class master techniques that will be useful to them as they attempt to solve problems.

In summary, your social studies instruction has a specific responsibility to promote citizenship education. You strive to accomplish this purpose through lessons drawing content from history and social sciences (and, sometimes, other disciplines), lessons that broaden student understandings to include global as well as local, state, and national perspectives. You seek to organize and present this content in ways that will facilitate the development of your students' reflective thinking and problem-solving abilities.

COMMON EMPHASES

For each of the four broad content categories, you will find your, teaching will revolve around three major emphases: knowledge, skills, and values. *Knowledge* refers to specific facts and understandings a person needs to know. *Skills* include processes of gathering and using knowledge. *Values* are attitudes and beliefs individuals use to justify their actions. When these three areas are combined with (1) citizenship education, (2) global-awareness education, (3) history and social science education, and (4) reflective thinking and problem-solving education, you gain a more comprehensive picture of social studies' purposes. Figure 1-2 displays these relationships as a matrix.

FIGURE 1-2 • **Matrix of Social Studies Purposes**			
	Citizenship	**Global-Awareness**	**History and Social Science**	**Reflective Thinking and Problem-Solving**
Knowledge				
Skills				
Values				

Emphases Within Citizenship Education

★ **Knowledge** Your pupils should be exposed to knowledge related to the American heritage; the Constitution; the Bill of Rights; political processes followed at the local, state, and national levels; and other basic information an educated adult citizen is expected to know.

★ **Skills** Pupils need to be taught processes associated with rational decision making. Lessons you develop with this focus will help them learn how to compromise, express their views clearly, and work productively with others.

★ **Values** Citizens do not make decisions only on the basis of information. They also consider social and personal values. Members of your class need to be exposed to values associated with democratic decision making and to values that collectively support the operation of our nation's local, state, and national governments.

Emphases Within Global-Awareness Education

Knowledge Your students need information about different world places, peoples, and cultures. You especially need to help them to understand that groups in various parts of the world often view common problems and events in different ways. Finally, content you introduce in this area assists your learners to appreciate that communication and transportation technologies are bringing the world's peoples into more frequent contact with one another. To cope with this reality, students need to appreciate worldviews of people in other places and cultures that may well differ from their own.

Skills Differences of opinion regarding "appropriate" actions to be taken to respond to common problems often produce tensions among people from different national, ethnic, racial, and cultural groups. To help your students deal with these kinds of disputes, you want to spend some time helping them develop negotiation skills that respect diverse points of view. In addition, you want to help your learners develop communication patterns that allow them to exchange views with individuals from diverse backgrounds in respectful, considerate ways.

Values When individuals find that people from national, ethnic, racial, or cultural groups different from their own see the world in ways that are at odds with their own views, sometimes there is a tendency for them to avoid further contacts with people "who are different." Given the increasing diversity within our own national population and the increasing interdependence of all the world's peoples, your social studies lessons should help your students understand that diversity is something to be welcomed, not feared. It is important for students to understand that an appreciation for diversity encourages consideration of multiple options when solutions to problems are being considered. Your instruction can help students understand that more lasting and stable solutions result when people give careful, considerate, and respectful attention to diverse points of view.

Emphases Within History and Social Science Education

Knowledge The academic disciplines, including history and social sciences, are repositories of information that have potential to give your students powerful insights into human behavior. You will draw heavily from information from these disciplines as you plan and deliver social studies instruction.

Skills Among skills you will emphasize with your students are those that academic content specialists use as they gather and assess the importance of information. Many specialists use variants of the scientific method as they seek to verify and modify hypotheses. These same skills often are useful to your learners as they begin to confront the kinds of personal and public dilemmas adults face in their daily lives.

Values Certain values are implicit in how academic content specialists go about their work. For example, historians and social scientists prize knowledge based on data more than knowledge based on intuition or feeling. You need to help your learners understand how values affect what individuals believe to be real or important.

Emphases Within Reflective Thinking and Problem-Solving Education

Knowledge Members of your class need to learn basic information about how rational decisions are made. Introducing them to procedures useful for bringing problems into focus and attacking them in a systematic, step-by-step way are important concerns of this part of the social studies program. As you introduce your students to ways of identifying relevant information and using it to solve problems, they acquire techniques for organizing and evaluating data and for formulating and testing hypotheses.

Skills Your learners' capacity for engaging in serious reflection and problem solving improves when they have opportunities to make decisions about real issues and to experience the consequences of these decisions. In the lower grades, problem-solving skills are developed as students work with issues important to individuals and families.

More mature elementary learners use these skills to work with a broader range of social and political problems affecting communities, states, the nation, and the world.

Many problems in a democratic society require collective decision making. Hence, part of your social studies skill-development program needs to focus on helping students to work productively in groups. Such experiences provide members of your class with opportunities to engage in the kind of give-and-take discussion that characterizes adult group decision making.

Values Instruction in this area is designed to help your students develop a commitment to rational approaches to reflection and problem solving. Your intent is to nurture the development in your students of feelings that good decisions come about as a result of using logical processes to consider reliable evidence. As a result of your teaching, you hope students increasingly will resist jumping to conclusions based on unexamined assumptions or restrictive biases. Helping your students develop a tolerance for diverse views is another important part of the values dimension of reflective thinking and problem-solving instruction.

Putting It All Together

The major social studies purposes of (1) citizenship education, (2) global-awareness education, (3) history and social science education, and (4) reflective thinking and problem-solving education and the subcategories under each—(a) knowledge, (b) skills, and (c) values—frame the overall elementary social studies program. If you want your own program to be well balanced, you will include some learning experiences directed to each of these areas. However, the attention you decide to give to each will depend on your reading of your own teaching context. You will consider the ages, interests, and aptitudes of your learners; expectations of your local community; and state and school district curriculum guidelines and achievement standards.

THE SOCIAL STUDIES CURRICULUM AND ACHIEVEMENT STANDARDS

Social studies educational goals and purposes are accomplished through the delivery of specific content. This is the social studies *curriculum*. Traditionally the curriculum has been organized around the concept of "expanding horizons." The rationale for this pattern was that students in the early grades would start by studying those elements most concrete and familiar to them and then move to less familiar and more abstract topics. Thus, in the primary grades the curriculum started with the family and school and by high school included world history and geography.

Present-day technology and mobility has challenged this traditional scheme. Every night on television students encounter people and places far different from their immediate experience. The increased mobility of people makes it likely that even young children have experienced places far away from their own neighborhood. Even in relatively rural areas it is likely that some children in a given class are either from places

FIGURE 1-3 • The Social Studies Curriculum

Grade Level	*Topic*
Kindergarten	Awareness of Self in a Social Setting
First Grade	The Individuals in Primary Social Groups—Understanding School and Family Life
Second Grade	Meeting Basic Needs in Nearby Social Groups—The Neighborhood
Third Grade	Sharing Earth and Space with Others—The Community
Fourth Grade	Human Life in Varied Environments—The Region (Note: in some states the topic is state history and geography.)
Fifth Grade	People of the Americas—The United States and Its Close Neighbors (Note: In reality many of the programs focus on the United States up to the Civil War. Little is done relating to Canada and Latin America.)
Sixth Grade	Pattern One: People and Cultures—World Regions
	Pattern Two: European Cultures in the Western Hemisphere
	Pattern Three: Land and People of Latin America
Seventh Grade	Pattern One: A Changing World of Many Nations
	Pattern Two: People and Cultures—Representative World Regions
Eighth Grade	Building a Strong and Free Nation—The United States (Note: In many states this is study of U.S. history from the Civil War to the present.)
	Pattern Two: Economics and Law-Related Studies
	Pattern Three: Interdisciplinary Study of the Local Region

far from the local community or have lived in other communities. However, the general pattern of the expanding horizons approach still forms the basic structure for the social studies curriculum. In some places it has been altered so that families and communities from across the world are included rather than just "my family" and "my community." The NCSS Task Force on Scope and Sequence (1989) conducted a comprehensive analysis of social studies curriculum patterns. They found many commonalities in the K–5 curriculum, with some alternative patterns for grades 6–8. Figure 1-3 illustrates the social studies curriculum patterns described in the NCSS Task Force report.

Each state decides the curriculum sequence for its schools. As a result, there are variations from state to state. As a teacher, you will be responsible for teaching the curriculum content prescribed by your state. You need to consider how you can address the basic purposes of the social studies through these curriculum topics. One way to begin thinking about what should be taught at a given grade level is to combine the curriculum topic of the grade level with the matrix of social studies purposes (see Figure 1-2). As you begin thinking about your teaching you can then ask, "How can I include citizenship, global awareness and history–social sciences within this topic?" "What knowledge, skills, and values should I include?"

In recent years the emphasis on accountability has led many states to conclude that just specifying the content of the curriculum was not sufficient. They needed specific, measurable statements of the achievement outcomes expected at each grade level. These outcome statements, called *standards,* attempt to define precisely what the state thinks every student in that grade level should know and be able to do. Achievement standards are related to curriculum topics and are used to develop assessments at each grade level. In some states and districts, teachers are required to identify which standard is being addressed in each lesson.

WORKING WITH SOCIAL STUDIES CURRICULUM STANDARDS

Historically, local officials and teachers have had a great deal of discretion in selecting and emphasizing the content of the school curriculum. However, several issues began to reduce the discretion of local educators, among them the following: (1) increased mobility and technology has led to dramatic social change; (2) funding for education began to shift from local jurisdictions to the state; (3) education became a political issue at both the federal and state levels; and (4) international assessments raised questions about the effectiveness of U.S. schools. Public awareness of and response to these issues resulted in increased calls for school accountability and for determining what students were learning.

If schools are to be held accountable for student achievement, the content students should be learning has to be defined with great precision and specificity. This is not new. As long ago as the early twentieth century some educators and policy makers were working hard to "specify learning outcomes, organize school programs in support of them, and to ascertain both performance levels of students and quality levels of instructional programs" (Armstrong, 2003, p. 83). However, the idea of a clear specification of educational outcomes was given a boost in with the publication in 1983 of *A Nation at Risk: The Imperative for Educational Reform* (National Commission on Excellence in Education, 1983). This publication charged that U.S. schools were failing and that this was placing the "nation at risk." The report called for increased rigor in the school curriculum and more school and teacher accountability. In response to this report, many states and professional organizations began developing curriculum standards that defined in quite explicit language what students should be learning in school.

The next impetus to the movement came in 2002 with the passage of the No Child Left Behind Act (Public Law 107-110, 2002). This act requires that states have in place challenging academic content standards. The law requires implementing student assessment tied to these standards to make sure that all students are making adequate yearly progress. Sanctions are put in place for those schools where students do not make adequate yearly progress. Initially, the assessments were to be in reading, language arts, and mathematics, with science testing to begin in 2007. While the No Child Left Behind Act requires assurances that all students are receiving solid academic instruction in subjects other than those tested, no specific timeline for testing is specified. There have been increased calls for tests in subjects such as the social studies.

Sources of Standards

Professional associations are often sources of curriculum standards. Professional groups interested in improving either the entire social studies program or the teaching of a specific subject have developed content standards and offered them for adoption by state and district boards of education.

The National Council for Social Studies (NCSS) developed *Expectations of Excellence* (1994) as a set of standards for the entire social studies curriculum. A number of other disciplines that included social studies content also have developed specific standards for their subject. For example, The National Center for History in the Schools produced *National Standards for History* (1996), a number of groups interested in geography collaborated in developing *Geography for Life: National Geography Standards* (Bednarz et al., 1994), the Center for Civic Education released the *National Standards for Civics and Government* (1994), and the National Council on Economic Education developed the *Voluntary National Content Standards in Economics* (1996).

Individuals who develop these standards, usually teachers and other content specialists, are typically committed to the importance of their specific subject, and are attuned to the developments in their field of interest. As a result, standards coming from professional organizations generally reflect the latest thinking in the subject and provide a credible overview of what the experts think is important in their specific content area.

You should review the national standards for the subjects of interest to you. They will give you a good understanding of how the experts define their subject. Be aware, however, that because these are developed at the national level, they may not specifically address the social studies curriculum of your state.

As a result of the No Child Left Behind Act, most states moved to develop a set of curriculum content standards and developed a process for making sure that they were being implemented in the classroom. In some places this took the form of standardized tests. In others it took the form of making sure that the textbooks used addressed the state standards.

The basic difference between standards developed by the state and those developed by professional organizations is that the standards developed by professional organizations are voluntary and are meant to be advisory in nature. State standards address the specific content required by that state for a given grade level and set forth obligatory academic achievement outcomes that all teachers in the state are supposed to address. Sometimes the state standards reflect standards developed by professional groups and sometimes they do not. State standards are usually developed by committees generally appointed by the educational division of the state government. These committees include an array of individuals representing different constituents such as teachers, parents, and content area specialists. Therefore, it is useful to think of state standards as political documents reflecting compromise between many competing interests.

Because you will be expected to implement your state's standards and they carry the force of law, it is imperative that you know the standards for the grade level and the topics you teach. Many teacher preparation programs require that student teachers identify the curriculum standards addressed in specific lesson plans. It is quite common for school district interviewers to ask potential teachers questions about the state standards. Most states post on the Internet the standards they have adopted; you often may locate these by going to the homepage of the state department of education.

Teachers often work together to plan how to meet standards.

Kathy Kirtland/Merrill

Issues Related to Standards and Standardized Testing

Supporters of standards believe that well-defined standards are a key to school improvement, for the following reasons:

- *Standards ensure that students will be exposed to important content.* Elementary teachers generally have a broad preparation in several subject areas. They may not understand what is important in all subjects and therefore may either ignore important aspects or teach only those topics they see as interesting or fun.
- *Standards ensure that acceptable levels of rigor characterize school programs.* Common standards allow for careful consideration of the sophistication of the content and levels of student performance. Programs not tied to a specific standard and a baseline of expectations do not provide parents and policy makers a way of judging program quality.
- *Standards facilitate school-by-school comparison.* If students in different schools have all been expected to study the same standards, then individual schools' effectiveness can be determined by comparing student achievement across schools.
- *Standards make it easier for students to move from school to school.* Increased mobility has meant that many students move from one school to another during a given school year. This has been viewed as a serious educational problem because students may encounter new curricula and expectations at each school attended. If all schools are teaching to the same set of standards, then the impact of student mobility should be diminished.
- *Standards promote efficient use of scarce resources.* This can mean a couple of different things. For example, policy makers at the state level are often reluctant to provide more money to schools unless they can clearly see an impact. Therefore, evidence regarding student achievement of standards allows them to

allocate resources to those places that are getting results. Others point out that evidence regarding student attainment of educational standards allows decision makers to pinpoint areas of weakness in the curriculum and allocate resources to address those weaknesses.

- *Standards promote educational equity.* There are often vast differences in the quality of education provided by individual schools and school districts. Often children from ethnic minorities and children of economically impoverished parents do not have access to school programs of the quality provided to other students. Establishing state standards that are expected of all students force state and local policy makers to address this problem.

Not everyone agrees with these propositions. In fact, the whole issue of standards generates considerable, often heated, debate. Some educators believe that the establishment of curriculum standards, and especially the implementation of standardized tests as a major indicator of student attainment of the standards, actually results in a lowering of educational quality.

Among the concerns of those opposing the enforced establishment of standards and standardized testing are the following:

- *Standardized tests are poor indicators of student achievement of standards.* Although it appears to be logical to clearly identify content standards and then test students to see if they are learning them, the reality is somewhat different. First, the test must be a valid and reliable indicator of the standards. This is not easy to ensure. It is time consuming and costly to develop valid and reliable tests, and the tendency is simply to select existing ones. However, these may be poorly aligned with state standards and the tests scores reported to the public not valid indicators of student achievement of the standards.

  Secondly, a test cannot test all standards. Any test is simply "a sample of all the exercises we could have posed if the assessment were infinitely long" (Stiggins, 2005, p. 68). Those constructing tests must choose what to sample. Developing valid test items that measure complex learning outcomes is very difficult. Therefore, the content measured tends to be the content for which it is easiest to construct test items, not necessarily what is most important. In addition, the general emphasis on standardized tests is to generate a spread of student scores. It does little good to have items that everyone gets right because this does not discriminate among students. What content are students most likely to get right? The content that has been emphasized in classroom lessons. This tends to lead to test items covering the more obscure and trivial content. Standardized tests are therefore seen as poor and inadequate indicators of student achievement of content standards.

- *Accountability that relies on standardized tests as a main measure of achievement promotes educational inequities.* While proponents of accountability and standardized tests claim that it will lead to more educational equity, those opposed claim it will result in exactly the opposite. Studies have indicated that students' achievement on standardized tests is directly related to their parents' socioeconomic status. Therefore, the claim can be made that these tests are not indicating the quality of the school, but the socioeconomic status of the community. If those schools that are achieving high test scores are rewarded and those that are not are punished, then additional money flows to the higher socioeconomic-status community and this only widens the gap between rich schools and poor schools. No Child Left Behind addresses the equity issue by requiring that parents in low-performing schools have the option to transfer their child to another school. Early indications are that few parents pursue this option and therefore the issue of equity and quality in poorer communities remains unaddressed.

- *Explicit standards and standardized tests narrow the curriculum focus.* It is very clear that teachers teach what is tested. This is especially true if there are high stakes, such as publicity and pay, attached to the scores. The predictable outcome is that teachers will teach to the test or to those standards most likely to be tested and eliminate topics that might be valuable but not likely to be tested. This is already evident in many places where there is no state testing of social studies content. In these places there has been a noticeable drop in the amount of time teachers spend teaching social studies or other nontested subjects.

- *Explicit standards lead to a loss of local control of schools.* The establishment of state standards means that curriculum control is taken away from local school districts and placed in the hands of individuals at the state level. This can be dangerous because the content of the curriculum can easily be influenced by a very few individuals. In addition, individuals at the state level cannot be expected to be aware of local needs and conditions. This makes it more difficult for educators to respond to the interests and needs of all students.

- *Standards ignore the reality of individual differences.* Critics of explicit standards claim that one size does not fit all. Their implementation in many places has meant that all teachers in a given grade level are supposed to teach to the same standards regardless of the prior achievement or individual differences of their students. This has led to a lockstep, production-line style of education. As one administrator said to one of the authors, "As I go from one fourth-grade classroom to the next, I ought to be able to see the same content being discussed and the sentence of the first teacher completed by the second teacher" (personal communication, 2005). However, the reality is that not all fourth-grade students are alike, and not all of them have completed the same academic prerequisites. Those who have not completed a subject's prerequisites are more likely to be frustrated; those who are advanced are likely to be bored.

See Stiggins (2005) for an in-depth discussion of the advantages and disadvantages of standardized tests and the controversy surrounding their use.

The Impact of Standards on Instruction

Regardless of your view of the advantages or disadvantages of standards, they will be a part of your professional landscape. You will be expected to teach to state standards and may well be expected to document how you are meeting them. Curriculum standards will impact your teaching in several ways, which we discuss in the following subsections.

Content Constraints State standards place constraints on what you include in the curriculum, and can limit your instructional freedom. This can be good, as it can provide teachers unfamiliar with the curriculum with a framework for designing lessons of consistent, acceptable quality. However, some expert teachers who understand both the curriculum and their students' needs are able to implement high-quality, innovative programs that do not in fact adhere to published standards. Thus, they may well view standards as limiting what they can do.

However, most state standards are not designed to prevent additional content from being added to the curriculum. In general, so long as your units and lessons address what is deemed essential content elements by the state, you are free to teach other topics that in your professional judgment represent responsible addition to your program. Therefore, although standards place some constraints, they still allow for some teacher judgment and creativity.

Over time it is likely that the current emphasis on standards might diminish. However, the current reality is that you must know the pertinent national and state curriculum standards and you will be expected to teach them in the classroom. Because of the political nature of state standards especially, we recommend that you also consult those standards developed by professional groups so that if needed, you can supplement the mandated curriculum and develop a sound, beneficial program for your students.

Time Allocations Pressures from school administrators and others concerned about how students will perform on tests related to state standards may result in a significant alteration of how you allocate instructional time. For example, you may have to weight the time invested in certain instructional activities against the potential outcomes. Instructional activities that might be interesting to students but that have little payoff in addressing state standards may have to be eliminated or reduced. You will be required to exercise some professional judgment in implementing both activities that are valuable for your students and those that address state standards.

Testing Most state standards are designed as the basis for a testing program that can provide evidence that students are actually learning what is mandated. This is often the basis for comparing schools. Thus, there will be attempts to "teach to the test." While teaching to the test might be justified if the test is a comprehensive and valid measure of achievement standards, this is seldom the case. Therefore, instructional time is certain to be spent on topics of questionable educational value.

While there is no doubt that high-stakes testing will have an influence on what you teach and on how much time you allocate to specific topics that are likely to be tested, we believe that a meaningful social studies program that students find relevant will result in solid test scores. While you need to be mindful of the content that is likely to appear on standardized tests, remember that research indicates that if what a person learns is meaningful to them, they will retain that information for a longer period of time. On the other hand, teaching isolated facts in which students find little relevance or meaning takes more time, and forgetting occurs rapidly. Therefore, teachers who implement an interesting social studies program are likely to be able to teach more content in a given amount of time and have students remember it longer.

Complying with State Standards

You may well be required to present evidence that you are actually teaching information contained in state social studies standards. Even without official requests about your compliance, it is in your own professional interests to keep track of this information. Compliance data can be very useful when you are evaluated by administrators and when you have conferences with parents. In the current climate of accountability, few people are willing simply to take the word of a teacher that everything is just fine. Most people want evidence. Therefore, we recommend you develop a documentation system. Developing and maintaining such a system is not difficult. It just means adding to or altering the records and documents that you already keep.

Referencing Standards on Lesson Plans One simple way of documenting how you include curriculum standards in your classroom is by simply making sure that you reference them on your lesson plans. In fact, referencing standards can help you as you prepare lessons. When preparing lesson plans, one of the most difficult steps is getting started. Many novice teachers ask, "What should I teach?" Reviewing standards can help you answer this question. The standard being addressed in the particular lesson can be one of the first entries on the lesson plan form. You may then use that standard to develop specific objectives for your lesson that are appropriate for your specific group of learners.

Your lesson plans should be filed away for future reference. At certain times during the year you might review your plans against the standards to make sure that you are addressing all relevant standards.

Preparing a Checklist Related to the Social Studies Standards This is a simple task that can prove beneficial not only in documenting the inclusion of state standards but in helping you do long-term planning. Before the school year begins, develop a checklist of the standards you will be expected to address during the year. As you plan units and lessons you can quickly review the standards and identify those that are appropriate for the unit or lesson. You can then simply provide the date when you addressed a particular standard. It might be that on a given date you addressed more than one standard and likely that over the course of the year you will have addressed some standards on multiple occasions. At the end of the year you will have a clear and concise record of your implementation of the standards in your classroom. If you also keep your lesson plans, you can then provide specific evidence of how you addressed the standards.

Implementing Alternative Assessment Approaches The major point of accountability is to change the focus from just what is covered to an emphasis on what students actually learn. In many states this evidence takes the form of a standardized test. As indicated earlier, there are some serious limitations to drawing conclusions from standardized tests. A number of educators who favor the use of standards oppose the use of standardized tests as the indicator of student achievement. These individuals generally advocate the use of multiple measures of student learning and alternative assessment techniques. *Alternative assessment techniques* are broadly defined as the variety of methods other than standardized tests that can be used to determine whether a student has learned. These might take the form of student products, such as completed assignments and other things they have produced, collected in what is called a *portfolio*. This portfolio contains multiple items that give a comprehensive overview of what the student has learned and accomplished during the year (see Stiggins, 2005). We suggest that you classify students' portfolio entries according to the achievement standards they address. You could also use a standards checklist for this purpose. At the end of the year you may thus easily review the achievements of a given student related to a specific standard. Many educators suggest that this would be a more valid way of documenting student learning than standardized tests. When presented clearly, parents frequently find this information more useful and informative than test scores (Stiggins, 2005).

In summary, in your teaching you will be required to address state and national curriculum standards established for your grade level and subject. While standards may limit the freedom that many teachers have had in the past to make their own professional decisions about what to teach in the social studies, they can have some important benefits. They can help you better define what is important to teach in a specific subject, they can provide specific guidance in the preparation of unit and lesson plans, and they can provide evidence to parents and other interested parties that you implementing a quality program. Because the standards define *what* to teach and not *how* to teach, good, creative teachers find that they can still design exciting and meaningful lessons.

KEY IDEAS IN SUMMARY

- Social studies lessons provide your students with tools they can use to think reflectively and make decisions about personal issues and social problems, citizenship responsibilities, and global issues. There are disagreements about what components should be present in a good social studies program. Varying views regarding what the priorities of social studies instruction should be energize the field and give you opportunities to participate in discussions about what learners should experience in this part of the elementary school curriculum.

- Some surveys of students' attitudes have revealed that large numbers of young people do not find social studies to be among their favorite subjects. In the view of the authors, where negative attitudes exist, they result not from the subject matter itself but rather from instructional approaches that are not well suited to either the content or the needs of elementary school learners.

- You may find it helpful to think in terms of four basic categories as you organize your social studies program: (1) citizenship education, (2) global-awareness education, (3) history and social science education, and (4) reflective thinking and problem-solving education.

- The *citizenship education* component embraces social studies instruction designed to (1) encourage students' commitment to such core values as democratic decision making, (2) help them think critically about existing government policies and practices, and (3) allow them to see the importance of citizens' becoming actively involved in public affairs.

- The *global-awareness* component recognizes that our world is becoming increasingly interdependent. Your instruction related to this theme helps to sensitize your students to perspectives of people in other cultures and lands.

- The *history–social science* component provides students with a knowledge base drawn from these academic disciplines that they will need as they make the kinds of rational decisions expected of good citizens.

- The *reflective thinking and problem-solving* component organizes your instruction to develop students' abilities to apply sophisticated thinking skills to problems.

- There are three important subemphases associated with the four major social studies program categories—knowledge, skills, and values. *Knowledge* refers to specific facts and understandings a person needs to know. *Skills* include processes of gathering and using knowledge. *Values* are the attitudes and beliefs individuals use to justify their actions.
- The accountability movement has had a tremendous impact on education. One outcome has been the development of specific curriculum content standards. Professional groups have developed standards for specific subjects that are beneficial in acquainting individuals with the outcomes that experts in the field think are important for students to learn. In response to the requirements of the No Child Left Behind Act, most states have established state standards for what should be taught in a given subject at a given grade level. State standards carry the force of law, and teachers must implement them in the classroom. In some states these standards have become the basis for standardized tests that are used to indicate how well students are achieving the standards.
- Standards do place some constraints on your freedom to teach content and they do influence your time allocations. You may well be expected to document how you are including standards in your instructional program. You may do this through references to standards on lesson plans, by establishing a checklist where you keep track of when you addressed specific standards, and by keeping evidence drawn from a variety of sources that indicate how well your students accomplished the standards.

CHAPTER REFLECTIONS

Now that you have read the chapter, think about these questions.

1. The chapter introduction refers to several challenges that social studies teachers face today. Which of these challenges do you believe will prove most difficult for you? How might you go about responding to them? What kinds of preparation might you begin now that will help you deal with these issues?

2. Initially, some of your students may appear to have little interest in your social studies lessons. What ideas do you have about connecting social studies instruction to their lives? Think about a particular topic you would like to teach. (Choose any grade level you like.) For this content, what are some specific things you might do to motivate student interest?

TWO

History and Geography

Courtesy of the Library of Congress

This chapter will help you to:

- Describe historical and geographical perspectives.
- Define *history* and the purposes of history in the elementary curriculum.
- Provide examples of history and geography lessons.
- State basic components of the national history standards.
- Define *geography* and the purposes of history in the elementary school.
- State the basic components of the national geography standards.

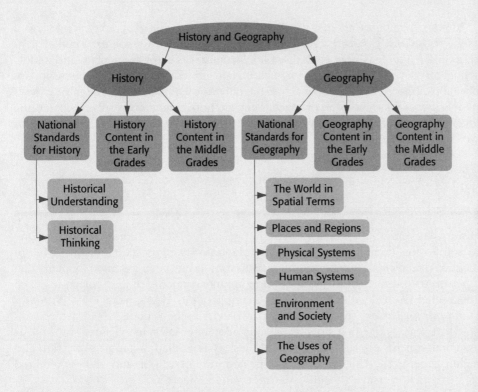

The major focus of the social studies is the study of people. Different disciplines have developed knowledge bases that help us understand humanity both in the past and the present. These knowledge bases form the foundation for the content taught in the social studies curriculum. These content sources provide a variety of perspectives that will help your learners understand and appreciate the great diversity of people and how they have responded to enduring and persistent issues.

It is useful to keep in mind the major purposes of the social studies when reviewing content drawn from history and the social sciences. As started earlier, the purpose is not to make junior historians and social scientists. Rather, the purpose is to provide them with a knowledge base that will assist them in reflective thinking and problem solving, developing a sense of global awareness, and in becoming involved and informed citizens.

In this chapter we address the disciplines of history and geography, long viewed as the two major foundation subjects of the social studies. We will explore key concepts and main ideas from each discipline that are useful for elementary and middle school teachers in planning for instruction, and provide examples of classroom applications. History views people across the dimension of time while geography views people across the dimension of space. They are both "integrative" subjects that bring together content from a variety of sources. History and geography content functions well in helping young people "make sense" of their world.

HISTORY

History has been the dominant subject in most of the social studies curriculum. One reason for this dominance is that history is often viewed as central to the development of citizenship competencies and patriotism. It has been assumed by many that a person who studies history will develop an understanding of their role as a citizen and a sense of loyalty to the nation. An example of this idea appears in the *National Standards for History* (National Center for History in the Schools, 1996), which contend that "knowledge of history is a precondition of political intelligence" (p. 1). This assumption helps explain why American history is studied in almost every fifth and eighth grade in the United States, is repeated in high school, and often is required as a part of universities' general education requirements.

A potential problem with the view that the primary purpose of history in the school curriculum is to develop patriotism and loyalty to country is that it can lead to a biased and distorted history. Events or actions that might not reflect positively on the nation may be omitted and the contributions of other people and nations overlooked. This practice is contrary to the goal of helping students become informed and reflective citizens.

This citizenship-development purpose of history often engenders controversy. For example, when the *National Standards for History* was published, some critics attacked it because they felt that the content deemphasized the American experience in favor of a more multicultural, non-Western emphasis. In other words, they did not think the standards were including the "appropriate" stories that would engender patriotism and loyalty. This pressure did result in some modifications of the original standards.

As a teacher, you may well encounter this controversy. Individuals have strong feelings about what content should be included in the curriculum. Some individuals may contend that you are not teaching the "right" stories or including the "right" facts. You will need a clear understanding of the purposes and the nature of history in order to meet these challenges and defend your decisions.

In addition to the citizenship purpose, other reasons have been cited for teaching history in the schools. One is that a study of history helps people avoid the mistakes of the past. Whether lessons focused on history can serve this laudable end depends largely on how you present the content. Memorizing names, dates, people, and events does not do much to help students apply the lessons of the past to the problems of the present. Development of functional insights based on past experiences requires instruction that engages learners in understanding different viewpoints about an event and in reflecting on the consequences of actions.

Another reason for learning history cited in the ***National Standards*** is that it contributes to the development of the "private individual" as well as the "public citizen." In this context, history is seen as a key to self-identity and personal belonging. History provides examples of how individuals are connected with all of humankind. Drake and Nelson (2005) state that history is important because it provides a powerful way to find out who and where we are in the human experience and in human affairs. History is a form of thinking that offers a method of inquiry about others. In the process, we may find out more about ourselves.

The beginning step in developing a solid history component in the curriculum is to have a clear understanding of the nature of history. Although most of us have had a fair number of history classes as we progressed though secondary school and college, many still have difficulty defining the subject and identifying what students should learn. As a result, the history curriculum is often filled with trivia that students fail to see as relevant or having any personal meaning.

What is history? ***History*** is often defined as the past and all that has happened in the past. While this is technically true, this definition is something of a distortion. It is "more accurately defined as an interpretive and partial account of some portion of the past" (Drake & Nelson, 2005, p.16). In addition, defining history as everything in the past is of little use to you as you plan your social studies program. Not even professional historians have a comprehensive knowledge of all that has happened in the past. There is simply too much content and not enough time in the school day to cover even a significant portion of the past. We need to ask the central question, "What is worth teaching and learning in history?"

A narrower definition of ***history*** states that history should study those things in the past deemed to be significant or worthy. This helps eliminate a lot of the trivia and narrows what should be taught. However, it raises another issue: What is defined as significant or worthy might be different from group to group. In addition, what is considered as significant and worthy changes over time. For example, some events that were viewed as significant 50 years ago are no longer considered that important while other events that might have been viewed as insignificant have taken on increased importance. One example is rock and roll music. During the 1950s, rock and roll did not sit well with many adults. It was called the "Devil's music" and much was written about its bad influence on young people. Rock and roll music was identified as the cause of increased teenage rebelliousness, delinquency, sex, and fast cars (Kashatus, 2002). Today, many look back with nostalgia on early rock and roll music and never think of blaming it for the social issues of the time.

This definition suggests that history is a dynamic subject that involves more than the memorization of names and dates. It also suggests that there is not a single correct history. Rather, history involves the study of what is significant and why it is deemed to be so. Commager (1965), an eminent historian, suggests that those who study history must engage in serious reflection. This reflection should first focus on the facts presented. Were all relevant facts presented? What was included and omitted and why? What is the bias of the historian who wrote the account?

What are alternative interpretations and patterns? The study of history thus becomes an active process somewhat akin to solving a mystery.

Gerwin and Zevin (2003) point out that mystery is a powerful technique for teaching history because it has certain inherent properties that motivate students. It arouses curiosity when individuals are confronted with the problem of sorting out clues and putting together evidence. In addition, the solution to a mystery becomes its own reward. Evidence of these contentions can be found in popular culture. Why are television shows that feature mysteries so popular? Why have high-profile trials captured the interest of so many people and been covered by hordes of reporters? Everyone loves a mystery and engaging in interpreting the evidence. Those properties can be used to help students learn history.

When you understand this dimension of history you develop a new attitude, and begin looking for ways to present history not as a bunch of facts found between the two covers of a book but as the active involvement of students in questioning, gathering data, and drawing conclusions. Historical episodes presented as interesting mysteries to be unraveled rather than as records to be memorized actively engage students in historical thinking. Learning to think in this manner will serve them well when they move out into a world where there are multiple interpretations of events and conflicting truth claims.

Good history also has a literary quality. This aspect of history helps you integrate history with subjects such as reading and writing. For example, the *History-Social Science Framework for California Public Schools* (1997) states that history should be a "story well told" (p. 4). In other words, good history means that the historian should present the material in a way that is engaging and compelling and that stirs the imagination of the reader. However, it is also important to remember is that there is not just one story, but many. In addition to understanding the literary quality of history, students should also consider *whose* story is being told, the *accuracy* of the story, and the *intended purposes* of the story. There are many well-told stories, some that are inaccurate and some that are intended to promote myths and stereotypes rather than reveal truth. Students need to be challenged to seek other stories about the same event and to question the selection of facts and the patterns of interpretation of the author or historian.

National Standards for History

The *National Standards for History* (National Center for History in the Schools, 1996) provides a comprehensive view of history developed by leading historians. The standards are organized into two categories, historical understanding and historical thinking.

Historical Understanding The *National Standards for History* (1996) gives guidance concerning what should be included in the curriculum. The standards promote inclusion of content with potential to bring history alive. They encourage teaching that will help students think historically, differentiate between past and present, stimulate curiosity and imagination, and engage students in the use of a variety of resources and artifacts. There are content recommendations that focus on the lives, accomplishments, struggles, and failures of real people.

Relating the past to the familiar, such as school, helps promote interest in history and the basic theme of change.

Courtesy of the Library of Congress

Standards for historical understanding are organized around five spheres of human activity:

- *Social history*—developing an understanding of society, including topics such as families, the changing roles of people, immigration, migration, class conflicts, slavery, and the relationships of groups within society
- *Political history*—the history of governments, the struggle to achieve and preserve basic human rights, and understanding the core principles and values of American democracy that unite us as a people
- *History of science and technology*—how science and technology has propelled change, the scientific quest to understand the world we live in, producing food, methods of transportation, and changes in communication
- *Economic history*—economic forces that influence the quality of life, the structure of society, and the course of human events
- *Cultural history*—religion, philosophy, art, and music and how they deepen our understanding of the human experience

A review of the five spheres reveals a rich and broad array of content sources that can be used for teaching history. They illustrate that history is not just the study of kings and queens, presidents and generals, war and conflict. These themes also support the claim that history can function as an integrative discipline that can include content from any area of the curriculum. The unifying thread is human behavior over time; the major focus concepts are **continuity** and **change**. Instruction is guided by questions such as, "How have things changed over time and why?" "What has continued over time and why?"

Historical Thinking The standards for historical thinking are useful because they expand traditional definitions of history. They help individuals understand that

═══ LESSON IDEA 2-1 ═══

TOPIC: Using Family Origins and Traditions (Social History)

OBJECTIVES: Students can (1) learn how to interview a family member, (2) identify examples of change and continuity, and (3) learn how to share with others.

ENGAGING THE STUDENTS: Implement this lesson near a holiday. Student can share some of the special things they do on a holiday. Then read some selections from the book, *We Celebrate Family Days*, by Bobbie Kalman (New York, Crabtree Publishing, 1986, ISBN 0-86505-058-0).

DEVELOPING THE CONTENT: Develop a chart that lists special days across the top and that contains examples of how each day is celebrated. Tell the class that they are going to find out how these special days were celebrated in the past. With the group, identify five or six central questions. Put these questions on a questionnaire along with directions for each student to take it home and interview parents or grandparents about how they celebrated these special days when they were young.

When the questionnaires are returned, add the responses to the chart. Discussion can center on which practices are similar and which are different. Students can be asked why they think some practices have changed and some have stayed the same.

BRINGING CLOSURE: Ask students to identify why some things change and others stay the same. Evaluate students based on the information they gathered in the interview, the participation in the classroom discussion, and their ability to identify at least one reason why things change or stay the same.

EXTENSION TO THE WEB: The History Buff homepage may help you create interesting lessons for students in the area of social history. It includes newspaper coverage of such topics as baseball, the Civil War, and the Old West.

URL—http://www.historybuff.com/index .html

history requires active participation that goes beyond memorization. These standards require learners to question and think when encountering historical accounts, documents, and artifacts. Historical thinking includes five categories:

- *Chronological thinking*—identifying the temporal sequence in which events occurred; distinguishing between past and present; creating and interpreting time lines; explaining patterns of change and continuity
- *Historical comprehension*— identifying central questions in a historical account; taking into account the historical context of events; using a variety of sources to clarify and understand historical events; identifying the characters, situations, sequence of events, causes, and outcomes in historical stories
- *Historical analysis and interpretation*—applying critical thinking to historical events; comparing/contrasting different perspectives of an event; separating fact and fiction; identifying bias, analyzing historical fiction for accuracy; analyzing illustrations for accuracy; explaining causes of historical actions
- *Developing historical research capabilities*—developing questions from encounters in historical accounts and artifacts; obtaining data from a variety of sources; determining credibility of historical materials; inquiring into and constructing historical accounts

LESSON IDEA 2-2

TOPIC: Resolving Conflicting Accounts (Historical Analysis)

OBJECTIVES: Students will (1) identify bias in historical accounts, and (2) state the importance of identifying bias in material they read.

ENGAGING THE STUDENTS: Have students relate a time when two different people had different explanations for something that happened, such as during a disagreement on the playground. Ask them why they think this happens.

DEVELOPING THE CONTENT: Place a chart on the board with two columns, one marked "Account 1" and the other "Account 2." The title of the account is "The Burning of Washington in the War of 1812." Give students account 1 to read.

ACCOUNT 1

Victorious troops of the crown swarmed into Washington. With cheers all around, torches were passed. Officers led their men on a block-by-block campaign to torch the rebel capital. Officers of the general staff believe that this action will soon break the back of the American resistance. There is talk that before the year is out these rebel colonies will be rightfully returned to the crown. American resistance is said to be crumbling. Loyal subjects of the king are said to be waiting in Canada for the signal to return south and reestablish proper colonial governments. (Report filed by a correspondent of the *London Gazette*)

When students have read the account, fill in the chart with answers to the following questions: Was this a positive event? Why was it viewed this way? How were the troops described? How were the Americans viewed? What words were used to describe both sides?

When the column for account 1 has been completed, give the students account 2.

ACCOUNT 2

The British barbarian showed his true colors today. Consistent with the pattern of 25 years ago when American rights were trampled into the ground, the undisciplined troops took Washington today with undisciplined savagery. With little regard for the safety of women and children, they went on a rampage that resulted in the burning of most of the buildings in Washington. American troops, shocked by the brutality, are rallying.

Determination has never been higher. All look forward to taking a revenge that will forever free this continent from the tyranny of the British. (Report filed by a correspondent of the *New York Review*)

Use the same questions and fill in the chart for account 2. After completing the chart, lead a discussion using the following questions:

1. How are the accounts similar?
2. How are the accounts different?
3. How do you explain the differences?
4. What are some recent incidents or events when there have been different views?
5. What do you think this means when you read about or hear an account of an event?

BRINGING CLOSURE: Either orally or in writing, have students identify at least one reason why it is important to consider different perspectives when reading accounts of past events.

EXTENSION TO THE WEB: Lots of material about historical events can be found at the Library of Congress—American Memory website. It is a very useful site with audio and video records and lots of material that can be used to create excitement and stimulate students.

URL—http://rs6.loc.gov./amhome.html

- *Analysis and decision making*—identifying problems, dilemmas, and issues that confronted people in historical situations; identifying the interests and values of those involved; evaluating alternative proposals for dealing with the problems; taking a position or course of action when confronting a dilemma

You will find these standards useful as you consider the history component of the curriculum. They provide a strong rationale for teaching history-related content and useful information about what to teach and how to teach it. You may think that some of these standards describe outcomes that are too advanced for many elementary students. In fact, most of them can be simplified and converted to language that is appropriate for the age and developmental level of learners in the individual elementary school grades. In the following sections, you will find examples you can use to appropriately incorporate history-related content into instructional programs for students in different grades.

History Content in the Early Grades

What are some challenges in teaching history-related content to learners in the early grades? First of all, you need to keep in mind that many young children do not yet have the ability to comprehend abstract time concepts. For example, many have difficulty understanding time intervals such as months or years, let alone decades or centuries. You simply cannot expect them to understand the significance of a time line covering an extended period of time. They have no concrete reference that will help them place events in some historical perspective.

In addition, they often lack the ability to recognize that dates designate a specific interval of time or to understand the meaning of intervals between two given dates (Seefeldt, 2005). Their foggy notions of time sometimes result in behaviors adults find humorous. They may even ask their grandparents about what they personally experienced when they were passengers on the *Mayflower*! It is only around age 12 that children begin to understand abstract concepts related to time in the same ways as adults (Elkind, 1981b; Erikson, 1982).

Analyzing artifacts gets students engaged in historical thinking.

© The British Museum

Although very young children have difficulty grasping abstract time concepts, they do understand differences among terms such as "yesterday," "last week," and "long ago." Children as young as 4 or 5 demonstrate some understanding of the sequence of events, particularly if they are recurring, sequential events that occur in their life. Therefore, you can help young children make the first steps toward understanding chronological time by relating historical content to time as it relates to children's personal lives (Seefeldt, 2005).

Young children are in a stage of development that is largely egocentric. Everything revolves around them. You can use this egocentrism as a starting point for developing historical thinking. Nothing is more interesting to young children than their own lives and those of their families. Elkind (1981a) suggests that historical study in the early grades should begin by helping children to discover their "personal history." This relates to the broad purpose of history in developing the "private individuals." Lessons you prepare that focus on events such as birthdays, family events, alterations in children's personal lives, patterns of interaction with parents and other relatives, and changes in the neighborhood can help establish a foundation for developing young students' historical comprehension and thinking abilities.

LESSON IDEA 2-3

TOPIC: Yesterday on the Playground (Historical Comprehension)

OBJECTIVES: Students will (1) write an eyewitness historical account and (2) state why historical accounts sometimes differ.

ENGAGING THE STUDENTS: Inform students that they are going to become historians and record a very important event: The events on the playground yesterday at lunchtime.

DEVELOPING THE CONTENT: Ask students, "What happened on the playground yesterday at lunch?" After a few share their experiences, state that it is clear that there were lots of things happening on the playground and there are lots of stories that can be told. Ask students what they think would be the best way to put together all of these stories and events so that people who were not there could understand what happened. For example, things could be arranged by time: What happened first? What happened next? Or they could be arranged by area: What happened on the ball field? What happened by the playground equipment? They can be challenged: Do they know everything that happened? They may need to interview others—the person on playground

duty, the principal, the school nurse, and students in other classes. At this point students can be grouped in groups of five or six to decide how they are going to write their account and whom they are going to interview. After several days of gathering information and writing their accounts, they can be asked to state why they think the accounts were different.

BRINGING CLOSURE: Conclude the activity by asking students what they learned about how history is written and what they think about when they read an account of an event. Evaluate the accounts that were written. They should have included data from different people and should have a clear organization. Students should be able to state how the feelings and background of a person could influence the account that is written.

EXTENSION TO THE WEB: Newspapers can be a source for locating different interpretations of the same event. The PaperBoy website contains online content from and links to more than 6,000 newspapers worldwide.

URL—http://www.thepaperboy.com

FIGURE 2-1 • Historical Elements in the Early Grades

KINDERGARTEN: AWARENESS OF SELF IN A SOCIAL SETTING

Historical Thinking — Time and Chronology
- Identify changes in seasons.
- Measure calendar time in terms of days and weeks.
- Distinguish between *now* and *long ago*.

Historical Thinking — Historical Comprehension
- Ask questions about past events.
- Read stories of past events.

Historical Understanding — Social History
- Chart personal growth.
- Dress up in clothing from the past.

GRADE 1: PRIMARY AND SECONDARY GROUPS-UNDERSTANDING FAMILY LIFE

Historical Thinking — Time and Chronology
- Begin a personal time line.
- Begin a family history using photos and artifacts.

Historical Thinking — Historical Research
- Handle and describe objects such as old toys, tools, etc.
- Create a historical narrative about a family event.

Historical Understanding — Social History
- Identify the impact of changes in the family.
- Compare families now with those in the past.

GRADE TWO: MEETING BASIC NEEDS: THE NEIGHBORHOOD

Historical Thinking — Time and Chronology
- Develop a school history time line.
- Identify new and historic buildings in the neighborhood.

Historical Thinking — Historical Analysis
- Observe the impact of change in the neighborhood (new homes, stores, etc.).
- Compare neighborhoods now with those from the past.

Historical Understanding — Social History
- Make inferences about change and continuity in the neighborhood.
- Predict the impact of change in the neighborhood.

GRADE THREE: SHARING EARTH AND SPACE — THE COMMUNITY

Historical Thinking — Time and Chronology
- Identify groups of people that settled the community.
- Identify important historical figures in the community.

Historical Thinking — Historical Analysis and Interpretation
- Hypothesize about the life of Native Americans and the early settlers.
- Construct historical narratives and plays about past events in the community.

Historical Understanding – Social History
- Compare life today in the community with life in the past.
- Explain important changes that have occurred in the community.

GRADE FOUR: LIFE IN VARIED ENVIRONMENTS – THE REGION

Historical Thinking – Time and Chronology
- Identify historical figures in the region.
- Prepare a simple time line of historical events.

Historical Understanding – Social History
- Identify how historical events have changed the region.
- Identify how different groups in the region have dealt with change.

Historical Thinking – Historical Research
- Research historical sites in the region.
- Construct historical narratives of people and events who have lived in the region.

Figure 2-1 presents ideas for lessons integrating history standards for the early elementary grades. Specific standards are identified for each grade level and some suggested activities are identified.

History Content in the Middle Grades

As students move into the middle grades, they begin to develop intellectual structures that allow them to deal with more difficult concepts. At about age 12, they begin to reach the formal operations stage in which they can think more abstractly about themselves and others (Elkind, 1981b; Erikson, 1982). Though these students can engage in more complex thinking than can younger learners, they still need lots of guidance and concrete experiences. Learning to think abstractly is an incremental growth process. You cannot simply assume that all your middle-grade students can grasp complex concepts presented in abstract written or verbal forms. They still will benefit from hands-on experiences and other instructional approaches that allow them to deal with new content in concrete ways.

To promote positive attitudes toward your social studies lessons, active involvement in learning is critical. You need to encourage your middle-grade students to explore possible answers to questions they think are important. Young people in this age group develop great satisfaction in doing things on their own, and when you can tie this kind of self-directed activity to your social studies program, your learners' attitudes toward this part of the curriculum will tend to be positive.

Figure 2-2 presents suggestions for history-related content for students in the middle years. You can challenge these students to begin dealing with more complex

FIGURE 2-2 • Historical Elements in the Middle Grades

GRADE FIVE: PEOPLE OF THE AMERICAS

Historical Understanding—Time and Chronology
  • Place historical events in an appropriate sequence.
Historical Understanding—Political History
  • Define the core principles of democracy and state how they were established.
Historical Thinking—Historical Research
  • Determine the credibility of sources about historical events.
  • Construct accounts of historical events.
Historical Thinking—Analysis and Decision Making
  • Identify the values and interests of major historical figures.
  • Compare different accounts of events.

GRADE SIX: PEOPLE AND CULTURES

Historical Understanding—Cultural History
  • Define how art and music reflect the history of a people.
Historical Understanding—Political History
  • Compare governmental structures of nations in different regions.
Historical Thinking—Analysis and Decision Making
  • Identify the interests and values of nations involved in conflict situations.
Historical Thinking—Historical Research
  • Develop questions about people and events through artifacts and conflicting accounts of events.

GRADE SEVEN: A CHANGING WORLD

Historical Understanding—Social History
  • Define the forces behind great migrations of people.
Historical Understanding—Science and Technology
  • Identify how changes in science and technology have impacted regions of the world.
Historical Thinking—Time and Chronology
  • Construct a time line of significant events in world history.
Historical Thinking—Analysis and Interpretation
  • Identify tentative causes and relationships between events.

GRADE EIGHT: BUILDING A STRONG AND FREE NATION

Historical Understanding—Political History
  • Identify the sequence of events that are the foundation of the nation.
Historical Understanding—Economic History
  • Develop a time line of important economic events.
Historical Thinking—Analysis and Decision Making
  • Identify example of problems and dilemmas that have confronted people in the development of a democracy.

dimensions of historical thinking. As they learn to cope successfully with more difficult ideas, they tend to grow in self-confidence and in their appreciation for the usefulness and excitement of studying topics associated with history.

When you prepare history-related lessons, you need to consider more than just curriculum standards related to this subject area. You also have to understand something about the developmental levels of your learners and about kinds of instructional approaches that make sense given students' interests and aptitudes. You also must be solidly grounded in the content you wish to teach. When all of these elements are in place, you are in a position to develop lessons that help your students develop historical understandings and encourage them to be curious about the past.

GEOGRAPHY

Along with history, geography has been a foundation for the social studies. History views people from the perspective of time. Geography views human affairs from the perspective of space and location. Risinger (1992) states that "geography is the stage upon which the human drama is played" (p. 4). This key social science discipline provides insights and tools that are useful in understanding and solving many important and vexing problems.

Geography is a subject that many people profess to understand. However, most have an incomplete and limited view of the subject. At one time, one of the authors held an academic appointment in a university geography department. He often was dismayed when people asked, "What do geographers do other than draw maps?" In fact, geography is a complex discipline, and its interests go well beyond such

The interaction between people and the environment makes each place unique.

Mark Downey/Getty Images, Inc.—Photodisc

applications as teaching students to recognize continents, memorize state capitals, identify landforms, and label topographic features on maps.

What, then, is geography, and how do maps relate to the discipline? In short, geography is an academic specialty that seeks to explain why things are located where they are and to identify patterns that can assist in problem solving. The map is a tool geographers use to display information. Specific concerns of geography relate to relationships among people, cultures, places, events, and environments, with special emphasis on spatial distributions and interactions of phenomena as they occur across space. Studies of distribution are important because people, resources, and other environmental features are not evenly distributed across the face of the earth. Some places lack things that other places have. These differences prompt flows of people and resources from place to place. These flows result in migration and trade. Geographers study the relationships among different regions of the world, paying particular attention to factors that enhance or inhibit the volume or the intensity of these interactions. These understandings help people grasp essential features of issues and problems to make better decisions.

National Standards for Geography

Professional geographers long have worried that too many school programs fail to introduce students to a comprehensive view of their discipline. To promote a more adequate understanding of what should be included in sound geography programs, several national organizations of geographers joined together to develop national standards for geography. These standards—*Geography for Life: National Geography Standards* (Bednarz et al., 1994)—were published to promote improved geography in the schools.

Geography for Life provides several reasons for studying geography. From a practical standpoint, the interconnectedness of the world makes geographic knowledge critical. Markets are now worldwide in scope. Businesses must understand the location of their potential customers, locations of resources, and transportation routes. They need to understand factors in one part of the world that will affect markets and resource flows.

You can draw on geography as you seek to help students overcome ethnocentrism and parochialism. Though our country is separated from other significant parts of the world by two large oceans, these bodies of water no longer isolate the United States from active involvement with people in distant parts of the planet. We live in an increasingly interdependent world, and our young people need to appreciate the nature of global relationships as they grow to maturity.

Geography for Life points out that geography is composed of three interrelated components: subject matter, skills, and perspectives. The *subject matter* component focuses on the earth as the home of humans. This includes the physical environment as well as the cultural dimensions and the interactions among the earth's peoples and between people and the environment. The *skills* component describes ways that geographers explore questions. Among geographic skills are those related to asking geographic questions; acquiring, organizing, and analyzing geographic information; and answering geographic questions. These skills can be applied to a huge variety of topics. Geographic subject matter and skills can be considered from two *perspectives*: spatial and ecological. The "spatial perspective" views the world by looking for

LESSON IDEA 2-4

TOPIC: Migration

OBJECTIVES: Learners can (1) locate places on a map, (2) identify movement patterns, and (3) state reasons for movement from place to place.

ENGAGING THE STUDENTS: As a homework assignment the night before the activity, have students find out from their parents the birthplaces of their parents and grandparents. Begin the lesson by asking students how many of them have moved during their life. Ask the reasons why their families moved. Begin to list the reasons for moving on a chart.

DEVELOPING THE CONTENT: Give each student six circles with "sticky backs." Have them put their initials on the front of each. On one circle write *mother*, on another write *father*, and on the other circles make two for grandfathers and two for grandmothers. Divide the class into groups of five or six. Provide each group with a world map and have them locate the birthplaces of their parents and grandparents. Each group will then share their map with the rest of the class. With the entire class, discuss the following questions: Can we identify any patterns of movement? What might explain those patterns? What were the reasons for the movements of our families? How do those compare with the reasons we put on our chart? What problems do people face when they move?

BRINGING CLOSURE: Conclude the activity by asking, "What did we learn about movement? What did we learn about members of our class? What other movements might be interesting to study? Evaluate students' abilities to locate places on maps and to identify movement patterns, and their participation in groups.

EXTENSION TO THE WEB: The Odden's Bookmarks website allows you to download maps and up-to-date information on every country in the world. This information can be useful in supplementing the family migration lesson.

URL—http://www.oddens.geog.uu.nl/ index.php

location, distance, direction, patterns, shape, and arrangement of human activities such as settlement, industry, land use, and economic activity. The "ecological perspective" looks at physical environmental characteristics such as climate, topography and landforms, vegetation, and the impact of human habitation on natural systems.

Geography for Life organizes the three components of subject matter, skills, and perspectives into six essential elements and 18 standards. A geographically informed person is described as someone who meets these standards and, as a result, who sees meaning and patterns in the way things are arranged, identifies the relationships and interactions among people, places, and environments, uses geographical skills, and applies the spatial and ecological perspectives to life situations (Bednarz et al., 1994, p. 34).

Element One: The World in Spatial Terms Thinking spatially involves using concepts such as location, density, distance, accessibility, flow, and distribution to investigate patterns and relationships. This requires the use of geographic representations such as maps, globes, aerial photographs, and satellite images.

Specific geography standards related to this element are:

- Using maps and other geographic representations, tools, and technologies to acquire, process, and report information from a spatial perspective

- Using mental maps to organize information about people, places, and environments in a spatial context
- Analyzing the spatial organization of people, places, and environments on the earth's surface

Element Two: Places and Regions The region is a central geographic concept. It refers to organizing areas of the earth's surface for various purposes, including investigation and research. A *region* is defined as an area of any size or shape that has a measure of cohesiveness or distinctiveness that sets it apart. Regions serve as a valuable tool for asking geographical questions.

Specific geography standards related to this element are:

- Understanding the combination of physical and human characteristics of places
- Knowing how people create regions to interpret the complexity of the earth
- Understanding how culture and experience influence people's perceptions of places and regions

Element Three: Physical Systems This element relates closely to the physical science and ecology components of the school curriculum. Physical processes

---

LESSON IDEA 2-5

TOPIC: Regions

OBJECTIVES: Learners can (1) identify criteria for establishing a region and (2) draw boundaries for a region.

ENGAGING THE STUDENTS: State to the class, "In our homes and in school we have certain places we go for certain activities. For example, if we want to eat, where do we go? We could call this the eating region. If we want to sleep, where do we go? We could call this the sleeping region. Today we are going out on the playground to see if we can identify different special places or regions."

DEVELOPING THE CONTENT: Provide groups of students with a simple map of the playground. Walk with the class around the playground and discuss what activities occur on different parts of the playground. Discuss a label that might be given to each region or area. Those might include:

- Swing region
- Tether ball region

- No-running region
- Primary-grade region

Have each group of students decide where they would draw the boundaries for each region and think of other regions they could create. After returning to the classroom, have each group's members share their maps and tell why they drew their boundaries where they did. Ask what problems they had in deciding where to draw the boundaries.

BRINGING CLOSURE: Ask students to state what a region is and what they have learned about regions. Evaluate the students' abilities to work together and to begin using simple criteria for establishing a region.

EXTENSION TO THE WEB: The National Atlas of the United States website provides a variety of maps on different topics that can be used to help students explore relationships among people, places, and environments.

URL—http://www.nationalatlas.gov

constantly shape the surface of the earth. Because the physical environment constitutes a background for all human activity, it is an essential component of geographic literacy. There are four basic physical processes. They relate to (1) the atmosphere (weather and climate), (2) the lithosphere (soils, erosion), (3) the hydrosphere (circulation of oceans, the water cycle), and (4) the biosphere (plants, animals, ecosystems).

Specific geography standards related to this element are:

- Knowing the physical processes that shape the patterns of the earth's surface
- Understanding the characteristics and spatial distribution of ecosystems on the earth's surface

Element Four: Human Systems The earth as the home of people is a major interest of geographers. Their study of human systems includes emphases on transportation, communication, economics, manufacturing, agriculture, religion, and culture.

Specific geography standards related to this element are:

- Understanding the characteristics, distributions, and complexities of the earth's cultural mosaics

This photo shows how humans interact with and change the physical environment.

Doug Wilson/U.S. Department of Agriculture

- Understanding the characteristics, distributions, and migration of human populations
- Knowing the patterns and networks of economic interdependence
- Knowing the patterns, processes, and functions of human settlements
- Understanding how the forces of cooperation and conflict influence the division and control of the earth's surface

Element Five: Environment and Society   Geographers have historically been interested in human–environment interactions. Many contemporary problems are the products of both intended and unintended consequences that result from human modification of the physical environment. Lessons you develop related to this element help students to understand the causes and implications of different types of pollution and resource depletion, and the effects of human choices on the environment.

LESSON IDEA 2-6

TOPIC: Environmental Perception

OBJECTIVES: Students can identify how their experiences influence their ideas and perceptions.

ENGAGING THE STUDENTS: Ask students to share the kinds of things they do in a park. Inform them that today they are going to get a chance to design a new park.

DEVELOPING THE CONTENT: Divide the class into groups. Have each group list what they think they would want in a "perfect park." Give them a diagram of a park and have each group draw on the blank diagram where they would put different things in their park. When they are finished, compare what each group included in the park, with special emphasis on the differences. Ask why they think there are differences in what each group included. Discuss the following questions:

- What do you think might be different if this park were in the middle of a city? If it were in a farming community? If it were in the desert? If it were in the mountains? If it were next to the beach?
- Why do you think it would be different? Do you think your ideas would be different if you lived long ago? Why?

- How do you think your ideas would be different if you lived in someplace far away?

Debrief the class by pointing out that the experiences that people have will influence the choices they make. People who live in a city might want to do different things in a park than people who live in the mountains. People who live in different lands and have different games and activities would want different things. People would choose to use the land differently based on their backgrounds and their needs and desires.

BRINGING CLOSURE: Ask students to state what they have learned from the activity. Focus on how well students make the connection between their own experiences and their choices. In addition, note how students decide to work together to resolve differences. They could be given another task in which they will have to resolve differences. Observe how they resolve these issues.

EXTENSION TO THE WEB: The U.S. Geological Survey website offers a number of lesson plans for different grades.

URL—http://mapping.usgs.gov/

Specific geography standards related to this element are:

- Understanding how humans modify the environment
- Understanding how physical systems affect human systems
- Understanding the changes that occur in the meaning, use, distribution, and importance of resources

Element Six: The Uses of Geography This element highlights the point that content from geography and methods of geographers can be applied to many problems. For example, insights from geography often are applied to challenges associated with wars, immigration, transportation, urban sprawl, economic growth, and disease control.

Specific geography standards related to this element are:

- Applying geography to interpret the past
- Applying geography to interpret the present and plan for the future

Geographic content as referenced in the elements and standards described in *Geography for Life* tie easily to outcomes associated with citizenship action and global awareness.

Geography Content in the Early Grades

Good lessons in geography help your students to "think geographically." Your intent is to nurture the development of their observation skills and to encourage them to ask questions about things they observe. To engage learners' higher-level thinking processes, you want them to go beyond asking "Where is it?" to also inquire, "Why is it there?" Pursuing answers to the latter question leads students to understand that there are patterns and reasons for the location of all sorts of things from schools to trees.

Many elements of geography are abstract and can pose special challenges for young children. You must remain aware of both possibilities and limitations imposed by children's levels of development. For example, information presented on maps and globes sometimes is hard for young learners to grasp. This difficulty occurs because these information sources convey information using abstractions, including specialized symbols, scales, directions, and perspective. Though young children may understand the idea of a map and be able to identify geographic features in simple maps and aerial photographs, moving beyond understanding the basics to making inferences and interpretations often is beyond their capabilities (Seefeldt, 2005). For example, the idea that a globe represents the earth can be confusing to very young children because from their perspective, the earth doesn't appear to be round. (We discuss maps and globes in detail in Chapter 7.)

Children begin to develop a more sophisticated understanding of concepts associated with geography as they increasingly explore their immediate environment and their daily lives. Lessons you provide that give them opportunities for numerous concrete exploratory experiences help build a foundation that enables them to cope with more abstract geographic concepts and ideas.

The elements suggested in Figure 2-3 are just a few of those that you might explore with learners at each grade level.

FIGURE 2-3 • Geographic Elements in the Early Grades

KINDERGARTEN: AWARENESS OF SELF IN A SOCIAL SETTING

Developing an Awareness of Spatial Organization
  • Locate objects in the classroom.
  • Construct a simple map of the classroom.
Becoming Aware of Physical Systems
  • Note the changing of seasons.
  • Relating specific seasons to human activities.

GRADE 1: PRIMARY AND SECONDARY GROUPS

Developing Spatial Awareness
  • Learn simple directions such as up, down, right, left, under, over, etc.
  • Learn directions from one place in the school to another.
Natural Systems
  • Classify human-made and natural objects.
  • Collect plants, rocks, etc.
Human Systems
  • Identify transportation types.
  • Define human uses of the environment such as factories, homes, parks, etc.

GRADE 2: MEETING BASIC NEEDS

Spatial Organization
  • Explain why things are located in different places in the neighborhood.
  • Predict the impact of a change in the community on the spatial organization.
Places and Regions
  • Define simple regions such as shopping areas, business district, school attendance areas.
  • Compare the local community with one in a very different place.
Physical Systems
  • State the changes caused by the revolution of the earth around the sun.
  • Identify important physical features such as mountains, oceans, rivers, etc.
Uses of Geography
  • Identify geographic features that attracted settlers to the region.
  • Compare the settlement patterns of now and long ago.

GRADE 3: SHARING EARTH AND SPACE—THE COMMUNITY

Spatial Organization
  • Identify the relationship of the local community to other places in the world.
  • Identify why things are located where they are in the local area.
  • Identify the interdependence of the community with other communities.
Places and Regions
  • Begin to locate places on maps using a grid system.
  • Begin to identify political regions such as city, state, and nation.
Physical Systems
  • Identify the impact of the revolution of the earth around the sun and the rotation of the earth on its axis.

Uses of Geography
- Identify geographical features that attracted early settlers.
- Compare the region of now with long ago.

GRADE 4: LIFE IN VARIED REGIONS

Places and Regions
- Identify different types of region (political regions, cultural regions, climatic regions).
- Define the uniqueness of different regions.

Physical Systems
- Identify the major physical regions of the world.
- Identify patterns that occur in the physical environment.

Uses of Geography
- State problems associated with the uneven distribution of people and resources.

FIGURE 2-4 • Geographic Elements in the Middle Grades

GRADE 5: PEOPLE OF THE AMERICAS

Spatial Understanding
- Make maps showing the distribution of different phenomena.
- Define the relationship between items such as wind currents and weather.

Physical Systems
- Define the impact of earth–sun relationships on seasons.
- State how physical processes change the earth.

Human Systems
- Identify migration routes in the westward movement in nineteenth-century America.
- Locate major cities and transportation routes.

GRADE 6. PEOPLE AND CULTURES

Spatial Understanding
- Locate patterns of world trade.
- Define the interdependence of different parts of the world.

Places and Regions
- Locate the regions of the world.
- Define the uniqueness of different regions as a result of the interaction of physical and human systems.

Uses of Geography
- Predict problems that may arise as a result of the unequal distribution of people and resources.

GRADE 7: A CHANGING WORLD OF MANY NATIONS

Spatial Understanding
- Identify the impact of changes in technology on human systems.
- Define how cultural regions change.

FIGURE 2-4 • (Continued)

Places and Regions
- Develop criteria for defining a region.
- State the problems that occur at the boundaries of regions.

Uses of Geography
- Define the relationship of persistent social and environmental problems.
- Predict the impact of climate change on selected regions.

GRADE 8: BUILDING A STRONG AND FREE NATION

Places and Regions
- Locate the spatial distribution of different cultural groups.
- Note the immigration and migration patterns of people in the United States.

Physical Systems
- Note the impact of major physical features on the development of the United States.
- Identify how the physical environment of the nation has been altered.

Uses of Geography
- Describe the relationship between environmental elements and historical events.
- Apply a geographic perspective to the discussion of a contemporary issue.

Geography Content in the Middle Grades

Middle-year learners' emerging abilities to engage in more abstract kinds of thinking provide opportunities for you to introduce more complex geographic concepts. Students during these years have a great deal of energy and prefer lessons that require their active involvement. They enjoy exploring and discovering new relationships. Generalizations they form from their investigations can be surprisingly sophisticated. Many lessons you teach should aim at encouraging students to develop hypotheses they can test and apply to state, national, and global settings. Active involvement rather than passive participation is a key to successful social studies teaching during these grades. Figure 2-4 shows elements you may explore with middle-year students.

KEY IDEAS IN SUMMARY

- History looks at people through the lens of time. Geography looks at people across space. Lessons associated with history and geography form an important component of a social studies program designed to produce thoughtful and reflective individuals who take a global perspective as they function as informed, active citizens.

- Skills and ideas drawn from history and geography are best learned when they are applied to enduring social questions.

- The steps in the development of historical accounts are (1) gathering relevant facts, (2) assembling them into a pattern, and (3) interpreting the meaning of the pattern. Because no two historians perform these steps in exactly the same way, people who read history must use critical thinking skills and analysis as they examine historians' conclusions.

- One reason often cited for including history in the social studies curriculum relates to citizenship education. The argument is that people with knowledge of the United States' past will tend to accept fundamental American values and beliefs. However, not everyone agrees about what these core values and beliefs are. Hence, history lessons sometimes engender controversy.

- Learning history can help young people develop a sense of connectedness and self-identity. Information from this discipline helps them understand how they fit with a larger community that has been shaped over time.

- The standards given in *National Standards for History* (National Center for History in the Schools, 1996) focus on two major purposes, promoting (1) historical understanding and (2) historical thinking. Historical understanding includes the study of five spheres of human activity, including (a) social history, (b) political history, (c) economic history, (d) cultural history, and (e) the history of science and technology. Historical thinking includes (a) chrono-

logical thinking, (b) historical comprehension, and (c) historical analysis and interpretation.

- Geography involves investigating relationships across space of people, places, events, and environments. Geographers seek to understand why things are located where they are and how patterns are related to each other.

- Geography is composed of three interrelated components: (1) subject matter, (2) skills, and (3) perspectives. The subject matter views the earth as the home of humans. Skills involve techniques required to explore the subject matter, and they include techniques for asking questions and organizing information. Perspectives involve those related to ecological issues and spatial issues.

- *Geography for Life: National Geography Standards* (Bednarz et al., 1994) identifies six elements of geography that are further divided into 18 standards. The six elements are (1) the world in spatial terms, (2) places and regions, (3) physical systems, (4) human systems, (5) environment and society, and (6) the uses of geography.

- As you teach, you need to take into account age and developmental levels of your learners. There are age-appropriate and developmentally appropriate ways of dealing with content derived from both history and geography.

CHAPTER REFLECTIONS

Now that you have read the chapter, think about these questions.

1. What is your understanding of the purposes of history? Are your views different now that you have completed the chapter than they were at the beginning? If so, how do you explain changes in your views?

2. How would you respond to a parent who questioned your teaching of history as not including the "right" focus on the "right" facts?

3. What is your response to the assertion that history and geography are not appropriate for young children and that their study should be postponed until later grades?

4. How would you now define *geography*?

5. How would you describe purposes of elementary school lessons that derive content from geography?

THREE

Political Science, Economics, and Related Social Sciences

Courtesy of the Washington Convention and Visitors Bureau

This chapter will help you to:

- Define the special perspectives of the social sciences.
- Identify content from political science, economics, and other social sciences useful for teaching elementary social studies.
- Develop active learning experiences that draw content from the social sciences.

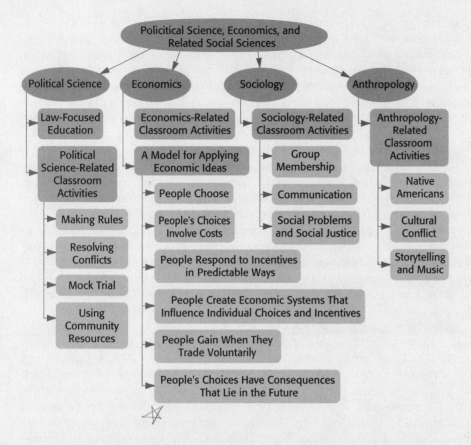

Have you ever been frustrated by governmental policies that seem to ignore the needs of individuals? Have you been upset with "red tape" at city hall when you attempted to do something that required a permit? Have you ever been frustrated while trying to read the small print on a contract or a warranty? Have you wondered why some things get more expensive over time and other things get less expensive? Have you wondered about why people behave differently in groups than they do when by themselves? Have you been puzzled about how such diverse cultures with such different values can develop in such close proximity to each other? Adult citizens encounter these and other similar questions on a regular basis. Understanding these questions and overcoming some of the frustration associated with them requires knowledge from political science, economics, and related social sciences.

Students are similarly puzzled and frustrated when confronted with the everyday issues related to such questions. There is a temptation for some individuals to simply give up and withdraw. For example, the low rate of voter turnout at many elections is viewed by some as an indicator that many citizens have given up trying to have an impact on the political process. Similarly, changes in prices of basic commodities such as gasoline lead many to a sense of being helpless victims of forces beyond their control. Advances in technology and transportation bring us into contact with a variety of individuals from different ethnic backgrounds and with different values and religions. This can lead to suspicion and division.

Living in the twenty-first century requires individuals to have some basic understanding of political science and civics, economics, sociology, and anthropology. However, researchers find that large numbers of young people have deficient knowledge of basic principles associated with these subjects (Branson, 2001).

For example, a report issued by the National Assessment of Educational Progress revealed that more than 30 percent of students in grades 4 and 8 scored below a "basic" understanding level of civics and political science (Lutkus, Weiss, Campbell, Mazzeo, & Lazar, 1999). There continues, too, to be disenchantment with our political system. The numbers of Americans trusting politicians to "do the right thing" has dropped dramatically during the past 40 years (National Commission on Civic Renewal, 1999).

Numerous reports also attest to learners' low levels of economic literacy. The National Council on Economics Education recently commissioned Lou Harris & Associates, Inc., to conduct a survey that included more than 1,000 students. Results of the *Standards in Economics Survey* revealed that large numbers of students lack basic information about concepts related to such issues as money, interest rates, inflation, governmental interventions, and trade (National Council on Economics Education, 1999). With support of the Federal Reserve Bank of Minneapolis, the Minnesota Center for Survey Research conducted a study designed to elicit information about understandings related to a number of economics-associated issues. Among other things, researchers found that more than 70 percent of respondents failed to recognize that determining the best use of scarce resources was an issue of high concern to economists. Few people also were able to explain economic principles behind differences in salaries paid to people in different occupations (Federal Reserve Bank of Minneapolis, 1998).

What does this mean for the future of our nation? Will our students be willing to be involved in the political process? Will they have the knowledge necessary to make decisions that will keep the nation economically strong? Will they live in harmony with those who are different or will they be alienated from one another according to ethnic, religious, or cultural boundaries? These are important questions for the future of our nation. In this chapter we give a brief overview of the social science disciplines that address these issues, and suggest ways to develop classroom lessons based on their content.

POLITICAL SCIENCE

In Chapter 1 we noted that developing civic competence is a primary mission of the social studies. The knowledge and skills required for competent and responsible citizenship are not acquired automatically. In fact, it might be argued that many role models students see in the popular media teach them the opposite of responsible citizenship. Each student must be taught civic responsibility through systematic instruction.

The discipline of political science logically relates to this mission. Political scientists study the systems humans have created for deciding which competing values and aspirations will be institutionalized and enforced among people. In every society, individuals and groups argue over which basic values should underpin the laws and the goals of that society, the best methods for achieving the goals and enforcing the laws, and how to accommodate those who disagree. For example, the electronic surveillance of phone calls of American citizens without a search warrant as a part of the "war on terror" has evoked heated debate. On the one side individuals claim that if a person is not doing anything wrong they should not be concerned and that this action is necessary to protect the nation. Others argue that this such activities are contrary to the Constitution and that such invasions of privacy can lead to misuse of power. Informed and well-meaning individuals disagree about these issues. As a result, societies need political systems to settle these conflicts. Political scientists study these systems.

The National Council for the Social Studies recognizes the importance of content from political science in its *Expectations of Excellence* (1994). This document identifies 10 thematic strands that should underpin all social studies programs (see Chapter 1). The political science emphasis is reflected in strand 6, "Power, Authority, and Governance." Political science is concerned with authoritative decision making and all of the processes by which a society allocates power, makes decisions, establishes rules and laws, and resolves conflict, and with who influences the decision makers. Political scientists investigate social, cultural, and political values; fundamental societal documents such as constitutions; political parties; the responsiveness of government to change; and the relationships of a people to their government.

The content of political science touches all of our lives. The dimensions of power, governance, and authority are not foreign to even the youngest child. Someone—parent, teacher, or other adult—is always making rules for them, telling them how act, and enforcing these rules. They know that different adults may have different rules; for example, their parents might have one set of rules and their teacher another. One teacher might have different rules from another teacher. Generally children don't have much say in the rules they must live by, nor may they understand the reason for them. They just know that because they are small and young they should obey them. Lessons involving political science concepts are meaningful for young children when they are allowed to investigate the need for laws and rules, why there are different rules at different places, and who has the power to establish them.

The *National Standards for Civics and Government* (Center for Civic Education, 1994) identifies three components that its authors assert should be addressed in this part of the social studies curriculum: content, intellectual skills, and participatory skills.

The *content* component relates to what students should know about civics and government. The component is stated in terms of a set of generalizations or

Comparing different forms of government helps students understand different ways that people have made rules and allocated power.

British Information Services

principles that individuals should know about government. Some of those generalizations follow:

- Politics is a process by which a group of people, whose opinions and interests might be divergent, reach collective decisions that are generally regarded as binding on the group.
- Different ideas about the purposes of government have profound consequences on the well-being of individuals and society.
- Constitutions may limit government in order to protect individual rights and promote the common good.
- The world is divided into nation-states that claim sovereignty over defined territory and jurisdiction over everyone within it.

The *intellectual skills* component identifies skills that help individuals think critically about political issues. Content and intellectual skills are inseparable—one does not think in a vacuum. The content forms the basis for the application of the intellectual skills. Intellectual skills are those that require students to explain, apply, develop a position, defend, or evaluate. They require students to do something beyond just reciting from memory.

Equally important to the civics–political science curriculum are *participatory skills*. It does little good for students to learn the content and then fail to participate as citizens. Participatory skills move the content from that of an intellectual exercise

FIGURE 3-1 • **Essential Ideas in Political Science**	
A Selection of Key Concepts	A Selection of Key Questions
Power Authority Equality Justice Rights Responsibilities Laws Liberty Conflict resolution Constitution Citizenship Compromise Democracy Legislature	• Who has power in the society? • How do individuals get power? • How are laws made? • How are the rights of individuals protected? • What are different forms of government? • How do laws change? • How are disputes handled? • What is the balance between the rights of individuals and the power of the government? • How are leaders selected?

to that of developing skills required for competent participation in the political process. Participation skills include the following:

- Building coalitions
- Negotiating
- Compromising
- Managing conflicts
- Making positions known to key policy makers

Figure 3-1 presents a selection of concepts and questions essential to the study of the civics–political science curriculum. Lessons in this component of the curriculum often relate to two basic themes: (1) government and governmental processes and (2) comparative political systems.

Government and governmental processes instruction emphasizes how decisions are made and how widely held values become formalized as laws. Lessons in this area focus on how political leaders are selected and how authority and power are distributed.

Lessons centering on ***comparative political systems*** help students understand that people at various times and places have organized themselves to make political decisions in different ways. These understandings are important given that today's students will live in a world in which contacts are common among people living under very different kinds of political structures. Your lessons should help students better understand that different approaches to government feature alternative arrangements for issues such as allocation of power, conflict resolution, enforcement, and rights of citizens.

Law-Focused Education

A component of political science that has become a part of some social studies programs is *law-focused education*. Law-focused education programs and lessons place special emphasis on our legal system, its relationship to individuals, and its responsiveness to change as a result of citizen action.

Law-focused education was developed to address a growing concern about the alienation of individuals from the law. These programs presume that if learners understand the laws and legal system that underpin our society, as adults they will be less likely to view themselves as victims of an impersonal system. Consequently, they will be less inclined to engage in destructive, antisocial behavior.

Law-focused lessons emphasize both common values of our society that draw us together and values conflicts that divide us. Students examine laws, social problems,

---

LESSON IDEA 3-1

TOPIC: Applying The Bill Of Rights

OBJECTIVES: Students can (1) define in their own words the meaning of articles in the U.S. Bill of Rights, (2) identify contemporary applications of the articles, and (3) work together in cooperative groups.

ENGAGING THE STUDENTS: Ask the class how many have heard of something called the Bill of Rights. Ask several if they know what it is, when it was written, and if it is important to know. Inform them that they are going to be involved in a project to learn about the Bill of Rights and how it applies to us.

DEVELOPING THE CONTENT: Divide the class into groups of four students. Assign each group the responsibility of becoming an expert on one of the first 10 amendments to the U.S. Constitution. Each group should be provided with a handout that includes its amendment and some questions to guide students' thinking about the amendment's meaning. The outcome of this phase of the group work is for students to state in their own words what the amendment means. Each of the definitions can then be placed on the top of a large sheet of paper.

The second assignment for each group is to search through newspapers and magazines to find headlines, articles, cartoons, letters to the editor, or advertisements related to the issues raised in its amendment. Members are to make a collage or a poster on the large sheet of paper that contains their definition of the amendment. When these have been completed, each small group shares its findings with the larger group. They may choose to do this by role playing one of the episodes depicted on their collage or through other creative methods.

BRINGING CLOSURE: This procedure will take several days. At the end of each day, review the group work skills demonstrated and what was learned during that day. At the conclusion of the lessons, students should state what they learned about the Bill of Rights. Ask them to cite at least three ways these protections continue to be relevant.

EXTENSION TO THE WEB: The Center for Civic Education website promotes learners' understanding of governmental affairs and civic responsibilities. Students can use this site to locate information they need to complete this lesson.

URL—http://www.civiced.org/

and controversial issues. It is important for them to realize that difficult problems seldom have absolutely right or wrong answers and that decisions result as much from a consideration of values priorities as from a consideration of evidence.

Law-focused lessons are not designed to turn members of your class into miniature lawyers. Rather, they seek to help them learn substantive content, how to identify and clarify values, and how to apply critical thinking and problem-solving skills. Some basic questions you and your students might pursue include the following:

- What are rules and laws?
- Why do we need rules and laws?
- Who makes the laws?
- What do I do if I think a rule or a law is unfair?
- What happens if a person breaks the law?
- What are my obligations as a citizen to follow the laws?
- How does the law protect my rights and me?
- What do I do if I feel I have been wronged?
- Why does the legal system seem so complicated?

You can choose from among a number of specific focus areas as you plan law-focused lessons. Your lessons may include such topics as (1) basic legal concepts, (2) the Constitution and the Bill of Rights, (3) criminal law, (4) consumer law, and (5) family law. Your specific topic choices should be based on learners' interests and backgrounds.

Understanding how the legal system functions is an important outcome of law-focused education.

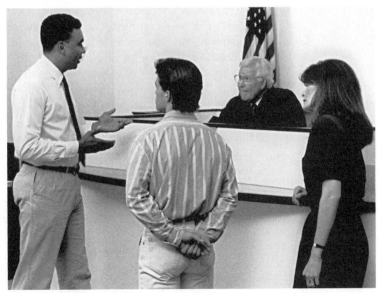

Scott Cunningham/Merrill

Political Science–Related Classroom Activities

Content from political science can help your learners understand the function of rules and laws. Students need to realize that there are honest differences among people regarding the goals and directions of a society and the role of government. Activities introduced here include ideas for helping young people see themselves as individuals who have the potential to influence political decisions. They also are designed to provide them with insights into how our government works.

Making Rules You want students to understand functions of rules and laws in our society. Among other things, lessons that focus on making rules help members of your class realize that people who make laws and people who enforce laws may have different views regarding their adequacy.

You can develop lessons focusing on making rules for use at all grade levels. If you are teaching in the primary grades, your instruction can center on establishing classroom and school rules. You may wish to engage your learners in discussions about how rules you or the principal make may differ from rules they might suggest. With older learners, you may find it useful to expand a rule-making experience to include development of a classroom constitution that all class members sign. This experience can help them learn important political science concepts and promote a sense of ownership in the adopted regulations.

Resolving Conflicts Another topic that is easily applied to the classroom is conflict resolution. Governments act to resolve conflicts between individuals and groups. Every society includes people who differ about what their nation's goals should be and about how they should be pursued. It is important for your students to understand that disagreement does not mean that one side must be "good" or "right" and the other "bad" or "wrong." There are honest disagreements between good and intelligent people concerning the best courses of action.

Lessons can focus on helping students understand that some people and groups try to resolve conflicts by force or violence. Conflict resolution is something that students of all ages confront. They regularly face conflicts on the playground and in the classroom. Because many students know no other ways to resolve disputes, they often resort to fighting or other forms of violence.

The basic issues of conflict and conflict resolution that involve students personally and that may involve their local communities parallel those that arise within and among nations. As students learn to develop effective strategies for coping with personal and local conflicts, their capacity grows to appreciate difficulties of resolving large-scale controversies that may involve whole nations. (In Chapter 7 we discuss conflict resolution in more detail and present methods for developing classroom lessons.)

Mock Trials *Mock trials* are simulation activities that feature enactments of trials. Because they include an element of competition between the contending parties, you will find that mock trials frequently stimulate high levels of student enthusiasm.

You can develop mock trial experiences from controversial issues that have potential to produce litigation at a future date or from reports of trials that already have occurred. If you are interested in engaging learners in experiences based on actual trials, you can draw on an enormous volume of materials developed by firms that

LESSON IDEA 3-2

TOPIC: Rule Making

OBJECTIVES: Students will (1) identify reasons for and advantages/disadvantages of rules, and (2) practice making decisions about issues that have alternative solutions.

ENGAGING THE STUDENTS: Identify a given area of the playground that the students enjoy using. Discuss why they like playing in that area. Then tell them that there have been some problems in that area. Several people have been injured, so school leaders have decided to make rules about use of the area. Several rules have been suggested. The class will discuss these rules and decide what to do.

DEVELOPING THE CONTENT: The first possible rule is to only allow older students to play in the area. Supporters believe this rule will reduce problems because the older children will not have to worry about younger children getting in the way. The younger children will be required to play in another (less desirable) area of the playground. Ask the class what they think about this idea. Use the following questions to prompt discussion:

1. What is good about this idea?
2. What do you think the people who thought about this idea liked about it?
3. Do you think this rule would solve the problem of people getting hurt?
4. Why do you think the upper-grade students like it?
5. What problems might this rule create?
6. Do you think this is a fair rule?

The second proposed rule is that only those people who have demonstrated that they are good citizens will be allowed to play in this area. Buttons will be made and those children who work hard in class and who follow the rules will be given a button by the teacher that they can wear. They can then go and play in the area and all others will have to stay out. People who misbehave will lose their buttons. Discuss this idea using the questions posed previously.

At this point, ask class members to suggest other rules for use of the area. Have them think about issues of fairness and equality as they propose their ideas. When they have identified a rule they agree with, ask them to think about what they might do to encourage its adoption. For example, they might decide to send a group to the student council or the principal or discuss the issue with other classes to get their support. The point is for students to grasp the idea that group action can influence decisions.

BRINGING CLOSURE: Ask class members what they learned about making rules. Why might different groups propose different rules? What should people consider when making rules? What are three or four things people can do when they do not like a proposed rule?

EXTENSION TO THE WEB: The Center for Civic Education website includes resources materials for teachers, lesson plans, and current articles on teaching civics.

URL—http://civiced.org/

---

produce mock trial materials for schools. An excellent general source for such materials is Social Studies School Services. For their elementary school social studies catalog, write to Social Studies School Service, 10200 Jefferson Boulevard, P.O. Box 802, Culver City, CA 90232-0802.

Using mock trials in a classroom involves the three stages of *preparation, enactment,* and *debriefing.* The success of a mock trial depends on careful attention to each of them.

LESSON IDEA 3-3

TOPIC: Conflict Resolution

OBJECTIVES: Students will (1) list steps that can be followed in resolving conflict and (2) define the potential role of governments in conflict resolution.

ENGAGING THE STUDENTS: Present to the class a newspaper report on a current issue in the news. It is best to present one with merit to both sides of the issue. Read the article to the class and have students discuss their thoughts and feelings. Tell them that an important role of government is trying to resolve conflicts such as the one presented while preserving stability and order. Tell them that the class is going to establish a mock government to try to find some solutions to the issue.

DEVELOPING THE CONTENT:

Step 1: *Assigning roles*—An important part of the mock government is assigning roles to class members. It is best if the whole class can be involved. One way of accomplishing this is to divide the class into at least three groups. One group is assigned to gather information and to make a presentation on one side of the issue. A second group is assigned the task of finding and presenting information on the other side of the issue. A third group is assigned the role of the governmental body hearing both sides of the issue and proposing a solution. This group's preparation task is to meet as a group and try to identify the criteria that should be followed in judging the arguments and in arriving at a decision. For example, they might identify "fairness" as an important criterion. They also need to set the rules for the hearing they will conduct.

Step 2: *Defining the issue*—At this stage, hold a discussion before students begin to work in their groups. Focus on identifying the specific issue and the goals of the opposing groups.

Step 3: *Establishing the hearing rules*—Before the hearing is to take place, the third group needs to present its rules on how the meeting will be conducted. Members need to state how long each side will be allowed to present its position and whether it will be allowed rebuttal time. The role of the members of the government in asking questions should also be presented and a person designated to chair the meeting. The power of that person to stop arguments also needs to be considered. When the rules are presented to the class, members are invited to discuss them. After listening to comments of class members, the government group can decide if some of their proposed rules should be changed.

Step 4: *Presenting the positions*—The hearing begins and the sides present their case.

Step 5: *Establishing decision criteria and deciding*—At this point, you and the governmental body discuss what the criteria should be in deciding the issue. Try to get the whole class involved in discussing the criteria. Class members should also decide how they propose to resolve the issue. Will they take a vote on one side or the other, or will they propose a third alternative that might then be voted on?

Step 6: *Debriefing*—This is an important part of the lesson and should not be overlooked. Lead a discussion of the entire decision-making process, noting how the process works in local, state, or federal governments.

BRINGING CLOSURE: Ask the students to review what they learned about conflict resolution during this activity. Ask them to compare this approach to other possible approaches, such as one authority (a king or queen) making the decision, or solving it using force. Require students to enumerate specific features of the conflict-resolution approach they have followed in this lesson.

EXTENSION TO THE WEB: The Center for Civic Education website contains an annotated bibliography of children's literature that can stimulate discussion of conflict resolution and violence.

URL—http://civiced.org/bibliography_violence.html

Preparation. You need to begin by introducing students to the purpose of a mock trial. They must know something about the focus of the trial and what they will do to prepare for it. Actions you take during this step motivate learners and inform them of rules or procedures they must follow. Once you have provided this basic information, you go on to explain the facts of the case. You may wish to prepare and distribute a simple "fact sheet" that explains facts related to both sides of the disputed issue. After you inform class members about the case's basics, you need to pause to take questions so you will know that learners have understood the information you have provided.

Next, identify the roles needed and assign them to individual members of your class. Typical roles include those of judge (or panel of judges), attorneys for both the prosecution and the defense, jurors, and court assistants such as court reporters and bailiffs. Some trials require witnesses and people to play the accused person or persons.

Once you have assigned roles, give individual students specific information about their roles and responsibilities. Do this by providing each person with a sheet that summarizes their role and provides suggestions regarding how it should be played. You may also ask learners to spend one or two class days doing additional research in preparation for the trial. If members of your class have never been involved in a mock trial, you may find it helpful to stage a short rehearsal trial. To do this, select a focus issue that will not require students to do much background preparation work. Assign learners roles. Guide them through the process, answer questions, and generally help them understand the flow of the activity.

Enactment. The enactment stage involves the actual running of the trial in the classroom. This general sequence is followed:

- The opening of the court
- Opening statements by attorneys, with the prosecuting attorney going first and the defense attorney following
- Witnesses for the prosecution, with cross-examination by the defense attorneys
- Witnesses for the defense, with cross-examination by the prosecuting attorneys
- Closing arguments, with the defense going first and the prosecution second
- Jury deliberations
- The verdict and adjournment of the court

During each step, the clerk and the judge make certain routine statements. You may want to give a basic script to students playing these roles so the enactment more closely resembles a real court session. During the enactment your basic task is to keep the activity on track.

Debriefing. You need to monitor time carefully so ample opportunity remains for this important component of the learning process. During debriefing, focus students' attention on issues that have been raised, logic that has been used, and processes that have been implemented. Lead a discussion in which you solicit observations and feelings of the different participants. Ask learners about what they have learned. Often they are tempted to dwell only on the verdict. Though this is an important component of the experience, you do not want discussion of the verdict to overshadow significant learning about the general trial process.

Using Community Resources In nearly every community there are people you can invite to school to help students better understand how governments and government officials operate. Resource people include those working for governmental agencies involved in law enforcement and corrections—police departments; highway patrols; corrections institutions; city, county, and district attorneys' offices; and all levels of courts. Personal visits from these people add an important dimension of reality to what you teach. For example, the problems of law enforcement and the decisions a police officer must make take on added significance when an actual officer comes to the classroom and explains them.

In addition to individuals with direct ties to governmental agencies, you may want to invite attorneys to talk to your class about various aspects of our legal system. Bar associations and law schools are possible sources of individuals who may be willing to come to the school. (There also may be an attorney who is a parent of a child in the class and who would like to talk to a group of elementary school learners.) Attorneys are in a position to share information related to a range of legal topics. Some of them may be willing to assist you in creating mock trials or simulations.

Judges are frequently willing to serve as guest speakers. Their comments can help students understand difficulties judges face as they grapple with complex issues. They can also help students understand that judges face certain constraints as they do their work.

A field trip to view a court in session is often an enlightening experience for learners. In planning for a court visit, you need to recognize that not all courtrooms are open to the public at all times and that there are some cases that are not appropriate for young learners. Usually, you can arrange a court visit by contacting the relevant court clerk.

You may have branches of the Better Business Bureau and the American Civil Liberties Union in your community. The Better Business Bureau has information that may help you develop lessons focusing on consumer law and consumer fraud. The American Civil Liberties Union is particularly interested in civil rights cases.

Finally, the local newspaper should not be overlooked as a useful community-based source of information. Newspapers provide material you can use in constructing rule-making or conflict resolution episodes, or in creating mock trials. You can also have older students read articles dealing with controversial issues that local community members are struggling to resolve.

ECONOMICS

Scarcity is the fundamental concern of *economics.* People's wants exceed the resources needed to satisfy them. Hence, individuals have to decide how to allocate limited resources to satisfy wants and needs. Patterns of decisions characterizing an entire society constitute its economic system. The system developed over the years in the United States attempts to respond to the central issue of scarcity and to accommodate the important social goals of (1) economic growth, (2) economic efficiency, (3) security, (4) stability, (5) equity, and (6) freedom.

One dimension of economics that has received increased attention in recent years is the need for students to understand issues of personal finance. Greenspan

FIGURE 3-2 • Essential Ideas in Economics	
A Selection of Key Concepts	A Selection of Key Questions
Scarcity	How are scarce resources allocated?
Capital	Who decides what is produced?
Labor	How does trade benefit everyone?
Division of labor	How do individuals who are unable to compete
Choice	get their needs met?
Costs	What happens when there is more demand than
Private property	supply?
Public property	What happens to production when individuals
Competition	specialize?
Supply and demand	What happens when there is an incentive to
Specialization	make a choice?
Market	How is it decided how much the work of an
Producer	individual is worth?
Consumer	What is a market economy?
Incentives	What is a command economy?
Price	How does competition influence cost?
Money	

(2005) states that learning financial management skills needs to start at the elementary level to provide a foundation for financial literacy that can help individuals from making poor decisions that can take years to overcome.

More than 140 corporations, governmental agencies, educational organizations, and nonprofit groups have formed the Jump$tart Coalition for Personal Financial Literacy to advocate for more financial literacy programs (Morton, 2005).

Although economics has received considerable attention in the standards movement as a part of the social studies curriculum, the emphasis has focused on broader principles of economics and has moved away from issues of personal finance. However, issues of personal finance certainly have great motivational appeal and should be used as a means for teaching broader economic issues. Figure 3-2 presents selected key economics concepts and questions to guide you in designing lessons.

Economics-Related Classroom Activities

Lessons you develop that draw content from economics help students understand that different economic systems have established different priorities. For example, some societies place more emphasis on the goal of economic security than on the goal of economic freedom.

Elementary economics lessons can focus on consumer and personal finance economics. Lessons in consumer economics center on teaching students how to be alert, careful buyers. Personal economics emphasizes skills such as personal budgeting, management of savings accounts, and (for older learners) balancing checkbooks.

However, it is important that comprehensive economics programs go beyond consumer and personal economics. A well-rounded economics-related program should provide students with a basic understanding of how the entire American economic system operates and how economic decisions affect everyday life.

You often can include economics-related content in lessons that draw most of their information from other subjects. For example, you might want to bring in economic motivations of immigrants in history lessons that focus on movement of people from other lands to the United States. Lessons you develop describing decisions of particular kinds of businesses to locate in given places may well draw content from both geography and economics. Problems governments face in making laws that do such things as (1) limiting choices people can make or (2) allocating tax revenues in certain ways involve both economic and political issues.

Interest in promoting economic understanding among schoolchildren has intensified in recent years. The National Council on Economics Education, founded in 1949, today comprises a national network of state councils and numerous university-based economics education centers. For information, write to the National Council on Economics Education, 1140 Avenue of the Americas, New York, NY 10036.

The National Council for the Social Studies recognizes the importance of content from economics in *Expectations of Excellence* (1994). This document identifies 10 thematic strands that should underpin all social studies programs. The economics emphasis is reflected in strand 7, "Production, Distribution, and Consumption" (see Chapter 1).

A Model for Applying Economic Ideas

Some people see economics as an abstract subject of interest only to those who like to work with complex graphs and mathematical formulas. This is not true. Perspectives of economics have great practical value. They proceed from this basic idea: Human behavior results from choices people make based on expected costs and benefits. Economics education experts Donald Wentworth and Mark Schug (1994) identify six key ideas that relate to this observation that you can use to organize economics-related lessons:

- People choose.
- People's choices involve costs.
- People respond to incentives in predictable ways.
- People create economic systems that influence individual choices and incentives.
- People gain when they trade voluntarily.
- People's choices have consequences that lie in the future.

People Choose   People choose. This statement assumes that your actions and those of others are rational. You make choices after considering alternatives and deciding how to use your scarce resources. The better you understand the alternatives open to you, the better your choices are likely to be. This suggests that one of your purposes in preparing lessons drawing content from economics is to help members of your class better understand pluses and minuses associated with options that are available to them when they have to make choices.

One approach you might take requires students to make decisions about how to spend money. In implementing a lesson of this kind, you first give each member of your class an imaginary sum of money. Ask students to list possible things they might buy. Then, involve them in discussions about advantages and disadvantages of spending their money on various alternatives. As they learn more about each option, the kinds of choices they make should improve. One insight they will acquire quickly is that the available money falls far short of what they would need to buy and everything they might like to have. They must make choices.

When your learners recognize that money is a scarce resource, you can lead them to consider other "desirables" that are scarce. For example, only limited amount of recess time is available. Members of your class must weigh alternatives and decide if they will "spend" this resource playing a game, talking with others, climbing on playground equipment, or engage in some other activity. A discussion related to decisions that students make every day helps them better understand the general human need to choose and allocate scarce resources wisely. Older learners may apply their understanding of positives and negatives associated with individual decisions to content from other kinds of lessons. For instance, you might discuss the choices that were available to people who, in the end, decided to move to a new community, a new country, or a new continent.

People's Choices Involve Costs   Choices involve costs. When you choose "a" instead of "b," you do so because you believe "a" will provide you with more benefits than "b." However, this choice also "costs" you whatever special benefits might have come to you had you selected "b." A choice of one thing denies you the opportunity to benefit from what you decided to reject. Economists use the term *opportunity cost* to explain that benefits you derive from a given decision come at a "cost" of the satisfactions you might have enjoyed from those things you decided not to choose.

You can use the opportunity cost idea to enrich many of your social studies lessons. For example, you might ask students to reflect on the costs borne by people in the United States during the previous two centuries who decided to move west. In addition to monetary costs, these people paid other prices. They gave up opportunities to visit old friends and relatives. They lost the comfortable familiarity of the terrain they had known for much of their lives. They gave up the relative safety of a well-developed society for the dangers of a rough-and-ready frontier. Why did they accept these costs? A discussion of this issue with learners might lead to several conclusions, including the possibility of riches from new lands, new opportunities for their children, and the ability to participate in setting up new governments.

People Respond to Incentives in Predictable Ways   Incentives encourage people to make a particular choice when they are confronted with alternatives. For example, you may find that the incentive of more recess time encourages your students to finish assigned tasks rather than talk to their neighbors. Changes in incentives often cause individuals to change the choices they make. If new incentives are attached to a particular option, this option is more likely to be selected. Similarly, when incentives associated with an alternative diminish, the likelihood decreases that that option will be chosen.

You can introduce members of your class to the idea of incentives through role-playing activities that require them to make choices. For example, you might have them act out roles in a situation you explain in the following way:

"All right, I want two people to play roles. This is going to be a situation involving two friends. One person wants to play a game that requires the other person as a player. The other person would rather watch a TV program. The student who wants to play the game must try to make the friend also want to play and give up the idea of watching television. Let's try and make this as real as we can. Do I have two volunteers?"

After class members finish role playing this situation, you can engage them in a discussion focusing on the incentives offered to encourage the person who wanted to watch television to play the game. Your students probably will suggest some incentives that did not occur to the person who took the part of the friend who wanted to play. The discussion might focus on *disincentives*, things designed to discourage the person from wanting to watch the television program. For example, the individual who wanted to play the game might have suggested that the program was going to be a rerun that the child who wanted to watch TV had already seen. As part of the discussion, you might point out the variety of incentives that are used to get people to do things. Coupons printed in newspapers are designed as incentives to encourage people to shop at certain stores. Advertisements regularly try to encourage a belief that their products will give more satisfaction or pleasure than those of competitors. To the extent individuals believe these claims, advertisements provide incentives for consumers to buy.

People Create Economic Systems That Influence Individual Choices and Incentives This statement speaks to the relationship between the issue of economic freedom and the role of government. To help your class grasp the complex nature of the relationship between the twin ideas of economic freedom and economic justice, you can use prompt questions such as these to spark a discussion:

- Do you believe people should be completely free to make any choices they like?
- What if someone exercises her or his freedom and makes a choice that hurts you? Is this right?
- What should be done about the problem of some people making choices that might hurt others?

Discussions related to these questions help students to appreciate that even in market economies where a high priority is placed on giving economic decision-making authority to individuals, there is a need to place limitations on economic freedom in the name of fairness and justice. Much governmental policy is directed toward this end. The idea is that the government allows the maximum possible amount of economic freedom while making sure that individual rights and freedoms are protected. For example, regulations place restrictions on where industries can dump certain waste materials. These rules prevent pollution and protect the health of the general population. Even elementary students need to understand that there is controversy

LESSON IDEA 3-4

TOPIC: Making Choices

OBJECTIVES: Learners will (1) identify choices they have to make and (2) explain how choosing one thing eliminates another that could have been chosen.

ENGAGING THE STUDENTS: Ask students what they like about events such as Christmas or their birthday. After discussing several things they like, focus on the receiving of gifts. Tell them that deciding what gifts to request involves making choices because people can't buy everything we might want.

DEVELOPING THE CONTENT: State to the class, "I would like you to pretend that I am going to get you a gift for one of those special occasions. I would like you to draw me a picture of five things you want." Collect the pictures when they are finished drawing.

Select one student's picture. Tell the class that the items in the picture are all good things; however, you don't have enough money to buy them all. The price of each item is two dollars and you only have four dollars. Ask the student who drew the picture to tell you which two things you should choose. Ask the individual why he or she chose those items. Make sure to discuss what the student is choosing to give up by not making the other choices. Help the class see that the learner is making choices based on

expected benefits assumed to be more important than what is being given up.

Repeat the process with several other students. Then discuss the following questions:

1. Why couldn't we get everything?
2. How do you decide what things you really want?
3. How do you feel when you have to choose?
4. Do you think people are able to get all the things they want? (This can lead to a discussion of how human wants expand more rapidly than the resources needed to satisfy them.)

BRINGING CLOSURE: Conclude the lesson by asking, "What did we learn about people's wants? Because people have many desires, what do they have to do? What do you need to think about when making choices? Do you have to give something up when you make a choice?"

EXTENSION TO THE WEB: The Foundation for Teaching Economics website offers good examples of lessons designed for use with children at different grade levels.

URL—http://www.fte.org/

---

regarding how much economic freedom is needed and how much government control is required. They will be thinking about and debating this general issue all their lives.

Students readily grasp the need for rules to limit choices. When they play games, they learn to follow rules that place restrictions on what they can do. Discussions of simple rules, such as "three strikes and you're out" in baseball, can lead them to consider governmental actions to limit choices for the purpose of promoting fairness. Role-playing exercises often work well to expand students' understanding of this issue. For example, you might try this idea: Set up a situation in which you make every rule with no reference to learner wishes or in which certain students, such as the oldest or all the boys or all the girls, are allowed to make decisions for the entire class. Follow up with a discussion in which you ask members of your class to share their feelings about these arrangements.

Understanding what is produced in different parts of the world leads to an understanding of the need for trade.

P.A. Pittet/F.A.O. Food and Agriculture Organization of the United Nations

People Gain When They Trade Voluntarily Because people are not self-sufficient, they need to trade. We do not make all of our clothes or grow all of our own food. People who are allowed to trade things they have in surplus for things they lack increase their ability to satisfy their needs. Many of your students will have an intuitive grasp of this idea. They frequently trade things such as lunch items and baseball cards.

You can devise simple activities for learners as young as those in the primary grades to reinforce the idea that trade provides benefits to people. For example, you might ask two people to come to the front of your classroom. Give one bread and the other lunchmeat. Ask students what lunch will be like for the two people if they cannot trade. They will point out that, without trade, one can eat only bread and the other only lunchmeat. However, if they trade, both can make sandwiches. You can have older learners investigate how communities, states, and regions trade things they have for things they want and need. These lessons can lead logically to such ideas as the interdependence of people and regions, the importance of transportation, and the function of money.

People's Choices Have Consequences That Lie in the Future The choices people make do not have perfectly predictable consequences. In your own life, although you try to make decisions that provide you with more benefits than costs, sometimes you are surprised by the results. Even when you make careful choices, unforeseen circumstances can lead to unanticipated consequences. This reality underscores the importance of conveying to students that they cannot simply "go to a book" to find out how they should make a difficult choice. At the same time, your lessons should help them understand that good thinking about choices reduces the probability of making an unwise decision.

To help students think about what goes into making smart decisions, you can initiate a discussion focusing on their recollections of personal decisions that have

LESSON IDEA 3-5

TOPIC: How Incentives Change Behavior

OBJECTIVES: Learners will (1) identify examples of incentives used to influence people's behavior and (2) apply the idea of incentives to understanding the behavior of people in the past.

ENGAGING THE STUDENTS: Begin by asking students if they would be willing to perform an undesirable task. Then ask them if they would perform the task if they received something they desired. Tell them that this is an example of an *incentive*, and that incentives are frequently used to get people to make choices they might not otherwise make.

DEVELOPING THE CONTENT: Divide the class into small groups and give each group a newspaper. Tell them you want them to go through the paper (especially the advertisements) and see how many examples of incentives they can find. Have them cut out the examples and paste them on a chart labeled "Incentives." Each group can then share their chart with the class.

Tell them that incentives can be anything that a person thinks will be beneficial to them. For example, the people who settled our community or our state had some incentives that led them to think that their life would be better if they settled here than at other places. Ask them what the incentives might have been for people to settle in our community or state. List these on the board and then tell them that in the next few days the class will do some research to see if their ideas about incentives are correct.

BRINGING CLOSURE: Ask class members to define *incentives*. Ask individuals to cite three examples of how incentives have encouraged them to act in certain ways. Have learners state how they are going to use their knowledge of incentives in their study of the local community or state.

EXTENSION TO THE WEB: The Economic Education website contains links to an outstanding selection of economics resources for teachers in grades K through 12, including lists of concepts and extensive descriptions of economics-related lessons and activities.

URL—http://ecedweb.unomaha.edu/

not worked out as expected. For example, at times individuals in your class may have chosen to play outside only to find that rain cut their games short. Or, they may have purchased a new game and found some pieces were missing when they arrived home and opened the package. These personal examples provide a link to the understanding that unanticipated events are a constant of life. Many examples from the social studies illustrate this point. For example, founders of new communities in thousands of locations across the American West were convinced that their towns would blossom into huge metropolises. Despite these high hopes, few of these places became thriving cities; many disappeared entirely after a few years.

SOCIOLOGY

Elements of sociology are found in different places in the school curriculum. Strand 5 of the NCSS (1994) curriculum standards is titled "Individuals, Groups and Institutions" (see Chapter 1). This content is directly drawn from sociology. Sociologists

The values, beliefs, and religious convictions of different people are a part of learning sociology.

Israel Ministry of Tourism, North America

study the norms and values of a society and how they are passed from generation to generation; the basic institutions of society such as families, religion, and education; the factors that influence social change; and how groups influence individual behavior. Lessons based on sociology content can help students understand and respond to a daunting array of social problems such as the influence of gangs, the presence of crime, and changing roles.

One of the key ideas of sociology is that of socialization. (Figure 3-3 presents a selection of key sociological concepts and questions.) All children are going through the process of *socialization,* which focuses on how individuals learn what is acceptable in society and what is not. It also includes the concept of *role*, or how individuals learn their place in society and what is expected of them. In an age of rapid change, traditional roles are constantly being challenged and some individuals become confused regarding societal expectations.

Sociology-Related Classroom Activities

Many primary-grade teachers find that a good portion of the social studies curriculum focuses on the family and the neighborhood. Both of these topics are closely aligned with sociology. Lessons on a simple and concrete level can help them understand the roles of individuals in families, how families differ, and how different families might emphasize different attitudes and values. In the neighborhood, they can begin to understand the interdependence and the role of people who live and work in their neighborhood and what happens when there is disagreement or conflict.

Group Membership One aspect of sociology that is useful in teaching elementary students is that of groups and group membership. As students move into the

FIGURE 3-3 • Essential Ideas in Sociology

A Selection of Key Concepts	A Selection of Key Questions
Roles Norms Sanctions Values Socialization Assimilation Primary institutions Social class Social stratification Discrimination Collective behavior Status	How are the roles of individuals defined in each society? What happens when people do not behave according to norms? How do individuals learn their roles? How do social institutions such as church, family, and school influence individual behavior? How do immigrants become assimilated into society? How are norms and roles changing? Why do people behave differently in groups than they do by themselves? How do individuals achieve high status in society?

lower elementary grades they start becoming group members. They may become members of many voluntary groups such as neighborhood play groups, sports teams, and religious groups. This provides you with an opportunity to discuss groups and the impact of groups on individuals. Some students may be tempted to join gangs or groups that generally reinforce antisocial behavior and negative attitudes and beliefs. Helping students understand such groups can help them make better decisions.

Communication Another topic that is frequently found in the elementary grades is that of communication. Being an informed citizen requires that individuals have what is known as *media literacy*. Individuals need to know how to identify and analyze the messages sent by television and movies just as they are able to identify and analyze the message in literature and the print media. Upper elementary and middle school students find content analysis of television programs an engaging activity because they see television as a part of the "real world." In performing content analysis, students look for specific items or activities that occur in a program. For example, they might list the gender roles in a variety of programs over several days. They could identify the instances of smoking or drinking behavior found in an evening of television. They then may discuss in class what messages on these topics the program produces might be sending. Students are often surprised at the subtle messages that people receive through the media.

Social Problems and Social Justice Students' lives are affected by many social issues, including racism, poverty, homelessness, littering, crime, delinquency, war, and substance abuse. These issues should not be avoided simply because they

LESSON IDEA 3-6

TOPIC: Learning Roles

OBJECTIVES: Students can (1) list the similarities of roles by gender and (2) describe the factors that teach people their roles.

ENGAGING THE STUDENTS: Either provide the students with a variety of magazines or have them bring some from home. With their parents' permission, if necessary, have them cut out pictures of men and women performing different tasks.

DEVELOPING THE CONTENT: Once the students have gathered a large number of pictures, have them stack the pictures according to gender and activity, grouping, for example, those pictures that portray men performing similar tasks and those that portray women performing similar tasks. Allow students to use their own criteria for deciding how to group the pictures. When all of the pictures have been grouped, ask the class to provide a label for each group that defines the types of tasks portrayed in the pictures. For example, groupings that show

individuals with children might be labeled "child care," those with food might be labeled "cooking," and so on. Then have the class compare the groups for men and women. What differences do they find? Why do they think there are differences? How do people learn what is expected of them? Should there be differences?

BRINGING CLOSURE: Use the following questions to bring the lesson to a conclusion: "What did you learn about how to group things? What did you learn about roles? What do you think should be done to help people change the way roles for men and women are taught?"

EXTENSION TO THE WEB: The Safe Healthy Schools' website promotes awareness of gender equity. You will find lesson plans on gender equity.

URL—http://www.safehealthyschools.org/sexuality_education/214.html

are unpleasant, controversial, or difficult. Students are aware of poverty, homelessness, and crime. At the upper elementary level investigating these topics give students an opportunity to become involved in the local community and to learn that they can make a difference. This makes social studies more than an abstract subject with little connection to everyday issues.

One lesson approach would be to identify social issues that are present in your local community. Students can choose an issue and gather data regarding its occurrence locally, and the community's response, if any. They can propose possible ways to address the issue and specific things they can do to help. It can be extremely satisfying for students when they believe they have made a useful contribution and made a difference in the community.

ANTHROPOLOGY

Anthropologists study human culture. They look at the ways people interpret and assign meaning to their social and physical world. In a world where images of other cultures appear nightly on television and where mobility has made it possible for

The various ways people have sought meaning and interpreted their physical world are included in anthropology.

Laima E. Druskis/PH College

people from different parts of the world to interact, it is important that individuals begin to appreciate the rich diversity of cultures.

One of the basic principles of anthropology is the idea of *wholeness*. This means that taken as a whole, the elements of a culture makes logical sense to the members of that culture. Understanding this idea is important for social studies teachers in order to get away from the "strange lands and funny people" approach to studying cultures across the world. This idea also relates to the concept of *ethnocentrism*. Individuals living in a given culture tend to think their way of viewing the world around them is the "right" and "natural" one, and view others as strange and unnatural. Students need to learn that no matter how different a culture might be from their own, that the people in that culture view it as logical and natural.

Certain topics associated with anthropology have long been a part of the elementary curriculum. Units with titles such as "Native Americans," "Early Civilizations," and "People of Other Lands" all have anthropological roots. Current emphases on ethnic studies and multicultural education also provide opportunities for teaching anthropological content. Figure 3-4 presents selected key anthropological concepts and questions you may use when developing lessons. There are numerous artifact kits available to teachers on topics such as ancient Rome and ancient Egypt that may help you teach the content and methodology of anthropology.

Anthropology-Related Classroom Activities

When developing anthropology-related activities for use in the classroom, a priority ought to be to provide experiences that will teach class members to respect other cultures. Care should be taken not to exaggerate unfamiliar customs or cultural practices.

FIGURE 3-4 • Essential Ideas in Anthropology

A Selection of Key Concepts	A Selection of Key Questions
Culture	What is human about human beings?
Cultural change	How did we get this way?
Cultural borrowing	How does a culture define what is right or normal?
Cultural lag	
Adaptation	How do cultural beliefs influence how the people view their environment?
Ritual	
Tradition	What happens when two different cultures come into contact?
Ethnicity	
Religion	How do traditions and rituals maintain a culture?
Invention	
Extended family	What happens if a culture is isolated from contact with others?
Nuclear family	
	How do religious practices affect values and behavior?
	How does the culture influence receptivity to changes such as new technology?
	Who is awarded high status in the culture?

Students should understand that there are legitimate ways to meet life's challenges that may differ from typical American practices.

Native Americans Studies of Native Americans is common throughout the elementary social studies curriculum. It is common to find a unit in the third grade as students study the history of the local area, in the fourth grade as they study the state and region, and in the fifth grade as they investigate the history and geography of the United States. Fortunately, contemporary units on Native Americans are getting away from stereotypes and myths. For example, contemporary units avoid communicating the myth that all Native Americans lived in tipis and were nomadic hunters of buffalo (although this statement is of course true for some groups).

An abundance of material is available that you can use to emphasize the rich cultural diversity of Native American cultures. There are, for example, numerous well-written children's books. These include Paul Goble's retelling of myths and legends of the Plains Indians in books such as *The Gift of the Sacred Dog* (Bradbury, 1980); Tomie De Paola's *The Legend of the Bluebonnet: An Old Tale of Texas* (Putnam, 1983); Leigh Casler and Shonto Begay's Chinook legend, *The Boy who Dreamed of an Acorn* (Philomel Books, 1994); Nancy Van Lann's telling of an Ojibwe legend, *Shinglebiss: An Ojibwe Legend* (Houghton Mifflin, 1997), and Michael Lacapa's

Apache folktale, *Antelope Woman* (Northland, 1992). These stories can help your students gain insight into varying cultural beliefs of Native Americans and how they developed functional approaches to meeting important life challenges.

Excellent nonfiction books are also available that can provide important information about Native American cultures, including *Buffalo Days* by Diane Hoyt-Goldsmith (Holiday House, 1997), *Songs from the Loom: A Navajo Girl Learns to Weave* by Monty Roessel (Learner Publications, 1995), and *Ancient Indians: The First Americans* by Roy Gallant (Enslow, 1989).

Cultural Conflict   Cultural conflict will be an issue that all of us will face throughout our lives. Changing times bring challenges to accepted customs and beliefs. Some cultures are able to adapt easily to changes and some are not. You can help students understand the important dimension of cultural change by focusing on prospective changes that affect individuals of their own age. For example, suppose there is a proposal to change the school calendar to a year-round scheme. Students can brainstorm what the changes might mean to them (e.g., impact on summer vacations, changes associated to moving to other places that retain the traditional calendar, the impact on family life, problems in maintaining school buildings if they are constantly in use, etc.).

One particular challenging dimension of cultural conflict is the adjustment that must be made when two cultures come into contact for the first time. Initial contacts are frequently disturbing for members of both cultures. Once again children's books, such as the *Lotus Seed* by Sherry Garland (Harcourt Brace Jovanovich, 1993) and *The Double Life of Pocahontas* by Jean Fritz (Puffin, 1983), explore the conflicts that occur when two cultures come into contact.

It is probable that there are people living in your community who have immigrated from other countries. You can invite them to come to class and share the difficulties they experienced when moving to the United States and tell about the things they saw and thought were strange or unusual.

Storytelling and Music   Storytelling is a common method for passing customs and beliefs from one generation to another. Gathering the stories of a culture is a major interest of anthropologists. Books such as *Why Mosquitoes Buzz in People's Ears* by Verna Aardema (Dial Books, 1975) can be used to illustrate how the stories people tell often communicate their values and beliefs. Music can also provide insight into the culture of a people. Song is often a form of storytelling. Class members can collect and share songs they have heard and stories they have been told that taught them something important. To make songs and stories from other cultures relevant to your students, you can challenge them to think about the stories that are included in their own popular music. Encourage them to ask, "What will future generations think about us by the stories that are included in our music?"

In this chapter we have provided a quick overview of some of the social sciences that provide the content foundation for social studies. Taken together they provide a variety of important perspectives and information about people and cultures. A good social studies program should include content from these different subjects to provide a comprehensive understanding of what it means to be human and of our responsibilities as citizens.

LESSON IDEA 3-7

TOPIC: Learning from an Artifact

OBJECTIVES: Students will make (1) at least one statement of the characteristics of a culture based on an investigation of an artifact, and (2) state how wrong conclusions can be drawn.

ENGAGING THE STUDENTS: Ask students how they think book authors know what conditions were like long ago. For example, how do they know how ancient Egyptians lived? How do they know about life in a Native American village? Have students brainstorm how we know about people and conditions from long ago. Inform them that one way is to investigate the things the people left behind such as pictures, tools, clothes, etc. Say, "We call these items *artifacts*. Scientists called anthropologists and archaeologists investigate artifacts to see what they can learn about these people. Today the class is going to investigate an artifact and see what we can discover." You might read to students Byrd Baylor's *One Small Blue Bead* (Charles Scribner's & Sons, 1992) to capture the excitement and significance of finding artifacts.

DEVELOPING THE CONTENT: Tell students, "Imagine that we are living 3,000 years in the future. We live on another planet and we have made a trip to a place called earth. As we are digging through the ruins on this planet, someone finds a jar full of coins. It is our job to see what we can tell about these people just by looking at these coins."

At this point, give each class member a coin (a penny, a nickel, or a mixture of pennies, nickels, dimes, and quarters). Say, "Look carefully at the coin and see what you can learn from it. Think about things such as the skills and abilities of the people, their government, their dress, and anything else. You may have to make inferences or guesses that go beyond just what you see on the coin."

After a few minutes of allowing students to talk among themselves, begin listing the conclusions they have drawn. Ask for their reasons.

Reinforce how inferences might be made from the fact that the coins are made with considerable precision. Ask, "What does that mean? What might it mean if we searched the area and could not find mines that contained the metals from which the coins were made? Who do you think the people are that are pictured on the coins? What can we learn by noting that the coins have a date on them? Why do different coins have different dates on them?"

Say to students, "Since we are living in the culture that uses the coins, we can tell which conclusions might be right and might be wrong. For example, does everyone dress like the figures we see on the coins? Do people live in houses or buildings like those pictured on some of the coins? Who are the figures on the coins? Are they pictures of gods?"

Discuss what might be done to check the conclusions drawn from artifacts. Ask, "What does it mean for us when we read about ancient civilizations where most of our knowledge is drawn from artifacts?"

BRINGING CLOSURE: Ask class members to state how artifacts can help us learn about people who lived long ago. How can we get them to tell us their story? Have them state how some conclusions might be wrong and what we need to remember when we study people from long ago.

EXTENSION TO THE WEB: The Smithsonian Institution website provide numerous resources for students K–12. The site gives many illustrations and pictures of artifacts that could be used to develop lessons.

URL— http://www.sil.si.edu/SILPublications/ Anthropology-K-12

KEY IDEAS IN SUMMARY

- In recent years, numerous surveys have revealed that young people as well as adult citizens lack much basic information about concepts associated with political science and economics. As a result, groups interested in promoting better understanding of concepts tied to these disciplines actively promote improved political science–related and economics-related school instruction.

- Many school programs associated with the discipline of political science feature *law-focused* lessons. These learning experiences introduce students to aspects of our legal system, its relationship to individuals, and its responsiveness to modification as a result of citizen action.

- Economists' fundamental concern is scarcity and, more particularly, how people respond to a world in which their wants exceed their capacity to pay for them. Knowledge derived from economics helps explain how people in different societies have responded to this fundamental human dilemma.

- Many economic programs in elementary schools help students to better understand that (1) people choose, (2) people's choices involve costs, (3) people respond to incentives in predictable ways, (4) people create economic systems that influence individual choices and incentives, (5) people gain when they trade voluntarily, and (6) people's choices have consequences that lie in the future.

- School lessons focusing on sociology and anthropology serve several important ends. Lessons that draw content from these disciplines provide learners with insights they will need to interact positively with people coming from ethnic and cultural backgrounds that differ from their own. Further, in their own classrooms, today's learners come into daily contact with young people from highly diverse backgrounds. It is important for them to learn to respect and value this diversity.

- Sociologists study groups, why they are formed, how they are organized, how they influence behaviors and values of their members, and why they sometimes fall apart. Insights from sociology can help members of your class understand that behavior patterns of individuals have multiple causes, and that among these, group and social norms play an important role.

- As they study human culture, anthropologists consider the diverse ways different people assign meaning to their social and physical worlds. Lessons associated with anthropology help your learners understand that there are a variety of legitimate ways people can approach common life problems. Instruction based on anthropology helps young people to become less ethnocentric and more tolerant of perspectives of other cultures.

CHAPTER REFLECTIONS

Now that you have read the chapter, think about these questions.

1. Are lessons derived from political science important as aids to promoting desirable characteristics of citizenship? Explain your response.
2. Is it possible both to promote loyalty to our government and society and at the same time focus on controversial topics about which there is little public agreement?

3. Few elementary school teachers take more than a single economics course as part of their undergraduate degree and teacher-preparation programs. Is it reasonable to expect people with so little background in economics to prepare lessons derived from this discipline?
4. Some issues associated with both political science and economics are controversial. How do you weigh a need to teach learners how to deal

with controversy and at the same time avoid upsetting parents and guardians who may not want their children to adopt opinions different from their own?

5. What do you see as merits and potential difficulties of implementing rule-making and mock trial learning experiences?

6. Should content related to political science and economics receive (1) more attention, (2) less attention, or (3) about the same amount of attention as you believe it typically receives today? On what do you base your conclusion?

7. What would you tell a parent about the "relevance" for learners who are in the *(choose a grade you would like to teach)* grade of content drawn from sociology and anthropology?

8. There are number of lesson ideas introduced in this chapter. Which of them particularly appeal to you? What elements of your favorite lesson ideas do you think would be especially good at motivating elementary students?

9. What do you think you need to learn about sociology and anthropology in order to develop good lessons based on these subjects?

10. Have your ideas about what should be taught in elementary social studies classroom changed as a result of reading this chapter? If so, in what ways?

FOUR

Active Learning: Giving Life and Meaning to Social Studies

Myrleen Cate/Index Stock Photography, Inc.

This chapter will help you to:

- Define the importance of providing your students with opportunities to put content they receive in their social studies lessons to active use.

- Identify challenges you may face in attempting to implement applied-learning approaches.

- Describe features of selected approaches that promise to provide students with concrete learning experiences.

- Implement necessary steps in planning service-learning experiences and indicate how students can be involved in indirect, direct, and advocacy service-learning activities.

- Demonstrate approaches to helping your students deal with controversial issues.

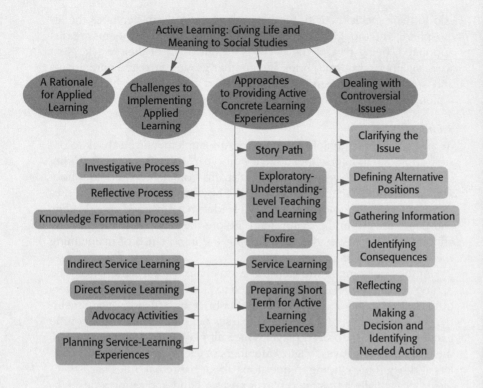

Is it important for the work students do in school to be connected to the community and the world beyond the school? Consider these two situations.

Scenario A

Jeffers is hosting today's basketball games between Jeffers Middle School and Lincoln Middle School. The boys' teams play first, followed by the girls' teams. Excited students, teachers, and administrators from the two schools, parents and guardians, and others from the local community fill seats in the gym. Members of the school pep bands and cheerleading squads pump up the crowd before the games, during timeouts and halftime breaks, and between the boys' game and the girls' game.

During halftimes, school dance squads entertain the crowd. Concession stand sales of snacks and soft drinks are brisk, and school administrators are pleased that they will have some additional money to add to their special activity fund. An air of enthusiasm pervades the atmosphere, and though players and supporters of the losing teams are disappointed, being part of the event is a high point of their week. Next week's games promise to bring out another group of excited participants and spectators. Members of today's crowd look forward to seeing a writeup of the games in tomorrow's newspaper.

Scenario B

As an experiment, administrative leaders are implementing a "back to basics" approach to interschool athletics this year. Today's games, featuring contests between boys' teams and girls' teams from Ashton Middle School and LaMar Middle School, begin with the boys' game. In an effort to preserve an academic atmosphere, school leaders have banned cheerleaders and pep bands from the gymnasium. Before the boys' game begins, the announcer admonishes the crowd about the importance of maintaining silence once the competition begins.

At the beginning of the game, five armchairs for the starters from the Ashton Middle School team are arranged to face five armchairs for starters from the LaMar Middle School Team. After brief introductions, team members take their seats, and the referee passes out pencils and copies of the game test booklets to each player. Once all players have their materials, the referee quietly says, "begin." Members of each team open their booklets and begin responding to questions about basketball rules and strategies. Occasionally a frustrated player raises a hand, indicating a desire to be replaced by a substitute.

At the end of the game, the referee picks up the exam booklets and corrects them with representatives of each team's coaching staff looking on. Once this is done, the results are announced, and the crowd files quietly out of the stadium.

Scenario "B" describes a hypothetical (and highly unlikely) situation in which a school district decided to restrict learners' competitive experiences to kinds of behavior that may have some meaning within the four walls of the school but that fail to connect in meaningful ways to the world beyond. "Learning the facts" about basketball and scoring well on a paper-and-pencil test over this material may produce evidence a teacher can use to sort learners and award grades. However, these facts in isolation from actions that require students to apply information in realistic ways have little practical utility. If a school district were ever foolish enough to implement a policy such as the one reflected in scenario "B," likely results would include diminished student enthusiasm for participating in athletic team activities and reduced parent and community interest in interschool competitions.

Contrasting situations depicted in these two scenarios have implications for your social studies program. If you want to generate student interest in your social lessons and build more community support for this part of the school curriculum, you need to build in opportunities for students to apply what they have learned.

A RATIONALE FOR APPLIED LEARNING

In addition to increasing student interest and community support, you serve important curricular ends when you imbed real world–oriented, application activities into your social studies program. Although many school philosophy statements claim that the entire school program seeks to promote democratic citizenship, the social studies accepts special responsibility for this task. If your lessons involve students in little more than discussing ideas related to democracy and the responsibilities of citizenship as abstractions, members of your class may include such information in a category labeled "stuff we need to know for school" and conclude that it has little importance for the real world. In time, class members may come to define education as an "accumulation of information to be tested in school" rather than as providing useful guidelines for behavior in the real world.

Edwards (2005) points out that one aspect of being an informed citizen is that of knowing how to build a better world. This requires more than just passing a test. It requires active involvement and participation so that students participate in solving important problems.

Individuals' habits of mind and heart take root in the early years (Wade, 2000). Lessons you develop that involve members of your class in activities that require them to act on their newly acquired knowledge promote development of the idea that individual actions can make a difference in the world. In addition, applied

Helping clean up a local park offers this student an opportunity to engage in participatory citizenship.

Pearson Education Corporate Digital Archive

learning often helps class members understand that what you are teaching has importance to their lives outside of school. This appreciation can engender positive student attitudes toward your social studies lessons. In addition, students find that lessons that require them to generate knowledge are more empowering than lessons that require them only to passively absorb information provided by others (Freiberg & Driscoll, 2000).

CHALLENGES TO IMPLEMENTING APPLIED LEARNING

In some schools, principals and other administrators do not regard social studies instruction as a high-priority component of the curriculum (Checkly, 2006). When such attitudes exist, they often result from pressures exerted by mandated standardized-test programs. Many elementary and middle school testing programs place much heavier emphases on reading, writing, and mathematics than on social studies. Low pupil scores on these tests bring heavy pressures on school administrators. As a result, some school principals divert more resources and general support to areas assessed by standardized tests in the hope that this support will produce increased student scores.

If you find yourself in a situation in which concerns about tests tend to undermine administrative support for your social studies program, you can take steps to support the importance of social studies. Areas such as reading and mathematics are skill areas. They provide individuals with skills to apply to real problems. The content for the *application* of these skills is found in such subjects as social studies and science. This helps explain why students' scores on standardized reading and mathematics tests often go up when they have opportunities to develop these proficiencies in different contexts. Applying these skills to content areas such as the social studies only makes sense. Prose materials are used to transmit much social studies content. Therefore, reading is an important skill that has wide application in the social studies. Similarly, social studies lessons often engage students in applying mathematical principles (computing differences in longitudes and latitudes, for example), in reading and interpreting numeric data from charts, and in preparing and analyzing graphs. Social studies lessons afford many possibilities for helping students acquire and apply important social studies knowledge and skill and, at the same time, sharpen their reading and mathematic skills.

Some of your students' parents and guardians initially may not be enthusiastic supporters of active, applied social studies activities. Often, attitudes of parents and guardians are shaped by their personal recollections of their own social studies lessons. Some of them recall instruction that featured nothing more exciting or challenging than filling in worksheets, outlining text chapters, and taking simple identification tests. One of your tasks is to bring parents and guardians up to date on features of a good contemporary social studies program, particularly one that works hard to engage students in applying what they have learned to the real world. You will need to defend these activities based on their impact on student learning. Parents and guardians often become strong advocates of programs they see as important in preparing their children for the realities of the world beyond the school.

APPROACHES TO PROVIDING ACTIVE, CONCRETE LEARNING EXPERIENCES

Although the instructional setting of the school where you teach will influence your decisions, making active, concrete learning experiences an integral part of your social studies program largely is a matter of your own determination to do so. This kind of instruction requires you to think carefully about how to promote active involvement of your class when new information is presented and, even more importantly, about what your students can do to make use of newly acquired knowledge and skills. Learning through concrete experience has deep historic roots. These learner-involving approaches have been promoted over the years by such theorists as John Dewey, Jean Piaget, Hilda Taba, Ralph Tyler, and Ernest Boyer (Wade, 2000).

Over the years, several labels have been used to describe learning orientations that embed these features. For a time, the term *project learning* was often used. More recently, educators have begun to use the term *experiential learning* to describe school programs that engage learners with practical situations, dilemmas, and perspectives that they can apply to real situations. Most discussions related to experiential learning point out that lessons organized according to this perspective have the potential to involve students in practical applications of newly acquired content.

You have many options available to you as you strive to build meaningful experiential learning experiences that provide a connection between your classroom and the world beyond. These options range from relatively simple activites that require a minimum of change to those that involve students directly in real-world activities that require considerable thought and planning.

Some of the relatively simple activities involve bringing outside speakers to the classroom, involving students in Internet activities, and by simulating real-world applications through the use of well-designed role-playing exercises and simulations.

In many communities, opportunities exist that allow students to be involved outside of the classroom. These can be relatively simple activities that require little or no time off of the school grounds such as making a presentation to a principal or inviting community leaders to the classroom to more complex activites that take students into the community.

Your choices will be influenced by the age and sophistication of your students, the kinds of content your social studies lessons are featuring, and the difficulty in having students involved in activities away from the school campus. More mature learners can be involved in complex service-learning activities or in various kinds of community-improvement initiatives. The activites in which they are involved should focus on important social studies standards and outcomes. If they do not, their effectiveness will be limited and you are likely to find more resistance from administrators and parents.

In subsections that follow, we explore the following approaches to providing active, concrete learning experiences:

- Story Path
- Exploratory-understanding-level teaching and learning
- Foxfire
- Service learning
- Short-term lessons featuring active, concrete learning

Story Path

Story Path is an active involvment learning approach that uses the elements of story in the design of units and lessons. It is based on a strategy that was developed and taught in the schools of Scotland. Numerous units using the Story Path method have been published and are available for purchase. Whole sets of material are available on topics such as "Families in the Neighborhood," "The Community Park," "A Pionner Community," "The Oregon Trail," "Ancient Civilizations," and "A Presidential Election." The availablilty of already developed sets of material with a teacher's guide and various forms and activities for students can be useful for new teachers who do not have the time to devote to the development of new units. However, the basic elements of the Story Path can be used to create your own lessons that are focused on your curriculum or your students.

Story Path combines problem solving with the elements of a story. As a teacher, your role is to define the setting and establish the plot. For example, the plot might be based on a historical episode or an issue or activity such as election or a controversial issue. Students get involved by identifying themselves with a character that they create and define.

Story Path then becomes an unfolding drama where the characters encounter problems that must be solved and decisions that must be made. Because they are characters in the story, it helps them take ownership for their own learning and requires that they apply and test the knowledge that they have and construct their own understandings as a result of their encounters. For example, "The Oregon Trail" (McGuire, 2005) places students in the role as members of a wagon train (the setting). They create their own unique character that then embarks on the trip to Oregon (characterization). Along the way they confront critical events that require problem solving and decisions (the plot). Lesson Idea 4-1 is an example of an activity based on the Story Path approach.

Exploratory-Understanding-Level Teaching and Learning

Instructional specialists Morris Bigge and S. Samuel Shermis (1999) use the term *exploratory-understanding-level teaching and learning* to describe a more complex and sophisticated approach to planning and delivering classroom lessons that feature concrete application experiences. When exploratory-understanding-level teaching and learning is successful, students emerge with increased knowledge; an enhanced ability to solve problems on their own; knowledge of what good thinking is; an increased ability to distinguish relevant from irrelevant information; and intellectual habits of curiosity, persistence, and carefulness.

This approach features a cycle that involves learners in a recurring pattern of involvement with four phases or processes: (1) the *investigative process,* (2) the *reflective process*, (3) the *knowledge formation process*, and (4) the *application process* (Bigge & Shermis, 1999). Components of this learning cycle are depicted in Figure 4-1.

Investigative Process During the investigative-process phase, your students, with your help, investigate high-interest problems that require active learner participation. To begin the investigative process, you establish conditions that allow students

LESSON IDEA 4-1

TOPIC: Changes in the Neighborhood

OBJECTIVES: Students will (1) identify various economic and social functions in the local community, and (2) predict the impact of change in one part of the community on other parts of the community.

ENGAGING THE STUDENTS: Develop a list with students of the various functions, businesses, and other locations that are found in a community, including houses, schools, hospitals, parks, stores, and so on.

DEVELOPING THE CONTENT: Present the students with a simple community map containing just the basic street pattern. Have the students identify where they would place some of the various functions and locations such as schools, parks, and so on. Inform them that they will be living in this community. Have them choose and define a role to take on for the activity. Some may choose to be store owners, others teachers, for example. Have them write a

short description of their character. Students are to also choose a place in the community where their character will live. Add these locations to the map.

After all students have described their characters and where they live, announce that the state has decided to build a new highway through the community. Have a predetermined route for the highway that you then place as an overlay on the existing map. The route may cut across some businesses, homes, or other functions that the students have placed on the map. Ask students what they think will happen to the community if the highway is built.

BRINGING CLOSURE: Review what the class did. Ask what some of the issues or concerns might be. Use these questions to build subsequent lessons. For example, the next lesson might be a public hearing where students can express their feelings about the new highway and the proposed route.

to have a concrete or highly real world–oriented learning experience. For example, you may choose to focus on an issue that is generating much interest in your local community. Another possibility might be to involve learners in simulated recreations of historical events. You might find it appropriate to take on the role of a particular historical figure yourself and deliver information to members of your class in a way that is consistent with the style and manner of the person you are depicting. You may be fortunate enough to live in an area where some local residents regularly participate in living history presentations. A class presentation by someone who regularly portrays Benjamin Franklin, George Washington, or another key figure from our history can generate high levels of learner interest. Some teachers have developed imaginative ways of involving members of their class in "relivings" of experiences from our nation's past.

One middle school social studies teacher involves class members as participants in a comprehensive Civil War enactment. Class members wear uniforms and even take part in an overnight encampment. A fourth-grade teacher turns her room into a wagon train and students spend a night together on the trail. It has been so popular that parents request this teacher for their children.

Reflective Process During the reflective-process phase, you work to help your students think about what they have learned during their investigations and make sense out of what they have discovered. Your work during this phase builds on the

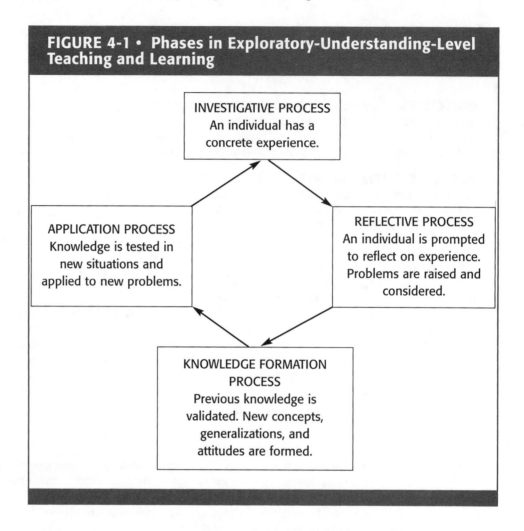

FIGURE 4-1 • **Phases in Exploratory-Understanding-Level Teaching and Learning**

INVESTIGATIVE PROCESS
An individual has a
concrete experience.

APPLICATION PROCESS
Knowledge is tested in
new situations and
applied to new problems.

REFLECTIVE PROCESS
An individual is prompted
to reflect on experience.
Problems are raised and
considered.

KNOWLEDGE FORMATION
PROCESS
Previous knowledge is
validated. New concepts,
generalizations, and
attitudes are formed.

idea that students' roles properly involve generating knowledge, not just taking in information transmitted to them by others. You need to use appropriate questions as prompts to get members of your class involved in the reflective process. Shanks (1998) identifies several different levels of reflective questions that can be used to help learners think about their experiences and make meaning out of them. These include (1) questions related to previous experience, (2) questions that probe for deeper levels of understanding, and (3) questions that elicit personal-meaning descriptions. Figure 4-2 provides examples of questions at each of these levels.

A critical element in any form of reflective thinking is problem posing. Framing and stating the problem accurately is central for productive reflection and resolution. For example, if a person driving a car experiences a flat tire and does not have a car jack, the problem can be posed in a couple of ways. One way of posing the problem would be how to get a jack. A second way of posing the problem is would be how to lift the wheel off of the ground so the tire can be changed. The first problem statement limits reflection and the search for resolution. The second opens several

---

FIGURE 4-2 • Reflective Questions

Questions Related to Previous Experience
- What can you tell us about your experience?
- How does this compare with other things you have done?
- What did you like/dislike about this experience?
- Would you have done anything differently?

Questions that Probe for Deeper Level of Understanding
- How did this experience make you feel?
- Have you had similar feelings? When?
- Do you think your feelings would have been different if you were a different gender? In a different culture?
- Can you give one positive and one negative thing about this experience?
- Can you give a metaphor for this experience?

Questions That Elicit Personal-Meaning Descriptions
- Was there anything unexpected in the way things turned out?
- Was there anything puzzling to you?
- What are some questions you need to explore or investigate?
- What impact did this have on your life?
- Is this something that you should care about beyond this experience?
- Were there issues of right and wrong that you should consider?
- What do you need to do next?

---

creative avenues for solving the problem. The basic point is that students need to practice posing problems. This can be facilitated by teaching them how to describe a problem by focusing on its elements.

Student engagement in problem-posing and reflection is enhanced if the selected problems relate to dilemmas students face in their own lives. You can develop a series of questions related to these issues to help members of your class develop a better focus on key issues and problems. Once students have developed such a focus, you can involve them in brainstorming and other techniques that will help them develop alternative responses. These provide you with possibilities for involving students in more reflection about the quality of suggested alternatives and for involving them in follow-up research activities to test the adequacy of their ideas.

Knowledge Formation Process The knowledge formation phase is a particularly important part of the sequence. During this component of the learning experience, you prompt students to identify inconsistencies, inadequacies, and discrepancies in their thinking (Bigge & Shermis, 1999). Part of their work here involves them in acquiring what might be called "traditional" knowledge. You do this for the purpose of providing students with opportunities to uncover information they

This class is actively engaged in playing roles and investigating artifacts.

Anthony Magnacca/Merrill

can use to verify and substantiate data and to reflect on the adequacy of their ideas and hypotheses.

As members of your class gather information, help them look for relevant patterns and relationships. You may find it desirable to have students work together as they seek to identify potential approaches to the problem. As class members engage in this work, you need to monitor them carefully and prompt them to look for relevant information both from the data sources they are consulting and from their own prior learning experiences. You need to be careful to allow students' insights and experiences, not your own, to guide generation and identification of knowledge they will later apply as they seek to shed light on the problem. Even if you believe that members of your class are developing flawed ideas, you should avoid the temptation to simply give them the correct information. Instead, you want to lead them to more adequate understandings by asking questions and making suggestions that encourage them to evaluate their ideas and recognize any flaws in their thinking.

Application Process During the application phase, students engage in verification, substantiation, and reflection as they test knowledge they have acquired in new situations. They build on what they have (1) identified during the investigative-process stage, (2) considered during the reflective-process stage, and (3) further investigated as they have sought information during the knowledge formation stage. The cycle then begins to repeat as students use validated information to work with new problems and situations that you introduce during a new investigative-process stage.

Planning for continued student use of newly developed knowledge and expertise is important (Wink, 1997). If your sequence appears to end with actions taken

LESSON IDEA 4-2

TOPIC: Teaching for Reflection

OBJECTIVE: Students will (1) identify elements of a recent experience that were most meaningful, and (2) develop a product that displays their reflection on their experience.

ENGAGING THE STUDENTS: This lesson is based on experiences of a fourth-grade class spent in a day on a field trip to a local operating historical farm. You easily may adapt it to other, similar field trips. Begin by asking students: What was new or surprising in your experience? What did you learn? What did you like about the experience? How did this experience make you feel? How did this experience change the way you think about people who lived in the past?

DEVELOPING THE CONTENT: After students share their answers, inform them that they are to

pretend that they were a student of their same age and gender living on the farm. They are to write a letter to a friend living in another part of the country describing a day in their life. They should include not just the tasks they do but also their hopes and feelings.

BRINGING CLOSURE: Allow one or two students to share a part of their letters.

EXTENSION TO THE WEB: The Best of History website provides links to many sites that include pictures, diary entries, and other resources. Students could be directed to one or more of these sites to compare their acounts with those of real people who lived in the past.

URL—http://www.besthistorysites.net/

during the application process, learning is incomplete. Few problems in life have permanent solutions or endings. As adults, we have to revisit situations that retain some essential characteristics from the past but that also take on new ones over time. It is important for your students to understand that problem solving is an ongoing activity and that completing one cycle of study related to an issue leads to opportunities to apply more sophisticated levels of understanding (1) to modifications of earlier problems and situations and (2) to new ones. Often when students have a chance to make follow-up applications of what they have learned, their levels of self-esteem and feelings of efficacy increase. These positive developments come about because learners recognize that previous experiences have given them tools they can apply as they successfully grapple with new dilemmas.

Foxfire

When you teach elementary and middle school learners, social studies lessons often seem to focus on places that are far away and people who lived long ago. For some students, these places and people have no more reality than scenes and characters they see in films and in television productions. This set of circumstances is particularly problematic when students live in areas that are remote from national centers (remote, for example, from places such as New York City, Washington, DC, Chicago, or Los Angeles) that routinely are featured in films and in media coverage of current events. There is danger that students may see the content of social studies lessons as having little practical significance for their own lives and really only about "strange lands and funny people." Foxfire is an attempt to help students connect to the world around them.

In 1966, Eliot Wigginton became concerned about the lack of connectivity of school learning to the world his class members knew in Rabun Gap, Georgia. He developed a community- and learner-centered program called *Foxfire* that has been the impetus for similar initiatives in many other parts of the country. This program strives to help learners understand that they are engaged in legitimate and academically important work when they study local places, people, and traditions.

If you implemented a lesson that incorporates key features of the Foxfire approach in your own classroom, you would (1) involve learners heavily in planning, (2) develop activities requiring students to become actively involved, (3) build in abundant opportunities for reflection, problem solving, and imagination, and (4) provide for rigorous evaluation of learning (Foxfire Fund, 2002). When interacting with members of your class, you would function more as a learning guide than as a primary source of information.

Foxfire programs always place heavy emphases on learners developing tangible products that summarize what they have learned and presenting this information in ways that can be easily accessed by community members and other interested parties. In the early years, these products often took the form of oral history reports that were summarized in a learner-produced magazine. Later many of these articles were gathered into Foxfire books.

The Foxfire Fund, Inc., a not-for-profit group headquartered in Rabun County, Georgia, works to maintain and extend the Foxfire tradition. This group supports publication of *The Foxfire News* and numerous books that feature learner work as well as contributions from professionals who are committed to Foxfire's active, community-based approach to learning. In addition, the Foxfire Fund offers training programs for teachers from throughout the country who wish to implement the approach in their own schools.

With advances in computers and with new tools such as digital cameras, students can now develop multimedia projects as a way of displaying what they have learned and communicating stories. Most students find doing these types of projects motivating and can produce some impressive projects that involve mixing a number of media.

Web Check. To learn more about the Foxfire approach, visit the homepage of the Foxfire Fund, Inc. You will be able to locate information related to all aspects of the Foxfire approach. **URL—http://www.foxfire.org**

Service Learning

Service learning was defined in the National and Community Service Act of 1990 (later reauthorized as the National and Community Service Trust Act in 1993 [U.S. Code. Vol. 10401-12700, Title 42 Section 12511, Chapter 23, 1995]) as a method where students learn through active participation in community service. The National Service-Learning Clearinghouse (2005) makes a distinction between volunteerism and service learning. A ***volunteer*** is defined as someone who performs a valued service.

Service learning involves linking the service to the acquisiton and comprehension of values, skills, and knowledge. In other words, service-learning activities are linked to important learning goals and standards. For example, gathering money or supplies to help victims of a natural disaster such as Hurricane Katrina is a worthwhile volunteering activity. However, if the activity is tied to developing an understanding about the geography of the Gulf Coast and New Orleans at the mouth of the Mississippi River or the interconnectedness of trade, then it becomes a service-learning activity tied to the curriculum and to learning standards.

Edwards (2005) notes that research on service learning indicates that the experience does have a positive impact on students. Some of the benefits of service learning include a heightened sense of personal and social responsibility, a more positive attitude toward others, more complex patterns of thought, improved learning of content, and improved self-esteem.

The importance of service learning in the social studies prompted the National Council of Social Studies (NCSS) to adopt a position statement titled "Service Learning: An Essential Component of Citizenship Education" (2000). You may find service learning a useful approach for establishing a meaningful connection between your social studies program and the world beyond your school. Today's conception of citizenship education requires you to do more than simply provide learners with information. You also need to engender in students a desire to put new knowledge to work in ways that are consistent with behavior patterns of responsible citizens.

Service learning can involve a range of activities that involve students of all ages. For example, even young children can find it exciting and rewarding to be engaged in simple service-learning activities such as picking up litter or helping community members who need assistance. Lesson Idea 4-3 provides an example of a service-learning activity for students in the upper elementary grades on Hurricane Katrina, in 2005, which you easily could adapt for other natural disasters.

Service learning can be divided into three types (Wade, 2000):

- Indirect service learning
- Direct service learning
- Advocacy activities

Indirect Service Learning Indirect service learning engages students in activities within the school or in groups involving school learners that connect to larger community initiatives or projects. For example, from time to time members of your class might participate in activities such as car washes, bake sales, fundraising walk-a-thons, or collections of canned goods or other items for needy families. Another example of indirect service learning involves situations in which you and your class provide needed support by "adopting" something. For example, following the tragedy of September 11, 2001, one middle school class made contact with a school in New York City that was located near the World Trade Center. The class adopted the school, created buttons with a unity theme, and sold them to people in the local community. The class sent the proceeds to the New York City school.

Direct Service Learning Direct service learning takes students out of the school and into the community for the purpose of providing assistance of some kind. This would involve activities such as picking up litter, cleaning up graffiti, assisting people with illnesses or disabilities, helping people learn English, or tutoring

LESSON IDEA 4-3

TOPIC: Helping Victims of Natural Disasters

OBJECTIVES: Students will: (1) describe Hurricane Katrina as a natural disaster, (2) locate the Gulf Coast on a map, (3) describe the economic consequences of a disruption of work and trade, (4) commit to finding ways to assist disaster victims.

ENGAGING THE STUDENTS: Discuss with the class the images and the information they have seen on television about Hurricane Katrina.

DEVELOPING THE CONTENT: Ask students, "What is meant by a natural disaster? What are examples of other natural disasters? What is an example of something that is a disaster but not a natural disaster (perhaps an act of terrorism)?".

Locate the Gulf Coast on a map of the United States. Ask the following questions: "What do you notice about the location of New Orleans? What do you know about the Mississippi River? How does travel and trade up and down the river influence places far away from New Orleans? What would happen if ships and barges carrying goods could not go up and down the river? How would that influence us? What about the people who live in New Orleans, what would happen if they are unable to work in the stores and businesses? Why do you think it would be important to help the people who live in New Orleans stay there and survive?"

Say, "We have identified that New Orleans is an important city, and the activities of the city influence many people. What can we do to help the people there who were hurt by the hurricane?" Have the class brainstorm possible activities that could be helpful. List these activities on the board and have the class begin planning what they could do.

BRINGING CLOSURE: Ask The following questions: "What did we learn today about natural disasters? What did we learn about this place?" Note that it is important to understand that, as citizens and people, we need to be sensitve to others in need and find ways of helping them. However, by helping them, we are also providing a service to many other people who were not directly influenced by the event.

EXTENSION TO THE WEB: An abundance of information about various natural disasters and events can be found on the web by using a search engine such as Google and typing in the name of the event. In addition, Web pages for organizations such as the Red Cross or the Salvation Army can provide information on how to help.

URLs—http://www.redcross.org/ and http://www1.salvationarmy.org

younger children. The best kinds of direct service-learning activities help your students make practical applications of the content you are featuring in the academic portion of the social studies program. Under these conditions, students gain satisfaction from knowing they are providing legitimate help to others and an appreciation that the content of the social studies program has practical relevance for the world outside the school.

Advocacy Activities When members of your class are involved in advocacy activities, they engage in work on behalf of a specific cause. For example, students may participate in efforts to raise community awareness about circumstances relating to an array of issues such as the need for new facilities, problems with transportation arrangements, and perceived injustices of various kinds. When students do this kind of work in the community, they have opportunities to deal with issues related to values as well as with academic content. The need to consider both issues of value and issues of fact make advocacy activities particularly suitable vehicles for developing your students' civic participation skills (Wade, 2000). Involvement in advocacy activities also helps learners to understand that citizenship involves more than talking about constitutional rights and responsibilities.

Planning Service-Learning Experiences If you are interested in involving members of your class in service-learning activities, you need to commit considerable time to careful planning. Indirect service-learning approaches require fewer prior arrangements because, for the most part, students work either within the school or in out-of-school conditions in which members of the class continue to function as an intact group. Direct service-learning and advocacy activities, because they often require students to work collaboratively with others in settings outside of the school, must be carefully planned and organized. You need to think carefully about what students are to do, who they will work with, how they will be monitored, and how their contributions will be evaluated.

A useful resource for planning service-learning activities is the *Service Learning Toolbox* developed by Geiger (n.d.) as a part of the Rural Education Program and the Northwest Regional Educational laboratory in Portland, Oregon. This guide identifies four stages—preparation, action, formal evaluation, and online resources. We have adapted the guide's suggestions and those of Wade (2000) based on our own experiences, adding celebration as part of the process because we have found it to be a valuable part of service learning. Our model thus consists of preparation, action, evaluation and reflection, and celebration.

Web Check. A useful resource for individuals interested in service learning is the Web page for the National Service-Learning Clearinghouse. Information about service learning and many lesson plans can be found here. **URL—http//www. servicelearning.org**

Preparation. The key element in any successful teaching activity is preparation. Time invested in preparation pays many dividends by helping eliminate management problems and in creating a motivating and rewarding experience for students. Service-learning activities require extra preparation. Some of the activities might involve off-campus activities that can have some important legal dimensions. *Preparation* involves identifying a service-learning activity, defining the objectives, developing a timeline, identifying the roles of the students, contacting relevant individuals who will be involved, scheduling activities, arranging transportation if needed, identifying any budget needs, and providing supervision. A major component in your planning is curriculum intergration. This establishes a clear tie between the intended community-service work and the academic content of your social studies program. This is what makes a service-learning project valuable as a part of an active, meaningful social studies program (Wade, 2000).

Although service learning is especially useful for accomplishing social studies goals, it can also be used to meet goals for other parts of the curriculum, such as language arts or science. You might begin the process of tying a proposed service-learning project to your academic program by looking at the content of your social studies curriculum and identifying service-learning opportunities that might relate to basic purposes or themes. For example, you could start with the basic themes of social studies introduced in Chapter 1. You might then begin listing service-learning projects related to each of these themes. After you identify some potential projects, you may want to look at content of other areas of the school program (mathematics, science, etc.) that might also logically tie to the proposed service-learning activity.

Action. This is the implementation phase of the project. During the action phase you must be sensitive to changes that need to be made. Frequently, the timeline proves not to be realistic, planned participants must cancel, or certain activities are not possible. Modification will just about always be needed.

Orientation of your students is essential if you are to reach your program's educational potential. Students need to be provided with a good overview that describes basic purposes of the project and tells them what each person will be expected to do. You need to seek a commitment from your students to pursue these activities. If you begin a service-learning experience under conditions in which class members approach the activity with little interest or enthusiasm, the prospects for success will not be good. Given this reality, it makes sense to select a project focus that ties into existing learner interests. If learners already have an affinity for the project focus, then you will find few motivational problems as you explain to students what they are to do and launch the new experience.

As you put the plan into action you need to explain to students the nature of the activity and what they will accomplish as a result of their participation. Individual students often are fearful about getting involved in something new when they are confused about what they are supposed to be doing. To win commitment from as many students as possible, you should allow students themselves to decide on some of the activities they will be doing as the project unfolds. You may want to approach this by providing learners with two lists. One of these might be headed "What Everybody Will Do," and the other might be headed "Some Options." On the second list, you might provide alternatives from which students might select, and, depending on the age and sophistication of your students, you may invite learners themselves to suggest additional possibilities.

Evaluation and Reflection. Active participation alone does not assure that students' involvement in service-learning experiences will contribute significantly to their educational development. The benefits of these experiences come to students who also are engaged in evaluation and reflection on what has happened. Reflection opportunities need to be provided throughout the entire project, not just as a summing-up activity at the end (Wade, 2000). You might find it useful to pose prompt questions at various stages that require students to stop, think, interpret, and synthesize. You may wish to ask students (1) questions related to previous experience, (2) questions that probe for deeper levels of understanding, and (3) questions that elicit personal-meaning descriptions. (For examples of questions associated with each category, refer back to Figure 4-2.)

In addition to asking questions, you might encourage students to engage in reflection and evaluation activities by keeping journals, debriefing with their cooperative learning group, writing articles for the newspaper, creating photo essays, making presentations to groups such as parents, developing portfolios related to their experiences, drawing or painting illustrations, or developing a guide for future participants. Many students enjoy these activities. They provide them with opportunities to reflect on their experiences and to integrate content from both their academic lessons in school and their service-learning work.

Celebration. It is very useful to have a celebration at the conclusion of a service-learning project. A celebration serves the purpose of providing for some reflection,

Involving students in service-learning activities helps them realize they can make a difference.

Mary Kate Denny/PhotoEdit Inc.

providing a sense of closure, reinforcing learning, and providing motivation for future projects. Celebrations that include community members as well as your students provide a means for thanking all of those who have assisted in planning and implementing the project. Celebratory events also give you opportunities to invite school administrators and parents so they can share in the excitement and observe how participation in the project has affected students. This can have great public relations as well as educational benefits. In some instances it is useful to invite representatives of the media. Public sharing of this kind provides concrete evidence of the benefits of the service-learning experience and functions as a satisfying capstone experience.

Preparing Short Term For Active Learning Experiences

Some lessons that give students opportunities to apply what they have learned do not require planning that is as sophisticated or detailed as the preparation you will undertake to implement Story Path or service learning. For example, you may find it sufficient to engage your students in a lesson focusing on information they get from handling an artifact or from interviews of adults who have had special kinds of experience. Lesson Idea 4-4 provides an example of a simple concrete learning lesson.

LESSON IDEA 4-4

TOPIC: Voyage to the New World

OBJECTIVES: Students will (1) make choices, (2) work cooperatively with others while they do so, and (3) seek additional information to use as they reflect on their choices.

ENGAGING THE STUDENTS: Ask if any students have moved from one place to another. Ask learners who have had this experience to explain to the class how they felt when they moved and what choices they had to make in deciding what they needed to take to their new location.

DEVELOPING THE CONTENT: Tell members of the class that today they are going to go back in history and that they will be moving from their home to a new place. In this move, they will have to travel across the ocean in a small ship. They are going to a new colony where there are no established stores where they can buy things. As a result, they will have to take what they need to survive in the new location with them when they head off on their journey. Provide students with the following handout. Take time to read the instructions, and check to see that all members of the class understand what they are to do.

VOYAGE TO THE NEW WORLD

You are about to leave the home you have known for your entire life for a new colony in a faraway land. Others first moved to this new place about 5 years ago. You know from reports that they have had a very difficult time. Some have died, and some have returned to their previous homes.

However, you and your family are determined to try and have a better life in spite of the hardships. You are now in the process of deciding what you will take with you to this new colony. Because the ship you are traveling on is quite small, you can take only a few things with you. You have a list of items that you can use as you decide what will go. Each item has a point value. You can only take 50 points worth of items. Go through the list and identify the items you will take.

Item	Points
Mattress	10
Hunting Knife	3
Bible	3
School Books	10
Dressy Clothes	8
Wool Blankets	7
Musket and Powder	5
Sled	10
Medicine Kit	5
Barrel of Flour	12
Extra Set of Warm Clothes	8
Candles	5
Fishing Pole	3
Ax	3
Hammer	3
Iron Pot	5
Sewing Kit	4
Table and Chairs	12
Dishes	10
Forks, Spoons	5
Shovel	3
Dog	7
Vegetable and Grain Seeds	7
Flower Seeds	3

Place a check mark by each item you will take. Then, add up your total points. Indicate your total here: _____. (Remember, your total cannot exceed 50 points.)

Once you have made your choices, meet with at least four others in a group. Compare your choices. What things did everyone seem to agree would be important? On which items was there disagreement? What else would you have liked to have known that might have helped you to make better choices? How could you get this information?

BRINGING CLOSURE: Ask members of the class to explain what they learned from this lesson. Ask them to explain what kinds of things people have to think about when they are forced to make choices. What kinds of evidence do they consider? Do they always know in advance that the choices they have made are good ones? What can they do to make sure their decisions are as good as they can be? Have students identify what else they would like to know about what people actually did when they moved to these new colonies. Use this to build motivation for research on colonization.

Other relatively simple activities that can be used to make social studies an active process can be built around selections of children's literature. For example, Miska Miles's **Annie and the Old One** (Little, Brown, 1971) is a book about a Native American girl and her grandmother. It can be used as a stimulus to get students to investigate senior citizens in their community. They can seek answers to questions such as, Are there senior citizen centers in the community? What activities are available to them? What are their stories? For example, in the San Francisco Bay area an organization called the "Digital Clubhouse" has paired students with senior citizens. The senior citizens are interviewed by the students, who record their stories. They then use computers to develop a multimedia presentation of each of the stories. One such project by the Digital Clubhouse, "Stories of Service," resulted in a number of digital stories of World War II veterans that have been placed in the Smithsonian Institution collection. Not only is a project like this of value to the students, it is valued by the senior citizens and makes a contribution to the oral history of the nation.

Another example involving literature uses Lynne Cherry's **The Great Kapok Tree** (Harcourt Brace Jovanovich, 1990) as a stimulus. This book is about cutting down a kapok tree in the rain forest. It can be used as a stimulus to investigate conservation in the local community. Are there things in the community that ought to be preserved? Why should they be preserved? They might be prompted to take action to help stop destruction of some of the valuable resources. Once again, this meets the criterion of a service-learning activity because it not only performs a service to the local community, it has a direct relationship to standards and objectives.

DEALING WITH CONTROVERSIAL ISSUES

One way of involving students in active and concrete learning is through addressing controversial issues. Getting students actively involved in service learning often leads them into controversy. Almost any selection of topics you might include in current events lessons will include issues that people debate. Classroom experiences you provide to your students that help them deal with issues about which people have varying opinions prepare them to deal with controversial issues that will be part of the political and social landscape they will face throughout their lives.

Controversial issues you will deal with are not restricted to current events. Content dealing with many kinds of issues generates debate, and one purpose of your teaching is to help members of your class appreciate that it is proper and normal for informed and well-meaning people to disagree about important issues. To reinforce this idea, you can point out that even experts hold multiple views of historical events and develop alternative hypotheses to explain social and economic forces.

This diversity of people and viewpoints makes the world an interesting place, and these varying perspectives potentially can make the social studies a rich and compelling subject. Unfortunately, in some places teachers and administrators avoid dealing with controversy out of a fear that such lessons will generate criticism from some members of the larger community. The thought that you can avoid complaints simply by avoiding controversy is an illusion. Even if you and your school administrators believe your program is avoiding controversy, the blandest social studies programs will include some topics and perspectives that are bound to meet with disfavor by some part of the community. Hence, avoiding controversial issues as a way to eliminate all public criticism of school programs will not work. In addition, such practices irresponsibly shelter your students from the diversity of opinion that is a natural feature of a democratic society.

In some cases, you also may find yourself confronted by school and political leaders who give lip service to the importance of introducing students to controversy, but who have highly restrictive notions regarding what kinds of positions respecting some issues are "legitimate" and therefore appropriate for introduction to elementary and middle school learners. For example, a number of years ago, a state senator stood and observed a large group of high school students who were rallying outside the capitol building to protest an action of the legislature. The senator turned to one his aides and remarked, "Look at all those students protesting! Let's face it, the schools are failing." These comments reflect the views of someone who does not recognize one of the key features of democratic decision making: the freedom of individuals to debate, support, and oppose any issue under consideration. The senator's views, instead, presumed that everybody should accept the decisions of political leaders on certain key issues and that the role of teachers was to teach them this unquestioned obedience.

The key point here is that, as a teacher, you do not want to shy away from controversy, but rather to deal with it in an open and professional manner. Although occasionally you may receive complaints about allowing many perspectives to be heard when specific issues become a focus of your lessons, you need to resist the temptation to limit consideration of diverse views. The cost to democracy of prohibiting certain views to be aired is too high. In addition, avoiding controversy sends an inappropriate message to your students. Such an action tells members of your class that you think that controversy is not a natural part of our society and that disputes about unsettled issues should be avoided. Your students will not be fooled. They know that there are controversial events and issues in life. If you avoid discussing these in school, you imply that school does not deal with the kinds of divisive topics that are everywhere present in the real world.

When you deal with controversial issues in the classroom, you do not try to impose conformity or to promote a particular viewpoint. Rather, your purpose is to help students face controversy respectfully and with open minds. Members of your class need to learn that people who are informed and good can have honest differences of opinions. One of your purposes is to help them appreciate that hearing expressions of varying views leads citizens to make wiser choices.

 You may find it useful to teach members of your class a sequence of steps they can follow that will help them better deal with controversial issues:

1. Clarifying the issue
2. Defining alternative positions
3. Gathering information
4. Identifying consequences
5. Reflecting
6. Making a decision and identifying needed action

Clarifying the Issue

When you ask students to focus on a controversial issue, you need to take care that they understand exactly what the points of concern are. Sometimes the exact nature of a "problem" is not obvious. For example, suppose you saw this headline in the local paper:

"More Uproar Over Low Math Scores"

The headline refers to a general area that is generating concern, but it fails to indicate exactly what is at issue. Controversies surrounding low math scores on a standardized test could be centered on concerns as varied as these examples:

- Concerns about the adequacy of instructional techniques used to teach mathematical content
- Concerns about the content of the mathematics curriculum
- Concerns about the format and/or content of the test used to assess learners' achievement levels in mathematics
- Concerns about the amount of time devoted to the study of mathematics during a typical school day

If you want your students to grapple with controversial issues in a meaningful way, you need to take time to explain carefully what is at the heart of the dispute. When your students have this information, they can focus more clearly on arguments and perspectives varying people bring to bear on the problem under discussion.

Defining Alternative Positions

Once the issues have been clarified, you need to help students understand varying positions and attitudes that have been adopted by individuals who are concerned about the problems. To give learners a sense of participatory ownership in a problem, you may find it useful to have them identify as large a number of possible responses to the problem as they can. A brainstorming technique would work well for this purpose. You may find it useful to have class members identify their own positions and then carefully explain positions (and supporting logic) that differ from their own. The purpose of actions taken during this phase is to help your students see problems from a variety of perspectives.

Gathering Information

After members of your class have identified alternative positions, you should challenge them to gather facts and information relevant to the focus problem and to a number of the positions and perspectives that were identified during the defining-alternative-positions phase of the lesson. One of your purposes is to help class members understand that, sometimes, positions people take are based more on emotions and personal values than on evidence. If some people in your class have strong personal feelings about the problem you are considering, actions taken during the gathering-information phase can help them step back from a purely emotional commitment as they consider evidence that supports (and that fails to support) their own views and the views of others.

Identifying Consequences

During the identifying-consequences phase of the lesson, ask your students to think about what might happen if specific alternative responses to the problem were implemented. In cases in which a large number of alternatives have been identified, you need to select only a few (perhaps three to five) for students to consider as they think about consequences of implementation. As your students look at results that might logically follow implementation of the selected alternatives, think about prompting them with questions such as these:

- Who will benefit if this alternative is selected?
- Who will be hurt if this alternative is selected?
- Are there things not related to the problem that might have to change if this alternative is selected?
- If the answer to the previous question is "yes," will the need for other things to change make it impossibly difficult to choose this alternative, or will the need for other things to change not present a big problem?

Reflecting

The reflection stage gives your students an opportunity to sort through information they have received and "make sense" of individual action alternatives. As class members consider various issues that have been raised, they have opportunities to reconsider facts and other evidence relevant to the problem and to think about their personal beliefs and values. Individuals should reflect on the information they have gathered, the possible consequences of a course of action, and their own personal values and beliefs. You might consider asking students prompt questions such as these:

- At this point, which alternative solutions seem to be best supported by facts and other kinds of evidence?
- As you think about alternative responses to the problem, which ones seem to fit best with your own beliefs, priorities, and feelings?

Making a Decision and Identifying Needed Actions

During the final phase of the lesson, individual members of your class make decisions and identify a needed course of action. In preparing them for this phase, you need to point out that sometimes immediate and decisive actions are not best. Complex problems often require deliberative and complex solutions. Often these complexities respond better to a series of relatively small actions, each of which over time makes a contribution to solving the problem. As prompts for your students, you might ask questions such as these:

- Suppose you decided that several things need to be done. How many different things would you recommend? Which would you do first, second, third, and so forth?
- Think about each of your action proposals. What problems might arise as each is implemented?
- Think about these problems. What might be done to solve them so your solution to the overall problem stays on track?

In summary, social studies should be an active process where students are actively engaged in going beyond just the gathering of information. Learning how to think and how to apply what they have learned in the school to the world outside. As one teacher remarked, we need to overcome 2 × 4 social studies—we need to get outside the two covers of the book and the four walls of the classroom.

KEY IDEAS IN SUMMARY

- Citizenship is a central goal of the social studies. Citizenship is not passive but requires active involvement. Therefore, the social studies ought to promote the active involvement of students and engage them in "doing something" with social studies content. Getting beyond the walls of the classroom gives the social studies a reality base and helps promote student motivation and interest.
- You may face challenges as you seek to build meaningful application activities into your social studies program. In some places, concerns about standardized testing in areas such as reading and mathematics have resulted in diminished administrative support for social studies instruction. In addition, parents and guardians often are unfamiliar with social studies programs that involve students in meaningful application activities. Among responses to these challenges you may consider are arguments to principals that social studies content often provides students with opportunities to develop reading and quantitative skills. You often can win support from parents and guardians by simply describing to them benefits of social studies lessons that involve students in real-world experiences.
- Many options are available to use as you think about providing your students with concrete learning experiences. These include involving learners in (1) Story Path lessons, (2) exploratory-understanding-level teaching and learning,

(3) community-linked lessons such as those promoted by Foxfire, (4) service learning, and (5) more simple lessons featuring practical applications.
- *Exploratory-understanding-level teaching and learning* is a particularly well-thought-out approach to providing students with active, concrete learning experiences. This approach takes students through recurring cycles that feature (1) an investigative process, (2) a reflective process, (3) a knowledge formation phase, and (4) an application phase.
- *Service-learning* projects link community service to your classroom. There are basically three types of service learning: (1) direct projects, (2) indirect projects, and (3) advocacy projects. Indirect projects require less planning time and organization than either direct projects or advocacy projects.
- Dealing with controversy is a routine activity for citizens in a democracy. You can help develop your students' abilities to deal with controversy by requiring them to deal with controversial issues in the classroom and by taking them through a discussion, learning, and thinking sequence involving these steps: (1) clarifying the issue, (2) defining alternative positions, (3) gathering information, (4) identifying consequences, (5) reflecting, and (6) making a decision and identifying needed action.

CHAPTER REFLECTIONS

1. Given today's emphasis on preparing learners for standardized tests, is it responsible for lessons to focus on application activities that may enrich students' understanding of a few subject areas, but deny them the time to develop even knowledge-level understandings of others?

2. Take time to reflect on your experiences in school with the social studies. To what extent did you have opportunities to apply what you learned? To what extent did your teachers try to connect your lessons to issues and problems facing the local community? As you think about your own social studies teaching, what do you see as some barriers to engaging students in active learning experiences, and how might you overcome them?

3. How do you respond to the assertion that learners must first acquire a body of information if they are to benefit from doing projects and getting involved in experiential learning activities?

4. What do you see as the advantages and disadvantages of service learning? What would you feel comfortable doing? What makes you uncomfortable? Are there actions you could take that will help you overcome any concerns about certain aspects of implementing service-learning projects? What are they, and what barriers may you have to overcome to take these actions?

5. Are elementary and middle school students too young to be confronted with controversial issues? Do they have an adequate knowledge base at this stage of their development to understand the issues and evidence that is marshaled in support of contending positions?

FIVE

Selecting Teaching Approaches for Knowledge Acquisition

Anthony Magnacca/Merrill

This chapter will help you to:

- Identify variables that you need to consider when choosing a teaching approach.
- Explain how the *structure of knowledge* organizes important categories of content.
- Describe functions of *facts*, *concepts*, and *generalizations*.
- Describe purposes of selected instructional approaches you might use.
- Define the difference between *knowledge acquisition* and *knowledge discovery*.
- State the importance of personally constructing knowledge.
- Identify the steps of a variety of instructional approaches.

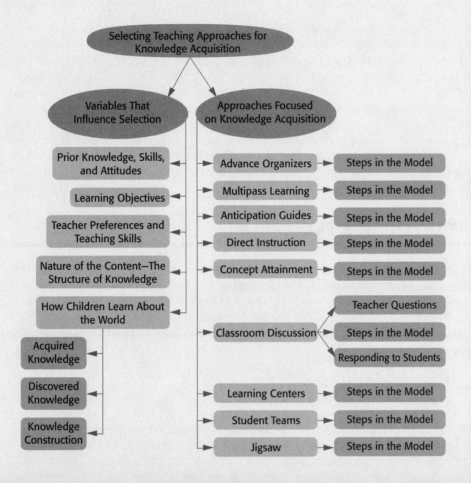

Teaching is at the core of your responsibilities as a teacher. There is evidence that too many individuals entering teaching tend to teach the way they themselves were taught. This is a risky approach. Your selection of teaching approaches needs to be based on the needs of your students, the type of learning, and your instructional objectives rather than on tradition. The national spotlight is focused on education and concern about the quality of teaching is widespread. The status quo is no longer possible. Teachers must move beyond simply teaching the way they were taught.

Student-to-student differences make it unlikely that any single approach you choose will respond adequately to the needs of every member of your class. This reality obligates you to use multiple approaches as you seek to accommodate these differences. The choices you make as a teacher influence what members of your class learn (Lasley, Matczynski, & Rowley, 2002; Sanders, 2001). Your selection of teaching approaches ranks among the most important of your professional decisions.

A variety of teaching approaches and teaching models will be useful to you as you face instructional decisions. In this chapter, we will focus on the instructional act and explore a variety of approaches that you can use to help students succeed in knowledge acquisition and to increase the probability of success in the classroom.

As you think about selecting approaches, begin by considering each prospective lesson as an instructional problem to be solved. The first step in solving a problem is to formulate a hypothesis. In essence, your hypothesis states, "I predict that using method A will achieve the desired outcomes." Note that your thinking focuses on the objectives or the outcomes to be achieved and not on what approaches look like fun or are "cute." If your hypothesis is sound, large numbers of learners will master your objective.

VARIABLES THAT INFLUENCE SELECTION

Successful problem solving requires a consideration of all important variables. This, too, is the case for selecting teaching approaches. To make a good hypothesis concerning what approach to use you need to consider the prior knowledge of your students, the learning objectives for the lesson, and the nature of the content to be taught. The choice of a particular approach often becomes quite clear once you have considered these variables.

Prior Knowledge, Skills, and Attitudes

When you think about your students' prior knowledge, you are interested in their present skill levels, their knowledge of content related to the unit, their general attitudes toward the content, the types of things that generally interest them, and their previous experiences. Brain scans have revealed that when new knowledge is connected to past experiences there is substantially more cerebral activity and increased retention (Sousa, 2001).

One of the most important variables to consider is students' necessary prerequisite skills. Even the most creative approach will have little impact if students do not have the background that will prepare them for success. For example, if you use an instructional approach that requires students to read material at too high a level of reading difficulty, you can expect a high failure rate.

Another aspect of prior knowledge that is of considerable importance to you is the experiential background of your students. Remember that members of your class may have had life experiences that differ greatly from your own. You cannot assume that these students know what you and others like you knew when you were the age of the young people in your class.

The worldview of members of your class has come about because of their personal experiences. The human brain constantly seeks to organize and make sense of the world people confront in their daily lives. Your students' interpretations of reality, based as they often are on very limited experiences, sometimes are at odds with what you want to teach. If you expect members of your class to learn the concepts you are teaching, you may have to challenge alternative, inadequate conceptions of reality that they initially bring with them to the classroom (Gardner, 1991). Such circumstances may prompt you to choose teaching approaches that will involve students in investigating and questioning their own ideas. This active involvement in the process of adopting a worldview is necessary if you really expect your students' misconceptions to change as a result of your instruction.

Knowledge of student attitudes and interests is also important to you as you work to select appropriate instructional approaches. For example, some techniques you select may require students to persevere for a considerable time on a particular task related to the lesson. This kind of approach may work well with learners who are highly motivated and interested. It probably is less well suited to less mature, less interested students, who may have shorter attention spans. Similarly, you need to think carefully about student characteristics when you consider approaches that give them lots of freedom of action. You probably will not want to use techniques of this kind with students characterized by little self-direction or self-control.

Learning Objectives

Learning objectives are statements that describe what you expect students to be able to do as a result of your teaching. Expectations contained in your learning objectives should guide your choice of instructional approaches. For example, if your objective will require students to engage in sophisticated patterns of thinking, you want to choose a teaching approach that requires them to demonstrate these behaviors. Focusing on your objectives for a particular lesson often indicates exactly which approach to use.

Teacher Preferences and Teaching Skills

A major variable that will influence your selection of a teaching approach is your own preferences and teaching skills. You will tend to choose instructional approaches that are most in line with your own preferences and experiences. The danger, however, is that an approach that appeals strongly to you may not always be appropriate for your students or consistent with the objectives you have established.

You need to be open to trying new approaches and to moving outside your "comfort zone." Over time, you will find it useful to become familiar with a wide-ranging repertoire of teaching approaches. In deciding which approach to use as you begin a given sequence of instruction, your primary consideration should be student learning. You need to ask, "Will this approach help members of my class master this material?" If you can answer "yes" to this question, you generally are on solid ground. The temptation you need to resist is to answer "yes" because you personally like a given approach. To be credible, your "yes" response has to come after you honestly have assessed your students' background and learning preferences.

Nature of the Content—The Structure of Knowledge

You need to understand the nature of the content you wish to teach when you select your teaching techniques. You may find the ***structure of knowledge*** helpful as you deal with this issue. The structure-of-knowledge approach is based on the work of such important learning theorists as Jerome Bruner (1960) and Hilda Taba (1962). The structure of knowledge organizes content along a continuum ranging from specific to general. It includes three basic content types: (1) facts, (2) concepts, and (3) generalizations.

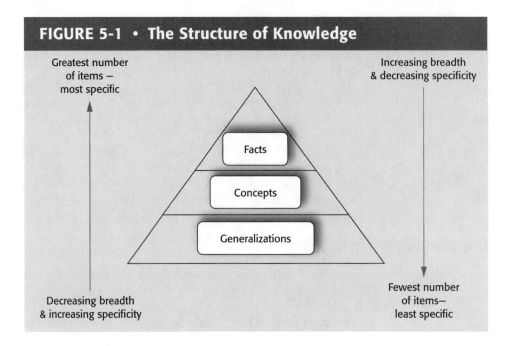

FIGURE 5-1 • The Structure of Knowledge

Figure 5-1 illustrates the structure of knowledge. This pyramid illustrates that in a given subject there are large amounts of specific bits of information called *facts*. These facts apply to a very specific set of circumstances. Therefore, they are of limited use in helping your students to apply knowledge to novel contexts. The following are examples of facts that relate to a specific event, time, place, or person:

- Abraham Lincoln was born in 1809.
- Mountains cover between 10 percent and 15 percent of New Mexico's land surface.
- Mexico City has a larger population than New York City.

At the next level are concepts. *Concepts* are word labels we give to categories of things that have some common attributes. Concepts are valuable because they help us organize the world into categories that are more transferable than facts. For example, once someone understands the critical attributes of something labeled *dog*, each new encounter with an animal of this category can quickly be labeled. Therefore, when facts are organized and grouped into concepts they can be applied and transferred to new situations. In social studies, concepts such as *peninsula, democracy, wants,* and *needs* are important ideas that help us understand and make sense out of our social and physical environment.

The following are examples of concepts emphasized in the social studies curriculum:

- Change
- Community
- Family

- Power
- Government
- Latitude
- Culture
- Tradition
- Trade

Generalizations, at the base of the pyramid, are usually statements that express a relationship between two or more concepts. Strong generalizations are statements that can be applied across time and space. They often take an "if-then" format.

Any subject is composed of a limited number of generalizations or principles. When a person has a good grasp of the basic generalizations or principles in a subject, they have a good degree of knowledge or mastery of the subject. For example, if we understand the political science generalization that states when people feel the government is unresponsive to their needs, they often revolt; we can apply this to past historical episodes as well as make predictions for the future.

The following are examples of generalizations that you might emphasize in your social studies lessons:

- Competition in the market leads to reduced prices.
- When the majority of people feel that a government no longer represents their interests, a revolution frequently occurs.
- Most change and conflict occur near the boundaries of regions.

You need to remember that facts are important. However, they are important as building blocks to concepts. Concepts are very valuable intellectual tools that help us understand the world. They become even more useful when they are organized into generalizations that help us understand and predict past and future events.

Teaching generalizations involves your students in the construction of personal meaning. Instructional activities you design that seek to help learners grasp generalizations require their active involvement. This kind of instruction, often highly motivating to students, engages learners in testing and making judgments about generalizations' predictive and descriptive powers.

How Children Learn About the World

Attending to how individuals learn is an important consideration when you select a teaching approach. Obviously, you want to select techniques that will help members of your class learn your lesson content. In recent years considerable research has focused on the learning process. The types of knowledge learned in social studies can be grouped into the categories of acquired knowledge and discovered knowledge (Carin & Bass, 2001).

Acquired Knowledge *Acquired knowledge* is socially transmitted knowledge acquired from others. It comes to students through direct interactions with others or through the media (books, television, films, and so forth). There is a body of knowledge in social studies that all students are expected to learn. However, knowledge acquisition requires much more than just telling the students the information or having them read it in a book.

Research has indicated that there are some approaches that facilitate the learning and retention of new information. Researchers have found that students grasp acquired knowledge best when (1) the information is presented to them clearly, (2) they have a need to understand the information, and (3) they have opportunities to practice what they have learned (Rosenshine, 1986).

Discovered Knowledge It is commonly understood that modern society requires individuals to be lifelong learners. Change is a constant and new knowledge is being created at an astounding rate. For education to be complete, individuals must learn how to sort through the mass of information available to them and learn how to discover new knowledge. Learning through direct experience is especially important for young children. Your students use their senses to explore the world around them. They observe, feel, touch, and taste. When you prepare your social studies lessons, you need to provide opportunities for members of your class to engage in direct experience and make personal discoveries.

You also need to keep in mind that your students may form patterns and organize their discoveries in ways that are different from yours or from "conventional wisdom." You may find it necessary to engage students in activities that encourage them to challenge and revise these alternative conceptions.

Knowledge Construction Regardless of whether the type of learning is acquired knowledge or discovered knowledge, students learn through personal construction. The brain does not function as a copy machine that takes a photograph and files it in a file somewhere. As an individual confronts new information and new situations, their brain analyzes, integrates, and synthesizes information. Existing knowledge is reorganized and new patterns are established. Basically, the mind is asking two questions: "Does this make sense?" and "Does this have meaning?" (Sousa, 2001, p. 46).

The question of whether the information makes sense is related to students' previous knowledge. Does it fit with the way students think the world works? To understand the power of students' previous knowledge, all you need to do is to engage in a discussion with preschoolers. No amount of argument on your part will change their minds when they are convinced they know how something works. All of us can probably remember times when we had difficulty learning because something contrasted with our previous beliefs or experiences. Therefore, when presenting new information to students, you need to know their previous background and to present the material in ways that help them understand how it makes sense.

The issue of meaning is related to the issue of relevance. The question here is, "Why is this information important?" It relates to the issue of motivation. Does the student have any need to know and remember this information? A student who does not understand the importance of what is to be learned is less likely to remember it.

There are several implications for planning lessons that follow from these basic questions. When planning lessons for students at all ages the lessons need be realistic and relevant, provide for social interaction, support multiple perspectives and multiple representations of content, nurture self-awareness, and encourage ownership of learning (Woolfolk, 2004).

This means that even if the goal is knowledge acquisition of content that all are expected to learn, the learning process still needs to be one where the information is imbedded in authentic tasks, where students are active and are assisted in finding meaning.

As you consider various instructional approaches, you need to remember that there is no single "best" approach. "Best" may well be different in the contexts of what type of content, for what objectives, and for which students.

Those who emphasize the use of standardized tests as indicators of knowledge acquisition tend to support approaches that present lots of information to students in the most direct manner. Those who emphasize broader measures of student learning place their emphasis on developing students' thinking skills and emphasize lessons designed to engage students in searches for discovered knowledge. You need to keep in mind that both approaches are important.

We do not need to rediscover everything in each generation. To do so would be foolish and would hinder progress. It only makes good sense to build on what others have discovered. However, it is clearly understood that modern citizens must be lifelong learners. Change is a common element in life and most of life outside of school is not organized around acquiring knowledge and giving it back on a test. In most of our lives, we need to discover knowledge and apply it to the unique problems at hand. Therefore, those who have learned only how to acquire knowledge created by others are at a distinct disadvantage.

To make good instructional choices, you need to be familiar with a large number of alternatives. In the next section, we discuss a variety of teaching approaches that you may want to include in your personal list of alternative techniques. Think about these questions as you read material focused on each described approach:

- What objectives might I best accomplish through this approach?
- How does this approach match the ways children learn social studies?
- What prior knowledge and skill might be required for students to be successful?
- How does the approach match my skills?
- What do I need to know to implement the approach effectively?

APPROACHES FOCUSED ON KNOWLEDGE ACQUISITION

The approaches in this section begin with those that help students acquire knowledge. Remember, acquired knowledge is knowledge that is socially transmitted from others. It is usually common or core information that has been identified as important for all students to learn. Remember that students acquire previously discovered knowledge best when they have a need to know the information, the information is presented clearly and logically, and students have an opportunity to practice and apply the information in a variety of contexts. The following approaches are ones that can be effective in helping students acquire and retain important information.

Advance Organizers

The *advance organizer* approach presents students with familiar concepts or analogies drawn from their previous knowledge that helps them establish a frame of reference or an organizing schema for the information they are about to learn. For example, if you were presenting the idea of government to young children, you might begin by reviewing how decisions are made in a family. There might be times when the family meets and decides together. Other times the decision or the rule is made by the parents without any input from others. These could be used as advance organizers for learning about two different types of government.

Steps in the Model You can follow these steps when applying the advance organizer model to the classroom:

1. *Identify the major concepts or ideas you want to teach*. Consider students' previous knowledge and brainstorm which aspects of it would provide useful organizers for the new concepts and ideas you want to teach. This might involve little more than reviewing previous lessons so that they call to mind important concepts and ideas.
2. *Plan how you will connect their prior knowledge to the new concepts*. There are numerous ways you might consider such as the use of questions and discussion, role playing, or graphic organizers.
3. *Present the new concepts or ideas in a systematic fashion, connecting the new learning to previous knowledge*. At each step ask for examples and applications to monitor their understanding.
4. *Apply the new learning*. Present students with a task or an activity where they will have to apply and demonstrate their understanding of the new information. Again, you may do this in a variety of ways. They might demonstrate their understanding through completing a worksheet, drawing a picture, performing a role play, constructing a diagram, or building a model.

The advance organizer is a powerful approach in helping students acquire knowledge in an efficient and meaningful way. It helps them continue to expand and refine their concepts and understandings. It can be used in connection with textbooks by providing context and vocabulary prior to students reading a text.

Multipass Learning

The textbook is a common feature in social studies classrooms. Although many experts urge teachers to use the text only as a resource, the fact is that texts are used extensively in most classrooms, and you will need to know how to use them effectively.

In the contemporary classroom, you are likely to have students at varying learning ability and reading levels, as well as English language learners. In other words, you cannot expect everyone to be able to read the text and comprehend the material. *Multipass reading* is one way of using the textbook to meet the needs of a diverse classroom. It incorporates some of the same basic principles of advance organizers, and is a way of providing a *scaffold*, or an organizing schema, for what is read. The basic concept is for students to make several passes through the material to be read. Each pass has a different purpose.

Steps in the Model

1. *Break the content of the text into relatively small steps that are appropriate for the age and ability of your students*. Identify logical beginning and stopping points.
2. *Provide students with an introduction that helps them fit what they will be learning in the text to their prior knowledge*.

3. *Instruct students to quickly leaf through the pages of the text looking only at the pictures and illustrations*. When they have done this, have them predict what this section will be about.
4. *Have students make a second pass through the material reading only the major headings and subheadings*. When they have completed this, discuss with them how this information compares with what they predicted. Help them see connections between the major headings, thus providing a scaffold or advance organizer to help them comprehend what they will read.
5. *During the third pass through the material, have students read the first sentences of paragraphs*. This can be useful because authors often state the main idea in the first sentence of a paragraph. Therefore, reading only the first sentences can provide students with the main ideas or the generalizations. In fact, in one class of fifth-grade English language learners one of the authors worked with, the students became excited when they discovered they could answer about 70 percent of the questions at the end of the chapter just by reading the first sentences! After students have completed this pass, discuss with them some of the main ideas presented in this reading selection.
6. *In a final pass students read the entire passage and identify information and the details that support the main idea or the generalization*. In essence, this is applying the structure of knowledge. Through the first three passes they identified the generalizations and the concepts. In this final pass they are identifying the facts and the details. This approach is useful in helping them see the relationships among generalizations, concepts, and facts.
7. *Review what students have learned*. This final step ensures that students have grasped the text's generalizations, the big ideas, and the relationships. This is a critical step in making sure that the lesson has been effective.

Anticipation Guides

Anticipation guides are useful tools for helping students understand and process new information. This new information might be presented in the form of a film, a portion of the textbook, or a guest speaker. Anticipation guides may also be called *prediction* or *reaction* guides (Savage et al., 2006). Anticipation guides are intended to build on students' prior knowledge and relate their previous understandings to the new material. Anticipation guides serve as a form of advance organizer by providing students with a framework for thinking about the new material they will encounter.

The basic concept in an anticipation or a prediction guide is to present students with some questions or statements related to the new material (Savage et al., 2006). They are to predict what they think they will find. There are a variety of ways of constructing anticipation guides. Those for early elementary students might use pictures or diagrams and minimize the use of vocabulary.

Steps in the Model

1. *Read or preview the material that students will be using*. Determine the important ideas and concepts you want them to learn.
2. *Write several statements about the concepts*. These statements should consider students' previous knowledge yet provide some challenge to this knowledge.

FIGURE 5-2 • Sample Anticipation Guide

The War for American Independence

Directions:

Before viewing the film respond to the following statements. When you have completed viewing the film, you will be asked to respond again.

Before Viewing		**After Viewing**
Agree		*Agree*
————	1. A major reason for the war was the issue of taxes.	————
————	2. During the war, all of the states were unified and supported George Washington.	————
————	3. Many Native Americans sided with the British.	————
————	4. Most African Americans supported the colonists.	————
————	5. The war thrust women into new roles and gave them responsibilities and privileges they had never had.	————

Write a couple of statements that are thought provoking enough to stimulate discussion or even disagreement.

3. *Prior to encountering the material, have students respond to the guide.*
4. *Discuss the responses with the whole class.*
5. *Present the new material to the class.*
6. *Students respond to the guide again and reconsider their original responses.*
7. *Review the material with the entire class and discuss what they learned and any changes that they made.*

Figure 5-2 presents a sample anticipation guide.

Direct Instruction

Direct instruction is probably the most commonly used model in teaching. In ***direct instruction***, the teacher clearly is in charge of the classroom and controls the presentation of new information by following a systematic step-by-step approach. Although direct instruction is primarily teacher directed, when properly implemented, there can be high levels of student activity and involvement.

Much of the tradition of direct instruction is related to the work of Madelyn Hunter (1976). During the 1970s she popularized a widely used approach to direct instruction. Her model was later modified by educational researcher Barak Rosenshine (1983), who used the term ***explicit teaching*** to describe this approach. More recently, Good and Brophy (2003) have described their direct instruction model as ***active teaching***. Although there are some slight differences in the models, they all generally follow the same basic steps.

Good social studies instruction in-volves gathering information from a variety of sources.

Anthony Magnacca/Merrill

Steps in the Model

1. *Daily Review* (first 6–8 minutes). During this step, review what was covered the previous day, check homework, and quickly reteach to clear up any misconceptions.

2. *Anticipatory Set* (3–5 minutes). The purpose of the anticipatory set is similar to that of an advance organizer. At this step, tell students what they will be learn-ing in the lesson. This might be in the form of stating the objective or mention-ing a topic that will stimulate interest in the content to be learned.

3. *Lesson Development* (15–20 minutes). Present new content in a systematic man-ner, in small, logical steps with frequent monitoring and checks for understanding. These checks can take the form of brief questions or a brief activity where students demonstrate their knowledge. If you spot misunderstandings, modify instruction and reteach it until students properly grasp the new material. During this phase of the lesson, provide frequent feedback to learners regarding their performance.

4. *Guided Practice* (10–15 minutes). During guided practice you give students an assignment that is related to the lesson objective. You quickly circulate around the room and check their understanding and help them apply their learning. In some lesson models this is called *seatwork*.

5. *Closure* (2–3 minutes). At the closure stage, reinforce and review the main points of the lesson. This is to ensure that students have learned the content and to build a bridge to the next lesson.

6. *Independent Practice* (Homework). Give students an assignment they are to complete on their own with minimum supervision. This often takes the form of homework. To be effective, it needs to be an application that is slightly different in context than the one presented in class. It is important that guided practice always precede independent practice and that you are sure students understand the target concept or skill before they engage in independent practice. You do not want them practicing incorrect responses.

There is evidence that direct instruction is most suitable when the material you want students to learn can easily be organized into a structure featuring sequential, logical steps. Direct instruction requires that you know exactly where the lesson is going and that you control the pace of the lesson and the flow of information. When done appropriately, direct instruction can be a powerful method of teaching basic information and skills. On the other hand, you will not find direct instruction to be an appropriate choice when your learning objectives seek to develop students' more complex thinking skills by involving them in activities that focus on discovery and personal construction of meaning.

Concept Attainment

Because concepts are so useful for students as categories for organizing large quantities of information, you will find it useful to include in your repertoire techniques for teaching them. One of these techniques is called *concept attainment*, which features the acquisition of concepts that the teacher has identified as critical for students to know or understand. For example, a concept-attainment approach would be a logical choice if your objective is to have members of your class master the geographical concept of *peninsula* or the economic concept of *trade*.

You will recall that *concepts* are labels given to groups of items that share common characteristics or attributes. The concept-attainment technique systematically builds students' understanding of these features. Although you are in control of the concepts to be learned, this model keeps students actively involved and pushes them to engage in sophisticated thinking.

Steps in the Model A prerequisite to using the model is to define the concept that you are going to teach the students. You need to identify the critical attributes of the concept, as these will guide you as you select the examples and nonexamples that form the core of your lesson. There are six simple steps in helping students understand a concept. This simplicity makes it easy to apply to a variety of subjects in the classroom.

Step 1: *Provide students with the concept name*—In this step you introduce students to the concept they will be learning in the lesson. This step focuses learners' attention and tells them why it is important to learn the concept. For example, if your target concept is *peninsula*, you might begin as follows:

"Those of us who live in the San Francisco area often hear news reports that mention events that occur on the peninsula. It is important for us to know what a peninsula is so that we can understand what they are talking about. Today we are going to learn how to identify and find a peninsula."

Step 2: *Give members of your class examples of the concept that have the essential or critical attributes*—At this point present several examples of peninsulas. Indicate that each example is a peninsula. You might involve your class in a short discussion of what learners see in your examples. You need to vary your examples so students see peninsulas of different sizes, shapes, and geographical orientations. These are all noncritical attributes of the concept *peninsula*. For example, some peninsulas are long, others

LESSON IDEA 5-1

TOPIC: How Far Is It?

OBJECTIVES: Students will be able to calculate distances on maps using the scale.

ENGAGING THE STUDENTS: Introduce the lesson by saying the following: "Yesterday we learned about maps. What are maps? What do maps show us?"

DEVELOPING THE CONTENT: Place a map of the local community on the board in front of the room. Point out that you have marked two places on the map. Ask students if they think they could walk from one of the places to the other. Ask, "How can we tell how far apart the two places are?"

Next, show them a model car. Ask, "What kind of car is this? If you had a real car like this, would it be this big? How much bigger would it be?" Inform students that what they are looking at is a *scale model*. This means it looks like the real car, but it is different in size. If possible, you might have another car at a different scale.

Ask students, "Do you think there is a way we could figure out the actual size of the real car this model represents?" After listening to their comments, say something along these lines: "There is something called a scale that tells us exactly how much bigger the real car would be. For example, if the scale is 1 inch equals 1 foot, and the scale model is 10 inches long, how long is the real car?" Listen to students' answers.

After students have wrestled with this problem for a few minutes, show them how to calculate the size of the car represented by the model. To do this, place a strip of paper 10 inches long on the floor beside the model car. Suppose your model is 5 inches wide. Say to your class, "We know our model is 5 inches wide. We also know our scale is 1 inch equals 1 foot. Now, who can tell me how many inches wide the real car is? Can anybody tell me how wide the car is in terms of feet?" Listen to students' answers.

Circulate to check for understanding. If learners are unable to make the conversion, do at least one more problem with the class as a whole. Explain that scale on a map helps us determine how far apart things might be. Point out the scale on the map. On some maps 1 inch represents 1 mile. Ask students to determine what distance on the map represents 1 mile on the ground. (To help learners better grasp the distance represented by the term "mile," provide them with a concrete example. For example, it may be about a mile from your school to a main highway or to a mall where students and their families regularly shop.)

Next, ask members of your class to calculate the distance in miles between two points on the map. Ask, "Could you walk between these two points?"

GUIDED PRACTICE: Give your students a few problems that require them to calculate the difference between two points on maps. Circulate and provide corrective feedback to those having difficulty. If the class is successful in understanding scale, give them a homework assignment such as measuring their room and drawing a scale model.

CLOSURE: Ask students to define *scale* and state why it is useful to know the scale on a map.

INDEPENDENT PRACTICE: Give students several pairs of cities on a map of the United States. Have them find the distances between the two cities and bring their work to class the next day.

EXTENSION TO THE WEB: The Maps.com website provides free outline maps and global images that can be downloaded as print images for students to use.

URL—http://www.maps.com/FreeStuff .aspx?nav=FF

are short. Some are narrow, others are wide. Some are oriented to the north, others to the south.

During this phase, you can accommodate different modes of learning by allowing students to gather information about the concept through different senses. For example, you can ask students to feel or trace a peninsula on molded relief maps. Other concepts you teach also may lend themselves to touching, smelling, hearing, or tasting.

Step 3: *Display nonexamples of the concept*—Show examples of geographical features that are not peninsulas. You might show them photographs of isthmuses, islands, and continents. You want to choose nonexamples that will help students identify attributes that are not associated with peninsulas. As each example is presented, say, "This is not a peninsula." At this point you may find it useful to engage learners in a discussion about why they think the example is not a peninsula.

Step 4: *Display examples and nonexamples and ask students to choose an example*—Present your students with a mixed set of examples and nonexamples of peninsulas. Ask them to identify which are examples of peninsulas.

Step 5: *Students define the critical attributes of the concept*—Ask members of your class to think about what they have seen and done. Encourage them to define characteristics of a peninsula using their own words. If students are unable to give a definition that includes the critical attributes, then provide them with additional examples and nonexamples so that they can clearly see the concept's defining characteristics.

Step 6: *Students apply the concept by finding new examples*—Conclude by asking members of your class to use a globe, atlases, or maps to identify examples of peninsulas. Provide help if either their definitions are a bit wide of the mark or they are having difficulty locating examples.

In this simple lesson focusing on the concept *peninsula*, you might present all the examples in one day's lesson. However, when you focus on more complex concepts, such as *democracy*, you may need several days to provide sufficient examples and nonexamples.

Classroom Discussion

There is probably no approach that shows up on lesson plans as frequently as discussion. However, often the term *discussion* covers a range of classroom activities, from that of asking a series of factual questions where the purpose is a review and the format is much like an oral examination to discussions where open-ended questions are used with the purpose of getting students involved in problem solving.

For our purposes, we define *discussion* as a learning activity where the purpose is to help students learn new concepts and relationships. This requires a purposeful plan that leads to students to identify important information and move to identifying new relationships or conclusions. Your role as the teacher is to set the purpose and the goal for the discussion and to structure the steps to accomplishing the goal.

LESSON IDEA 5-2

TOPIC: What Is a Nomad?

OBJECTIVE: Students will identify the critical attributes of a nomad.

ENGAGING THE STUDENTS: Begin the lesson by asking, "Which of you have moved from one house to another?" Have students discuss reasons why people move and the advantages and disadvantages of moving. Inform them that today they are going to be learning about some people who move frequently.

DEVELOPING THE CONTENT: Collect a number of pictures of groups of people. One set should include pictures of people who can be classified as *nomads*. This might include pictures of Plains Indians, Eskimos, Bedouins, and so on. Another set can include people living in permanent residential groups.

Present one of the pictures of a nomadic group to students. Tell them, "The people in this picture are called nomads. What are the things you notice about them in the picture?"

Present a picture of a different nomadic group. Inform students that these people are also called nomads. Ask them to identify what they see and how they think these people are like the people they saw in the first picture.

Present students with a third picture. This picture should not be of a nomadic group. Tell the students that these people are not nomads. Have them state what they see as similarities and differences to the first two pictures.

Provide students with two pictures, one of a nomadic group and one of a group that is not. Ask them to choose which picture is of a nomadic group.

Ask students to respond to the question, "What is a nomad?" List the criteria that they would use in defining a nomad.

CLOSURE: Review what the students have learned about nomads. Ask them to find another example of people who might be called nomads and bring the example to the next class.

EXTENSION TO THE WEB: The Saskatoon (Canada) Public School Division website presents detailed information on concept attainment. It contains links to a number of concept-attainment lesson ideas for various grade levels and curriculum areas (including social studies).

URL—http://olc.spsd.sk.ca/DE/PD/instr/strats/cattain/

Direct instruction is one of the most common teaching approaches.

Anne Vega/Merrill

Although some new ideas might be introduced, the essence of the approach is the interaction that occurs as class members, under your guidance, reflect on and share individual insights related to your lesson's content focus.

To create the conditions for productive classroom discussions, you need to commit considerable attention to planning. Among other things, you need to think about questions you will ask, how you will sequence your questions, and how you will respond to student contributions. Initially, you may find it useful to write down some of the questions you will use to guide your discussion. These will help you keep the discussion focused and get the discussion back on track should it bog down at some point.

Teacher Questions   Good teacher questions have long been identified as an important component of effective teaching. There are several dimensions associated with high-quality questioning. Among other considerations, you want to ask questions that are clear, concise, and appropriately sequenced.

Clear questions clearly communicate to students the kinds of answers you are looking for. When your questions lack clarity, incorrect responses may be the result of the failure of your students to understand what you seek. When you ask questions, you need to avoid vague and ambiguous language.

Your questions should be concise and brief. Verbose, long-winded questions will confuse your learners. Lengthy questions often lack a clear focus, and students tend to struggle to understand what response is expected of them. In addition, long statements often contain more than one question. This condition confuses students, who wonder which question they should answer. When this occurs, many students resolve their confusion by refusing to volunteer any response out of fear that their response will be inappropriate.

Questions serve many purposes. Among other things, they can help you develop learners' higher-level thinking abilities. Marzano (1992), a specialist in instructional design, identifies eight distinct categories of questions that can help your students develop more sophisticated patterns of thinking.

- *Comparison Questions:* Questions in this category focus your students' attention on similarities and differences.
- *Classification Questions:* These questions ask your learners to group things according to some common characteristics.
- *Induction Questions:* These questions help your students to arrive at conclusions based on their own analysis of specific information.
- *Deduction Questions:* These questions help your students to see whether specific information is consistent with a general principle.
- *Error-Analysis Questions:* These questions ask your students to look for errors in logic or in a procedure. For example, you might want them to spot errors in propaganda or to identify instances of data distortion.
- *Constructing-Support Questions:* These questions ask your students to support a conclusion or position they have taken.
- *Abstracting Questions:* These ask your students to identify patterns and relate them to new content. Often these questions relate to analogies and metaphors.

- *Analyzing-Perspective Questions:* These questions ask your students to identify their personal positions and to consider the merit of other views. They seek to help learners identify values.

Now let us look at how you may sequence these question types in a classroom discussion model.

Steps in the Model

1. *Review previous learning and clarify the topic of the discussion.* For discussions to be productive, they must have a clear focus. Too often, discussions flounder because the opening question does not provide a clear focus. It is usually best to open the discussion with a quick review of previous learning in order for students to have a context for the discussion. Then introduce the issue to be discussed in a clear and unambiguous manner. State the focus much as you would state your objectives. For example, you might introduce a discussion of changes in the local community by stating, "Today we are going to see if we can identify what might happen if that new store we mentioned yesterday is built across the street from the school."

2. *Present an opening question.* Opening questions to a discussion should have a couple of purposes. They should elicit information students will need to think about in the course of the discussion and they should be nonthreatening, to encourage maximum participation. Following the focus of the discussion started in the first step, an appropriate opening question might be, "How many of you have gone shopping in a store like this? What did you notice about the number of people? What did you notice about the different activities at the store?"

3. *Ask a classification question.* An example might be, "Based on your experiences, what do you see as the problems that are associated with large stores like the one you visited?" Students might now classify their observations into areas such as traffic, noise, litter, and so on.

4. *Ask a comparison question.* "In what ways would this new store planned for across the street be like the ones you have visited? Do you think it would have the same types of problems? Would it create new traffic? Would there be more noise?"

5. *As appropriate, follow up the previous question with constructing-support questions.* "Why do you think it would be different? Why do you think there would be more or less traffic?"

6. *Ask an analyzing-perspective question.* Now that students have identified basic information and issues, ask them to take a position and support it. An example might be, "Now that we have identified what some the advantages and disadvantages might be of a store like this, do you think this store should be built? Why or why not?"

7. *Debrief and bring closure.* At this step, quickly summarize the main points made and the issues that were raised. The intent here is to reinforce what the students have learned as a result of the discussion.

Responding to Students Successful classroom discussions include careful and appropriate reactions to learner responses to questions. You need to do the following as you respond to students during a class discussion.

Wait for Student Responses. When you ask a question, you may find it difficult to tolerate the extended periods of silence that may follow. Researchers have found that many teachers tend to either answer their own question or ask another when students do not answer immediately. You need to avoid this pattern. Students need time to think about their answers. If you wait even a few seconds (try to go as long as six or seven), you will increase the likelihood that one or more students will volunteer an answer. Increasing time results in higher levels of class participation, more appropriate learner answers, and higher rates of student learning (Good & Brophy, 2003).

Refocus. This is an important skill as a means of keeping a discussion "on track." Discussions are prone to wander away from the main focus unless you make a specific effort to keep them focused on the objective of the lesson. This skill involves listening to student responses, reinforcing their participation, and then refocusing the discussion by restating the original question or by reminding the class of the original intent of the discussion.

Clarify. You will find that many of your students have trouble expressing themselves or making their point. As the discussion leader, you need to clarify students' answers to keep the discussion moving forward. Unclear or "off the wall" learner comments have a tendency to stop discussion because students get confused and do not know what to say. When this happens, you can help learners clarify their responses by paraphrasing. After someone in your class has made a contribution, you can simply say, "Are you saying that . . . ?" Another aspect of clarifying is to ask

Group discussions can engage many students in meaningful activity.

Scott Cunningham/Merrill

LESSON IDEA 5-3

TOPIC: Why Prices Vary from Place to Place

OBJECTIVES: Students will be able to identify at least one reason why the price of an item might be different in different places.

ENGAGING THE STUDENTS: Introduce the lesson by asking if anyone in the class has purchased something that they later found was cheaper in another place. Ask, "Why do you think the price of something might be different in different places?"

DEVELOPING THE CONTENT: Tell the students that today they are going to read about prices of the same thing in two different communities. Give all students a copy of the following case study.

Different Prices

Directions

The following is a story of people who live in a small town. Read through this story and see if you can identify why things cost more in their town than in a nearby city.

SMALLVILLE: In the Central Valley there is a town named Smallville. There are only a few stores in the town. One of the stores in the town is a nursery that sells plants and flowers that people can plant in their gardens. This year the nursery was selling new rose bushes for $15.95.

About 50 miles away from Smallville is a larger city with lots of shops and stores. There are several nurseries in the large city. Some of the people who live in Smallville were shopping in the city. They discovered that the nurseries in the large city had a lot more rose bushes and they cost only $12.95 each.

Why do you think the nurseries in the city charged less for their rose bushes?

Why do you think they had more rose bushes?

Why don't the people in Smallville do all of their shopping in the city?

What might be some reasons why the owner of the nursery in Smallville charges more money for rose bushes?

Group Work After students have had a chance to read the account and think about the questions, have them meet in groups of 4 to 6 and share their conclusions. Each group will present their answers to the entire class.

CLOSURE: Review with the students their conclusions. Make sure that special attention is paid to the issues of competition between stores and how that can make prices cheaper. Another concept that could be emphasized is that of volume of business. A store that can sell lots of something can often sell it cheaper than a place that sells only a small quantity. You might also emphasize that if people have to take time and pay for gas to drive some distance for something, it might be cheaper for them to pay the higher price in their own community.

Independent Practice Give students an assignment to compare the prices of something in at least two different stores or places. They will report their findings in a whole-class discussion.

EXTENSION TO THE WEB: You can find more information on teaching economics in the classroom at the website for the National Council on Economic Education. They have material and lessons for all grades K–12.

URL—http://www.ncee.net/

the student to give more information or to define ambiguous or vague terms. You might make comments such as, "Could you tell us a little more about that?" or "Who are the 'they' you mentioned?"

Summarize. As a teacher, another important skill to learn is when to stop at critical stages in the discussion and ***summarize***, or recapitulate with your learners the information that has been brought out to this point. Sometimes when a discussion seems to have bogged down, you can get it moving again by taking time to summarize. This may inspire students' thinking and get the discussion back on track.

Learning Centers

Up to this point the approaches described generally take place in the context of a whole class working together under the teacher's guidance. However, some approaches to acquiring content knowledge can be accomplished through individualized and group contexts. The learning center is an individualized learning approach that can help you differentiate learning to accommodate differences. Learning centers have long been a popular approach in elementary schools.

A ***learning center*** is a designated place within the classroom where materials related to a single topic are arranged. It serves as an environment for learning all the required information about a topic. Students are usually given assignments that require them to visit one or more learning centers and use the material to complete an assignment. In some instances, students might have time or reason to visit only one learning center. In others, there might be multiple learning centers, each with an independent focus, and a designated time when all students are working at a center. Some learning centers might have an assignment required of all students, others might have alternative assignments that students might choose.

Learning centers can be used for different purposes. Among the major types of learning centers are enrichment centers, reinforcement centers, and alternative-materials centers.

Enrichment centers are designed as an alternative for students who have completed other assigned work. They usually focus on the same topic or the same ideas being studied by the rest of the class. Those students who master the material quickly can then go to the enrichment center. The activities here should be challenging yet fun activities that motivate students and encourage them to extend their learning.

Reinforcement centers are established to provide reinforcement for the topics being studied in the class. They might be implemented near the end of a unit for students to review what they have learned earlier in the unit. Reinforcement centers should provide alternative materials and activities for those parts of the curriculum that students may have found difficult.

Alternative-materials centers focus on content that you want all students to learn. They respond to diversity in the classroom by including a variety of learning materials related to the common topic. Students can be allowed to select materials and activities consistent with their own interests and abilities. For example, you may have some students who are not proficient readers. An alternative-materials center might include things such as CD-ROMs or easy-to-use software that would help these students succeed. We use the alternative-materials center model in the following subsection.

Steps in the Model

1. *Identify content that can be learned independently through a learning center*. This should be content for which there is an abundance of study material.
2. *Develop a task sheet that identifies all of the options and the steps that a student must perform at the learning center.*
3. *Gather and display at the center all of the material that students will need.*
4. *Explain to the entire class what they will be expected to do at each learning center*. Establish class rules for using the center and its materials.
5. *Identify a schedule for students to work at a center*. If you are using more than one center, you can establish schedules so that different students are using different centers at the same time. This will help prevent overcrowding.
6. *Monitor student use of the center*. If several centers are in use at the same time, move from center to center to answer questions and solve problems. Develop a recordkeeping system to monitor which students have completed which centers.
7. *When all students have completed the activities of a center, review with the class the central ideas* that students should have learned as a result of their work and what was effective for those who were successful.

Student Teams

This is a cooperative learning approach that is useful when there is a wide ability range in the classroom. Based on the work of the Johns Hopkins Team Learning Project (Slavin, 1980), the approach applies two variables that have been shown to be effective in learning—peer tutoring and competition between classroom teams.

Student teams works best when there is a given body of content that all students need to learn. (For example, all students in the classroom usually are required to take the same examination at the end of the learning sequence.) The student teams plan requires that you have some prior knowledge of the achievement level of each student in class. Based on their prior learning, each student is given a baseline score indicating their achievement level. The success of each team is based on the improvement level of each student in the team over their baseline score. The team in the classroom that has the highest gain is the winner and is given some special recognition or privileges.

Steps in the Model

1. *Break the entire class into teams of four or five*. Team members should consist of a mix of high, average, and low-achieving students, based on their baseline scores.
2. *Ordinarily, begin by introducing the content you expect all students to learn in a whole-group setting.*
3. *Provide to all of the teams task sheets and support material for the material to be learned.* Each team must work on tasks until they believe that all members of the team understand the content. During the team work, it is important for team members to help each other. Those who understand the content should be helping those who have difficulty. Teams can be given some freedom to determine what they need to do to make sure that all of their team members learn the content.

4. *When the team decides that all members have a good grasp of the material, they can take the test*. You can either give each group the test or the criterion task when they request it, or give the test or task to the whole class at the same time.

5. *Score the test and award the group points*. A special scoring system is used to emphasize the importance of cooperation and the active peer tutoring of all team members. An individual team member may contribute up to 10 points for the team total depending on how well they do on the final test. To determine how many points is awarded to the team, the score of this person is compared to their baseline score. For example, suppose a student entered with a baseline average of 50 percent. On this particular test, they got 55 percent correct. This means that their team gets 5 points. However, if a student with a baseline of 50 percent gets 65 percent correct, the team would only receive the maximum of 10 points. Perfect papers are given 10 points regardless of the baseline score. This provides an incentive for the high-scoring students to continue to do well. Suppose a high-scoring student has an average of 95 percent. If they get 100 percent correct, they can win 10 points rather than just 5 points for the team. Do not take away points for students who score below the baseline. They simply do not earn any points for the team. Add together the total points for each team and the team with the highest number of points is the winner for this activity.

6. *Debrief when the activity is over*. Focus on the quality of the interactions between team members and what the successful teams did to help everyone learn the content. This will help less successful teams learn how to use teamwork and how to become effective peer tutors. It is best to change the composition of the teams at intervals. After three or four rounds with the same team, regroup the students. At this point you would also want to recalculate the baseline scores to take into account those who had improved.

Table 5-1 shows a sample scoring summary for a student team.

TABLE 5-1
Scoring Example for Student Teams

STUDENT	BASELINE SCORE	TEST SCORE	TEAM POINTS
Abby	57	64	7
Benji	63	60	0
Carol	40	55	10
Dale	83	88	5
Eddie	75	95	10
		Team Total	32

Jigsaw

Another cooperative learning approach useful for knowledge acquisition is the *jigsaw* method, in which each person in a group accomplishes part of a larger assignment. Jigsaw is especially useful when the content you want to teach can be divided into several components. For example, it could be used in a middle school class where the class is studying a topic such as South America. The content could be broken into different groups according to different nations. Jigsaw capitalizes on peer tutoring and the notion that individuals learn most when they have to teach the content.

Jigsaw includes two different groupings of students, the "home" group and the "expert" group. The home group is the basic unit of organization. Like student teams, the class should be divided into groups with a range of abilities, although you do not need to generate baseline scores for students to participate in jigsaw. Individuals in the home group are then designated to become an "expert" on some dimension of the topic. They do this by meeting with corresponding members of other home groups to study, share information, and become "expert" on their assigned aspect of the topic. Home groups are then regrouped and it is the role of each expert to teach their home group what they learned in the expert group. The whole class is given a test or criterion task at the end of the learning sequence. Teams that do the best are given special recognition.

Steps in the Model

1. *Identify the major headings for the topic to be learned*. Gather material and provide instructions and overviews for each of the expert groups.
2. *Divide the class into home groups*. Provide the home group with an overview of what is to be learned and accomplished. Each home group then designates one or more people to be members of each expert group. (Sometimes it is good to have two members on each expert group in case someone is absent. If only one member of each home group is designated to be in an expert group and they are absent, you may need to meet with this home group and review the material with them.)
3. *Expert groups meet*. They are given the material and assignments and work together until all members of the expert group feel they have a good understanding of the information.
4. *Home groups reconvene and each expert teaches the home group what they learned in their expert group*. When the home group feels they have learned the material from each expert, they can take the test or perform the criterion task.
5. *The tests or criterion tasks from each home group are evaluated and the outstanding home groups are given recognition or rewards*.
6. *Debrief by focusing on what helped groups operate smoothly and why some groups were successful*. You may then also review the major understandings that all students should have as a result of their work in groups.

Web Check: If you would like more information on how cooperative learning can be useful in accommodating diversity in your classroom, you might try the California Department of Education and National Institute for Science Education websites, which provide information on how cooperative learning approaches have been useful in promoting learning in diverse classrooms. **URLs—http://www.cde .ca.gov/sp/el/er/cooplrng.asp** and **http://www.wcer.wisc.edu/archive/CLl/CL/ doingcl/DCL1.asp**

The approaches discussed in this section all focus on knowledge acquisition. They are appropriate when there is a body of content that all students need to learn. They are appropriate for discovery learning or problem solving, which will be discussed in the next chapter. Given the recent focus on accountability and testing, the approaches discussed in this chapter are likely to take on increased importance.

KEY IDEAS IN SUMMARY

- As a teacher, you have an opportunity to exercise great influence over your students' learning. In part your effectiveness will depend on your ability to choose teaching approaches that are appropriate given your objectives and your learners' characteristics.

- There is no one best teaching approach. To be effective, a contemporary teacher needs to use a variety of instructional approaches. Instructional approaches need to be selected based on important variables rather than on how you were taught or on what appears to be "cute" or "fun."

- There are several variables you need to consider when selecting a teaching approach. These include (1) learners' prior skills, knowledge, and attitudes; (2) the particular orientation to knowledge acquisition you wish your learners to use; (3) the nature of your learning objectives; (4) the nature of the content; and (5) your own preferences and teaching skills.

- The types of information you want students to learn can be grouped into two types, (1) discovered knowledge, and (2) acquired knowledge.

In both types students need to be personally involved in constructing their own meaning.

- The structure of knowledge may be helpful to you as you think about the nature of the content you wish to teach. The structure of knowledge organizes content along a continuum ranging from specific to general. Its major components, from most specific to most general, are (1) facts, (2) concepts, and (3) generalizations. Your teaching in social studies should focus on helping students use facts to form concepts and to acquire generalizations that describe relationships among concepts.

- Knowledge acquisition approaches range from those that focus on the whole group, often involving cooperative learning, to those that are individualized.

- Helping students acquire knowledge requires more than merely telling them or having them read information. To be effective, approaches that focus on knowledge acquisition need to inform students why they need to learn the information, to actively involve them in the learning process, and to present them with multiple perspectives.

CHAPTER REFLECTIONS

Now that you have read the chapter, think about these questions.

1. Suppose someone asked you to describe the "best" technique for teaching your social studies lessons. How would you respond to this question?

2. In the chapter you learned about several variables you should think about when you select an instructional approach for a particular lesson. Do you think you will have more difficulty gathering information about some of these

variables than others? If so, which ones do you think may cause you initial difficulties? How might you begin preparing yourself to overcome these potential challenges?

3. You may well have been in classes when so-called "discussions" basically were little more than teacher lectures. What steps would you take in planning and implementing a classroom discussion that would result in higher rates of active student involvement?

SIX

Selecting Teaching Approaches for Knowledge Discovery

Scott Cunningham/Merrill

This chapter will help you to:

- State why both knowledge acquisition and knowledge discovery should be part of the social studies program.

- Describe common elements of knowledge discovery approaches.

- List the steps of the concept formation approach.

- Identify how the inferring and generalizing approach can be used in the existing curriculum.

- State the relationship between role playing and simulations.

- Describe how the inquiry approach is related to the scientific process.

- Describe the purposes and characteristics of creative thinking and critical thinking lessons.

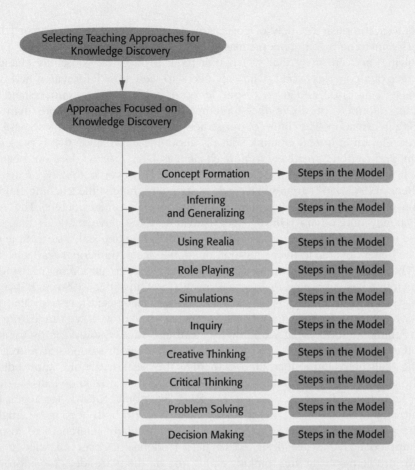

Selecting Teaching Approaches for Knowledge Discovery

Approaches Focused on Knowledge Discovery

Concept Formation	Steps in the Model
Inferring and Generalizing	Steps in the Model
Using Realia	Steps in the Model
Role Playing	Steps in the Model
Simulations	Steps in the Model
Inquiry	Steps in the Model
Creative Thinking	Steps in the Model
Critical Thinking	Steps in the Model
Problem Solving	Steps in the Model
Decision Making	Steps in the Model

- Differentiate between kinds of problems that are better approached using (1) a problem-solving technique or (2) a decision-making technique.

In the early years of our country, few people held out high educational expectations for the general population. You may be surprised to learn that many citizens in those years considered educational institutions to be doing a good job when schools produced graduates who could write their own names (Scheid, 1993). Later on, a primary goal of education, especially that beyond the basics, was to provide academic preparation for the small number of individuals who attended institutions of higher education (Altenbaugh, 2003). This sort of preparation emphasized the acquisition of those bodies of knowledge that were common in colleges and universities.

However, contemporary society has much broader expectations for education. Nearly all the children in the United States are attending school and we expect our schools to accomplish a variety of goals. Among other things, you and your fellow teachers want to help young people master processes associated with thinking, problem solving, and creativity that will permit them to face the constantly changing challenges of a complex world. One only needs to view how information had been manipulated, distorted, and given a "spin" in recent political events to understand that being an informed citizen in the contemporary world requires more than just acquiring information. The future of our society may well depend on those who can discover relevant information, think critically about the information that is presented to them, and respond creatively to new challenges. This process does not begin in high school, it must begin in the elementary grades. However, not everyone agrees.

Cheney (1987, 1997) argues that teachers spend too much time teaching children learning processes and too little time teaching them important content. The argument Cheney and others (Hirsch, 1987; Ravitch, 1985) have made is that time devoted to teaching children process skills, including thinking skills, steals time that could be better devoted to the acquisition of knowledge in traditional academic subjects. The recent emphasis on standardized testing as an important measure of accountability has supported this view. However, Perkins (1993–1994, p. 84) counters this position by noting, "You can often answer fact-based questions that you don't have answers for by extrapolating from what you know. If we can learn more facts by thinking about what we know, we can also know more facts by thinking about them as we learn them." In other words, helping your students acquire good thinking skills helps rather than hinders them as they seek to acquire knowledge.

The argument over whether we should be teaching either knowledge acquisition or knowledge discovery is based on a false dichotomy. Knowledge acquisition and knowledge discovery are not mutually exclusive, and both need to be taught.

The professional literature in education contains many references to instructional approaches that are designed to help students discover knowledge and improve problem-solving and thinking skills. Among them are ideas for improving students' abilities to do the following:

- Form new concepts
- Make meaning out of data and form generalizations
- Learn through use of realia, role playing, and simulations
- Use inquiry approaches
- Be creative
- Think critically
- Solve problems
- Make decisions

APPROACHES FOCUSED ON KNOWLEDGE DISCOVERY

Teaching approaches that focus on knowledge discovery have several common characteristics. Generally, they are best used when the outcome is not a "right" answer or "correct" conclusion that is expected of all students. There are many instances in teaching social studies where there are no right answers. For example, historians suggest that all of history is subject to the interpretation of the historian who wrote the account. Gerwin and Zevin (2003) note that history should be viewed as a puzzle, a set of conflicting viewpoints that creates a suspicion of ready-made interpretations.

To facilitate knowledge discovery a classroom environment needs to be created where students feel free to search for new understandings without fear of being wrong. One of the biggest blocks to knowledge discovery is the view that school is about finding the right answer. For example, one individual in a teacher education program noted, "Mostly, though, I did not speak because I was afraid of being wrong. . . . The pressure to give the right answer has been ingrained in me so deeply through the years of schooling that it has paralyzed me from fully participating in class" (Nelson & Harper, 2006, p. 7).

Students need to learn that there are unknowns and that there is new knowledge to be discovered. Furthermore, they need to learn that they do have the ability to think and solve problems. Learning *how* to learn is at least as important as *what* is learned. The emphasis in knowledge discovery approaches is on how to learn.

Another common characteristics of knowledge discovery approaches is that they place more responsibility on students for their own learning. This changes the teacher's role. Rather than being simply an information dispenser, the teacher's role becomes one of stimulating exploration, helping students discover relevant information, questioning their conclusions, and providing guidance.

In this section we discuss a number of different approaches that are useful in helping students engage in the processes of knowledge discovery, problem solving, and critical thinking. These approaches can be both stimulating and threatening to teachers. It is very stimulating to observe even very young students engage in thinking and reaching conclusions. Many of us who regularly observe and teach young children are constantly amazed by the quality of their thinking. However, in many of these approaches, you cannot predict the outcome. Different groups of students will go in different directions. In addition, you are turning over more control of the learning process to students. These can be threatening to teachers who always want to be in control and know exactly what the outcomes will be.

Concept Formation

In Chapter 5 we discussed the concept attainment approach. That approach helps students learn concepts identified as important for all students to learn. *Concept formation*, on the other hand, focuses on the *process* of forming concepts. It helps students analyze data by seeking common attributes and organizing the data into categories based on these attributes. The importance of this process was underscored a few years ago by a speaker at a scientific conference one of the authors attended. This speaker noted that advancement in science was dependent on the formulation of new concepts and new ways of organizing data. This is exactly the approach of concept formation.

Steps in the Model

1. *Present students with an open-ended question related to the topic.* For example, if the unit relates to the local community, the question might be, "If you had a friend moving to our community, what would you tell them about it?" The intent is to elicit an array of information about the topic.

2. *List student responses.* At this point you want to simply record responses and not judge them as right or wrong. You can record them by listing them on the board, on chart paper, or on a transparency. If students are old enough you might have a couple come to the front and help you record the responses. You may ask for clarification to get concise, recordable statements. Some discussion skills will be needed. Sometimes the group may focus on just one narrow dimension of the topic. You will need to prompt them to think more broadly.

3. *Group the items on the list.* This can be done by asking, "As you look at the list, which items can be grouped together. Why?" You should also let them know that any item can be in more than one group. An efficient way to group items is to use a coding system such as letters, numerals, symbols, or colors to indicate which things are grouped together. As students state which things they would put together, make sure they give their reasons. The purpose of this step is to get students to focus on common attributes or characteristics of the items in each group. Be aware that they may not group things as you would. Younger children often group things together that occur together. For example, a very young child might group items such as a *fork* and *salad* together because a fork is used to eat a salad. Remember there are no incorrect groupings as long as the students can give a reason.

4. *Label the groups.* Ask students to give a label or a title to each group based on the kinds of things in each group. A problem that sometimes occurs at this step is that students may supply broad labels that would include everything they have listed. You may need to prompt them that they need to come up with a label that is appropriate only for the items in the group. Figure 6-1 provides a sample set of items students have grouped and labeled.

5. *Debrief.* Once students have developed groups and labels for each group, bring the lesson to a close by reviewing what they have done. Focus on the process of listing, grouping, and labeling. Inform them that they have developed some concepts that will be useful as they continue to learn about the topic.

The concept formation approach is often useful at the beginning of a unit of instruction. It helps orient students to the topic. This can also be useful to the teacher for diagnostic purposes. The items students suggest and the way they group them communicate what they already know about the subject and any misconceptions they may have. For example, one of the authors did a concept formation activity with a group of sixth-grade students using the open question, "If you were to visit Brazil, what do you think you would see?" Among the items listed were *dark-skinned people, Spanish-speaking people, jungles,* and *shacks.* This indicated misinformation because learners did not know that Portuguese, not Spanish, was the language of Brazil. In addition, it helped the teacher diagnose that the students were unaware of the diversity of landscapes and people. They were not aware of modern cities such as Rio de Janeiro and Brasilia, that there were agricultural regions in addition to the jungle, and that all citizens of Brazil are not dark skinned. The teacher could then plan to correct these misconceptions and stereotypes and provide accurate information in subsequent unit lessons.

Some teachers have used this approach also at the end of a unit of study. They review what has been learned in the unit and compare this with the list and the concepts formulated at the beginning of the unit.

FIGURE 6-1 • Grouping and Labeling

An elementary grade class listed following items in response to the question, "What are some of the things that people use land for in our state?"

Houses	Baseball fields	Railroad tracks
Stores	Orchards	Mining
Schools	Forests	Airports
Growing corn	Lakes and dams	Growing vegetables
Raising cows	Zoos	Soccer fields
Parks	Roads	Factories

Their next task was to group items together on some basis and give each group a name. They developed the following groups:

BUILDING THINGS	GROWING THINGS	PLAYING ON
Houses	Growing corn	Parks
Stores	Raising cows	Baseball fields
Schools	Growing vegetables	Soccer fields
Factories	Orchards	

USING	NATURE
Railroad tracks	Forests
Mining	Lakes and dams
Airports	Zoos
Roads	

What might be other possible groupings? What other category labels might be used?

In summary, concept formation provides a model for helping students learn how concepts are formed. It provides them with a unique learning experience. In addition, it can be a good beginning before new content is introduced.

Inferring and Generalizing

You will recall that *generalizations* are statements that describe relationships among concepts. They have great explanatory and predictive value. Generalizations are important outcomes in the social studies. We want student to grasp the key ideas that will help them understand their environment and predict future actions. The inferring and generalizing approach is designed to help students take information they have acquired, organize it, and look for relationships.

LESSON IDEA 6-1

TOPIC: Life in Our Community Long Ago

OBJECTIVES: Students will group and label at least three categories of things observed in a recent field trip to a local museum.

ENGAGING THE STUDENTS: Have a brief overview of the field trip the class took to the museum.

DEVELOPING THE CONTENT: Say, "Yesterday we saw many exhibits that showed us what it would have been like to live in our community about 100 years ago. What were some of the things you saw in our field trip?" (As students share what they saw, abbreviate their contributions and list them on the charts taped to the front chalkboard.)

After the students have developed a list of 10 or so things they observed, have them group the items. Say, "Okay, yesterday we saw quite a few interesting things. I've listed those things on the charts. What I would like you to do now is to see if you can identify how some of these things we observed might be grouped together. As you look at the lists, do you see some things that might go together as a group? Why do you think they go together? Remember, something can be in more than one group."

When they have placed most of the items on the charts in groups, have them give labels to each group. Say, "We have grouped things on our list together in groups. Now we want to give each group a name. Look at all of the items in the "A" group. What could we call that group? We want to give it a name that describes the reason why we put those things together in that group."

CLOSURE: Say to the class, "What did we do today? What steps did we follow? Now that we have formed some groups and given them some labels that indicate some of the ways people lived long ago, we are going to do some more reading, watch a film, and look at some pictures of our community long ago. We are going to see if we can put some of the new things we learn in the groups we have formed and see if we need to form any new groups. So as we continue our study, we need to ask: What is this like? How is it like things we have already learned? Does it fit into our groups?"

EXTENSION TO THE WEB: The Just Think Foundation website provides numerous resources that can help you teach lessons to improve your students' thinking skills. There are lesson plans and links to other web resources.

URL—http://www.justthink.org

Steps in the Model

1. *Organize the information students have learned into a form where relationships can be identified.* This can be done by referring to the generalization that is the major focus of your unit of instruction. Then develop a model that identifies the various components of the generalization. For example, suppose that you wanted students to understand the generalization, "Change in one part of the community leads to changes in other parts of the community." A model of this generalization might look like this:

	Change	**Impact**
Community 1		
Community 2		

What this model indicates is that two community samples will be presented. In each community the students will identify a specific change. Then they will note the impact on other parts of the community. This helps you, the teacher, understand that the students can be presented information on these two communities through knowledge acquisition approaches. They might view films, read texts, or go on field trips. An important step of inferring and generalizing is to organize information visually so that relationships can be noted. In some instances, for example a story that is read in one sitting, a chart such as the one shown would be unnecessary.

2. *Compare the information in the categories by using a questioning technique focusing on each cell of the chart.* ("What do you notice about the change in Community 1? What happened as a result of that change? What do you notice about change in Community 2? What happened as a result of that change?")

3. *Develop an explanatory statement.* The purpose of this step is to get students to go beyond the information gathered and to identify patterns and relationships. ("What similarities and differences do you note between Community 1 and Community 2? How do you explain those similarities and differences?")

4. *Develop a generalization.* The purpose here is to look at the similarities and differences they noted and develop a generalization that might be applied to other places. ("What statement can we make that explains what we found out about change in these two communities? Can we apply that statement to other communities to predict what might happen?")

5. *Test the generalization.* At this step, take the generalization the students formed and apply it to a new example. ("Here is another community. In this community, they built a new hospital. Let's take what we learned about Community 1 and 2 and predict what we think will change in this community.")

The inferring and generalizing approach is very powerful. It does not require a lot of new material or a change in the curriculum. All it requires to be successful is that you have a focus on generalizations and that you organize information in a way that reflects

A data retrieval chart helps students organize information so that relationships can be more easily identified.

Anthony Magnacca/Merrill

LESSON IDEA 6-2

TOPIC: Nations of Latin America

OBJECTIVE: Students will develop a generalization that explains the relationship among literacy, income level, and life expectancy by comparing data presented on a chart.

ENGAGING THE LEARNERS: While pointing out the location of Latin America on a large wall map or globe, say to learners, "As you think about countries in Latin America, would you say they are all pretty much alike, or do you think there are important country-to-country differences? How do you think these countries compare to the United States?" Record some students' responses, and keep them available for use at the conclusion of the lesson.

DEVELOPING THE CONTENT: Provide students with individual copies of this chart:

Selected Characteristics of Four Countries in Latin America and the United States

Country	Languages	Percentage of People Who Can Read and Write	Life Expectancy in Years	Percentages of People Who Live in Poverty
Bolivia	Spanish and various Native American Languages	83.1	64	70.0
Costa Rica	Spanish	94.8	76	20.6
Ecuador	Spanish and various Native American Languages	90.1	71	50.0
Honduras	Spanish	72.7	69	53.0
United States	English and other languages including Spanish	97.0	77	12.7

Source of data: Central Intelligence Agency, World Factbook 2001, Washington, DC: CIA, 2001.

Ask students to look carefully at the chart and respond to the following questions:

1. What are some similarities you notice among these countries? Possible student responses:
   • The label at the top refers to all of them as Latin American countries and the United States. So they're all in the same part of the world.
   • Spanish seems to be spoken by some people in each of these countries.
2. What differences do you note? Possible student responses:
   • More people are able to read and write in some of these countries than others. Honduras has the highest percentage of people who cannot read and write.

- Life expectancies are different. In Bolivia, the age is only 64.
- Poverty levels are quite different. In Bolivia, 70 percent of the people live in poverty; in the United States, 12.7 percent live in poverty.

3. You have identified several important differences. Can you suggest some causes of these differences? Possible student responses:

- It seems people tend to live longer where there is less poverty.
- People also seem to live longer in places where higher percentages of the people can read and write.
- Poverty rates go down when more people in a country can read and write.

(These are only examples. Members of your class may develop different generalizations from the chart.)

Next, make these comments: "These are all good ideas. Let me write them on the board. We are going to be studying Latin America for the next several weeks. As we do, let's try to find evidence to test the accuracy of our statements. I want each of you to take notes on these ideas. When you find new information, think about whether it supports or does not support these generalizations. When we finish the unit, we'll look again at these ideas to see whether we need to revise any of them."

CLOSURE: Ask students to compare their ideas about these countries before they used the charts with those they have now that they have recorded and thought about the information they have learned. Ask them to identify ideas that have stayed the same and those they have changed. Challenge them to think about where any misconceptions they had may have originated.

EXTENSION TO THE WEB: The Social Science Models website provides some excellent examples of the data chart technique. See examples provided in the description of Lesson 3, relating to a unit on the presidency of George Washington.

URL—http:www.//auburn.edu/pctl/models/ SocialSciences/Washington/materials.html

the relationships contained within the generalization. Lesson Idea 6-2 presents an example of a inferring and generalizing lesson using a data chart for recording the information.

Using Realia

There are many *realia,* or real objects, that you can use in your social studies lessons. Using real objects in the classroom helps make the subject concrete and can stimulate a great deal of interest. The realia could be artifacts, art prints, pictures, documents, or even music. One teacher we know begins some of his units by posting pictures around the room, and groups of students have to write a story of what they think is happening. The basic question to pose when in using realia is, "How can I get this object to tell me its story?"

There are several commercial sources offering artifact kits on topics such as ancient Greece or Egypt, and others that have collections of documents and cartoons on topics such as the Civil War. The *TCI "Brings Learning Alive!"* series (Bower, Lodbell, & Owens, 2006) includes a variety of transparencies of things such as cartoons, photographs of buildings, and pictures of artwork that can be used to get students involved in analyzing and discovering information.

Steps in the Model

1. *Begin by identifying opportunities in your curriculum where you could use realia.* You might begin by surveying the media centers in your school district to see what is available. Experienced teachers often build their own realia kits, collecting objects, pictures, charts, and so on and storing them for classroom use.

2. *Decide how to present the realia to the class.* You may do this as a whole group where you lead the students in an analysis of the object, or in learning centers where students individually record their observations.

3. *Present each object to students.* Have them identify what they see. Ask such questions as, "What shape is this? Are there any distinguishing characteristics? What does it look like? How was it made? How old do you think it is? Who do you think might have made it?"

4. *Interpret the object.* Ask, "What does this object tell us about the people who made it? What does it tell us about the way they lived?" Try to get the students to move beyond the obvious characteristics to more subtle inferences.

5. *If you have knowledge of the object, you might share your information with them.* Ask them how this information related to their hypotheses about what the object was and who made it. If it is a mystery object, ask the students what they might do to find out more about the object.

6. *Bring the lesson to a close by reviewing what they did.* Ask, "How can we use objects to learn about the people who made them and used them?"

Role Playing

Role playing is an approach that can be used at all levels. Young children often enter role playing eagerly, as it is an extension of what many of them do at play. When introduced properly, even students in the middle grades will engage in role-playing scenarios, although they often need a little more encouragement because they are self-conscious and sensitive to how they will appear to their peers.

Role playing is best used in helping students develop an understanding of values and attitudes and learn the complexities of interpersonal decision making, and is most effective in situations where personal action is required and where there is no simple right or wrong answer.

Role playing can vary from a very short impromptu activity that comes up as a part of a lesson to complex preplanned activities that include well-defined roles requiring considerable interaction. For this discussion we will approach role playing as a preplanned activity.

Steps in the Model

1. *Identify situations in the curriculum where the dynamics of an interpersonal decision is critical for understanding.* Define the conflict or the issue and identify the roles needed.

2. *Develop a character profile for each role.* These should consist of relatively simple instructions to each student concerning their identity and their goals.

3. *Introduce the situation in the classroom.* Choose the students who will play the roles and set up the situation.

4. *Perform the role play.* Have the role players act out the situation.

5. *Discuss and evaluate the enactment.* Identify what happened and why the students think it happened in that way. Encourage the role players to discuss what they were thinking and feeling as they acted out their parts.

6. *Reenact the situation with a different set of players.* After some discussion it is often useful to have others perform the role play and try some different strategies.

LESSON IDEA 6-3

TOPIC: Being a History Detective

OBJECTIVES: As a result of this lesson, students will learn to make inferences from an artifact.

ENGAGING THE STUDENTS: Ask students, "How many of you have seen television shows such as *CSI* that involve detectives? What do detectives do? How would you like to be a detective? Being an historian is much like being a detective. The historian has evidence and from that evidence has to try and figure out what happened. Today we are going to see if we can be good history detectives."

DEVELOPING THE CONTENT: Present a photograph, art print, cartoon, or image that is related to the topic you are teaching. (Note: there are lots of downloadable images of photographs, artifacts, etc. at the Smithsonian Institution Libraries website. You should be able to find something that is relevant to your unit.) Present the image to the class and ask, "What do you think this image is about? What are the different things you see? What could you tell about this event by looking at this image? If you were going to tell a story about this image, what would you say?"

At this point one option would be to break the class into groups and have them develop a short narrative about the image presented.

Have members of the class share the story they developed. Challenge them to point out elements of the image that support their story. After several have shared their stories, tell them about the image and have them check their conclusions.

CLOSURE: Ask, "What did we do today? How is an historian like a detective? What might this mean when we read an account of something in history? (The interpretation could be wrong.) What do we need to do when reading about something that happened in history? How might we use what we have learned when visiting a museum?"

EXTENSION TO THE WEB: Hundreds of downloadable images can be found at as many different websites. In addition to pictures and images, the text of articles or the lyrics of songs can be presented as artifacts that can be investigated for clues. The Smithsonian Institution website referred to in the lesson is the following:

URL—http://www.sil.si.edu/SILPublications/ anthropology=K12

7. *Have a final discussion comparing the two enactments and how they were alike and different*.
8. *Debrief with the class focusing on what they learned.* Make sure to include not just information but feelings and emotions.

Simulations

Simulations have some similarities with role playing, and might be described as elaborate role playing. In a *simulation* students each assume a particular role, make decisions, and experience the consequences of their actions. In recent years computer simulations have increased the awareness of this approach. Many simulations have been developed by commercial companies and can be found in catalogs of social studies materials. Simulations have been created around such themes as an archaeological dig, the Gold Rush, the Oregon trail, creating a business, a political campaign, and others.

Simulations can add a "real-world" dimension to your teaching that many students find highly motivating. Keep in mind that the purpose of a simulation is not to learn lots of facts and acquire information, but to put students in roles where they learn to use information to make decisions and experience the consequences of their decisions.

Some simulations can be done in a single class session, others may take several days to complete. When deciding to use a simulation you need to think about the time required and whether the outcomes are worth the time invested.

Steps in the Model

1. *Select the simulation.* Because of the time involved and the cost for a commercially prepared simulation, you need to carefully choose simulations that best fit your curriculum. While you can create your own simulation, they usually take so much time to create that most teachers use those that are commercially developed. If possible, work through the simulation prior to introducing it to your class, as you will want to know exactly how it works and where problems or confusion may occur.

2. *Provide an overview to the class.* In this step you introduce the students to the simulation. Describe the problem to the students, their objectives, and the rules they need to follow. You might want to give a quick demonstration of a part of the simulation to provide them with a model.

3. *Provide a training phase so that students can walk through their roles and discover any potential problems.* Encourage students to ask questions and allow them to make mistakes. Some simulations involve students working in groups. If this is the case, then you need to make sure they understand the role of the group and how to work together.

4. *Conduct the simulation.* This is the *activity* phase. You serve as a coach, explainer, and referee. Sometimes disputes will arise and you will need to serve as a referee and make up a rule or a decision. Occasionally, if there is too much confusion, you may need to stop the activity and discuss what is happening and why. You may also want to stop the activity at certain spots to reflect on the actions and the strategies of some of the players.

5. *Conduct a debriefing.* Research has indicated that the debriefing time is one of the most important components of a simulation. It is here that you help students critique their actions and solidify their learning. You want them to leave the debriefing understanding at least some of the main principles that they have learned. Do not neglect the values and attitudes dimension. Simulations are especially powerful in helping students develop attitudes and values.

Inquiry

Inquiry approaches have a long history in the social studies. The eminent American educational philosopher John Dewey suggested basic steps for sequencing inquiry instruction in his classic *How We Think*, originally published in 1910. Fifty years later, inquiry became a central component of many of the social studies projects that were developed in the reform movement in the 1960s. Inquiry approaches have faded with the emphasis on standardized tests and accountability.

Over the years there have been a variety of inquiry approaches. Some, such as the Suchman (1962) style, have specific rules that are to be followed. For example, in Suchman inquiry, students work as a whole group to gather the infomration they need.

The teacher is in control of the data and students can get it by asking the teacher questions that can be answered "yes" or "no." Other inquiry approaches are much more flexible and allow for a variety of ways for the students to find the information they need.

Basically, inquiry approaches involve inductive reasoning. One way to look at inquiry is to view it as the scientific method applied to teaching. The approach is based on the theory that learning takes place when we are confronted with something that doesn't fit with the way we have ordered the world. As we strive to accommodate this new information, learning takes place. In addition, inquiry advocates contend that individuals do not change their minds and become open to new understandings by merely being told they are "wrong." Individuals become open to new learning when they test it and find that their model doesn't work very well.

The basic inquiry approach involves stimulating students to (1) form hypotheses that might explain a puzzling or discrepant occurrence, (2) gather data related to the hypotheses, and (3) test their hypotheses against the data. This might result in the acceptance, rejection, or modification of their hypotheses.

Steps in the Model

1. *The key to successful inquiry lessons is having a proper stimulus or focus.* This focus should be a puzzling or discrepant event, and should be something that does not have an easy answer. However, you need to make sure that there is an abundance of material that students can access in the data-gathering phase. If there are few sources of data, students will become frustrated and discouraged. The following situation can be used to create a discrepant event. Tell students, "We've noticed that many of the largest cities in the United States such as New York, Los Angeles, Chicago, Miami, Houston, Boston, San Francisco, and Seattle are port cities. Why do you think this is so? Now let's look at what has become the largest city in the world, Mexico City. Where is it located?" Note that in this example you build a model around the way many people have constructed the world. They see port as natural places where large cities will grow. While this is true, there are other reasons related to city growth. Presenting Mexico City provides a discrepant event that can push students to develop a deeper understanding about the location of centers of population.

2. *Students generate hypotheses*. Introduce to students and define the term *hypotheses* (a testable guess or theory about why something might be the way it is). At this stage students state guesses or hypotheses that might explain the puzzling situation or the discrepant event. Accept and record all guesses. In some cases, you may need to help students restate their hypotheses to make sure they are clear and concise and can guide data gathering.

3. *Gather data relating to the hypotheses*. At this step you have a couple of alternatives. One alternative is to follow Suchman inquiry where you, the teacher, have the data and students need to ask you questions to gather what they need. This has the advantage of keeping things under your control so that you can clarify the type of information needed, model the inquiry process, and help students learn how to ask good questions that are related to their hypotheses. A disadvantage is that it can be frustrating to students and challenging for you. For example, students who are not used to asking questions often want you to answer broad theory questions such as, "Is the reason Mexico City grew so large

Effective thinking and problem solving are important components of social studies instruction.

Tom Watson/Merrill

because . . . ?" They don't know how to ask questions such as, "Are there oil wells within 50 miles?" Therefore, they get frustrated very quickly. You need to develop skill in helping students learn how to frame questions and how to use the data they get from questions to evaluate their hypotheses.

Another alternative is to have the class identify the kind of information they need to have for each hypothesis and then break into groups to seek that data from sources you provide. One source that has greatly facilitated inquiry is the computer. Many students have learned how to use keywords to search for specific information. Keyword searching is an integral part of computer-assisted inquiry lessons.

4. *After data is gathered, students come back together as a group and evaluate each hypothesis using the data.* For example, using the Mexico City location problem, you might state, "We thought that one explanation for the location of Mexico City was that it was located near some valuable resources such as gold or oil. What did you find out about the location of valuable resources near Mexico City? What does that mean for our guess?"

5. *The next step is for students to modify or accept their hypotheses.* Once they have reflected on all of their guesses using the data they have gathered, you can ask, "Did we find any of our guesses that explained this? Given the new information we have, how might we change our guesses?"

6. *Review and debrief the lesson.* The important part of debriefing an inquiry lesson is to focus on the process of facing a puzzling situation, forming hypotheses, identifying what information is needed, gathering the data, and then testing the hypotheses.

You can use inquiry lessons at all grade levels. The difference will be in the type of puzzling situation you present and manner in which students define and gather the information.

Creative Thinking

Creative thinking features novel approaches to perplexing problems. Many inventors are creative thinkers. The inventor of the forklift truck was inspired to build it after watching mechanical fingers remove doughnuts from a hot oven (Ruggiero, 1988). The usefulness of the forklift makes an important point about the object of creative thinking. It is not thinking devoted to the creation of something bizarre for which there is no immediate or potential use. To be a legitimate "creative product," something must be both new and useful (Slabbert, 1994).

When you teach members of your class to employ creative thinking strategies, you help them accommodate to change. Slabbert (1994), an authority on creativity, argues that it is just as important for you to teach young people creative thinking skills, which will have lifelong relevance, as to teach them traditional subject content, which may soon become outdated. There is disagreement about the nature of lasting effects of lessons focusing on developing students' creative thinking skills. Some recent studies have found that the "cognitive abilities underlying creative performance differ from task to task" (Baer, 1993–1994, p. 80). This conclusion suggests that no single creative thinking lesson that you teach has the capacity to give your students the ability to develop creative solutions to all kinds of problems. This means that you need to prepare creative thinking lessons that focus on many different kinds of problems and tasks. By exposing students to a variety of creative thinking experiences, you increase the probability that they will develop thinking responses with practical value for different kinds of problems they will encounter as adults.

A number of creative thinking techniques have been developed. One that is widely used is *brainstorming*. Brainstorming developed first in the world of business. It is designed to help people develop original solutions to problems. It places an initial premium on generating a huge volume of possible answers. When you use brainstorming, you encourage students to develop as many responses as possible to a focus problem.

Steps in the Model

1. *Present a focus problem.* This needs to be a clear problem, one for which there is no clear answer and one that is interesting to the students. For example, "What do you think would happen if a rule was passed that said cars could no longer be driven in our community?"

2. *Students state their ideas as rapidly as possible.* A person is free to speak whenever someone else stops speaking. The idea is to generate a rapid outpouring of ideas. Students are encouraged to say whatever comes to their minds so long as it is relevant. No judgments are made about the plausibility or the value of a contribution. All ideas are accepted. This rule helps break down students' fears about "saying something stupid."

3. *Write down (or assign a designated recordkeeper to write down) every idea.* You may use a chalkboard, a large piece of butcher paper, a blank transparency, or some other means of doing this. It is essential that information from students be written down quickly. Responses from participants often come fast and furiously.

4. *Stop the idea-generation phase when the rate of presentation of new ideas noticeably slows.*

5. *Bring closure with a general discussion of all ideas presented.* This discussion may stimulate a need for additional study. (For example, given the focus question used to illustrate these procedures, there might be follow-up on topics such as alternative transportation systems, pollution, and so forth.)

Critical Thinking

You use lessons designed to promote students' critical thinking abilities to improve their abilities to evaluate ideas. Critical thinking always involves judgments based on informed opinion. Properly, these judgments should be supported by defensible criteria (Lipman, 1988).

Critical thinking encourages generation of new ideas. At times, you will wish to link critical thinking and creative thinking instruction. When you take this approach, you will first engage members of your class in exercises requiring them to use creative thinking. During this phase, you involve students in generating new ideas. During the second part of the lesson you require them to use critical thinking skills to make judgments about these ideas.

Dunn and Dunn (1972) developed an analytic brainstorming approach that encourages learners to think critically. The following steps are adapted from their recommendations. Note that your students must brainstorm responses to questions posed at each step. As the lesson progresses, you write student responses in a place where they can be seen easily by all class members.

Steps in the Model

1. *After brainstorming responses to a problem, encourage students to consider what the "best" solution to the problem might be.* Suppose you are teaching a group of fifth graders. You might use this question to begin the activity: "What would be the best thing we could do to make sure first graders don't get hurt on the playground?"
2. *Next, ask why these ideas have not already been implemented.* ("What things are preventing us from doing any of these things to help solve this problem?")
3. *After students have responded to this question, ask a follow-up question designed to help students begin thinking about what might be done to overcome any obstacles.* ("How could we overcome some of these difficulties?")
4. *Ask students to consider problems they might encounter in implementing responses to the previous question.* ("What might keep us from overcoming any difficulties we may face in trying to keep first graders from getting hurt on the playground?")
5. *Finally, ask students to decide what should be the first step toward a realistic solution of the problem.* ("Let's think about everything we have considered. What action should we take first to solve this problem? Be prepared to explain your choices.") Class members respond and defend their choices by referring to appropriate criteria.

Problem Solving

Throughout our lives we are confronted with problems. Although the nature of the problems change as we grow, they are always with us. It is important for students to realize that problems will not just disappear as they reach adulthood. What they

can do is to learn how to approach problems so that their anxiety is lessened. Therefore, learning a problem-solving approach can be one of the most important
outcomes of school.

Steps in the Model

1. *The most important step in solving any problem is problem identification.*
   When the problem is poorly defined or incorrectly identified, efforts to solve it
   will be unlikely to succeed. The way the problem is defined will influence the
   solution. Suppose you are driving a car and have a flat tire. You discover that
   there is no car jack. What is the problem? If we define the problem as that of
   getting a jack, that will lead us to one set of solutions. However, if we define the
   problem as how to get the wheel off the ground, that may lead to a whole new
   set of solutions. Defining the problem should also take into account the context.
   If the flat tire occurs on a busy highway or street, that context offers possibilities that are not present if you are in a rural area where there is little traffic.

   When problem scenarios are presented in the classroom, have students
   clearly define the problem and the issues they need to consider in seeking a solution. You may need to prompt them to go beyond the obvious by asking, "Is
   there another way we can state this problem?" Clearly write the problem so that
   the students have a reference to what they are trying to solve.

2. *Identify possible approaches to the problem.* Once the problem is clearly identified, ask students to suggest solutions, perhaps by brainstorming to get as many
   suggestions as possible. (Remember, while brainstorming do not spend time
   evaluating the suggestions.)

3. *Evaluate the proposed solutions.* At this point it is useful to review the requirements for a solution. What must the solution accomplish? Then evaluate each
   proposed solution to see which of them may accomplish the desired outcome.

4. *Decide on a defensible solution.* There might be more than one possible solution to a problem. Students will then need to choose and provide the reasons
   for their choice.

5. *Debrief the lesson.* Review the steps taken to reach a solution. Ask students to
   identify other places where they might use the same process.

You will find an example of a problem-solving exercise in Lesson Idea 6-4.

Decision Making

Many questions your students will face throughout their lives have no "right"
answers. Various responses may prove to be appropriate. Issues of this kind force
people to choose from among alternatives without assurance that their choice will
be the best. We all have to learn to make choices in the face of ambiguity and
uncertainty.

To develop your students' proficiency in dealing with issues of this kind, you
need to provide them with experience in working with thinking processes associated with decision making (Beyer, 1988). Many of the steps in the decision making
format are the same as those in problem solving. The major difference is that in
decision making we are calling on students to make a personal choice. A part of

LESSON IDEA 6-4

TOPIC: Where Should We Build the Playground?

OBJECTIVES: Students will be able to apply the problem-solving model to the problem of building a playground.

ENGAGING THE STUDENTS: Ask students about their favorite playground activities. List the various activities on the board.

DEVELOPING THE CONTENT: Announce to the class that the school has just been notified that the existing playground is going to be changed. All the equipment and the entire playground area are going to be changed. Students now need to identify how the playground will be rebuilt. The size of the playground will remain the same and it will have to be useful to all of the students in the school.

Defining the Problem Ask, "What is the problem that we need to solve to make sure that the playground is one that we can use and will like? What are the special things that we need to consider to make sure the playground is a safe one that can be used by all students?"

Identifying Possible Approaches Ask, "How can we go about solving the problem of how

to build the playground? What information do you think we might need to gather? Should we survey other students? Do we need to think about cost? Are some activities noisy, and should not be close to the neighboring houses? Do we need to make sure the older children are not playing in ways that might injure younger children?"

Evaluating the Suggestions Say to students, "Several ways of solving this problem have been identified. Let's look at each approach and decide what seems good and what might not be so good about it."

Choosing the Best Approach Say, "As we look at what we have identified as good and bad about each approach, which approach to do you think is best? Why do you think so? Will it make sure that the things we think are important are considered?"

BRINGING CLOSURE: Ask students, "What did we do today? Why did we do it this way? Can you think of some other problems where we could use these same steps?"

the decision-making process requires that individuals think about their values and what is important to them. Therefore, different individuals may arrive at different decisions. For example, you may have faced a choice of deciding where to go to college. There weren't any "right" or "wrong" choices. Your decision was probably influenced as much or more by what you value than it was by the reputation of the institution.

Steps in the Model

1. *Present a dilemma to students, ideally one containing a difficult choice.* This might be a moral dilemma that prompts individuals to consider their beliefs and values. For example, a common dilemma that many young children face is getting involved with a friend in an activity that parents have expressly told them not to do. The child is faced with a dilemma. Do they want to please their friend and maybe even do something that looks like it might be fun, or should they follow the instructions of their parents to avoid getting in trouble?

2. *Clearly identify the importance of making a decision.* When we face difficult issues there is a tendency to try and avoid making a decision. We hope that maybe the decision will be made for us. However, this avoidance tendency carries with it several dangers. If we are not making a choice, others may make a choice that is not in our best interest. We may discover too late that our inaction has placed us in an even more difficult situation.

3. *Discuss alternative decisions.* Like problem solving, it is useful to try and identify a number of possible decisions. Stress that taking time to identify alternative decisions rather than impulsively acting on the first thing that comes to mind can help us avoid many difficulties.

4. *Identify the possible consequences of each choice.* Making productive choices requires that we reflect on the alternatives. What is the logical outcome of each choice or action? This might require that each student gather data in order to predict potential consequences. What happened in the past? What has happened in similar circumstances?

5. *Identify values implicit in each alternative choice.* This means identifying clearly what is important to us in the choices we make. For example, in the previous example, what is important if the child chooses to follow their friend? It might be they value the friendship and don't want to harm that or that they value having fun. What do they value if they follow the instructions of the parents? Do they value avoiding punishment? Do they value having a good relationship with their parents over the relationship with their friend?

   With students in the upper elementary grades, this step could involve the use of case studies. You might want to include cases or examples of others in history who have made difficult choices. Discussion should center on what was most important to these individuals when they made their choices.

6. *Choose from the alternatives.* At this step it is important to get each student to make a choice. Because of the influence of peer pressure, this is best done individually. Before you initiate group discussion of the choices made, students need to individually think about what they would do and why.

7. *Have individuals share their choices and their reasons.* This group discussion may open up new values and considerations. During the discussion, individuals might identify new alternatives that would be even more productive.

8. *Debrief the lesson by focusing on the process of making a decision rather than on any specific decision made.* The objective of the decision-making strategy is to teach a process of making a decision, not to identify specific "right" or "wrong" choices.

There are many ways to use decision-making lessons. For example, as part of their effort to help develop students' citizenship skills, many schools have a student council. Suppose a group of fifth and sixth graders in your school decide that upper-grade council members (from grades 5 and 6) ought to be students who have been attending the school for at least three years. Their idea is that newcomers are unfamiliar with the school's traditions and won't be able to represent its true interests well. Present school policy allows any student in grades 5 or 6 to run for membership on the student council. If you were presented with this idea, you might capitalize on the situation and engage your students in a decision-making lesson.

LESSON IDEA 6-5

TOPIC: Deciding How to Vote

OBJECTIVES: Students will identify the reasons for and the actions they would take in voting. They will identify the steps to follow in making a decision.

ENGAGING THE STUDENTS: Ask students to share a time when they were faced with a difficult decision where they had to make a choice. (Examples may include the choice of clothing to wear to school when they wanted to wear one thing and their parents wanted them to wear something else, having two friends where each wanted to play at the same time, deciding what to buy with their money when there was more than one attractive choice.) Ask students to share what they decided to do.

DEVELOPING THE CONTENT: Present students with the following dilemma.

Student elections are just about to occur. Two students are running for election to the student council. One of the students is your best friend. You play together after school and have lots of fun. However, the other student has some really good ideas about some things that could make the school better. This person has also said they would like you to help them if they get elected.

- *List possible choices.* Ask, "What could you do if you were faced with this choice?" List the possible actions on the board.

- *Identify consequences.* Say, "Let's take each of the possible actions and think about what might happen if you chose each one. What might happen if you voted for your friend? What might happen if you voted for the other candidate? What if you decided not to vote for either one?"
- *Identify values.* Ask, "If you decided to vote for your friend, what would be most important to you? If you decided to vote for the other person, what would be most important to you? If you didn't vote, what would be most important to you?"
- *Students make an individual choice.* Say to students, "Now that we have discussed these alternatives, I want you to write down what choice you would make and whay you make it. You may have an idea about a choice we didn't list on the board. That's okay, write it down and state why you would do that."
- *Students share their choices.* Ask, "Who would like to share what they would do?" Have as many students who are willing share what they would do and why.

BRINGING CLOSURE: *Review what was done.* Ask students, "What did you learn about making decisions? Why is it important to think about alternatives and consequences when making a choice?"

In summary, you have a variety of approaches available to help students discover knowledge. Learning how to discover new knowledge and learning how to inquire, solve problems, and make decisions are important outcomes. The approaches discussed here can be used at different grade levels. The approach does not vary by grade level but rather, the type of content included and the nature of the problems posed will change. You will need to present younger students with concrete problems that focus on their immediate environment. Their level of sophistication might be less than older students, but they can still apply the processes. Although you may face considerable pressure to focus most of your efforts on knowledge acquisition in order to prepare your students for standardized tests, you need to realize that students will not be prepared to take their place in the world as productive citizens if they do not know how to think and solve problems.

KEY IDEAS IN SUMMARY

- Should teachers spend time teaching thinking skills directly? Today, many people think so. Some critics, however, argue that time spent teaching thinking skills diverts time from instruction that could better be spent on more purely academic subject matters. In response, some authorities claim that students learn academic subject content better when they also receive instruction focusing specifically on thinking-skills development.
- *Concept formation* approaches take knowledge that students already possess and help them organize it into categories with common attributes. This approach helps students learn how to engage in an important process that is rarely taught.
- *Inferring and generalizing* focuses on helping students look for relationships and go beyond specific information to form generalizations. It is an especially powerful approach that can help students understand why gathering information is important. Using this approach does not require a radical change in the curriculum.
- *Role playing* can be used as a quick supplement within a lesson or as a complex, preplanned activity. It places students in a particular role and has them act out the choices they would make. Role playing works well when there is more than one enactment of the role play. Students usually enjoy doing it because it contains elements much like play.
- *Simulations* are complex role playing. In recent years simulations have been developed on computers. These can offer some exciting opportunities for students to become actively engaged in social studies lessons and to experience the consequences of their choices. Debriefing is an important part of simulations because this is where the main ideas and concepts can be clearly expressed.

- *Inquiry approaches* utilize inductive learning processes. They begin by introducing students to isolated pieces of information. Students proceed through a series of steps that culminate in their developing an explanatory generalization. General steps in an inquiry lesson are (1) describing essential features of a problem or situation, (2) suggesting possible solutions or explanations, (3) gathering evidence to test these solutions or explanations, (4) evaluating solutions or explanations in light of this evidence, and (5) developing a conclusion based on the best evidence.
- *Creative thinking* requires learners to consider perplexing problems in novel ways. The "product" of good creative thinking must be both new and useful. *Brainstorming* is one technique teachers use to develop students' creative thinking skills. This procedure encourages them to generate responses in a lively, uninhibited way.
- *Critical thinking* requires that judgments be made in light of defensible criteria. Dunn and Dunn (1972) developed an analytic adaptation of brainstorming that is useful for developing students' critical thinking abilities.
- *Problem-solving* techniques are used when issues have "correct," "right," or "most appropriate" answers. A typical problem-solving lesson includes four steps: (1) identify the problem, (2) consider possible approaches to its solution, (3) select and apply approaches, and (4) reach a defensible solution.
- Some problems have several possible solutions. The specific decision a person reaches results from considering evidence and weighing personal values. You will find that you can use *decision-making* lessons in a variety of circumstances in your social studies program.

CHAPTER REFLECTIONS

Now that you have read the chapter, think about these questions:

1. Some critics contend that it is irresponsible to spend any of your instructional time teaching students thinking-skills processes. They allege that such lessons divert valuable time away from important academic content, particularly from the kinds of content that appears on standardized tests. How do you react to these concerns, and on what do you base your position?

2. Should tests be designed that focus on students' abilities to use specific higher-level thinking techniques, or should the success of these techniques be measured indirectly by looking at student scores on more traditional content tests?

3. Are there really differences among what we call "inquiry approaches," "critical thinking," "problem solving," and "creative thinking," or are these just fancy labels used to describe processes that are more alike than different?

4. What are your thoughts about developing lessons for primary-grade students that focus on developing their higher-level thinking abilities? Are these children too young to benefit from this kind of instruction? Why, or why not?

5. Interest in developing higher-level thinking skills has been a priority of many educational leaders for decades. If this is true, why do you suppose researchers over the years have found relatively little classroom instructional time dedicated to this kind of teaching?

SEVEN

Teaching Social Studies Skills

Scott Cunningham/Merrill

This chapter will help you to:

- Identify social skills that students need to learn.
- Explain problems often experienced by elementary students when they work with maps and globes.
- Identify key map, globe, and graphing skills.
- List research skills that students need to learn.
- Use time lines to help your students better understand issues associated with time and chronology.
- Help learners recognize differences between responsible and irresponsible ways of displaying information on graphs and charts.
- Introduce your students to basic symbols used in political cartoons and approaches to interpreting meanings of political cartoons.

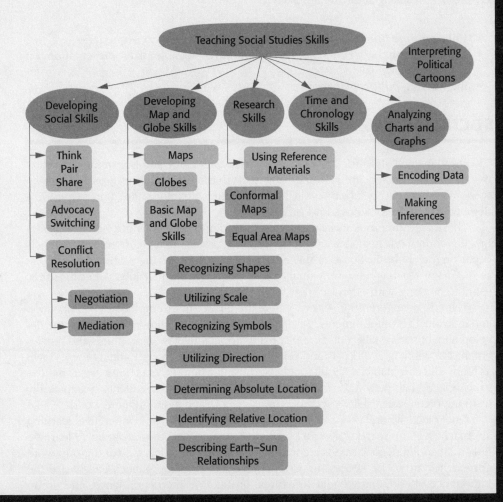

Teaching Social Studies Skills

- Developing Social Skills
  - Think Pair Share
  - Advocacy Switching
  - Conflict Resolution
    - Negotiation
    - Mediation
- Developing Map and Globe Skills
  - Maps
  - Globes
  - Basic Map and Globe Skills
    - Conformal Maps
    - Equal Area Maps
    - Recognizing Shapes
    - Utilizing Scale
    - Recognizing Symbols
    - Utilizing Direction
    - Determining Absolute Location
    - Identifying Relative Location
    - Describing Earth–Sun Relationships
- Research Skills
  - Using Reference Materials
- Time and Chronology Skills
- Interpreting Political Cartoons
- Analyzing Charts and Graphs
  - Encoding Data
  - Making Inferences

When you teach social studies lessons, what your students learn should not be limited to knowledge acquisition and discovery. Students need to learn a variety of skills that will be of use throughout their lives. These skills are "processes that human beings acquire in order to access knowledge" (Dynneson & Gross, 1999, p. 309). In its publication *Expectations of Excellence: Curriculum Standards for Social Studies,* the National Council for the Social Studies (1994) strongly endorses the idea that social studies skills should be an integral part of the social studies program.

A number of important social studies skills should be included in the curriculum, starting in the early grades. These include social skills, research skills, and map and globe skills. The following specific outcomes are among those that should be addressed:

- Working productively with others
- Resolving interpersonal conflicts
- Using *maps and globes* to understand spatial relationships

- Utilizing *time lines* to gain a better sense of chronological sequences
- Distinguishing between responsible and irresponsible data presentation on *charts* and *graphs*
- Interpreting *political cartoons*

DEVELOPING SOCIAL SKILLS

Two fundamental skills for a person living in a democracy and becoming a productive member of society are learning how to establish good relationships and how to work with others. Social cohesion and working with others are important for a democratic nation to survive and prosper.

There are numerous indications that these important skills are not being adequately addressed. A glance at any newspaper reveals that interpersonal conflicts occur on a daily basis. Some of these have tragic results. In the world of work, one of the major reasons why individuals are dismissed from their jobs is because they cannot get along with others.

There is a danger in our society, where there is so much emphasis on competition and individual accomplishments, that students will develop attitudes that hinder the development of social skills. For example, many popular television programs and movies emphasize winning at all costs and portray humiliating others and putting them down as funny and acceptable. It should not be surprising when students bring these attitudes to school and interpersonal conflicts result. It is imperative that students systematically learn important social skills if we hope to create a better, more humane world.

One place where you can begin is through the use of cooperative learning approaches. Many social skills can be taught in the context of a cooperative learning lesson. In addition, social skills are important if cooperative learning and group work approaches are to be successful. Cooperative learning approaches emphasize the importance of cooperative goal structures, productive interdependence, and group accountability.

In Chapter 5 we discussed formal cooperative learning approaches such as jigsaw and student teams. Several other group approaches also can be used in developing social skills, including two-by-two, think-pair-share, advocacy switching, and conflict resolution. These are relatively simple to use and can be implemented without a lot of the preparation normally required for cooperative learning approaches.

Two-by-Two

Two-by-two is especially useful for breaking the ice when forming new classroom groups. Its purpose is to help students learn about others in the classroom. Students usually learn new things about each other, which prompts additional interpersonal contact.

To initate this activity, students are paired together. In each pair, each student is asked to find out a specific bit of information about the other person. In earlier grades this can be done using a specific prompt such as, "Find out one thing your partner likes to do outside of school." You might use a prompt to help identify a basis for future student groupings. For example, you might ask students to share something about

*Learning to work together is
an important social skill.*

Dorrey A. Cardinale/Parker Boon Productions/Silver Burdett Ginn

school they enjoy. This can help you identify students with similar and different abilities, which can be useful when grouping students for cooperative learning projects.

Once the pairs have met and have shared with each other, they form into groups of 4. In these groups, each student shares what they learned about their partner. The goal is for all 4 members to share and for all of them to know one specific thing about all the others in the group. Once they have done this, regroup them into groups of 8, where each student tries to learn a specific bit of information about the other 7 people in the group. The groups of 8 are then organized into groups of 16 and the challenge is for each student in the group to remember something about each of the other 15 members of the group. Finally, the groups re-form in one large classroom group and students challenged to see if they can remember one thing about every other member of the class.

The multiplication of the group size can be conducted up to a size you feel appropriate for your class and the age and maturity level of the students. This activity is one students usually enjoy.

If you have not used this activity, you may be surprised at the number of students who will be able to provide information about everybody in the classroom at the end of the activity. The activity makes students more comfortable with each other and can build a sense of cohesion.

Think-Pair-Share

Think-pair-share begins by presenting students with a problem or question, preferably one with no clear right or wrong answers. The best questions are those that stimulate imagination and creativity. You want a question or problem that will not be threatening to the students and that will stimulate maximum student participation.

The first step is to have each student think about the problem independently. Older students might be asked to write their response. Your purpose here is to have students do their own thinking without peer pressure. This is the "think" portion of the activity. Giving individuals time to think free of peer influence will result in better answers and a wider variety of answers.

The next step is for each student to pair up with another person. You may either let them choose someone to work with or assign them to a partner. Allowing them to choose their partner often results in more involvement and discussion. However, sometimes good friends who choose each other might tend to get off task. You might challenge the pairs to discuss the ideas of both people, identify what they like about each idea and, if they wish, put both ideas together to come up with what they think might be a better response.

The final step is to have the pairs share with the entire class (McTighe & Lyman, 1988). This should be done without an evaluation of the suggested solutions, as your purpose here is simply to stimulate involvement. Evaluating solutions will inhibit students' willingness to share. This also is why open-ended questions or questions focusing on creativity are useful, because there are no "right" answers.

Advocacy Switching

One problem in contemporary society is that people are unwilling to listen to or accept positions on issues contrary to the one they hold. The result is a polarization of indviduals who are convinced they are "right" and are therefore unwilling to compromise. *Advocacy switching* is an approach that requires students to take different sides on an issue. The intent is that when they are forced to defend each side of an issue, they will develop the ability to view issues through the eyes of others and will reach more productive alternatives.

The first step in this process is to identify an issue for which there is adequate information to support two points of view. The issue should be one that is of personal interest to the students. For example, your issue might be, "Should the length of the school year remain the same or be lengthened?" This is a topic where nearly all the students at all grade levels will have a response. Other good issues will arise during the year as things occur in the school and the community that affect students.

Once you have presented the issue or focus question to students, divide the class into groups of four, subdividing each group into pairs. Assign one pair one side of the issue and the other the opposite position. Give each pair information supporting their side of the issue. After each side has completed their review of the issue and the information supporting their side, they present it to the other pair in their group. When one pair is presenting their side, the other pair listens carefully and identifies the key points. After both presentations, have the pairs switch sides. They are given the information on the side of the issue opposing the one they orginally took. Using the key points the first group made and the new information they are now given, they try to make as strong a case as possible in support of their new position.

LESSON IDEA 7-1

TOPIC: Understanding Another's Perspective

OBJECTIVES: Students will be able to identify the perspectives and feelings of different individuals in a conflict situation.

ENGAGING THE STUDENTS: Ask students to identify the villain in selected fairy tales. For example, they might identify the wolf in "The Three Little Pigs" or the wicked witch in "Hansel and Gretel."

DEVELOPING THE CONTENT: Ask students, "How do you think these characters might have felt?" Take a scene from one of the children's books in the classroom that has a conflict situation in it. Read the excerpt to the class. Then have them retell the story from the perspectives of the different characters.

BRINGING CLOSURE: Ask students, "What have you learned in this activity?" Ask how they might use their new understanding when they are in conflict with another person.

EXTENSION TO THE WEB: This page of the University of Georgia website describes a program in Georgia that successfully implemented group learning.

URL—http://www.ovpr.uga.edu/research news/summer2001/kids.html

---

When all groups have completed this second phase, it is useful to come together as a class and review not only the two sides of the issue, but what was learned by taking both sides. This activity is especially useful in social studies, where learning to view issues through multiple perspectives is important.

Conflict Resolution

A very important social skill that all students need to learn is that of conflict resolution. Students face numerous instances of interpersonal conflict and if they do not know how to respond, serious conflict can occur. Although conflict resolution is not just the province of social studies, because the social studies focuses on people and history is filled with examples of conflict, it provides a good context for learning conflict resolution.

Negotiation One approach that can be used to help resolve conflicts is negotiation. Negotiation is a process that individuals can use throughout their lives. It can be taught as a step-by-step process that uses communication and thinking skills to reach a mutually acceptable resolution. There are several steps to negotiation:

- Agree to negotiate
- Gather points of view
- Find common interests
- Describe feelings
- Create win-win options
- Evaluate options
- Develop an agreement (Savage, 1999, p. 241)

Agree to Negotiate. Negotiations cannot work unless those involved in the conflict agree to negotiate. If one individual holds a firm stance and will not budge, then negotiation will not work. The best way to get individuals to agree to negotiate is for them to see that it is in their best interest to do so. At this step, it might be your responsibility as a teacher to help each participant understand how they may meet their needs by negotiating.

When an agreement to negotiate is established, you need to determine a few ground rules. These should include no putdowns, no name calling, and allowing the other person to express opinions without interruption.

Gather Points of View. At this step one person listens while the other presents their point of view. When they have completed their statement, the second person must first summarize what the first person said and then present their point of view. When the second person is done, the first person must now summarize the point of view of the second person. At this point, you may wish to use advocacy switching to get each person to look at the conflict through the eyes of the other.

Find Common Interests. At this step each person needs to express what they want or need. They should alternate in sharing their wants and needs as in the previous step; however, the focus here should be on wants and needs, not on positions. It is easy for people to get so locked into a position that they overlook options that will help them achieve their wants and needs. At this point, the individuals in the conflict should be helped to find some compatible interests. At the conclusion of this step, those involved in the conflict should be able to identify the interests they have in common.

Describe Feelings. Sometimes simply identifying wants and needs is not enough. Conflict situations usually involve intense feelings, and these feelings can get in the way of productive resolution. The difficulty is increased because students are rarely encouraged to share feelings. They are fearful that sharing feelings will open them up to ridicule or rejection. You may need to intervene by helping each student describe how they are feeling. Are they angry? Fearful? Do they feel threatened? Are they humiliated? Sharing feelings is a key step because people in conflict generally are so caught up in their own feelings that they do not see how others are feeling. Once they do so, they begin to appreciate a different perspective and the door of understanding and compromise begins to open.

Create Win-Win Options. Unfortunately, too many individuals in our society view conflict as something that must culminate with a winner and a loser. This stance blocks the search for productive resolution. Individuals are afraid to negotiate because they are afraid they will "lose." However, approaching conflicts with the idea that there can be a ***win-win situation***, where both parties get their needs met, provides a framework for creative and productive problem solving.

At this step, participants focus on wants and needs and brainstorm as many ideas as possible for how both people can get their wants and needs met. It is useful to have them focus on trying to identify at least three options. This is a realistic number that prevents them from quickly settling on the first idea that pops into mind.

Evaluate Options. Once several win-win options have been identified, those involved in the conflict need to evaluate each option in terms of how it will benefit each person and help them meet their wants and needs. If they cannot agree on any of the options, then they are challenged to reformulate the options, combine parts of the options, or come up with new ones. It might mean that each person is going to have to prioritize their wants and needs and identify those that are most important and those that are of minor importance. They should evaluate the options against reality. What are the strengths and weaknesses? What does each person gain? How does each option benefit both people?

Develop an Agreement. After evaluating options and arriving at the one they both think best meets their wants and needs, both parties develop an agreement that is mutually satisfactory. It must be clear and understood by both people. In some instances it is useful to write up the agreement in simple language and have each individual sign it. This can provide a record that can be referenced if additional problems occur.

Negotiation is one of the more important outcomes of school. The steps of the negotiation process can be used in social studies when investigating current and past conflicts between groups and nations. They can use the negotiation framework to identify how the participants in these conflicts attempted to find a win-win resolution. Historical examples can also be used to illustrate why negotiations sometimes fail and the possible consequences of failure.

Mediation. Mediation has become a popular approach in resolving conflicts. *Mediation* is the application of the negotiation process with the assistance of a third party to facilitate. Some schools have had great success in teaching students how to be mediators. In these instances, student mediators go through training to help them learn the associated skills, and are then given forms and guidelines to follow in the process.

The parties involved in a conflict must agree to mediation, and must agree to ground rules. Those ground rules usually are as follows:

- We agree not to interrupt each other.
- We agree not to use putdowns or name calling.
- We agree to be honest and to tell the truth.
- We do want to solve the problem.

Once both parties accept the ground rules, the mediator guides them through the negotiation steps. The goal of mediation is not for the mediator to solve the problem; rather, it is to facilitate the process so that students can learn how to solve problems on their own.

Once an agreement has been reached, it should be written down and everyone, including the mediator, signs it. The mediator keeps a copy and may call the students back together if it appears that the agreement is not being kept. If there is a breakdown and agreement cannot be reached or kept, the mediator informs the teacher and the teacher may step in as the mediator (Powell, McLaughlin, Savage, & Zehm, 2001).

In summary, learning social studies implies learning social skills. Active participation in citizenship and in the world of work requires that individuals learn how to get along with others. Social skills need to be included in the curriculum. Teaching social skills can pay off for teachers in helping reduce interpersonal conflict in the classroom.

DEVELOPING MAP AND GLOBE SKILLS

One of the sets of skills unique to the social studies program is that of learning to use maps and globes. Learning how to interpret information from maps and globes is essential for students to understand the spatial dimension of the world. Map and globe skills help us answer these questions: Where is it? Why is it there? How is it related to other factors? Map and globe skills help learners plot information and discover relationships that might otherwise go unnoticed. Although a teacher once stated that she could not read maps and had survived, these skills can help students arrive at a better understanding of the world around them and improve their decision making.

Maps

Maps are used more frequently than globes in most elementary social studies classrooms. When maps are used properly, they are effective instructional resources. Maps of various kinds can help you accomplish many purposes. In addition, they cost less than globes and consume little storage space. However, in the typical classroom there are only one or two maps, generally political maps, hanging on the wall. This severely limits what can be learned from maps. It is best to have several maps focusing on different topics so that they can be compared and relationships identified.

You need to understand, however, that the strengths of maps as teaching tools are counterbalanced by the imperfect representation of the earth's surface they present to learners. A three-dimensional surface cannot be projected—transformed into a two-dimensional surface—without distortion. You can help students understand why flat maps distort information presented on globes by working with half of the peel you have removed from an orange. Place the peel on a flat surface and push down. Learners will quickly see that something has to "give" before the spherical surface can be converted to a flat plane.

Many maps illustrate only a portion of the earth's surface. More maps on display in U.S elementary classrooms depict the United States than other parts of the world. Students' continuous exposure to such maps has the potential to lead them to erroneous conclusions. For example, many middle-grade students, as a result of many years of looking at classroom walls featuring flat maps of the United States hanging on the wall, have erroneously concluded that on maps "north is always up" and "the Atlantic is always found on the right-hand side." These mistakes result from a failure to distinguish differences among north, south, east, west, up, down, right, and left. This confusion often leads to other misconceptions. You may even have students who are convinced that no rivers in the world flow from south to north. This is only a natural conclusion because water cannot flow up!

It is useful to get maps down from the walls. Place them on the floor and orient them so that individuals can see that north and south are directions quite different from up and down. Use a variety of maps so that students also note that features such as the Atlantic Ocean may be in a position other than on the right side.

Constant exposure to a large wall map of the United States also has the potential to confuse students about the proper size relationships among world places. Some of your students may overestimate the physical size of the United States (this is also a problem with some adults). This misunderstanding may lead them to dismiss the magnitude and importance of other places in the world. You can address this problem by placing transparencies of maps of different parts of the world (drawn to the same scale) on top of each other in order to make comparisons of size.

When your students work with maps, they need to recognize certain basic design features. Regardless of what parts of the world they depict, maps tend to sort into two basic types: conformal and equal area.

Conformal Maps Your students need to understand that *conformal* maps keep shapes of the land areas the same as they appear on a globe. This means that there will be some distortion of the area. Projecting the shape of something from a sphere to a flat surface while keeping the shape the same requires some adjustments in area. An important example of a conformal map is the Mercator projection map, named for a famous sixteenth-century mapmaker.

To understand how a Mercator projection map is made, imagine a clear glass globe with land areas outlined in dark ink and a tiny light in the center. The globe is placed on a table so a line passing through the North Pole, the light in the center, and the South Pole is perpendicular to the tabletop. A cylinder of paper is slipped over the globe. The light source causes shadows to be cast on the paper cylinder from the boundaries of the land areas. The mapmaker carefully traces these shadows. When the cylinder is unwrapped, the result is a Mercator projection map of the world. (In reality, the process is done mathematically, but the principles are as described here.)

The Mercator projection produces a world map that maintains accurate shapes of land masses. However, relative sizes of places are not accurately portrayed; as the distance from the equator increases, the amount of distortion is greater. You need to help students understand that Mercator maps make land areas in extreme northern and southern areas appear much larger than they are depicted on a globe.

The distortion in land areas on Mercator projection maps can lead to unfortunate misunderstandings. As noted previously in this chapter, students who do not often work with globes and who see a Mercator map every day often mistakenly conclude that Greenland is as large as or even larger than South America. Greenland's apparent size on a Mercator projection map is a result of its great distance from the equator. South America, on the other hand, lies across the equator and hence is relatively undistorted.

When conformal maps are the only world maps available, it is particularly important to give students opportunities to work with globes. When you involve them in such lessons, you need to explain why the sizes of landmasses in extreme northern and southern regions are distorted on Mercator maps.

Modifications of the Mercator projection reduce some of these extreme area distortions. In general, though, these modifications give up the Mercator projection's total consistency with the shape of landmasses as depicted on the globe as a tradeoff for less distortion in area. Such maps are not truly conformal.

Equal Area Maps *Equal area* maps of the world are drawn in such a way that the relative size of landmasses, as reflected on the globe, is preserved. This means that the shape as it appears on the globe will have some distortion. For example, Greenland is approximately one-ninth the size of South America; thus, on an equal area map of the world, South America would be nine times as large as Greenland.

Because there tends to be greater emphasis on shape in elementary school, fewer equal area maps than conformal maps hang on classroom walls. However, as noted, this does result in some prevalent misunderstandings. For some questions and issues, it is more important to understand the relative size of places in the world. Therefore, equal area maps are the best resource for displaying this spatial relationship.

Because of the enormous distortions of areas of some important world landmasses on conformal maps, equal area maps should be available in every elementary classroom. Ideally, your classroom should have at least one world map of each type. Exposure to both conformal and equal area maps and to globes will help your students understand both relative sizes and areas of landmasses. You can also work with maps of both types to reinforce the idea that all renderings of a sphere onto a flat surface result in distortions.

Globes

Globes deserve more attention than they receive in many social studies classrooms. Some of the misunderstandings individuals have about the world can be eliminated if they are provided with more experience in working with globes and relatively less in working with maps. Globes provide the best representation of our spherical planet. Maps, dealing in only two dimensions, distort shapes and areas; this distortion can lead to serious misconceptions.

For example, many flat world maps use a projection that makes Africa look smaller in area than North America. However, the entire United States can fit into the Sahara Desert region of North Africa. Such maps also make Greenland look as large as South America. In fact, South America is nine times larger. When plotting a direct route between two spots in the world, the route on a flat map may appear to be curved or somewhat circular. Using a globe rather than a flat map can help students understand these distortions.

Although the increased use of globes can help your students gain a better appreciation of size relationships, their use poses some difficulties. First, globes are bulky. Ideally, you need enough of them so that no more than three or four students at a time need to work with a single globe. If you have 25 students in your class, optimally you should have six or more globes. Often, there is simply not sufficient space to accommodate such a large number. Another problem is cost. Globes cost more than maps and are generally kept for a long time. However, the world is in a constant state of change. For example, many globes still in classroom use have incorrect labels of parts of the world that have changed.

The cost and space issues can be addressed using technology. There are several good computerized alternatives. CD-ROM software can be purchased for use on the computer (you may wish to consult your school's technology specialist). In addition, several websites provide a variety of maps and images. One interesting newer site is Google Earth (**http://earth.google.com/**). The online alternatives also address the issue of keeping labels and names current, as most websites are kept rigorously up to date. However, it is still important for students to have access to a globe that they can handle and manipulate, for the reasons given.

There also are problems associated with using globes to teach certain kinds of content. Suppose you wanted to teach students about Romania. Romania is about

425 miles (684 kilometers) across from east to west. On a standard 16-inch globe, Romania occupies less than 1 inch of space from east to west. Little detail can be included in such a small space. A larger globe would involve other difficulties. A globe large enough for Romania to be 36 inches across would be 48 *feet* in diameter. Such a globe would need to be installed in a special building. A map of Romania would better serve your instructional needs.

Though they do have limitations when your purpose is to emphasize small parts of the earth's surface, globes are ideally suited to helping learners grasp other kinds of content. They are excellent vehicles for displaying proper area and locational relationships. For example, on a flat wall map of the world, it appears to be a great distance across either the Atlantic Ocean or the Pacific Ocean from the United States to Russia. However, on a globe the route across the North Pole illustrates that the distance is much shorter.

You can use globes as you help your students develop skills associated with the location of some part of the world with other parts of the world and how to use latitude and longitude to find the absolute location of a place. The concept of the ***great circle*** route is much better taught by using a globe rather than a map. Earth–sun relationships—as they relate to issues such as day and night, the seasons of the year, the 24-hour day, and time zones—are best taught using globes.

The information presented on globes is of no use unless students understand what it means. There are substantial differences in the types and amounts of information introduced on various kinds of globes. By the end of their elementary social studies experience, learners should recognize the major features of the globe. These include the equator, the Tropic of Cancer, the Tropic of Capricorn, the North Pole, the South Pole, the International Date Line, the Prime Meridian, horizon ring, the distance scale, and the world time zones.

As students progress through the elementary social studies program, they should become increasingly proficient in their abilities to use globe skills. For example, they should be able to find locations using latitude and longitude, explain seasonal changes in terms of earth–sun relationships, point out the function of the international dateline, and explain the time difference between selected pairs of world locations.

Basic Map and Globe Skills

There are seven basic map and globe skills that should be included in a good map and globe skills project:

- Recognizing shapes
- Utilizing scale
- Recognizing symbols
- Utilizing direction
- Determining absolute location
- Identifying relative location
- Describing earth–sun relationships

Globes have the least distortion and help students understand the size and shape of various parts of the world.

Scott Cunningham/Merrill

Recognizing Shapes   Recognizing shapes is one of the most fundamental map and globe skills. Though the skill may appear to be simple or even simplistic, many sophisticated analyses in geography require a grasp of the importance of physical shapes, particularly those of landmasses. Students need to recognize shapes such as those of islands, continents, and oceans. By the time students reach the upper elementary grades they should be able to recognize the continents of the world and their home state by their shapes. The kinds of learning associated with recognizing shapes increase in complexity as children move through the elementary program. As students move to higher levels, they should start learning how the shape of a place impacts other dimensions of life such as transportation, politics, and growth.

Utilizing Scale   Scale is an abstract and difficult concept. You may find that teaching students to understand and use this concept is one of your most challenging assignments. However, scale is a part of the life of most students. Many of them play with toys. Those toys depict real objects; however, they are only a fraction of the size of the objects. It is important to reduce the size if we are to represent real objects so that we can manipulate and play with them. Thus, toy trains, toy airplanes, and toy cars are "scale models" of real objects. The *scale* tell us how much smaller they are than the real thing.

Scale can be difficult because it requires the concurrent understanding of two subordinate understandings. Each of these can frustrate students, especially those in the early elementary grades.

First, to appreciate scale, learners need to know that geographical features (mountains, rivers, oceans, and so forth) can be visually depicted in a convenient way. For example, it is possible to represent a mountain by taking a photograph of the mountain. Students need to understand that the mountain is real; they need to know the photograph is real; and, most importantly, they need to appreciate the connection between the mountain as depicted in the photograph and the actual mountain itself.

Second, a child looking at a photograph of a mountain needs to recognize that there is a knowable physical size relationship between the size of the mountain as it exists on the earth's surface and the size as it is depicted in the photograph. A sound understanding of the principle of using small, convenient representations as reliable indicators of the size of large phenomena is fundamental to an appreciation of scale. Students who lack this basic knowledge have a difficult time grasping the idea that the scales on maps and globes can be used to make accurate statements about the actual sizes of the physical features of the earth.

To help your learners better understand scale, you might bring a camera to school that produces instant prints. Photograph familiar objects in the classroom from different distances. Ask your students to measure the real object. Then, have them measure the size of the objects as depicted in photos you have taken at various distances. Help students to develop scales that describe size relationships among the real object and the photos taken at various distances. This exercise can help them appreciate that scales vary with distance from the depicted objects. You can use this insight as you begin to help students understand differences between large-scale and small-scale maps.

The importance of learning scale is that when we are faced with a geographical problem, we need to choose a map at the appropriate scale. For example, if we are facing a question about a particular street in a specific city, a globe or a large-scale map of the nation will not be sufficient. If we are interested in a question about the spatial relationships of two nations in the world, small-scale maps of specific places will not be useful.

Recognizing Symbols Everything on a map or a globe is a symbol. The colors are symbols, the lines are symbols, all of the information on the map is communicated through a symbol. Learning how to decode symbols is critical if students are to understand the information included on maps and globes. *Symbols* provide a convenient shorthand representation of the kinds of phenomena that exist in the world. Although the idea of symbols is somewhat abstract, even very young children understand the concept. How many students reach kindergarten without understanding what is represented by "golden arches"? Similarly, very young children quickly learn the meaning of the symbols of a "red light" and a "green light." Your challenge is to help students understand that different symbols can be used to indicate a variety of things. Actually, understanding symbols is a prereading activity that can help students begin to learn that letters and words themselves are symbols that represent certain sounds and combinations of sounds. Figure 7-1 shows a selection of symbols as depicted on a student-produced map.

As you help your students to interpret map and globe symbols, you need to help them understand that while a symbol represents something real, they can have limitations in representing reality. Less mature students may have difficulty with this idea. For example, if they see Kansas depicted in orange, they may conclude that everything in Kansas literally is orange.

Utilizing Direction It is useful to know how to orient yourself in the environment no matter where you are in the world. For example, one of the authors was attending a conference with a couple of colleagues in an unfamiliar city. One individual rented a car at the airport. Upon arrival, the group proceeded to the car with directions on how to get to their destination. The directions began, "Take the north exit

FIGURE 7-1 • A Student-Produced Map Featuring Simple Symbols

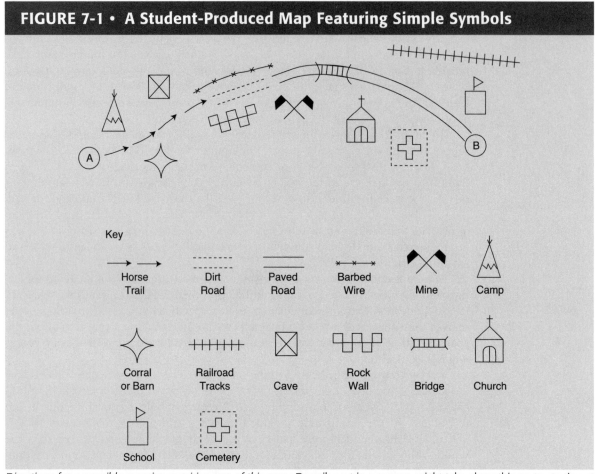

Directions for a possible exercise requiring use of this map: Describe a trip a person might take along this route starting at point A and finishing at point B. Use the key to interpret the meaning of each symbol on the map.

from the airport." If you have just landed in an unfamiliar place after having been on an airplane for several hours, how would you know which direction was north?

The process of learning how to orient yourself in your environment begins in the classroom and can be carried over into the world. Learning direction is much more than learning that the *compass rose* on a map helps you identify which direction is north. Students need to understand that directions on a map are not just arbitrary symbols, they relate to the real world and involve understanding other dimensions such as earth–sun relationships. The sun always comes up in the east, moves across the sky from east to west, and sets in the west. They can learn that when the sun reaches the highest point in the sky, our shadows in the northern hemisphere always points north. (The author used this knowledge to determine how to get out of that airport parking lot.)

One of the map and globe skills related to directions that students should learn is how to orient the map in the proper direction. This means getting the map off of the clasroom wall and putting it on the floor of the classroom with north on the compass

LESSON IDEA 7-2

TOPIC: Learning About Map Symbols

OBJECTIVES: Students will create symbols to represent real objects.

ENGAGING THE STUDENTS: Cut out well-known symbols for businesses and other organizations from newspapers and magazines. For example, you might select symbols representing the Olympics, the United Nations, McDonalds, Texaco, and many other organizations, firms, and groups. Ask how many youngsters recognize each symbol. Explain why symbols are used (to save time, to provide for ready recognition, and so forth). Does the school have a mascot? Is there a symbol that represents a favorite sports team? Lead into the idea that mapmakers and globemakers use many symbols.

DEVELOPING THE CONTENT: Assign students in groups to do one of the following:

1. Have one group of students find as many symbols as possible around the school. They might use symbols of automobiles, symbols on packages of paper, symbols on pencils and pens, and so on. They might cut symbols out of magazines you provide. Their job is to create a poster containing only the symbols. They will post this in the class and students will then see who can identify the most symbols.
2. Have another group develop symbols for the real objects in the local community. For example, what symbol might they create for a church, a factory, a market, a school, or a park? Have them place the symbols they create on flash cards. On one side will be the symbol. On the other side will be the thing for which the symbol stands. The rest of the class can then place these symbols on a map of the local community at their approximate location.
3. A third group is to make two-part puzzles. These can be made from construction paper. From sources such as *National Geographic*, find pictures of things that are depicted by symbols on maps. Paste a picture on the top half of a sheet of construction paper. On the bottom, draw the symbol used for the thing depicted. Then cut the sheet into two parts. Give students a mixed group of top and bottom sheets. Ask them to try to fit the sheets together by using their knowledge of symbols. When a sheet fits properly, they know they have matched the symbol to the thing it depicts (Figure 7-2).

BRINGING CLOSURE: Review with students the use of symbols in the world and on maps.

EXTENSION TO THE WEB: At the homepage of the U.S. Geological Survey you can find information related to maps, globes, and mapmaking, and maps that can be downloaded. There are also links to other places where you can find maps.

URL—http://www.usgs.gov/

rose pointing north. This can help students overcome confusing north with up. *North* is the direction from the equator toward the north pole. *Up* is the direction from the surface of the earth toward outer space.

Using common objects on the playground can help students move learning about directions outside the four walls of the classroom. For example, how does the direction of the shadow of the tetherball pole change during the day? How can you use that shadow to establish direction?

It is also useful to note that, due to the rotation of the earth, the stars also cross the skies in an east to west direction. Therefore, identifying the movement of the stars at night helps you identify directions when there is no sun. The ancient Polynesians

FIGURE 7-2 • A Simple Symbol for a Church

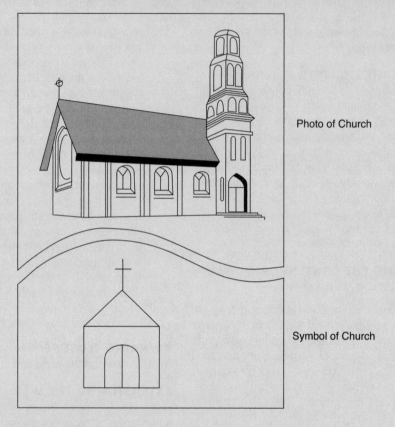

Photo of Church

Symbol of Church

These two pieces are part of a puzzle set you can use to help students see connections between symbols and the objects they represent. You ask learners to fit together pieces that belong together. When properly completed, one piece will feature a photo of the object that is represented symbolically on the other.

used this information about stars to navigate the long distances between islands in the Pacific.

Determining Absolute Location Students use *absolute location* to pinpoint the exact position of any point on the earth's surface. To adequately perform the skill, your learners must be familiar with the lines of latitude and longitude. Specifically, they must understand how a longitude–latitude grid system can be used to identify the "address" of every location on earth. If you are teaching younger students, you may wish to have them work with very simple grids before you introduce the global system of latitude and longitude. Figure 7-3 presents a sample grid activity.

A Major beginning point for students in understanding absolute location and the grid system is knowing the significance of the equator and the Prime Meridian. These are reference points from which all other locations are established.

FIGURE 7-3 • An Example of a Gird Activity to Help Students Locate Places Using the Coordinates of Longitude and Latitude

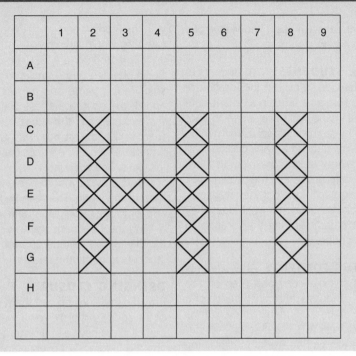

Directions: Find the secret word by placing an X in each of these squares: *C2, C5, C8; D2, D5, D8; E2, E3, E4, E5, E8; F2, F5, F8; G2, G5, G8.*

Identifying Relative Location *Relative location* refers to the location of one place in terms of one or more other places. When Chicago is described as being north of Houston, east of Omaha, and west of New York, we are referring to Chicago's relative location. You can begin building the skill of pointing out relative location by helping students to recognize their own relative location in terms of familiar places. For example, you help them understand the relative location of your school by pointing out its position in terms of nearby parks and homes. You can go on to discuss where your local community is located compared to other places in your state. Later, you can expand this understanding by pointing out your community's location relative to places in the nation and the world.

Describing Earth–Sun Relationships Earth–sun relationships impact our understanding of such things as day and night, the seasons, and different times in different parts of the world. Your learners initially may be frustrated by content related to earth–sun relationships. Part of the problem relates to our language.

In casual conversation, people speak about the sun "rising" and "setting." This terminology is based on an illusion that makes sense. Residents of the earth's surface are not physically aware that the globe is spinning on its axis. Hence, the "rising" and "setting" terminology does accurately describe what individuals see, but this language does not properly describe what is going on. Adults (most of them, at least) know that it is the movement of the earth, not the sun, that make the difference.

═ LESSON IDEA 7-3 ═

TOPIC: Learning About Absolute Location

OBJECTIVES: Students will apply knowledge of a grid system to locate places on maps.

ENGAGING THE STUDENTS: Ask students to think about how they would explain the location of your community to someone living in a distant state or in another country who has never been to your community. Begin by saying, "Suppose that person was on the telephone and had a blank outline map with no city names. Your task is to explain to them where your community was so that they could mark the location on their map." Point out the local community on a map and ask students what ideas they would have about communicating the location to this person on the phone.

DEVELOPING THE CONTENT: After students have shared ideas, place a copy of a map on the overhead projector. Then place a transparency of a grid system on top of the map. Identify the columns as 1, 2, 3 and the rows as A, B, C and so on. Ask students, "How might this grid be useful in explaining the location?"

Give the students a piece of graph paper. Have them label the columns with numerals and the rows with letters. With older students you may make it a little more challenging by having them label a line across the middle as the "equator" with 0 and one down the middle as the Prime Meridian with 0. They would begin their numerals and letters beginning

with the 0 points and going in both directions. Therefore they would have both east 1, 2, 3, 4, and west 1, 2, 3, 4, and north A, B, C, D, and south A, B, C, D. Begin playing a game similar to the game of "Battleship." In this game one person chooses a location and describes it to the rest of the class in terms of the numerals and the letters. Each student places a mark in the correct box. This can be done several times and then students can check to see how many locations they got right.

Next, provide your students with a simple outline map of the world. The map should include latitude and longitude designations and a compass rose. Play a "Find the Continent" game with the members of the class. Give latitude and longitude and ask the students to name the nearest continent.

BRINGING CLOSURE: Review with students how the grid lines helped them identify the location or the address of places on a map. Point out to them that all maps have a grid system that can be used to find the "address" of every place in the world.

EXTENSION TO THE WEB: The National Geographic Society website includes a variety of maps that you may incorporate into your social studies program.

URL—http://www.nationalgeographic.com/

Elementary children, especially those in the lower grades, lack this understanding. Many of them are quite ready to believe that the sun, not the earth, moves.

As your students progress through the elementary program, they encounter the idea of "seasons." They learn that seasons change because the angle of the sun's rays strikes some parts of the earth's surface more directly at certain times of the year than at others (Figure 7-4). Many children who grasp this basic idea have trouble understanding exactly how this happens. Some conclude erroneously that the earth wobbles back and forth on its axis, thus causing a change in where the sun's rays strike most directly. You need to be aware of this potential problem and help your students grasp how seasonal change can occur without "global wobble."

One way of helping them understand this relationship is to place four globes in different parts of the classroom. Make sure that the four globes are all oriented in the

FIGURE 7-4 • Earth–Sun Relationships

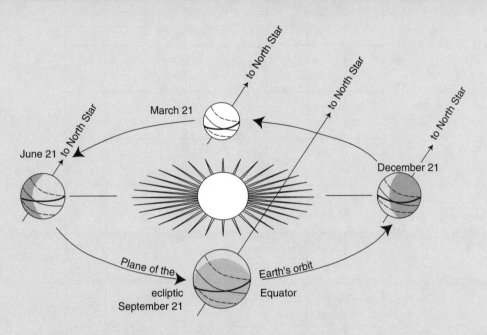

The figure depicts the location of the earth in relation to the sun on key dates. Some elementary students have difficulty understanding that the earth does not swing back and forth or wobble on its axis. A figure such as this can help you explain what actually occurs. The earth's axis always points toward the North Star. Note that sun strikes the earth's surface directly at different points on different dates during the year.

same direction. This means that the top holder of the horizon ring on the globes, or the North Pole, are all pointing in the same direction. These four globes represent the revolution of the earth around the sun. Stand in the middle of the globes with a strong flashlight. As you shine the flashlight on one of the globes have the students identify which part of the globe on a north-south axis is receiving the most light and which part is receiving the least. Move to the next globe and follow the same process. When you get to the one where the horizon ring is pointing toward you, have a student spin the globe and show that in the circle of illumination from the flashlight, the North Pole always has light. In the one pointing away from you and the flashlight, when the globe is spun, it never gets any light. Explain that this shows how the sun strikes the earth at different angles to form different seasons. During a part of the summer, the North Pole always has light and during a part of the winter, it never gets light.

For older students you can use an analemma to trace the path of the sun during the year. On a globe, the *analemma* is a figure eight stretching between the tropic zones. The *tropic zones* mark the northern and southern boundaries of where the sun is directly overhead (Figure 7-5). They can notice that in the northern hemisphere the

FIGURE 7-5 • The _Analemma_

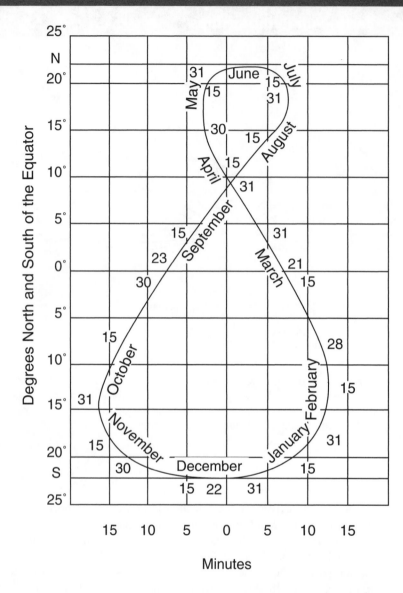

An _analemma_ indicates latitudes at which the sun is directly overhead at noon on each day of the year. The northern limit of the analemma is the Tropic of Cancer, where the sun is directly overhead on June 21–22. The southern limit is the Tropic of Capricorn, where the sun is directly overhead on December 21–22. The sun is directly overhead at noon at the equator twice each year: once on March 21–22. and again on September 21–22. The apparent movement of the sun results from the earth's annual movement around the sun. Because the earth's axis always points to the North Star, at some times of the year the sun's rays strike most directly at various points of the earth's surface. To better understand why this happens, see Figure 7-4. Your students may be interested in where the sun is directly overhead on their birthdays.

date June 21 appears on the figure eight at the Tropic of Cancer line. In the southern hemisphere the date December 21 appears on the figure eight at the Tropic of Capricorn line. These indicate the dates the sun reaches the tropic lines during the year. By following the dates on the analemma, students can identify where on the planet the sun is directly overhead for any day of the year.

Map and globe skills are important components of a solid social studies program. Understanding maps and globes helps students understand spatial dimensions and how they affect our lives. They can also help students understand natural phenomena such as day and night and the seasons.

Some teachers have found it useful to start each year with a unit on maps and globes. This unit might take up the first couple of weeks of the new academic year. This can provide a foundation for applying maps and globes for the academic year and provides the teacher with a good starting point with each class until they can diagnose students' prior knowledge and other important variables such as reading level that might impact how they plan and deliver the content of their social studies program.

RESEARCH SKILLS

Learning how to gather information and how to analyze it are important lifetime skills students need to learn. Throughout our lives we need to know how to research and collect relevant information, such as that related to decisions about products we might purchase or finding jobs we desire. Once again, while the development of research skills is a responsibility for the entire curriculum, the nature of the social studies makes it a subject where research skills can be naturally included.

With the growth of personal computers, an abundance of data can be found on just about any topic. This has made it much easier for students to research topics. However, because of this abundance, students need to know what data is of value and how to interpret what it means.

Using Reference Materials

Conducting research requires students to use a variety of reference materials. Reference materials commonly used in elementary and middle schools are atlases, yearbooks, encyclopedias, and newspapers. It is important for students to know what can be found in different types of reference materials.

For example, an *atlas* contains maps on a particular topic. If the task requires investigating the spatial distribution of something like population, then an atlas is the place to look. *Yearbooks* usually give a detailed account of something on a yearly basis. For example, the *Statesmen Yearbook* gives a brief account of every nation in the world on a yearly basis. If up-to-date information on some nation in the world is needed, the *Statesmen Yearbook* is a good source. There are a variety of encyclopedias on different topics. *Encyclopedias* give concise summaries of specific topics. Some students are familiar with the multivolume sets of encyclopedias that provide information that covers a range of topics. Some encyclopedias also have summaries related to a specific topic.

For example, there is an encyclopedia of explorers and explorations and one on nations that gives basic information on every nation in the world. If what is needed is a short summary of a topic, an encyclopedia is a good beginning point. Newspapers provide daily or weekly information on a variety of topics of local, regional, and national interest.

One of the skills that needs to be taught to students is how use reference material to find the information they need. One approach is to provide interesting or unusual questions and have students use reference materials to find the answer. This can be a fun activity for the students if they are finding interesting or amusing answers.

Many reference works are available on CD-ROMs. These can be especially useful because they can also include visual and audio features such as animation and music. They are easy to store and use. You may want to review social studies resource catalogs for CD-ROMs that would be useful in your classroom.

There is a wealth of information available on the Internet that can be used to assist students in learning research skills. However, there also are risks that need to be addressed. One problem is that information on the Internet can be incorrect. Students need to learn to evaluate sources of information. In addition, URLs tend to change rapidly. A site that is a good source at one time may be missing or totally inappropriate the next time it is consulted. There is also the possibility that students can wander into pornographic sites. Using the Internet requires considerable supervision. First, you need to conduct some preliminary searches so you know what is available and where. Then, when students are involved in searching for data, you need to be constantly monitoring what they are doing.

TIME AND CHRONOLOGY SKILLS

For students to develop an understating of history, they need to understand time. This is usually done in the elementary school through the use of time lines. *Time lines* provide a system for organizing events in a meaningful pattern or sequence. Time lines are a concise way to summarize information. They can be very useful in helping students see a relationship between events over time. A time line might be the sequence of events for a day or for centuries. It is best if time lines have a particular theme to which the items on the line are related. A time line of random or unrelated events has little meaning or relevance.

A challenge for teachers in the early grades is that students do not have a well developed sense of time. For a young child concepts such as *decade* or *century* simply have no meaning because they have no concrete references that will help them place them in perspective. They do understand relative terms such as *yesterday*, *last week,* or *long ago*. For them, long ago might be last month or last year. A number of years ago, one curriculum project tried to help young children develop a perspective on time and chronology by giving them a concrete reference. Events in the past were referred to as "two grandparents ago" or "five grandparents ago." They reasoned that young children would recognize that grandparents had been around a long time. If they realized that something happened five grandparents ago, that would be a lot longer than two grandparents ago.

LESSON IDEA 7-4

TOPIC: My Personal Time Line

OBJECTIVES: Students will place personal events and events of significance on a time line.

ENGAGING THE STUDENTS: Ask students, "How many of you have heard your parents or relatives talk about events that happened before you were born?" Let them discuss some of the things they have heard. Inform them that they are going to organize some of the events that have happened in their families on a time line. Explain to them about time lines.

DEVELOPING THE CONTENT: Provide students with the following chart:

Decade	2000	1990	1980	1970
Birthdates (family, friends)				
Important family events				
U.S. Presidents				
Important national events				
Other events of interest				

Have students take the chart home and fill it out with their family's help. They then bring it back to school and from the chart construct a time line. They may have to do some research or have some help in identifying the dates of presidential terms or important events.

When they have completed their time line, they then identify what it illustrates. How does it summarize their family? How are some of the events linked?

BRINGING CLOSURE: Review with the students what they have done and what they have learned. Ask, "How can time lines be useful?"

EXTENSION TO THE WEB: The History Buff homepage has a library of newspaper coverage of many historical social, political, and sporting events. This could be a source of information students could research to fill in and supplement their time lines.

URL—http://www.historybuff.com/index. html

The point is that, when using a time line, try to establish time intervals that have some meaning to your students. When using time lines in the early elementary grades, start with simple lines that have some meaning for students. Chapin and Messick (1999) suggest that in grades K–2 students should be able to identify the beginning, middle, and end to stories and daily events. By grades 3–4 they should be able to construct time lines of significant developments in the community and the state and should be able to group historic events into broadly defined eras. By grades 5–6 students should be able to construct multiple time lines of important developments and be able to interpret the data.

ANALYZING CHARTS AND GRAPHS

The vast amount of information available to the average person can be overwhelming. We live in a society in which data and statistics are commonly used to convince and persuade. Many times this information is presented in the form of charts, graphs, or tables.

These specialized forms of data presentation can help your students with certain kinds of social studies content. Because so much visual information confronts people today, you need to help members of your class to understand how to represent and interpret information in charts and graphs.

Encoding Data

To understand data presented in graphic form, students must know something about how information is encoded. This kind of instruction can start as early as kindergarten and the early primary years. With children this young, you will work with concrete data that have personal meaning for these children. For example, as a class you might develop simple graphs displaying information about the numbers of boys and girls in the class, the numbers of students who have birthdays in each month of the year, the number of rainy days in a month, the temperatures for each day, or the numbers of students who ride the bus or walk to school.

As students mature, they need to learn about three basic types of graphs: *bar graphs*, *pie graphs,* and *line graphs*. The choice of the type of graph to use relates to the type of data to be encoded and the possible uses of this information. For example, charting the number of boys and girls in a given classroom could be accomplished using either a pie chart or a bar graph. Both types could show the relationship. However, a pie graph usually requires an understanding of the sophisticated concept "percentage." Students who are not yet familiar with percentages find bar graphs easier to understand.

Web Check: If you are interested in activities to help students learn more about interpreting graphs, go to the Mega Math website. At this site you will find a variety of games and stories that can be used to help students explore graphs and their properties.

http://www.c3.lanl.gov/mega-math/workbk/graph/gractiv.html

Making Inferences

Once your students learn how to construct charts and graphs, you can help them develop information interpreting skills. Your purpose is to help them think about displayed information and make appropriate inferences. You might begin by asking simple questions about graphically displayed information. For example, if you had developed a bar graph depicting numbers of class members' birthdays for each month of the year, you might ask such questions as, "Which month has the most birthdays? Which has the fewest?"

If you and a group of older students work with graphs and charts, you need to challenge them to engage in more sophisticated kinds of thinking. For example, if you and your class have developed a graph depicting numbers of cars of different makes and models in the school parking lot, you might challenge students to explain depicted patterns. ("Why are there large numbers of some makes and models, but only small numbers of others?") There is a wealth of information in graph form that can be used as a focus for inquiry. For example, graphs on the life expectancy of U.S. residents by state shows some intriguing variations among the states. You might find it useful to build a lesson that requires students to form hypotheses to explain these differences.

You need to help your students understand that poorly prepared graphs and charts can lead to faulty interpretations. Many irresponsibly drawn bar graphs appear in newspapers and other publications. One basic design problem is found in bar graphs that fail to start at zero. To see how this poses a problem, consider this situation. Suppose that two classrooms had a contest to see how many books students in each room read during a school year. At the end of the year, students in Classroom 1 read a total of 110 books, and students in Classroom 2 read a total of 120 books. Although students in Class 2 read more books, the difference between the two classes is not a huge one.

If these differences were plotted on a bar graph that began at zero, someone looking at the bar for Classroom 1 and the bar for Classroom 2 would recognize that there is not a huge gap between numbers of books read by students in one of the classrooms as opposed to the other. However, suppose that the chart started with a baseline of 100 books instead of 0 books. Such a chart would show only the number of books in excess of 100 read by each class. The resulting chart would imply to an unsophisticated observer that one class read more than twice the number of books than the other. (This would happen because there would be a graph that was only 10 books high for the class that read 110 books and a graph that was 20 books high for the class that read 120 books.) Figure 7-6 illustrates responsible and irresponsible bar charts that display this information about these two classes.

Understanding problems associated with irresponsible visual representations of information will help students throughout their adult lives. As you help them to spot poorly designed charts and graphs, you may find it useful to encourage members of your class to look for examples of data distortions in advertisements and in the media.

INTERPRETING POLITICAL CARTOONS

Interpreting a political cartoon requires that you know something about the topic the cartoonist is addressing. In addition, you have to recognize some symbols cartoonists regularly use to depict certain ideas or categories of people. Finally, you have to have some experience in making inferences. These interpretive complexities make political cartoons extremely difficult for elementary and middle school learners (Steinbrink & Bliss, 1988). You can make ideas embedded in these cartoons much

FIGURE 7-6 • Irresponsible and Responsible Representations of Data on Bar Graphs

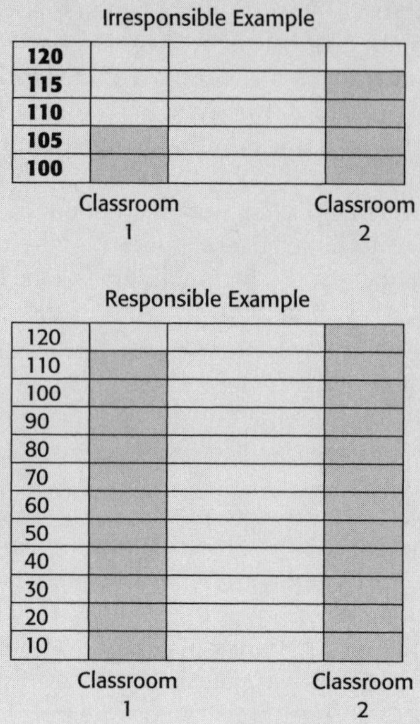

Irresponsible Example

120		
115		
110		
105		
100		

Classroom 1   Classroom 2

Responsible Example

120		
110		
100		
90		
80		
70		
60		
50		
40		
30		
20		
10		

Classroom 1   Classroom 2

more accessible to students if you engage them in lessons designed to increase their proficiency in working with symbolic images and with issues that engage their higher-level thinking abilities.

Some images that routinely appear in cartoons are widely known by adult newspaper readers. For example, Uncle Sam with his top hat and striped pants is easily recognized as a stand-in for the United States. Figures such as John Bull, representing the United Kingdom, and Marianne, representing France, are less widely known in the United States, perhaps because they appear in cartoons much less frequently than does Uncle Sam. Sometimes nonhuman figures are used as symbols of countries. For example, in the days of the old Soviet Union, American cartoonists frequently used a bear to symbolize the Union of Soviet Socialist Republics. Symbolic representations often confuse students. When you initiate instruction related to political cartoons with your class, you need to take time to provide them with information regarding symbols they may not understand.

The challenge of understanding symbols represents only a part of the problem students face when they come face to face with a political cartoon. The cartoonist provides few details about the general topic the cartoon addresses. People who look at the cartoon are expected to have considerable prior knowledge. Therefore, political cartoons can be difficult for students (Martorella, Beal, & Bolick, 2005). You need to provide learners with some context information that helps them understand the general situation the cartoonist is addressing. If they know something about symbols and about the particular happening or happenings the cartoonist is using as a focus for his drawing, then they are better positioned to "get the point."

You could use the following questions to help students understand political cartoons:

- What do you see in the cartoon?
- What are the different characters or figures that you see?
- If we think of those characters as symbols, what could they represent?
- How are the symbols interacting or relating to each other?
- What idea do you think the cartoonist is trying to present?

You will find that students who are able to grasp meanings of political cartoons take pride in their ability to think like adults. Many of them also become more interested in the political affairs that provide material for political cartoonists.

In summary, skills are important tools that help individuals learn how to gether information. They are tools that can help people througout their lives. Social studies skills have important relevance to helping students achieve the goal of being informed and productive citizens. They should be considered an important component of any social studies curriculum starting in the early grades.

KEY IDEAS IN SUMMARY

- *Social skills* are those that focus on individuals working together productively. Popular culture may communicate to students certain social skills and social values that are counter to positive social skills.
- Social skills need to be systematically taught. Many of them need to be taught in the group context where students are required to work with others to arrive at solutions.
- Many adults have confused ideas about locations of places on the globe. Elementary students are even more likely to have an inadequate grasp of map and globe skills needed for the proper understanding of geographical location. Some misunderstandings result from a complete lack of information, others from inadequate information. For example, large wall maps sometimes distort shapes and sizes of landmasses.
- Maps are useful for teaching certain kinds of content, such as the study of relatively small areas.

Typically they are less expensive than globes and are much easier to store. All maps include distortions. On *conformal* world maps, shapes of land areas are as they are on the globe, but the areas of landmasses distant from the equator are greatly distorted. On *equal area* world maps, areas of landmasses are consistent with areas as they appear on the globe, but shapes may be distorted.

- Globes should receive more attention in elementary social studies classrooms. Only the globe shows places on earth with a minimum of shape and size distortion and with accurate relative placement of water and land areas. To be useful as teaching tools, there should be at least one globe available for every three or four students. Globes have disadvantages as well as advantages. They are bulky and rather expensive. They do not lend themselves well to teaching content related to small geographic areas.
- There are seven basic map and globe skills: (1) recognizing shapes, (2) utilizing scale,

(3) recognizing symbols, (4) utilizing direction, (5) determining absolute location, (6) pointing out relative location, and (7) describing earth–sun relationships.

- *Time lines* are tools that you can use to help students better understand issues related to time and chronology. You may find it particularly useful to develop time lines that, among other things, contain information related to learners' personal lives.

- Charts and graphs are other special ways that important information is presented. Today, much information is presented in graphic form. Consequently, students need to learn how to create and interpret data presented in this way.

They need particular help in recognizing differences between graphs and charts that present information in responsible and irresponsible ways.

- Many students find political cartoons incomprehensible. There are two major difficulties they face. First of all, they frequently do not recognize standard symbols such as Uncle Sam. Second, the students lack information about the topic the cartoonist is addressing. You can work with students to make content of political cartoons more accessible by teaching them some standard cartoon symbols and helping them to know something about the issues individual cartoonists are addressing.

CHAPTER REFLECTIONS

Now that you have read the chapter, think about these questions.

1. Suppose you wanted to purchase some additional globes for your classroom. Your principal points out that globes are expensive and suggests that you order maps instead. What kind of a case might you make in support of spending the extra money to purchase globes?

2. The example of a time line in this chapter suggests including personal information about students and their relatives. What other ideas do you have for personalizing time lines? If a parent, guardian, or administrator saw one of your personalized time lines and asked you to explain why you included information about students, how would you respond?

3. Suppose you have taught a lesson on "recognizing distortions" on graphs and charts. What would you tell your students to look for in a follow-up assignment requiring them to look for "responsible" and "irresponsible" presentations of data in charts and graphs published in newspapers and magazines?

4. Political cartoons compress a lot of basic information and opinion into a single graphic presentation. To understand them, viewers must be familiar with numerous symbolic representations and with specific events or issues. Do these features make political cartoons too challenging for elementary-level students? Why or why not?

EIGHT

Planning for Diversity—Culture, Gender, and Exceptionality

UN/DPI Photo

This chapter will help you to:

- Recognize that your lesson planning must respond to the diverse personal characteristics of today's students.
- Prepare learners for a world in which they will interact with people whose values, perspectives, and capabilities vary from their own.
- Identify examples of how different cultures give children specific sets of assumptions about how they should view and react to the world.
- Appreciate that diversity of our population is one of our nation's strengths.
- Develop lessons related to multicultural issues that focus both on single-group and multiple-group perspectives.

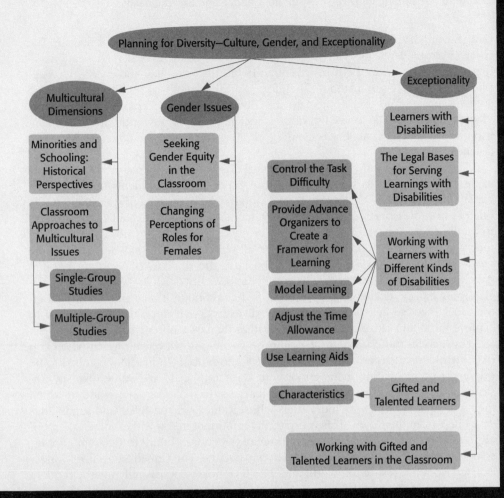

Planning for Diversity—Culture, Gender, and Exceptionality

Multicultural Dimensions

Gender Issues

Exceptionality

Minorities and Schooling: Historical Perspectives

Classroom Approaches to Multicultural Issues

Single-Group Studies

Multiple-Group Studies

Seeking Gender Equity in the Classroom

Changing Perceptions of Roles for Females

Control the Task Difficulty

Provide Advance Organizers to Create a Framework for Learning

Model Learning

Adjust the Time Allowance

Use Learning Aids

Learners with Disabilities

The Legal Bases for Serving Learnings with Disabilities

Working with Learners with Different Kinds of Disabilities

Characteristics

Gifted and Talented Learners

Working with Gifted and Talented Learners in the Classroom

- Identify issues associated with gender equity and describe approaches for dealing with this topic in the social studies classroom.
- Prepare lessons designed to help students understand how generally accepted roles for females have become more numerous over time.
- Describe various categories of learners with disabilities and point out some classroom approaches that you might use in working with students with specific disabilities.
- Explain legal requirements for providing educational services to learners with disabilities.
- Describe characteristics of gifted and talented students and point out some approaches you can take in working with these students in your own classroom.

One of our basic themes of this book is that the social studies is about people. The study of people leads us to a recognition of their incredible diversity. Our nation values equality. However, both in school and out, this value has not always been applied in a socially just manner. Therefore, social studies should focus on helping students understand and appreciate this diversity, and on exploring how people view themselves, make sense out of their social and physical worlds, and make contributions to society. An understanding of diversity includes culture, gender, and ableness.

The diversity of individuals in the typical classroom has increased tremendously in the past few years. A typical teacher can expect to have students representing a variety of cultures and backgrounds, and students with a variety of special needs. As one of our professors frequently stated, "Remember, you will have all of the students from all of the homes." Those involved in public education do not choose whom they will teach. Their charge is to educate all who come. This has been one of the great strengths of American education because the door to opportunity is often the classroom door. However, dealing with the diversity of students and needs in the classroom can be challenging. Our point is that although it may take additional effort, social studies teachers should view diversity as an important opportunity to achieve important citizenship objectives rather than as a burden to be avoided.

Diversity in the classroom does impose two types of obligations on when you plan instructional experiences. First, some of your social studies lessons need to be oriented toward helping members of your class appreciate and value diversity. Instruction of this kind helps prepare your learners for their lives in a world in which they will interact often with individuals whose values, perspectives, and capabilities may differ from their own. This is especially important in a world of increased globalization. The very survival of the nation may depend on future leaders who understand diversity and who possess a global perspective. The United States is no longer isolated from the rest of the world and, like it or not, is increasingly interdependent with the rest of the world.

Second, some categories of learners in your class may require different approaches to instruction than others. This recognizes the fact that the learning experiences of the students in your classroom will be influenced by their culture, their language, and their prior experiences. Your efforts to adapt instruction to fit special characteristics of individual learners enhance the probability that large numbers of them will profit from your teaching.

MULTICULTURAL DIMENSIONS

In the latter part of the twentieth century, a new wave of immigrants began entering the United States. More than a million immigrants entered every year so that by 1996 they accounted for roughly 10 percent of the total U.S. population. It is predicted that by 2020 the foreign-born population will be as many as 1 in 7 people. What is at least as significant as the numbers of immigrants that are entering the United States is the composition of the population. Today, Latin American and Asia have replaced Europe as the place of origin for many immigrants. Mexico continues to be the largest source of immigrants, with China, Cuba, India, and Vietnam also making important contributions (Garcia, 2002).

The diversity of cultures represented in today's classrooms underscores the importance of knowing something about the background of your students. It is important for you to have information about the specific cultural backgrounds of individuals in order to design lessons that will be effective for all students.

Minorities and Schooling: Historical Perspectives

Traditionally in the United States, a major goal in the education of multicultural populations has been what is called "Americanization." *Americanization* has been defined as an approach that seeks to merge ethnically and linguistic diverse groups into a single dominant culture (Garcia, 2002), and has sometimes been labeled the "melting pot" theory of assimilation. A basic assumption behind this approach was that individuals from different cultures must learn American values and ideals in order to preserve national unity and national identity. Too often this has been interpreted to mean that these individuals must give up their culture, their language, and their ethnic identity.

The social studies has often been used as a tool to bring about Americanization. Textbooks primarily emphasize U.S. perspectives, and the contributions and experiences of other groups have been either omitted or distorted. For example, Native American and Hispanic contributions have seldom been included in the curriculum in a meaningful way. The story of the building of the transcontinental railroad is often told with minimal mention of the bravery and hard work of Chinese and African American laborers.

Attempts to include broader perspectives in the social studies program have been met with some resistance. Some critics of a broader inclusion of multicultural content see this as "watering down" the curriculum. They are worried that if the experiences of other cultures are included, some "traditional" American history content will be excluded and this will weaken the social glue that holds the nation together. This has led to what some have called the "culture wars." There are some who believe that Americanization is a desirable goal. They contend that individuals from other places need to recognize they are now in the United States and therefore have an obligation to learn the dominant language and to accept the dominant culture.

Altough any person moving to a different culture must necessarily make some changes, should they be expected to give up their own language and culture? Should they come to feel as if their culture is inferior? Should individuals be expected to reject their heritage and give up their cultural pride to be considered a "true" American? Is it intellectually honest to diminish the contributions of some groups to elevate the status of others? Can we not work to develop shared values and a common national vision while also allowing individuals to retain pride in their own heritage? These questions need to be addressed as we consider our future as a multicultural society.

Throughout history, diversity has been a key ingredient in maintaining the health and vitality of a society. Multicultural perspectives lead to innovation and cultural change. Those nations that discourage diversity usually become stagnant. We need to recognize that diversity is a strength. As a social studies teacher, you should work to ensure that your students appreciate the many cultural and ethnic threads that go together to make up our national tapestry.

A beginning point for including multicultural perspectives in the classroom lies with you. As a teacher, you must be aware of your own cultural perspectives in order to develop a healthy multicultural curriculum. For example, if you are a member of the Caucasian majority, you may well live in a world where perspectives of your own group are so dominant that you may fail to recognize that your worldviews may differ from those of your students. This means that you need to think clearly about your own assumptions and to reflect on how students might interpret your actions (Savage, Savage, & Armstrong, 2006). You need to consider your answers to the following questions:

- How do I view various cultural groups? What are my biases and assumptions?
- What are my views about what the curriculum ought to be? How is that view influenced by my cultural perspectives?
- What assumptions am I making about the previous experience and the background my students bring to school?
- How might my ideas of good teaching and learning be influenced by my background?

CLASSROOM ACTIVITY 8-1

DIAGNOSING STEREOTYPES

This procedure can be used with all but the very youngest students. Children in the primary grades should be asked to respond verbally. Middle- and upper-grades students can write their responses.

To prepare for the exercise, gather together 8 to 12 photographs of members of different racial and ethnic groups. Ask students to look at each photograph and assign one of the following descriptive words that they believe might "go with" the person who is depicted:

a. helpful
b. troublesome
c. doctor
d. teacher
e. janitor
f. delivery person
g. friendly
h. hot-tempered
i. lazy
j. generous
k. energetic
l. hardworking
m. poor
n. wealthy
o. dirty
p. kind
q. ignorant
r. wise
s. sad
t. helpless

Terms *a, c, d, g, j, k, l, n, p, and r* are associated with people who are viewed positively or who are perceived as having higher status. Terms *b, e, f, h, i, m, o, q, s,* and *t* are associated with people viewed negatively or as having lower status.

THINK ABOUT THIS

If large numbers of students assign negative/low-status terms to photographs of nonwhite American men and women, this suggests that a negative stereotyping problem exists. You can respond to this situation by preparing lessons that are designed to break down these narrow, unrealistic views.

You may wish to use this exercise before and after you teach one or more lessons directed at eradicating stereotyping. Compare results to indicate whether students have developed more appreciation for groups that they initially negatively stereotyped.

In thinking about how you might help your students to acknowledge the dignity of people from a variety of backgrounds, you need to know something about existing attitudes and perspectives of members of your class. Classroom Activity 8-1 introduces one approach you might use to gather this information.

In recent years the emphasis in teaching social studies to ethnically diverse populations has centered on the idea of culturally responsive pedagogy (Garcia, 2002). Culturally responsive pedagogy is based on the idea of accepting and valuing diversity and seeks to eliminate educational experiences that label some groups as inferior. Research indicates that what is especially important in culturally responsive pedagogy is the development of a "culture of inclusion" (Good & Brophy, 2003). This is an attitude that accepts all students, communicates positive expectations, and includes learning experiences that are meaningful to all students.

Specific teaching practices related to culturally responsive pedagogy and a culture of inclusion include the following:

- Diversity is viewed as an asset.
- Lessons and programs are designed to promote an appreciation for cultural differences among all learners.
- Lessons and programs are designed to preserve and maintain perspectives of individual cultures and ethnic groups while including important dimensions of the dominant culture.
- Lessons and units respect students' prior knowledge and integrates the home culture with planned school experiences.
- Lessons and programs elicit ideas from students for activities and experiences.

Classroom Approaches to Multicultural Issues

Approaches used in developing lessons with a multicultural emphasis often feature either a single-group or a multiple-perspectives focus. When you use a single-group focus, you and your learners look at a single group or culture in depth. For example, one instructional sequence might center on lives of a certain Native American group during a specific historical period. Another might focus on experiences of immigrants from Southeast Asia.

Typically, multiple-perspectives lessons take a given issue or problem and explain how two or more groups see it. These lessons help students "step into the shoes" of others and become more sensitive to their views. For example, you might select "European Settlement of the United States" as a theme and introduce the topic by contrasting how English, French, Spanish, and Native American men and women viewed this process.

Single-Group Studies Single-group studies have the advantage of helping students understand a culture as a whole, and see the interrelatedness of values, beliefs, and attitudes. However, care needs to be taken to make sure the study is free from damaging stereotypes and distortions. In preparing lessons of this kind, you have to become well informed about the group to be studied. Single-group studies are designed to help students learn more about special perspectives of the group they are studying. Optimally, learners will complete their study with a good idea of how group members

Understanding the music and celebrations of a group helps us gain insight into their beliefs and values.

Eugene Gordon/PH College

interpret reality. To accomplish this purpose, your lessons have to go beyond superficial introduction of the group's clothing, food, and religious preferences. There has to be careful attention to the group's values, ethics, and special cultural traditions.

Your single-group lessons should provide learners with information about the group's history. This content helps them identify with struggles and experiences that, over time, have helped to shape attitudes of group members. Additionally, historical content highlights relationships between the group and the larger society of which it is a part. Changes in this relationship over time often reveal much about present perspectives of group members. For example, individuals who are suspicious of the motives of others may be members of groups that have been systematically and officially repressed in the past by representatives of a larger, majority culture.

Often, you will wish to include information about the focus group's contributions in such areas as art, music, literature, science, mathematics, and government. The study of cultural adaptation affords opportunities for students to learn that some groups have made innovative responses to trying conditions. For example, studies of certain Inuit groups (native peoples living in the far north, from Alaska across Canada to Greenland) often emphasize their adjustment to extremely cold climatic conditions. Early European explorers of the far north adopted many of their practices. Without the contributions of the Inuit, successful exploration of the world's polar regions by people from other areas would have been impossible.

You can also use single-group studies to focus on issues that reveal values of the group. Positions taken on key issues help define the group's priorities and help members of your class appreciate that individual groups have their own agendas. This insight can contribute to their understanding of the idea that healthy conflict is a defining feature of our democratic society.

Children's literature provides a rich source of material for lessons focusing on single groups. The example introduced in Lesson Idea 8-1 focuses on Native Americans.

LESSON IDEA 8-1

TOPIC: How Legends Help Us Understand People

OBJECTIVES: Students will (1) identify two or three specific aspects of Native American cultures as reflected in their legends, (2) cite one or more examples that illustrate how Native Americans view their relationships with nature, and (3) point out one or more aspects of Native American cultures that might conflict with aspects of the dominant Western culture.

ENGAGING THE STUDENTS: Ask the class whether anyone has had experience riding or taking care of horses. Encourage students to share their experiences. Ask them to tell how they feel about horses. Introduce them to *The Girl Who Loved Wild Horses,* by Paul Goble. Tell the class that you are going to read them a Native American legend about a girl who loved horses.

DEVELOPING THE CONTENT: Read the story. Stop as needed to clarify meanings of words, respond to questions, and share illustrations with the class. Ask questions such as, "What do you think this story means?" "What does it tell us about how Native Americans feel about their world?" "What things are important to them?" Read aloud the two songs at the end of the book. Then, ask questions such as, "What do these songs tell us?" "Do they reveal feelings that are different from those most of us have?" "What are the differences?"

Next, read aloud *The Legend of the Bluebonnet,* by Tomie DePaola. Ask questions similar to those you asked about *The Girl Who Loved Wild Horses.* Ask students what they think these people might have felt if others arrived and began hunting wild horses and plowing under bluebonnets to make room for houses and factories.

Follow up by helping students find other books dealing with lives of Native Americans. Ask them to think about traditional Native American customs as they read these materials. Particularly, urge students to consider how these customs might conflict with dominant Western cultural practices.

BRINGING CLOSURE: Ask class members to suggest what people in our country might do to promote understanding of minority cultures. Ask students to describe three "first steps" that need to be taken to begin implementing these ideas.

EXTENSION TO THE WEB: The Multicultural Pavilion website provides links and activities for developing multicultural understanding in the classroom.

URL–http://www.edchange.org/ multicultural

It draws on two well-known, popular books for young people, *The Girl Who Loved Wild Horses,* by Paul Goble, and *The Legend of the Bluebonnet,* by Tomie DePaola.

Music can be another useful resource for developing cultural understanding. Music of individual cultures and peoples reveals much about how they see the world. In addition, students often find music more interesting than merely reading about a group. In the example provided in Lesson Idea 8-2, the national anthem of Mexico serves as a point of departure for learning about Mexican values and culture.

Multiple-Group Perspectives When you develop lessons using a multiple-group perspectives approach, you establish a focus on a single issue and introduce it in terms of how it is viewed by several groups. For example, you might choose to introduce a given event, such as the early European settlement of the Atlantic coast of what is now the United States. Ask members of your class to examine this event from the perspectives of both the settlers and the Native Americans.

LESSON IDEA 8-2

TOPIC: What a National Anthem Tells Us About a People

OBJECTIVES: Students will (1) develop one or more hypotheses about the history of Mexico, (2) identify two or more values or basic beliefs of the Mexican people, and (3) identify two or more sources that they can consult to validate and clarify their hypotheses.

ENGAGING THE STUDENTS: Ask class members if they know what is meant by the term *national anthem*. Discuss "The Star Spangled Banner" with the class. Ask students why the song is important. Go over the words. Ask members of the class to try to identify what the song tells us about the history and values of people of the United States.

DEVELOPING THE CONTENT: Provide learners with copies of the English translation of the words of "Himno National," the national anthem of Mexico. (If available, play a recording of the anthem to familiarize students with the music as well as the words.) Review some of the unfamiliar words and symbols. Answer any questions. Ask students to state several hypotheses about what the anthem reveals about the history of Mexico. Write their ideas on an overhead transparency and project for all to see or, alternatively, write them on the chalkboard.

Himno National

Mexicans when the trumpet is calling,

Grasp your sword and your harness assemble.

Let the guns with their thunder appalling

Make the Earth's deep foundations to tremble.

May the angel divine, O Dear Homeland,

Crown thy brow with the olive branch of peace;

For thy destiny, traced by God's own hand

In the heavens, shall ever increase.

But shall ever the proud foe assail thee,

And with insolent foot profane thy ground,

Know, dear country, thy sons shall not fail thee,

Ev'ry one thy soldier shall be found, thy soldier ev'ry one shall be found.

Blessed Homeland, thy children have vowed them

If the bugle to battle should call,

They will fight with the last breath allowed them

Till on thy loved altars they fall.

Let the garland of life thine be;

Unto them be deathless fame;

Let the laurel of victory be assigned thee,

Enough for the tomb's honored name.

Spanish lyrics by Francisco Gonzales Bocanegra, music by Jaime Nuño (this translation is not verbatim from the Spanish)

Ask members of the class what the anthem suggests is important to the Mexican people. Write their ideas on another transparency or on the chalkboard.

Ask students where they think they might get information about Mexico that they could use to test the accuracy of their ideas. Encourage them to think about such resources as books, films, interviews with people who have traveled to Mexico, and guest speakers of Mexican descent.

Divide the class into cooperative learning groups. Ask each group to work with one or more of the hypotheses generated by the class. Have each group find information relating to their hypotheses and make a report of their findings to the whole class. Challenge group members to present information in interesting and creative ways. For example, some groups may wish to use role playing as a way of making their reports.

BRINGING CLOSURE: Ask class members to decide which of their initial ideas should be retained, modified, or rejected. Then ask them whether, as a result of what they have learned, they wish to generate any new hypotheses. Conclude by asking students to name two or three things that people can learn about a country by studying its national anthem.

EXTENSION TO THE WEB: The National Association for Multicultural Education website provides resources, material and teaching materials for teaching multicultural perspectives.

URL—http://www.nameorg.org/resources.html

LESSON IDEA 8-3

TOPIC: Moving Westward

OBJECTIVES: Students will (1) identify two or more groups of people who were living in the western United States before the arrival of pioneers from the eastern United States, (2) identify several customs and ways of living of these people, and (3) state at least two influences on the ways of life of these people that were a direct result of the pioneers' arrival.

ENGAGING THE STUDENTS: Have the class view a film or read a romanticized account of the westward movement or of the Old West. Ask students to think about what they saw or read. Ask them whether they would have liked to have lived at this time. Follow up with a question about the extent to which their opinions are based on what they have just seen or read. Introduce students to the idea that there were people already living in the western United States before the arrival of the pioneers.

DEVELOPING THE CONTENT: Divide the class into several groups. Ask each group to find locations of people inhabiting the Old West in the early 1800s. One group might be assigned to identify places where different groups of Native Americans were living. Another might focus on locations occupied by settlers who originally entered the area from Mexico. Others might focus on European groups, such as the British, French, and Russians. Each group should be given a small outline map of North America. A spokesperson from each group should plot the location of the assigned population on the group's map.

After the small-group work has been completed, reconvene the class as a single large group. Ask spokespersons from each group to plot the location of the group's assigned population on a large map. If possible, make copies of this map and distribute them to everyone in the class.

Next, reconstitute the small groups. Ask each group to find additional information about its assigned population. In particular, have students find out the following:

- When members of the assigned population first began to occupy the area they settled

- What their motives for coming were
- How they made a living
- Interesting customs and lifestyles of these people

Bring the students back together as a single large group. Pose the possibility that pioneers from the eastern United States are about to move into the lands occupied by the people each group has studied. Challenge students to think about the probable reactions to this situation of the people who are already occupying these lands.

Ask students to go back into their small groups. Tell people in each group to develop a response to the movement of the pioneers into the area their assigned population occupies. Ask them to prepare this response from the perspective of members of the assigned population. Give students options. For example, some groups may wish to write a simulated editorial as a way of sharing their views. Other groups may elect to have one or two students deliver reactions verbally.

To follow up on the presentations of the individual groups, add the perspective of yet another group of people who were involved in the westward movement: the women. Read the following account to the class. It comes from the diary of a young woman who moved west with her husband:

> Only women who went west in 1859 understand what a woman had to endure. There was no road, no stores, and, many times, no wood for a fire. I had a new baby, and it was teething and suffering from fever. The child took nearly all my strength. I became weak. My weight fell and fell. In the end, I was all the way down to ninety pounds.
>
> After reaching Denver, we heard that gold had been discovered in the mountains. On the nineteenth of February, 1860, I was taken from my sick bed and placed in a wagon, and we started for the new mines. No woman had yet been there. After several days' travel we came late at night to Salt Creek. We tried the water and found it was no good. We tied the oxen to the

(Continued)

wagon so they couldn't drink. Then we went to bed with nothing to eat. That night it got very cold.

The next day we moved to Trout Creek and found the water good. Several men had left Denver a few days ahead of us. We wanted to join up with them but had seen no sign of them. Our men decided to mount a search. They shouldered rifles and headed out looking for footprints. Each went in a different direction. The men had not returned by dark, and I felt very alone. I allowed the small donkey to come into the tent with me. I put my head on him and cried in the loneliness of the soul.

(Adapted from W. M. Thayer, Marvels of the New West, *Norwich, CT: Henry Bill Publishing, 1888, pp. 246–253)*

BRINGING CLOSURE: After students have finished making their group reports and have read and

thought about the diary excerpt, ask them to make general statements about the impact of the westward movement on different groups of people. As a culminating activity, involve students in developing a play, drawing a wall mural, or writing a personal history of the westward movement. Ask them to include specific examples of interactions between new settlers and original settlers of these lands.

EXTENSION TO THE WEB: A good source for getting information about immigrants and how they reacted to their new country can be found at the University of Minnesota's Immigration History Research Center.

URL—http://www.ihrc.umn.edu/

Multiple-perspectives lessons help your students realize that different people often interpret common episodes in varied ways. Values of groups to which individuals belong influence their understanding of events. Solutions that make sense to people in one group because they are consistent with this group's values may not seem logical at all to members of other groups whose values are different. To appreciate how values shape interpretations, consider how many films and books treat the westward movement of settlers across lands that today comprise the continental United States. Many accounts fail to give serious attention to the impact of the arrival of newcomers on people who were already occupying these lands. Lesson Idea 8-3 provides an approach you might use to help members of your class understand that a common event often affects some people differently than others.

Other multiple-perspectives lessons you prepare might use other means to introduce students to conflicting accounts of historical events. For example, you might have class members read letters to the editor or editorials from different newspapers that present conflicting views of contemporary issues. Or, you might expose your students to opposing viewpoints by scheduling class speakers from groups with different views on controversial issues.

Multicultural education ought to be a part of any quality social studies program. Changes in the relationships between nations of the world and the growing interdependence of people make this important. Fortunately, there are many resources available to teachers if the textbooks they use are lacking in this important dimension.

GENDER ISSUES

Gender issues in the social studies are similar to those of multicultural education. Too often the content of the social studies has not included the contributions of women. Women have made important contributions in all phases of our history. The omission of the contributions of women have had a negative impact on both males and females. Gender stereotypes still exist and interfere with the development of healthy attitudes and the solution of important social problems and issues. The development of gender equity is an important part of learning citizenship skills and perspectives that are crucial to the future of our nation. In recent years, a considerable amount of instructional material has been developed for including gender issues in social studies programs.

Seeking Gender Equity in the Classroom

One of your purposes as a social studies teacher is to help your students confront gender-based biases. School programs and practices have not always worked to nurture the development of gender equity. For example, researchers have found that teachers (who may be unaware of their own behavior patterns) interact more with female learners during reading instruction and more with male learners during arithmetic lessons (Good & Brophy, 2003). These varied amounts of teacher–student contact, over time, may result in different female and male achievement levels in these subjects; an outcome that fails to well serve the long-term interests of either female or male students.

Gender discrimination tends to restrict choices more for females than for males. To combat this situation, in your social studies lessons you need to provide students with examples of females who occupy a variety of responsible roles. Girls must recognize that increasing numbers of females play leadership roles in government, engineering, the physical sciences, and medicine. It also is helpful to emphasize contributions of women as well as men in lessons drawing content from history.

One of the important goals of multicultural education is to help students develop respect for the rich diversity of human experience.

Embassy of Finland

Changing Perceptions of Roles for Females

Outdated attitudes related to so-called "strengths" and "weaknesses" of each gender led to assumptions that today enjoy little support. For example, in the past certain occupations were widely believed to be the "property" of one gender. Many more roles were open to males than to females. Today, many gender-based employment

---

LESSON IDEA 8-4

TOPIC: Jobs for Females: Yesterday and Today

OBJECTIVES: Students will (1) recognize that today there is increasingly broad support for the idea that all jobs are open to women who qualify for them and that gender of applicants is no longer a critical factor, (2) describe differences in kinds of jobs open to women today and those open to them 30 or more years ago, and (3) suggest two or more reasons why women enjoy more employment choices today than they did in the twentieth century.

ENGAGING THE STUDENTS: Involve class members in a discussion you prompt with this question: "Are there some jobs that only women can hold, and others than only men can hold?"

DEVELOPING THE CONTENT: Ask class members to think about kinds of jobs women can have today. Write ideas on the chalkboard under the heading "Jobs Women Can Hold." Then, ask if there are any jobs women cannot hold. Write any student responses on the chalkboard under the heading "Jobs Women Cannot Hold." Save this information.

Next, divide class members into groups of about five students each. Provide each group with one or two copies of magazines that are at least 30 years old. (These can frequently be found at rummage or garage sales. Often they are available at modest cost from used bookstores and from resale shops such as Goodwill Industries.) Ask learners in each group to look for pictures of women at work. For each woman pictured, ask students to write down the nature of the occupation shown (teacher, nurse, steelworker, and so forth).

Ask a spokesperson from each group to report the group's findings. Write this information on the chalkboard next to the information in the "Jobs" lists. Lead a discussion that requires students to examine both the original lists and the list developed after their work with the magazines. Ask them to point out differences and similarities between the lists.

Have students re-form into groups. Give each group several copies of current magazines. Again, ask them to look for illustrations of women at work and to note the occupational roles.

Ask a representative from each group to share the group's findings. Write the information on the chalkboard. Repeat the discussion outlined previously. Students should find more job roles represented in the current magazines than in either of the previous lists.

Next, ask students to compare the kinds of jobs for women found in magazines 30 or more years old with those found in current magazines. Ask them if they can explain any differences.

BRINGING CLOSURE: As a follow-up activity, some students may enjoy preparing a bulletin board featuring women in a variety of occupational roles. Require each student to write a short paragraph beginning: "As I think about jobs available to women 30 years ago and today, I conclude that . . ." Look for at least three specific differences.

EXTENSION TO THE WEB: The homepage of the American Association of University Women provides information that can be used in constructing gender-equity lessons.

URL—http://www.aauw.org

requirements have disappeared, and there is a trend for employers to focus on qual-ifications of applicants without considering whether they are males or females. In this country, as throughout the world, women now represent a higher percentage of people in management positions than they did 20 years ago (WEEA Equity Resource Center, 2000). However, even though much progress has been made, there contin-ues to be disparity between numbers of males and females in certain professions. Lesson Idea 8-4 suggests one approach you might take to help students better un-derstand changes in roles of women over time.

EXCEPTIONALITY

If we believe that the content of the social studies program is important in helping individuals assume their roles as productive citizens, then we should also believe that it is important content for all students. This includes not only individuals of dif-ferent cultures and gender, it also includes individuals that might be labeled as "ex-ceptional" students. It is estimated that about 13 percent of the schoolage population receives special education services (U.S. Department of Education, 2000). Federal legislation has required that, whenever possible, exceptional students are to be ed-ucated in the "least restrictive environment." This means you can count on having exceptional students in your classroom.

The term *exceptionality* refers to a condition that differentiates specific charac-teristics of a given learner from those commonly found among typical school learn-ers. Given this definition, it is possible to identify many groups of "exceptional" learners in schools. Typically, though, school professionals use this term most often when they describe educational needs of learners who fall into three major cate-gories: (1) learners with disabilities, (2) learners who are gifted and talented, and (3) learners who are native speakers of a language other than English. In this sec-tion, we will introduce you to approaches for working with learners with disabilities and learners who are gifted and talented.

Learners with Disabilities

It is a given that you will have students in your classroom that have learning problems. These problems may range from obvious disabilities involving speech, hearing, sight, orthopedic impairments, and emotional disturbance to specific learning disabilities. *Specific learning disabilities* refers to a group of disorders that interfere with the abil-ity to listen, think, read, write, spell, or do mathematical calculations (Vaught, Bos, & Schumm, 2003). This category includes attention deficit disorder, hyperactivity disorder, and dyslexia. These students are usually identified because of their difficulty with some learning tasks and a discrepancy between their expected achievement and their actual achievement. They often appear to be just like other students as they participate in classroom discussions and seem to understand the material presented. However, assignments and tests quickly reveal that something is wrong and the content is not being understood or applied. Many of these individuals have great potential to succeed if they learn how to adjust. Famous people such as Thomas Edison and Albert Einstein are reported to have had specific learning disabilities.

The presence of students with disabilities in your classroom is assured for several reasons. From an ethical standpoint, educators today believe that these youngsters are just part of the population that parents send to school to be educated and that they deserve educational services just as much as children who are unburdened by disabling conditions. Further, existing federal regulations place strict legal requirements on schools that require them to follow strict guidelines in working with learners with disabilities.

The Legal Bases for Serving Learners with Disabilities

Legal guidelines for serving children with disabilities originally were delineated in Public Law 94-142, the "Education for All Handicapped Children Act," of 1975. This legislation was modified and, in 1990, renamed the "Individuals with Disabilities Education Act" (P.L. 101-476). These laws and subsequent updates lay out seven key principles that schools must follow in serving learners with disabilities.

- *Zero Rejects.* Schools must enroll every child regardless of the nature or severity of his or her disability.
- *Nondiscriminatory Testing.* Multiple indicators must be used to determine whether a child has a disability and whether special services are needed.
- *Appropriate Education.* Schools must develop and implement an "Individualized Education Plan" (IEP) for each child with a disability. A learner's regular classroom teacher must participate in the development of the IEP.
- *Least Restrictive Environment.* A child with a disability must be educated in the setting that is the least restrictive environment. Often this means that learners with disabilities spend at least part of each school day in regular classrooms.
- *Due Process.* Rights of children and parents/guardians in planning and placement decisions must be protected by due process procedures.
- *Parental Participation.* Parents/guardians must participate in decisions regarding educational plans developed for children with disabilities.
- *Inclusion Principle.* Public school classrooms have not only a legal obligation to serve learners with disabilities, they are obligated to welcome these learners as valued and wanted members of the regular class community.

Working with Learners with Different Kinds of Disabilities

You will make specific adaptations of your social studies lessons to accommodate students with special needs according to the specific needs of the students. One of the most common, and often perplexing, problems for the classroom teacher is dealing with individuals with specific learning disabilities. Because these students often appear no different from others in the classroom, their learning needs can be overlooked. The result is a great deal of frustration on the part of both student and teacher.

When you have students with specific learning disabilities in your classroom, there are some things that you can do to accommodate them and help them achieve success. These are sound instructional practices that are important for all students. However, they are especially important for students with specific learning disabilities.

Control the Task Difficulty Be aware of the types of frustrations that the student encounters in learning. Adjust the learning task into steps that match the learner's motivation and frustration level so the student attains a high level of success. In social studies, it is often possible to design alternative tasks at different levels of challenge that focus on the same content.

Provide Advance Organizers to Create a Framework for Learning Advance organizers are tasks or explanations that help students anticipate what they will be learning. Good advance organizers often take a concept or idea that the student has already learned and use it to provide a context for the new learning. They can also take the form of graphic organizers or structured overviews (see Chapter 5).

Model Learning Making learning visible is effective for all students but can be especially useful for those students who have learning disabilities. One powerful way of modeling learning is to use "think aloud" strategies. This is where you or some other students talk through what they are thinking and how they are approaching a task. Cooperative learning approaches can be a good way of helping students model thinking and problem solving for others.

Adjust the Time Allowance We are all different and learn things at different rates. What happens if you need a week to master a skill but are only given four days? You fail. What happens if you master the skill in two days? You get bored. Although there are those that argue that completing a task quickly is an important indication of ability, there is considerable evidence that if students are given sufficient time, a high percentage will achieve success. When planning for classroom instruction you need to find ways of accommodating both types of students. What are you going to have to offer those students who master the material quickly? How can you allow additional time for those who need it?

Use Learning Aids One of the most common learning aids that teachers use today is the computer. Wonderful programs are available that can help students overcome learning difficulties. However, other "low-tech" options also can be useful:

- *Audiotape reading material.* This became a common practice for one of the authors, who began teaching in a classroom with a high percentage of English language learners. Most of the students had reading levels far below reading level of the textbook. Therefore, failure was directly related to reading level, not with ability to learn. It is relatively simple to make audiotapes that students can use to learn the needed content. This can be useful in helping students improve their reading skills by having them follow along in the text or the reading material.

  When making tapes, use good instructional strategies such as inserting questions to keep the students alert and having them stop at critical points to respond or complete an activity. You do not need to read the material of a textbook chapter verbatim. You can condense it by emphasizing the main ideas and by paraphrasing less important content. If you do this, be sure and let students know which sections they should be following (Vaught et al., 2003).

- *Provide a structured outline.* This is simply providing the student with an outline of the content to be learned. As the teacher, you fill in some portions of the outline to provide a structure. The task of the student is to fill in the blanks. Not only is this a good way to assist students who have trouble comprehending material, it helps all students learn how to outline and identify main points.

- *Use multipass reading.* Our instructional practices often convey to students the idea that a person should be able to learn the material by reading something once. However, successful students learn this is not true. Multipass learning engages students in reading through a reading selection more than once with a specific purpose in mind each time. For example, the first pass through the material might be just to look at the pictures or illustrations. This is followed with a discussion on what the students think the material is about. This also serves as a good advance organizer. The second pass might be to read just the first sentences of paragraphs (many of the main ideas of reading material can be found in the first sentence). Once again, a discussion follows on what the passage is about and what the main ideas might be. The third pass could be to read for details. This would be a complete reading of the material to validate their ideas and to provide a detailed picture. You will be surprised at how much the students can learn by just reading the first sentences and how much more meaningful the text becomes when they then read for details. (See Chapter 5 for a fuller discussion.)
- *Present material in multiple ways.* Expecting all students to learn only through reading or hearing is not a realistic expectation. The material needs to be presented in mulitple ways. This might include using visual imagery such as pictures or graphic organizers, demonstrating the material by providing models, and engaging students in role playing. The key is to try and engage several of the senses.

While these ideas are useful to all students and can be applied to those with obvious disabilities such as speech, hearing, sight, orthopedic impairments, and emotional disturbance, there are some specific adaptations that need to be made for these students. Table 8-1 provides instructional-settings statistics on students with selected classes of disabilities.

TABLE 8-1
Percentages of Students with Selected Disabilities Receiving Instruction in Various Settings

LEARNER DISABILITY	INSTRUCTIONAL SETTING		
	In Regular Classroom 79%-100% of the School Day	In Regular Classroom 40%-78% of the School Day	In Setting Outside of Regular Classroom for 60% or more of the School Day
Speech and Language Impairments	87.8%	7.3%	4.9%
Visual Impairments	46.6%	21.3%	31.8%
Specific Learning Disabilities: ADD, etc	43.8%	39.3%	32.1%
Orthopedic Impairments	46.6%	21.3%	32.1%
Serious Emotional Disturbance	24.9%	23.3%	51.8%

Source: Table 54, *Digest of Educational Statistics,* Washington, DC: National Center for Educational Statistics, 2001, p. 67.

As noted in the table, learners with disabilities associated with speech will probably spend more of the instructional day with you in your regular classroom than will students with other kinds of disabilities. Difficulties these young people have range across issues having to do with problems in articulating certain sounds, stuttering, and maintaining an appropriate voice quality. Because of frustrations they have in communicating via the spoken word, many students with speech impairments suffer from low self-image. If you have access to a speech therapist who has worked with these individuals, ask about specific ideas for helping them in the classroom. Often speech therapists recommend actions such as the following:

- Call on students with speech impairments only when they have raised a hand or otherwise indicated a willingness to speak.
- Praise these students when they make a verbal contribution.
- Make time for these students to speak to you one on one. Such conversations give you opportunities to raise their morale and give them opportunities to verbalize concerns about school work in a "safe" atmosphere in which other class members won't ridicule their communication problems.

Learners with visual impairments have difficulties associated with sight. To help your visually impaired students, consider doing the following:

- Take care to communicate instructions slowly and orally to visually impaired students that you provide to others in written form.
- If instructions are complex and lengthy, consider providing visually impaired students with an audio recording of the information you want them to have. They can play back the cassette later (repeating the process, if necessary) to get the details they need.
- Realize that moving around the school and the classroom can be a problem for visually impaired students. Allow them to explore various areas of the classroom when they first join your class so they can develop a good mental picture of its layout. Consider asking them to come into the room at a time when other students are absent so they can better learn locations of chairs, desks, tables, and other classroom furniture.

Students with orthopedic impairments have limitations that often affect their motor control. Your challenge is to make modifications to your instructional program that will allow them to overcome obstacles associated with these physical limitations. For example, students with some orthopedic impairment find it difficult to provide written responses to assignments. Their challenge, and yours, is to find ways to work around any limitations imposed by their impairment and allow them to credibly demonstrate to you what they have learned. Though there are great individual-to-individual differences among learners with orthopedic impairments, general guidelines for working with these learners include the following:

- Recognize that some orthopedic impairments interfere with students' abilities to complete assignments as rapidly as other learners. You may need to allow these students more time to complete their work.
- Some learners with orthopedic impairments use walkers, crutches, and other specialized aids. You need to arrange classroom furniture in ways that allow

them to use this equipment. You also may need to allow these students to leave your class a few minutes before others because often it takes them longer to go from place to place.

Hearing impairments range from total *deafness* (a loss so thorough that individuals with the condition have extreme difficulty in producing and understanding normal speech) to *hard of hearing* (a loss that is serious, but not so profound as to prevent people with the condition from acquiring normal patterns of speech). In general, learners with identified hearing impairments have problems becoming proficient users of verbal language. In working with learners in this category, you may want to do the following:

- Some learners with hearing loss have been taught to read lips. You need to be sure you face these students when you speak so they can see your lips moving. Also, do not move around. Lip readers find it difficult to follow someone in motion.
- Some hearing-impaired learners may have mastered a sign language. At some point, you may find it useful to take a course in signing to help you communicate with them.
- As you introduce new information, consider writing key points on an overhead transparency or a chalkboard. With older students, you may occasionally give a short lecture. When you do this, consider distributing a sheet to class members that contains an outline of your comments. Such written clues provide a useful backup channel of communication for hearing-impaired students.

As noted in Table 8-1, many learners with severe emotional disturbance spend a good part of each instructional day in settings outside of your regular classroom. However, you still will have individuals with this condition in your classes, and you need to be prepared to deal with them. Young people with severe emotional disturbance are characterized by patterns that are inconsistent with age-appropriate behaviors. Characteristics of individuals within this group vary. Some students will be defiant, loud, rude, and desperate seekers of attention. Others may be quiet, fearful, and withdrawn.

Students with emotional disturbance often provide a serious challenge for classroom teachers. Many of them have had a history of failure and confrontation that has produced poor self-images. These young people need lessons that allow them to succeed. In working with severely emotionally disturbed students, you may wish to do the following:

- Develop lessons that students with severe emotional disturbance will see as giving them a "real chance" to succeed.
- Reduce distractions as learners do their work.
- Take extra care in giving directions. These learners must know exactly what they are to do, and they need to understand that you will insist that they follow the instructions you provide.
- As opportunities arise, help these students understand that there is a definite connection between their behaviors and the consequences flowing from these behaviors. Many of these learners approach school (and, indeed, life) with a belief that rewards and punishments are more the result of good luck and bad luck. Your efforts to help them better grasp cause-and-effect relationships can help them develop more mature ways of interpreting the world.

CLASSROOM ACTIVITY 8-2

MODIFYING LESSON PLANS TO MEET THE NEEDS OF STUDENTS WITH DISABILITIES

Because of the special needs of students with disabilities, you will need to modify lessons to provide them with legitimate opportunities to master your material.

Choose any lesson plan in this book as a focus. Then, develop these two lesson modifications:

1. A modification for learners with speech and language impairments

2. A modification for learners with specific learning disabilities

Feel free to draw on information from this chapter as you complete this task. You may also want to seek additional ideas from the World Wide Web and other sources.

Gifted and Talented Learners

The immediate reaction of many teachers is that gifted and talented students don't require much attention. The assumption is that because these students are gifted, they can easily adapt to any classroom situation. Many teachers think they would like a classroom full of gifted and talented students. However, these students have specific needs that are often ignored.

Long-standing pressures from parents, guardians, and others interested in school programs to better serve needs of such learners led Congress to establish the Office of Gifted and Talented in 1972. Subsequent federal legislation, particularly the Jacob K. Javits Gifted and Talented Students Education Act of 1994, provided for additional federal support for school programs to serve the needs of gifted and talented learners. This support takes the form of (1) grants to states to provide educational services for these learners and (2) nationally supported research focused on generating information related to better meeting the educational needs of this special group of young people.

Characteristics If you review the history of school programs for gifted and talented learners, you will find that ideas have changed regarding defining characteristics of this population of young people. Early selection procedures focused heavily on standardized IQ scores (Savage et al., 2006).

This narrow definition drew fire from critics who charged that such practices discriminated against minorities, who often have not scored well on standardized IQ tests. Others argued that the terms *gifted* and *talented* implied more than a high IQ score. More recent definitions have emphasized the notion of multiple intelligences (Gardner, 1993). The implications of this definition is that there is no one easy classification or response for gifted and talented students.

A leading expert in the education of gifted and talented learners, Joseph Renzulli (1978), argues that individuals in this group should be clearly different from more typical school learners in three distinct categories:

• *Intelligence.* Information about this variable should be gathered from multiple sources (e.g., past grades, examples of work the student has completed previously, comments from teachers and others who have worked with the student, and so forth).

- *Task Commitment.* This characteristic refers to the student's tenacity. Gifted and talented learners push through frustration they encounter as they work to finish an assigned task. They tend to be thorough and to see projects through to completion.
- *Creativity.* Gifted and talented learners look at problems in unusual ways and attack them in a manner that varies from traditional or expected approaches.

Working with Gifted and Talented Learners in the Classroom

You need to be familiar with two general approaches to working with gifted and talented learners. *Acceleration* programs serve these young people by allowing them to go through the existing school program at a quicker-than-normal pace. For example, a gifted and talented student in such a program might complete the grades 1 to 6 program in three or four years rather than the traditional six. Because learners in acceleration programs will end up in classes with individuals who are much older (a circumstance that concerns many parents, guardians, and educators), acceleration programs are not popular.

Enrichment programs keep gifted and talented learners with other young people in their age group. However, these learners receive instruction that is more sophisticated and demanding than that provided to so-called "regular" school learners. In some schools, special gifted and talented teachers work with gifted and talented students for part (and, in some cases, all) of the school day. In others, regular classroom teachers devise enrichment experiences for selected gifted and talented learners, who remain as members of regular classes students throughout the entire instructional day.

Enrichment is an especially useful approach in the social studies. Nearly any topic or concept in the social studies can be developed at multiple levels of concreteness and sophistication. When planning, identify the important concepts and generalizations you want students to learn, as opposed to a list of specific facts. Then consider a variety of activities or tasks at different intellectual challenge levels. This will allow you to differentiate your assignments while maintaining a common content focus. You need to make sure that the tasks you provide to gifted students do not consist merely of doing more. Gifted students will react negatively to assignments if they see that "enrichment" amounts to nothing more than an obligation to "do more" of what others in the class are doing. If this happens, your gifted and talented students may conclude that the reward of being gifted and talented is a kind of "academic punishment" that requires them to work harder than others in the class. What you need to strive for are tasks that will challenge these students and to go beyond the obvious and engage their creativity. Remember, however, that some of these students may be uncomfortable "stepping outside the box" and doing something creative. They have learned that school pays off if you have the "right" answers and they are reluctant to take risks unless they are sure they have that answer.

Another useful approach to gifted students is to use learning contracts to enrich their study of the curriculum. A *learning contract* is an agreement between student and teacher that spells out what is expected of both, and the assessment criteria. This is especially useful when some students master the content of the curriculum and have some special interests that go beyond what others in the class might be able to do. For example, one of the authors once conferenced with a student and asked about the apparent lack of motivation the student was demonstrating in class. This fourth grader responded that he was really interested in the Greeks and Romans and he was not being allowed to study them. A special learning contract with this student allowed him to expand his social studies learning into the study of these cultures, a situation that not only provided motivation for the student in question but, also stimulated some interest from the rest of the class.

You may have your own ideas about a learning contract for gifted and talented learners. For example, you may want to take advantage of information available on the World Wide Web as you prepare lists of enrichment activities for your learners. The following learning contract features are adapted from Winebrenner and Berger's (1994) suggestions:

- Learners will be given a list of the concepts and learning outcomes for the focus unit that the whole class will be expected to learn.
- There will be a section describing a selection of extension and enrichment activities from which students may choose.
- Learners will be expected to document how they spend their time. They will be expected to maintain a written record describing what they did each day.
- Learners will agree to be tested over content being studied by regular class members and enrichment content at regular check points.
- Learners will prepare a final product, as described in the description of the selected enrichment activity, that will be due on a specified date and that will comprise part of the data used to assess performance on the unit of study.

CLASSROOM ACTIVITY 8-3

PREPARING A LIST OF ENRICHMENT OPTIONS FOR GIFTED AND TALENTED STUDENTS

Identify a grade level you would like to teach, and select a title for a social studies unit you will teach. You have decided to prepare some learning contracts for three or four gifted and talented members of your class. Develop a list of enrichment activities for these students. They each will be expected to select and complete one of the activities. Be sure to include some activities that require students to use the World Wide Web to seek out information.

Include the following components in each of your enrichment options:

- A title and overview
- Descriptions of what students are to learn

- An explanation of activities you expect students to complete
- A description of what kinds of "learning products" you expect students to complete as evidence of what they have learned
- Due dates for specific components of the activity

(Feel free to add additional components of your own choosing.) Ask your course instructor to critique your ideas.

KEY IDEAS IN SUMMARY

- Because of the nature of social studies it is a natural subject to address concerns of diversity. Addressing issues of culture, gender, and exceptionality should be a part of the curriculum. Although addressing these concerns will take more time and effort, the results in increased motivation and reduced problems is well worth the effort.

- The diversity represented among students in public schools is greater than the diversity of the general American population. You will find students from many cultural and linguistic backgrounds in your classes. In addition, learners with varying disabilities will be in your classroom, as will gifted and talented students.

- Traditionally, learners from cultural and ethnic minority groups have not been represented fairly in school curricula. Educators are trying to remedy this situation. Because diversity is recognized as one of our nation's strengths, one of your obligations is to recognize and respond to student differences by preparing lessons that are responsive to their needs.

- Varying approaches exist for organizing instruction focusing on multicultural issues. Two of these are single-group and multiple-perspectives approaches. *Single-group* lessons focus students' attention on contributions and perspectives of one cultural group. *Multiple-perspectives* lessons often center on a common episode and describe its differential effects on varying groups and the reactions of these groups to these circumstances.

- In the past, our society had a much more restricted view of the kinds of roles that females should play. Lessons you prepare in the area of gender equity help students understand how these attitudes have changed and that, today, both females and males can aspire to a variety of adult roles.

- Many lessons focusing on gender equity attempt to remedy the deficiency found in many traditional textbooks and other information sources regarding important contributions females have made to political, social, and economic life throughout history.

- The term *exceptionality* refers to a condition that differentiates a characteristic of a given learner or a group of learners from those commonly found among average school learners. Among "exceptional" learners you will find in today's schools are learners with disabilities of various kinds and gifted and talented learners.

- For moral reasons and for reasons associated with important legal requirements, increasingly learners with disabilities are spending time in regular school classrooms. Many of them are never taught in any other setting. As a teacher, you need to understand your legal obligation to differentiate instruction to meet these learners' needs and the specific approaches you might take to assist students with varying kinds of disabilities.

- Programs for gifted and talented students, for the most part, involve them in *enrichment* activities that allow them opportunities to study content in depth and to approach it in novel and creative ways. You may be interested in strategies such as *learning contracts* that allow gifted and talented learners to pursue enrichment activities while, at the same time, mastering content you are providing to other members of the class.

CHAPTER REFLECTIONS

Now that you have read the chapter, think about these questions.

1. What do you see as the major purposes of lessons focusing on topics related to multiculturalism and gender equity? What are some strengths and weaknesses of arguments supporting and opposing increased emphases on these topics?

2. Is it possible for social studies programs to develop students' sensitivity to cultures other than their own and still develop an appreciation for

their own culture? What problems might you face as a teacher in dealing with this potential difficulty, and what ideas do you have for responding to it?

3. When you were in school, were you or any of your friends directed to take certain courses because they were "better for boys" or "better for girls"? If your answer is "yes," how did you or your friends feel, and what are your thoughts about the long-term consequences of this kind of gender-based advice?

4. How well prepared do you feel to modify your learning environment and your instructional practices to meet the needs of students with various kinds of disabilities? Do you have particular concerns about helping learners with certain types of disabilities? If so, how might you go about building your confidence in your abilities to credibly serve these students?

5. Some critics of programs for gifted and talented learners argue that these young people will be successful even in the absence of special programs to serve their needs. It would make more sense, these critics suggest, to put scarce educational funds to work serving needs of less able learners who are less likely to succeed in the absence of help they might receive from school programs designed to meet their unique needs. How do you feel about this issue? Do programs for gifted and talented learners irresponsibly divert funds away from programs for "more deserving" students?

NINE

Social Studies for Limited-English-Proficient Learners

Anne Vega/Merrill

This chapter will help you to:

- Identify kinds of difficulties that limited-English-proficient learners face when they deal with elementary social studies content.

- Point out the importance of considering cultural perspectives of students who are nonnative speakers of English.

- Apply techniques associated with sheltered instruction (specially designed academic instruction in English) when you work with limited-English-proficient learners.

- Explain principles of second-language learning and how they can assist you in developing meaningful instructional programs for nonnative speakers of English.

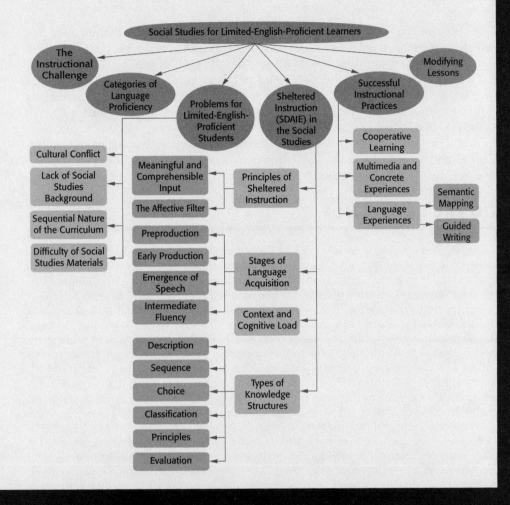

Social Studies for Limited-English-Proficient Learners

- The Instructional Challenge
- Categories of Language Proficiency
- Problems for Limited-English-Proficient Students
  - Cultural Conflict
  - Lack of Social Studies Background
  - Sequential Nature of the Curriculum
  - Difficulty of Social Studies Materials
  - Meaningful and Comprehensible Input
  - The Affective Filter
  - Principles of Sheltered Instruction
  - Preproduction
  - Early Production
  - Emergence of Speech
  - Intermediate Fluency
  - Stages of Language Acquisition
  - Context and Cognitive Load
  - Description
  - Sequence
  - Choice
  - Classification
  - Principles
  - Evaluation
  - Types of Knowledge Structures
- Sheltered Instruction (SDAIE) in the Social Studies
- Successful Instructional Practices
  - Cooperative Learning
  - Multimedia and Concrete Experiences
  - Language Experiences
    - Semantic Mapping
    - Guided Writing
- Modifying Lessons

- Describe examples of specific instructional approaches that you will find useful when teaching limited-English-proficient students.
- Suggest specific ways you can modify lessons to accommodate needs of limited-English-proficient learners.

When you begin teaching, you are almost certain to encounter students who have a primary language other than English. Since the United States dropped the immigration quota sytem in 1965, immigration patterns have changed. In 1980 about 11 percent of the of the U.S. population reported speaking a language other than English at home. By the year 2000, this had grown to over 17 percent. The proportion of English language learners is growing more rapidly than overall student growth (Echevarria & Graves, 2003). In addition, these patterns are not resticted to large urban school districts. Rural and suburban districts are reporting a need to develop programs especially for students at various levels of English proficiency.

These students generally are referred to as *limited-English-proficient students.* Not everyone likes this term. Some critics believe it implies that there is something wrong or deficient with young people who do not speak English as their first language.

A substitute term that some people suggest as a replacement is *English language learner.* Other terms that, from time to time, have been suggested as replacements for "limited-English-proficient" learner include *English learners, nonnative English speakers,* and *second-language learners* (Peregoy & Boyle, 1997). Because you probably will encounter *limited-English-proficient* more frequently than other alternatives and because the federal government uses this term in its official publications, we will use this term throughout the chapter.

THE INSTRUCTIONAL CHALLENGE

What challenges do the presence of limited-English-proficient students pose for you when you teach social studies lessons? In general, most problems you face will relate to difficulties many of these students have in grasping nuances of the English language. Others will relate to difficult cultural interpretations of seemingly common concepts and vocabulary. You need to take into account potential communication difficulties and prepare instructional experiences that give these young people legitimate opportunities to succeed. Many of them are sensitive to their lack of proficiency in English. As a result, they may lack confidence. Experiences they have in school that lead to failure simply reinforce negative self-perceptions and act to interfere with further learning. Because many limited-English-proficient students fail to receive instruction that takes into account their communication difficulties, large numbers of them drop out of school. To be more specific, they leave school early at nearly twice the rate of learners who come to school as native speakers of English (Garcia, 2002).

One of the goals of your social studies instruction is to prepare young people for their roles as citizens. If limited-English-proficient learners do not profit from the school program and drop out before graduating from high school, their potential to contribute as citizens diminishes. As a society, we can ill afford to tolerate this underdevelopment of talent. Happily, there is evidence that if you plan your instructional programs to accommodate special characteristics of limited-English-proficient learners and work hard to support the personal and academic development of these young people, they will profit from your instruction and will be inclined to stay in school (Garcia, 2002).

The issue that needs to be discussed relative to limited-English-proficient students and social studies is whether learning social studies instruction should be delayed until students have acquired English proficiency. This question has taken on increased importance in times of high-stakes testing. Most states have implemented accountability plans and testing for all students. Little or no accommodation is made for individuals with special needs or those with limited English proficiency. This makes it even more important that students learn academic content along with improving their English proficiency.

CATEGORIES OF LANGUAGE PROFICIENCY

Your students need two types of language proficiency to succeed in content-area classes. One of these focuses on the development of basic interpersonal communication skills. This kind of language proficiency allows your students to participate in everyday conversation in informal situations. These skills are what they need to communicate on the playground, in the store, or in other settings.

The second type of language ability they need is cognitive/academic language proficiency. This type of language expertise allows students to understand and communicate in classroom discussions in which the contextual clues are reduced and unique terminology is used.

Individuals who arrive at school with very little English may require several years to acquire a cognitive/academic language proficiency on a par with students who are native speakers of English. As you seek to help students who are not native speakers of English, you need to be alert to a reality that sometimes escapes classroom teachers. Often, these young people will pick up English conversational skills quickly. On the playground or in other informal situations, they may appear to be having little or no difficulty communicating in English. This kind of conversational English expertise, however, by no means suggests these students have sufficient command of the language to grasp the complex ideas that might be included in academic content instruction.

One natural merging of the social studies curriculum and the teaching of limited-English-proficient students is that the study of culture is a major ingredient in language-acquisition programs. Members of your class who are receiving assistance in bilingual programs or limited-English-proficient programs will be the beneficiaries of instructional experiences that tie closely to content of many of your social studies lessons. For example, some of your students who spend part of the day in bilingual classrooms may be able to use content from your social studies lessons as they prepare for assigned conversational exercises. You and the bilingual teachers who work with your students may wish to work together to plan a series of learning experiences that feature social studies content as an integral part of activities designed to improve learners' proficiencies with verbal and written English.

The social studies curriculum has the potential to give students from different cultures insights into values and perspectives that differ from their own. You will find that students from different cultures will be important resources for you as you design lessons that seek to broaden learners' understanding of and appreciation for varying cultures. Lessons that feature many opportunities for students to interact in an active manner function as good vehicles for helping students develop pride in their own heritages and appreciation for the heritages of others.

Another advantage your social studies lessons have for limited-English-proficient students is the opportunity these lessons provide for students to learn and understand basic American cultural values and beliefs. This kind of learning helps limited-English-proficient students sort through the mysterious behavior of others in society and helps them avoid embarrassing mistakes.

Today, many school programs that seek to aid students whose first language is not English are committed to the principle of additive bilingualism. *Additive bilingualism* favors assisting students to master a new language under conditions in which there is little or no pressure on them to diminish their proficiency in their first language or to devalue their primary language and culture. Additive bilingualism contrasts with *subtractive bilingualism,* which includes practices that devalue language skills in the first language and suggest that some negative characteristics associate with the student's cultural group. You will not be surprised to learn that researchers have found that students who experience additive programs have a more positive self-concept than those who experience subtractive programs (Baker, 1996).

PROBLEMS FOR LIMITED-ENGLISH-PROFICIENT STUDENTS

Your limited-English-proficient students face some special challenges when they confront social studies content. One problem is that social studies is a "language-bound" content area. Approaches to social studies often rely heavily on written and oral language to convey concepts, ideas, and key points. This is because many social studies programs rely on the textbook as the major feature for delivering content. It is not just the amount of reading that creates problems; the type of reading also contributes to the difficulty. Much required social studies reading is expository in style and filled with abstract concepts and unfamiliar terms and names. Even students with English as a primary language often find the expository style of social studies textbooks difficult.

Language problems represent just one difficulty that limited-English-proficient learners face. These students also often encounter difficulties with the following:

- Differing cultural backgrounds
- Lack of adequate content background
- Lack of connection with the content-organization pattern used in many social studies curricula
- Difficulty of language used to introduce some social studies content

Cultural Conflict

Anthropologists define *culture* as the attitudes, values, beliefs, and traditions shared by a group of people. Culture gives direction to life and helps people make sense out of their environment. Culture influences how people perceive themselves and others and exerts a powerful influence on the way they behave. All of your students, regardless of race, creed, or social class, come to school as culturally whole individuals with a language and a set of values, attitudes, beliefs, and knowledge.

Limited-English-proficient students often find the dominant classroom culture different and even threatening. The assumptions they make regarding classroom conduct and classroom participation may be different than those of the teacher. For example, they may be afraid to speak up for fear that their command of English is inadequate and they will be embarrassed. This relates to what is known as the *affective filter.* The affective filter hypothesis contends that when such affective factors as anxiety, embarrassment, or boredom are present, the input of new information is blocked. The filter becomes a barrier that hinders learning and progress.

These students may not understand how they are expected to relate to you and to other members of your class. For example, teachers may value questions and comments when students have been taught it is disrespectful to question a teacher.

Some may have cultural backgrounds that focus on individual accomplishments and therefore they are uncomfortable in cooperative learning groups. As a result, your limited-English-proficient learners may find themselves in a situation of cultural conflict where what they have learned in their primary culture is contrary to what you expect of them. They may respond to this situation with withdrawal and a refusal to participate, the opposite of what they need if they are to make progress in learning English.

To overcome these difficulties, you need to try and understand the cultural backgrounds of your students and to use this information to plan culturally responsive instruction. This can begin with such simple steps as learning how to correctly pronounce student names. A Vietnamese student of one of the authors recounted her embarrassment in elementary school when her teacher persisted in incorrectly pronouncing her name. She interpreted this as a rejection of her and her culture and withdrew from interacting with others. Abundant evidence exists that learners who receive instruction consistent with the norms of their home culture will have better learning opportunities (Au & Kawakami, 1994).

Lack of Social Studies Background

Prior knowledge is an important component in learning. New knowledge must be related to previous learning if it is to be meaningful. Many limited-English-proficient students lack the prerequisite social studies knowledge that facilitates success. For example, limited-English-proficient youngsters whose families have come to the United States as immigrants may not have had previous instruction in some topics that are featured in most U.S. social studies programs. When this is the case, these students have no conceptual base they can use as a foundation when you introduce new information to them. You need to be particularly careful to diagnose entry-level understandings of your limited-English-proficient students.

In addition to lacking formal instruction in topics familiar to most American students, recent immigrants to this country may know little about traditions and events that become part of the shared cultural heritage of people who have lived here for some time. For example, some of your limited-English-proficient learners may have no understanding of the familiar American holidays as the Fourth of July or Thanksgiving. References to these holidays may confuse and mystify them. Even some native speakers of English may not be familiar with traditions and events you presume they know. An example of this problem confronted one of the authors when his family moved to Texas. One of his sons had difficulty in a seventh-grade Texas history and geography class because the teacher assumed "everybody knew" about such people and places as Stephen F. Austin and the Alamo. Imagine how much more difficult it is for a child who comes from another culture and who speaks another language!

Finally, even those limited-English-proficient learners who have previous experience in American schools may have difficulty because of an inadequate understanding of central concepts taught in classes. Research indicates that it takes from five to seven years for limited-English-proficient students to achieve a level of language proficiency that is on a par with students who speak English as their first language (Cummins, 1981; Short, 1994). Therefore, even though these students have been exposed to certain ideas and concepts in previous years, there is no assurance that they have comprehended them. This point reinforces the need to monitor carefully what your limited-English-proficient students really know. You need to be cautious about assuming your limited-English-proficient students are comprehending academic content simply because they appear to be proficient users of English in informal, conversational settings.

Sequential Nature of the Curriculum

The social studies curriculum and the texts that accompany it lay out topics in a predictable sequence. This sequence assumes your students have been continuously enrolled in American schools. For example, nearly every school in the United States teaches U.S. history in the fifth grade and the eighth grade. The eighth-grade curriculum usually extends what was taught in the fifth grade. The cumulative and sequential nature of the elementary social studies curriculum may create problems for your limited-English-proficient students. These difficulties are especially serious for these students in middle schools and high schools. Although they may have been in a fifth-grade classroom that studied the early history of our nation, their conceptual understandings are likely to be very limited. Those who did not attend fifth grade in the United States might be totally lost.

To counter these kinds of problems, you have to think beyond the limits of the prescribed grade-level content when you work with limited-English-proficient learners. You need to take time to assess ideas introduced in earlier grades that these students may have missed. Once you identify them, you need to plan ways to fill in the gaps.

Difficulty of Social Studies Materials

Another major problem your limited-English-proficient students may face relates to the nature of the material often used in social studies classrooms. In many social studies classes, much content is embedded in prose materials that some limited-English-proficient learners find difficult to comprehend (Short, 1994). Typically textbooks do not supply the concrete references these students need. As you introduce content to these learners, you need to include visual, hands-on, manipulative kinds of activities.

Social studies lessons often include specialized terminology that can create confusion. For example, the term *strike* as used in a social studies lesson on labor relationships is very different from *strike* as used in describing a battle or a baseball game. Similarly, names and phrases we asume everyone will know can cause them much difficulty. One student who actually knew a fair amount of English when he moved to the United States humorously related how he was totally confused and thrown into a panic when the teacher made a reference to "Scooby-Doo." After a couple of days of intensive searching, he finally got enough courage to ask another member of the class about "Scooby-Doo."

In addition, some of your limited-English-proficient students may have understandings of terms or events that differ from your own. For example, a student coming from another country with a different form of government might interpret the term *democracy* in ways that are unfamiliar to you and to others who have always lived in the United States.

In summary, your limited-English-proficient students may encounter many problems in learning social studies. You can help them overcome many of these difficulties by being sensitive to their needs, working hard to understand their entry-level understandings, monitoring their progress carefully as lessons develop, and creating a responsive climate so they are not embarrassed or afraid to ask questions.

SHELTERED INSTRUCTION (SDAIE) IN THE SOCIAL STUDIES

Mastering academic content while becoming more proficient in English has led to what has been called *sheltered instruction*. This mode of instruction is also called *SDAIE* (specially designed academic instruction in English). Sheltered instruction is a means for making subject matter content, such as social studies, accessible to limited-English-proficient students (Echevarria & Graves, 2003). The primary goal of sheltered instruction is to make subject matter comprehensible.

Making the subject matter equally comprehensible for all students can be especially difficult in diverse classrooms. Limited-English-proficient students come from enormously varied backgrounds. Languages they speak at home are diverse. It is not uncommon for school districts to have students in their district with 20 or 30 different primary languages. It is simply not possible for school districts to employ teachers who are proficient in all of these languages. Sheltered instruction is based on some general principles that allow the diverse population to succeed in learning academic content.

An outline of key points helps to make lessons more comprehensible to LEP students.

KS Studios/Merrill

Principles of Sheltered Instruction

There are several basic principles of sheltered instruction that can help you teach social studies content to limited-English-proficient students. These principles are basically just good teaching. However, they are especially important for these students.

Meaningful and Comprehensible Input A key ingredient in all learning is comprehensible input. This means that individuals learn when they receive information that makes sense to them. For example, even if you are a native English speaker, you would have difficulty making sense out of the content of quantum physics unless you had the required prerequiste knowledge. The material would simply be incomprehensible. No amount of practice or review would help you succeed. This situation is similar to that experienced by many English language learners. The input is simply incomprehensible and they cannot make progress until they are have some understanding of what is being presented.

One of the ways to help make input comprehensible is to simplify it. Think about your speech patterns and the material you present to students. You should attempt to use high-frequency words, eliminate slang, speak in shorter sentences, include more repetitions, slow down your rate of speaking, and have longer pauses (Freeman & Freeman, 2001).

When you provide language instruction to limited-English-proficient students, you follow a pattern similar to that followed by young children when they first learn a language. Infants begin by mastering words and phrases that are important and meaningful to them. Their motivation to learn is driven by their understanding that mastering the language will provide them with specific benefits. Your task in the classroom is to think of ways to "build a case" in support of acquiring better English skills that prompts your limited-English-proficient learners to do the assigned work because they personally value the expertise that they will acquire. If these students see your lessons as too abstract or as dealing with topics too remote from their everyday lives, they are not likely to make desired gains in their proficiency in the use of English or in their mastery of social studies content.

You need to select learning materials for limited-English-proficient students that are at a level of difficulty they can understand. They will have difficulty with material using language that is too abstract or too technical. Ideally, complex content should be introduced in ways that begin with information that these students can comprehend with minimum difficulty. As their levels of understanding increase, then new and more complex information can be introduced. In addition to finding resource materials that carefully move from simple to more complex understandings, you also need to take care to diagnose the entry-level abilities of individual limited-English-proficient students. Your purpose should be to establish as good a match as possible between an individual's entry-level skills and the demands of the learning assignments you will ask this person to complete.

The Affective Filter The social–emotional component of your classroom environment is very important when facilitating the growth of limited-English-proficient students. Specialists who have studied how the social–emotional component of a classroom influences limited-English-proficient learners often refer to the impact of the affective filter on individual learners. As mentioned previously, the *affective filter* refers to the combination of the variables in your classroom related to self-concept, motivation, and fear of ridicule or failure that facilitates or blocks learning. When a student has anxieties related to these variables, the affective filter is likely to be high. When this happens, this student will have trouble processing information that would be comprehensible if the affective filter were lessened.

The same set of classroom conditions may produce different affective-filter levels for different students. Members of your class who have a positive self-concept and who are motivated to learn English tolerate more anxiety and generally move quite quickly through the early stages of language development. On the other hand, those filled with anxiety or fear struggle and encounter frustration as they attempt to learn a new language.

Information about negative effects of high affective-filter levels underscores the importance of actions you take to establish a classroom climate that your limited-English-proficient students will see as safe and encouraging. These students need much positive reinforcement, and you need to take time to celebrate their successes. Any corrections you make must be made in ways that do not cause fear of ridicule or failure.

Stages of Language Acquisition

Understanding the stages of language acquisition will help you to plan and implement meaningful and comprehensible social studies lessons. The following stages are based on what has been termed the "natural approach" to language development (Terrell, 1981):

- Preproduction
- Early production
- Emergence of speech
- Intermediate fluency

Preproduction Preproduction is the first stage of receptive language acquisition. This stage often is found among people from non–English-speaking countries who have recently arrived in the United States. The name comes from the idea that even though these individuals may know a few English words, they are too shy to respond and generally prefer to remain silent. They may point to items, use gestures such as nodding, or use other actions to communicate with others. Somewhat later, they may respond with "yes" or "no" or with single words in their primary language or in English. It is normal for this stage to last for six months or longer. You need to recognize that it is normal for students in this stage to be reluctant to speak, and you should not place undue pressure on them to do so. Speaking will emerge naturally.

At this stage, people focus their attention almost exclusively on aural comprehension. They observe gestures and try to make sense out of the input by using context clues. They guess about the meaning of vocabulary words.

You can assist students at this stage by using contextualized language. Gestures, realia, or pictures provide context clues that can help them find the meaning of what is spoken. You need to speak at a slow rate and to articulate words clearly. Short, simple directions and questions such as, "Point to the _____," or "Is this a _____?" are useful in helping to determine the comprehension of students at this stage. It is also a good idea to write the key terms in an oral presentation on the board or an overhead.

Early Production At the early production stage, individuals begin to try limited production of the language. They are starting to develop basic interpersonal communication skills. They can communicate with short verbal statements that may be memorized to fit certain contexts. The result is that these attempts to produce language contain many mistakes of pronounciation and word usage. These students may have a receptive vocabulary of about 1,000 words but can produce only about 10 percent of these. This stage may last from 6 months to 1 year.

Progress of these students is facilitated when you introduce them to written words and phrases that they find meaningful. They should not be ridiculed because of their misuse of language. Modeling correct usage is an appropriate way to provide correction. The purpose is to help lower the affective filters of these students so that they are not afraid to attempt communication in their new language. Patterned language usage and the use of contextual language is critical. Graphic organizers, story maps, and language experience charts are all helpful to these students as they seek meaning in the language they hear.

Emergence of Speech At the emergence of speech stage, individuals begin to feel more comfortable with the language and are more willing to attempt to speak sentences and participate in conversations. There is a noticeable expansion of comprehension. They have now broadened their receptive vocabulary to about 7,000 words, with about 10 percent production. They still need help in continued vocabulary development and in the development of their basic interpersonal communication skills. This stage tends to last for about 1 year.

Because students are more confident about their abilities to use the new language at this stage than at earlier stages, there are fewer worries about undermining their self-image when correcting their mistakes. At this stage, it makes sense to direct correction efforts to improving their levels of comprehension. Some sensitivity remains regarding their abilities to pronounce all words in the new language correctly, and you have to be careful about drawing too much attention to this kind of difficulty. Graphic organizers are still useful in helping students discover meaning in a text.

Students who have arrived at this stage of language proficiency can begin to participate in group writing activities and in reading literature they select themselves. Your major task is to provide many opportunities for these students to use English in a variety of contexts. They need to participate in discussions and conversations and should be challenged to respond to questions that require them to make fairly lengthy verbal responses.

Intermediate Fluency It often takes students three or four years to arrive at the intermediate fluency stage. These individuals engage in everyday conversations with ease. However, individuals in this stage may be reluctant to speak in front of large groups. They still make some mistakes and, although there appears to be a high degree of fluency, comprehension of content in academic areas such as social studies may be a problem. At this stage, your students have developed a fairly high level of development in the language domains of listening and speaking.

However, they still need assistance in achieving native-like fluency in reading and writing. They can engage in extended discourse and can give oral reports. They can benefit from working with peers on activities requiring reading and writing. These students often enjoy using their new communication skills in small groups. You can challenge these youngsters with tasks requiring quite sophisticated thinking skills. Correcting mistakes can be done in a much firmer manner than in previous stages.

Even at this stage, students' levels of language proficiency in some areas are likely to fall short of that of native speakers of English. Because many of these students speak the language well, you may be tempted to confuse verbal fluency with total mastery of the language.

Context and Cognitive Load

One way of beginning your planning for social studies instruction is to consider the context and the cognitive load of your classroom activities. The four stages of language acquisition emphasize the importance of context in helping your limited-English-proficient students comprehend lessons presented in English. *Context* refers to providing clues or hints that will help individuals identify the message and the key points. *Cognitive load* refers to the complexity or the sophistication of thinking required of students as they attempt to learn new material.

Students at the beginning stages of language acquistion need information presented to them that has a clear context and is relatively undemanding cognitively. This would include such situations as buying lunch, getting materials, following simple directions, and drawing a picture. Social studies content provided to these students needs to be basic, concrete, and embedded in classroom and school activities. You should assume your students have command of only a fairly limited and basic vocabulary.

As students progress, lessons can be presented that are still context dependent but more demanding cognitively; for example, activities that require students to go beyond recall or simple repetition of language patterns, or simple tasks. Social studies lessons you develop for these students still need to be supported by concrete objects for them to handle, pictures, graphs, story webs, games, opportunities for pupils to dramatize events, or possibilities for learners to construct models or objects that draw on the new knowledge they have acquired.

It is important to remember that more cognitively demanding material is generally more interesting and challenging to students. Therefore, you need to try to move to this type of instruction as soon as possible. However, it is important that the cognitive demands not be so high that they raise the affective filter to levels at which progress is blocked.

At the next stage, students begin to comprehend language relatively free of context clues. A good example of a language behavior consistent with this stage is talking on the telephone. When people are on the phone, they must make sense of the message using only what they hear. There are no external context clues. However, often phone messages often do not involve complex or cognitively demanding content. Hence, people often can understand the essence of the message even in the absence of context clues to supplement what they are hearing.

An assignment you give to your students that requires them to follow written instructions is an example of a classroom activity of this type. Unless you choose to supplement these written directions with charts or diagrams, your students receive no additional context clues to help them sort out the meaning of the message. This type of instruction is appropriate for your limited-English-proficient students who have made considerable progress in the speech-emergence phase and who may have reached intermediate fluency.

The highest level of fluency is when students are able engage in activities and tasks that have few context clues and that are cognitively demanding. Activities of this type would be reading the textbook, taking a test, and listening to a speaker or a lecture. In general, students at this level are operating at the level of cognitive/academic language proficiency.

As you plan activities, consider how cognitively demanding the content is and how you can provide context clues for those students who need them. Do not expect students in the early stages of language acquisition to have success in reading the textbook, comphrehending a lecture, or taking a test unless they are provided with an abundance of context clues.

Types of Knowledge Structures

Mohan (1986) proposed a framework that you can use when you are thinking about what types of activities to provide for your limited-English-proficient students. His framework is based on the idea that knowledge is structured similarly from situation to situation. If your students learn types of knowledge that apply to certain situations, then they can transfer this understanding to different content areas to enhance their comprehension of the content. Mohan also states that features of these knowledge structures facilitate transfer of learning from one language to another. There are six key knowledge structures that you can use to help learners organize and simplify content:

- Description
- Sequence
- Choice
- Classification
- Principles
- Evaluation

In working with individual learners, you can frame questions related to each of these categories.

Description *Description* requires students to observe, identify, locate, or describe persons, objects, settings, or events. The types of questions you can ask in this category relate to issues such as who, what, where, and how many. Key visuals are pictures, slides, diagrams, maps, and drawings.

Sequence *Sequence* requires students to organize things in order, note changes over time, follow steps in directions, or note recurring cycles. Questions you might ask in this category include, "What happened first? What was next? What was the order?" Important visuals that can help your students understand issues associated with sequence are flowcharts, time lines, and filmstrips.

Choice Students are required to make decisions, select from alternatives, propose alternatives, and take action when they are confronted with issues associated with *choice*. Some questions you might ask related to choice include, "What are the alternatives? What would you do? What other choices could be made? What would be the consequences?" Important visuals for displaying relationships are flowcharts and decision trees.

Classification Activities associated with *classification* require your students to identify common attributes and group and define items with common characteristics. Lessons associated with classification often feature many characteristics of the concept-formation approach described in Chapter 6. Some classification questions you might ask are, "What things go together? How are these items alike? How are these items different? In what other ways could these things be grouped?" Important visuals include charts, webs, tables, and semantic maps.

Principles Your lessons that seek to familiarize students with *principles* require learners to explain, predict, interpret data, formulate hypotheses, test hypotheses, apply information, and note cause and effect. Questions you might ask related to principles include, "How do you explain that? What caused that? Why do you think it happened that way? What do you think would happen if . . . ? How could you apply this information to solving problems?" Important visuals that can facilitate mastery are Venn diagrams, cycle charts, and data retrieval charts.

Evaluation Learning activities associated with *evaluation* require your students to make a judgment about the worth or relative strength of something. Questions that you might ask include, "Which is the best choice? What evidence would you look at to judge its worth? Which one is right?" Important visuals useful for displaying this type of thinking are rating scales, grids, and rank ordering.

You will find that your students have an easier time dealing with some of these knowledge types than with others. These differences have implications for you as you plan learning experiences for your limited-English-proficient learners. For example, content related to description, sequence, and classification often is not as complex as content related to other knowledge categories. For this reason, you might want to focus on content of this kind when preparing lessons for students at the early production stage of acquiring English. Lessons focusing on more demanding content, for example those associated with categories such as principle formulation and evaluation, need to be reserved for your limited-English-proficient students who have developed to fairly advanced levels of English usage and comprehension. When you take care to match knowledge types to limited-English-proficient students' individual levels of English facility, you improve the prospects that they will master the content. You want these learners to do well because every academic success they experience has the potential to enhance their self-images and motivate them to learn more.

SUCCESSFUL INSTRUCTIONAL PRACTICES

Researchers have identified several common characteristics of classrooms in which teachers have experienced success in their efforts to help limited-English-proficient students. These findings suggest that you should work to place great emphasis on promoting functional communication (1) between you and your learners and (2) from learner to learner. You should strive to organize your instruction around a theme and work to integrate individual subjects in such a way that individual lessons draw content from multiple content sources. You should work to maximize student collaboration on almost all activities and seek to avoid lessons that require students to work alone. You will also find it useful to develop a warm, somewhat informal atmosphere in your classroom. You should draw heavily on instructional techniques such as cooperative learning, and your lessons should feature concrete experiences, multiple examples of new content, and abundant opportunities for students to use their developing English language skills.

Cooperative Learning

Why are cooperative learning techniques so well suited for lessons you develop for limited-English-proficient learners? The strength of cooperative approaches lies in the opportunities they provide for students to interact with each other and to use language in a nonthreatening environment. Students in your class who might otherwise be silent because of embarrassment are more likely to communicate in a small group. In cooperative groups that include both native speakers of English and limited-English-proficient learners, you will find that group members will devise inventive ways to communicate even with members with very limited English language skills. More proficient users of English often work hard to help limited-English-proficient students comprehend the focus content. Additionally, the group rewards that often are a feature of your cooperative learning lessons serve as strong incentives for limited-English-proficient students. Overall, cooperative learning lessons help your limited-English-proficient learners avoid the fear of failure and provide them with opportunities to succeed in spite of their language difficulties.

Cooperative learning approaches facilitate interaction and lead to improved language usage.

Scott Cunningham/Merrill

Multimedia and Concrete Experiences

Because many social studies ideas are communicated in written form and are abstract, you will find that your students benefit when your instruction features concrete experiences and uses various types of media to illustrate new material. Incorporating these elements into your lessons will help all of your students. These features are particulary helpful for your limited-English-proficient students, who often are challenged both by the difficulty of abstract content and by the necessity to learn in a language they do not yet know well.

Many social studies concepts can be conveyed through the use of pictures. You will find it useful to develop a good picture file that features objects and scenes related to social content. Maps, globes, artifacts, and computer programs featuring good visual representations are also useful. One emerging technology that can be useful is the use of *i-movies,* short movies you can create that can be viewed on a computer. You can use visuals and pictures as you create i-movies that can illustrate concepts and ideas. These are often fun to make and can be viewed over and over by students who might need a more concrete representation of social studies concepts. Most students enjoy making i-movies, and you can enlist them to help you prepare a script and film the i-movie.

You may also find it useful to make and provide your limited-English-proficient students with audiotapes of classroom discussions. When these tapes are available, you can assign these students to carrels or other listening stations in the classroom where they can replay the tapes as many times as needed to comprehend the material. You will want to invite them to stop the tape and ask you questions when they encounter words or phrases they do not understand. Sometimes you may find it useful to have a student who is a native speaker of English listen to the tape with a limited-English-proficient learner. Often the native speaker will be able to help the limited-English-proficient learner understand any content that they initially may not grasp.

Flashcards and sentence strips are also useful when you work with limited-English-proficient learners. You prepare flashcards by writing important names, dates, concepts, and terms on blank cards. Sentence strips contain more information than flashcards. Typically, they will include a complete phrase or a brief description of a complete idea. You can use flashcards and sentence strips both to preview new vocabulary terms, concepts, and ideas at the beginning of lessons and to review and reinforce them as you teach lessons.

It can be useful to have your limited-English-proficient students develop their own sets of flashcards. Ask them to prepare cards that feature terms that are giving them difficulty. Over time, each student will have a personal "word bank" that they can use to gain control over new and difficult words and phrases. Flashcards with phrases students master can be discarded and new ones prepared with other unfamiliar and difficult terms. Sometimes your limited-English-proficient learners will want to keep track of the number of flashcards they have discarded or no longer need to use. Such data give them tangible evidence that they are becoming increasingly proficient users of English.

Field trips represent another way you can give your limited-English-proficient students concrete learning experiences. Visits to stores, parks, factories, and the local neighborhood forge links between everyday tasks and language acquisition. Other concrete activities for social studies classes include construction of social studies projects such as models, dioramas, and murals. Dramatizing events and role playing represent still other approaches you can use to embed social studies content in contexts your students will view as "real." For example, the principle of taxation without representation is commonly included in fifth-grade lessons. This abstract idea may prove difficult for second-language learners. If you involve students in acting out a dramatization in which individuals are required to pay a fee with no opportunity for input or discussion, the no-taxation-without-representation idea becomes more concrete, and students will experience less difficulty in grasping the meaning of the phrase.

Language Experiences

Most students have a natural desire to communicate. You need to include abundant opportunities for your limited-English-proficient learners to exercise communication skills (King, Fagan, Bratt, & Baer, 1992). However, many limited-English-proficient students are embarrassed and fearful about communicating either verbally or in writing. Two approaches you can use to encourage limited-English-speaking students to utilize their communication skills are semantic mapping and guided writing.

Semantic Mapping *Semantic mapping* encourages visual representation of connections among ideas. Sometimes it is useful to prepare semantic maps in two stages. The first one is developed from learners' preconceptions about a topic you want them to study. They use this map as they study assigned material. Then, at the conclusion of their study, have them revise the semantic maps in light of what they have learned. To implement this two-part sequence, do the following:

1. Present your students with a focus topic.
2. Ask them to use a brainstorming technique to identify as many ideas as they can think of that are related to the topic.
3. Next, ask them to organize these associations into a graphic that serves as an advance organizer for the material presented.
4. Assign students material related to the focus topic of the semantic map.
5. Once the students have completed their study of the content, ask them to revise their maps and engage them in a general discussion that functions as a review of the material.

Several features of semantic mapping make the approach particularly well suited to the needs of limited-English-proficient learners (Reyes & Molner, 1991). Benefits come because semantic mapping involves your learners in a systematic process that encourages communications of many kinds. These include discourse when the initial semantic maps are prepared, note-taking when content related to the map is studied, and review discussions that occur at the end of the instructional sequence. Figure 9-1 shows an example of a semantic map.

Guided Writing *Guided writing* promotes generation of ideas in a verbal context and integration of reading and writing in social studies. It is a technique that appears to be effective for older elementary limited-English-proficient students (Reyes & Molner, 1991). You begin the procedure by encouraging students to

FIGURE 9-1 • Example of a Semantic Map on the Concept Nomad

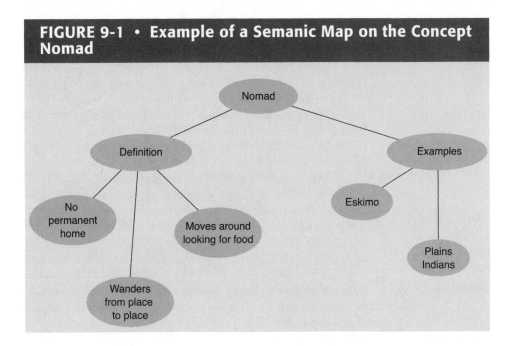

brainstorm their ideas about a topic you provide. Follow with a general discussion of learners' ideas. From information generated during this discussion, you work with your class to prepare a brief outline or web of the topic. Next, assign learners to groups and ask each group to write a short prose article following the outline or web. Limited-English-proficient learners profit from this kind of an arrangement because it gives them opportunities to share their thoughts with others and to learn more about connections between spoken and written English.

After your students complete these short written assignments, quickly read and analyze their initial drafts. Then return them to the groups with a checklist containing suggestions they can incorporate into a more polished second draft.

Next, ask students to read additional material on the focus topic. Ask them to take notes using their outlines or webs as guides to note-taking. Then, have them meet again in their groups to discuss new information they have acquired from their reading. Following their discussions, ask members of each group to generate a revised draft of their papers. Encourage them to incorporate new material and ideas they learned from the reading. The various parts of this activity act to help your limited-English-proficient students to appreciate relationships among the four language arts processes of speaking, reading, writing, and listening.

As your limited-English-proficient students grow more proficient in their use of English, you can encourage them to keep content journals. In these journals, they write down information and questions about the content they are learning. Occasionally collect the journals and look over what students have written. The journals give limited-English-proficient learners more practice in communicating in writing. Also important, they provide you with insights regarding possible misconceptions or "fuzzy" understandings of content.

MODIFYING LESSONS

Although you do need to think about special needs of your limited-English-proficient learners, you do not need to worry that you will be required to generate lesson plans that have nothing in common with those you develop for members of your class who are native speakers of English. Planning for learners with limited proficiency in English largely is a matter of making a few modifications to plans designed for other students. In most cases, these modifications require you only to build in more concrete learning experiences and to provide more examples of new concepts and ideas.

For an example of how you might change a basic lesson to build in learning experiences that are aimed at limited-English-proficient students, see Lesson Ideas 9–1 and 9–2. Lesson Idea 9–1 is the original, unmodified lesson. Lesson Idea 9–2, as you will see, includes more examples of new ideas and features more concrete experiences for learners than does Lesson Idea 9–1. These additions enhance its prospects for success with learners who are still working to develop their English language skills. The kinds of modifications embedded in Lesson Idea 9–2 represent simple adjustments to the original lesson design. Typically you will find that such adjustments can be made fairly easily, and they do not greatly increase the time required to put together your instructional plans.

LESSON IDEA 9-1

TOPIC: Cardinal Directions (Unmodified Version)

OBJECTIVES: Students will use cardinal directions to indicate the relative location of places on a map.

ENGAGING THE STUDENTS: Ask the class, "How many of you have asked someone for directions about how to get somewhere?" Allow students to share stories of problems with unclear directions. Tell them, "Today we are going to learn about something called cardinal directions. These can help you learn how to find places on maps and help you give better directions to people."

DEVELOPING THE CONTENT: Show the class a compass. Ask if anyone knows what it is and how it is used. Illustrate how to find *north* using the compass. Inform them that north is one of the cardinal directions. Show students the compass rose on a wall map. Inform them that the compass rose tells the direction that north is on the map.

Place the map on the floor of the classroom and orient to north using the compass and the compass rose. Ask the class if they know what direction is the opposite of north. Introduce them to the concept of *south*. Point out the direction south on the map. Tell them there are two other cardinal directions. If they are facing north, the direction to their right is east and the direction to their left is west. Have them identify those directions on the map.

For guided practice give them a few questions verbally. Examples might be, "What direction is Chicago from New Orleans? What direction is Los Angeles from New York?"

When it appears that students understand the concept, give them a worksheet that asks them to identify the direction of one place on the map when they are traveling from another.

BRINGING CLOSURE: Ask, "What did we learn today? How is understanding cardinal directions useful?" Evaluate how well students understand the use of a compass and a compass rose to indicate direction from one place to another. They should be able to identify the four cardinal directions and give the correct direction approximately 70 percent of the time.

LESSON IDEA 9-2

TOPIC: Cardinal Directions (Modified Version)

OBJECTIVES: Students will use cardinal directions to indicate the relative location of places on a map.

ENGAGING THE STUDENTS: Take the class outside during the middle of the day. Have students look at directions of their shadows. Show them a compass and ask if anyone knows how it is used. Use the compass to show them that at about noon their shadow points roughly to the north.

DEVELOPING THE CONTENT: Return to the classroom and find north using the compass. Give students a card with *north* printed on it and have them place the card on the north wall of the classroom. Show them a wall map and point out the compass rose. Tell them that the compass rose tells the person using the map which direction on the map is north.

Take the map off the wall and orient it on the floor of the classroom. Ask which direction is opposite of north. Provide one of the students a card with *south* printed on it. Have a student place the card on the south wall of the classroom. With the map on the floor, call on individual students to stand at one place on the map and then walk either north or south. For example, "John, where is Los Angeles on our map? Please stand on Los Angeles. Now walk north from Los Angeles." "Maria, find Chicago on the map. Walk south from Chicago." Call on some of your limited-English-proficient students to perform the task.

Introduce *east* and *west* by giving two students cards labeled *east* and *west*. Ask them to place the cards on the appropriate walls. Repeat the exercise of walking from one point to either east or west. Then mix the directions and have them walk in one of the four cardinal directions.

BRINGING CLOSURE: Ask, "What did we learn today? How is understanding cardinal directions useful?" Evaluate how well students understand the use of a compass and a compass rose to indicate direction from one place to another. They should be able to identify the four cardinal directions and give the correct direction approximately 70 percent of the time. Call on limited-English-proficient students and check for understanding by giving learners such directions as, "Juan, point to the north."

EXTENSION TO THE WEB: The following websites offer information about adapting lessons to meet the needs of limited-English-proficient students.

1. This is the home page for Teachers of English to Speakers of Other Languages. You will find useful information about planning lessons and additional links to other websites.

   URL—http://www.tesol.org/

2. This is the National Clearing House for English Language Acquisition and Language Instruction Educational Programs. We highly recommend this site, as it provides much useful information in preparing lessons for students who are not native speakers of English.

   URL—http://www.ncela.gwu.edu/

Note: As you will note, all modifications are in the "Developing the Content" sections of the two lesson plans. All other components remain the same.

In conclusion, many teachers are nervous about having limited-English-proficient students in their classroom. However, it is highly probable that you will have such students. These students deserve to have a quality education. A little bit of work in modifiying lessons for these students can pay large dividends. Many teachers discover that all students in the class, not just the limited-English-proficient students, benefit from these modifications

KEY IDEAS IN SUMMARY

- The rapid increase in the number of limited-English-proficienct students in public schools has increased the need for teachers who know how to meet their needs. Optimally, lessons you plan for them in content areas such as social studies will be designed in ways that allow them to progress academically and, at the same time, to improve their English language skills.

- Two types of language proficiency are important for students to succeed in content-area instruction. First, your students need to be helped to acquire basic interpersonal communication skills. These skills allow students to interact with others and to communicate their needs, and they usually develop in a relatively short time. Second, you need to help your learners develop their cognitive/academic language proficiency, which allows students to understand a subject when the context clues are reduced and when unique vocabulary is present. Students who are not native speakers of English typically take several years to reach this level.

- Social studies is an appropriate subject for limited-English-proficient students because it has the potential for providing meaningful learning experiences. Teaching in this area of the elementary curriculum allows these students to use their own backgrounds as resources for lessons and to engage in instructional experiences that can help them become more proficient users of English. In addition, these students provide you with a useful resource when you introduce other cultures to students who are native speakers of English.

- Many school programs designed to assist limited-English-proficienct students are based on the principle of *additive bilingualism.* This principle promotes the idea that students should master a new language under conditions in which there is an absence of pressure to diminish their proficiency in their first language. This approach contrasts with *subtractive bilingualism,* which describes practices that devalue students' first language and, often, devalue their home cultures.

- There are potential problems for limited-English-proficient students in social studies classes. Among these difficulties are those associated with (1) the differing cultural backgrounds of these students, (2) students' lack of adequate content background, (3) students' confusion when they encounter unfamiliar patterns of content organization, and (4) the difficult language used to present some social studies information.

- Sheltered instruction, sometimes also referred to as specially designed academic instruction in English (SDAIE), is an approach designed to make content instruction more comprehensible to your limited-English-proficient students. Sheltered instruction involves simplified speech, providing a context for the instruction, focusing on a task–function relationship, and providing for numerous interactional activities.

- When teaching limited-English-proficient students, you need to take action to keep levels of the affective filter low. This term refers to a complex of classroom and personal variables that, when present in significant quantity, can interfere with students' abilities to learn. When the affective filter is low, students' receptivity to instruction increases.

- One of your tasks in planning instruction for limited-English-proficient learners is to design lessons that they find meaningful and comprehensible. In doing so, you need to understand that there is a natural sequence or series of stages people go through as part of language acquisition. These stages are (1) preproduction, (2) early production, (3) emergence of speech, and (4) intermediate fluency.

- Varying the context clues present and the cognitive complexity of your communications with limited-English-proficient students helps them better understand your instruction. *Context clues* refer to hints and suggestions you provide that assist students to grasp key points. *Cognitive complexity* refers to the sophistication levels of thinking required of students as they grapple with new material.

- Certain knowledge structures are similar across situations and share common linguistic features. Teaching these knowledge structures to limited-English-proficient students facilitates their learning across content areas. They include (1) description, (2) sequence, (3) choice, (4) classification, (5) principles, and (6) evaluation.
- Successful instructional practices for limited-English-proficient students involve the use of cooperative learning, multimedia and concrete experiences, and active language experiences, including those involving semantic mapping and guided writing.
- You will not find it difficult to prepare modifications of lessons you develop for native speakers of English that will succeed with limited-English-proficient learners. The modifications typically will include more emphases on concrete learning experiences and will expose learners to more examples of new ideas.

CHAPTER REFLECTIONS

Now that you have read the chapter, think about these questions.

1. What is your position on the inclusion of limited-English-proficient students in social studies classes? Some critics suggest that time required for teachers to respond to needs of these students takes time away irresponsibly from the needs of native speakers of English. What are your thoughts about this concern?

2. What specific things might you do to make certain that the atmosphere in your classroom results in a low affective filter for your limited-English-proficient students? What problems or challenges do you anticipate in establishing such an environment?

3. What are some general principles you will follow in adapting lessons designed for native speakers of English in ways that will enable limited-English-proficient students to profit from your instruction?

4. Have you modified your ideas about teaching limited-English-proficient students as a result of reading this chapter? If so, which of your specific ideas or perspectives have changed?

TEN

Planning for Success

Anne Vega/Merrill

This chapter will help you to:

- Recognize the importance of planning and appreciate that planning facilitates decision making.
- State the function of *aims* in instructional planning and define why controversy often surrounds discussions of aims.
- Describe the relationship of *goals* to *aims* and explain the function of goals in the planning process.
- Define the function of *learning objectives* as guides to lesson planning and point out their relationship to goals.
- Point out important categories of information you need to consider as you begin to plan your instructional program.

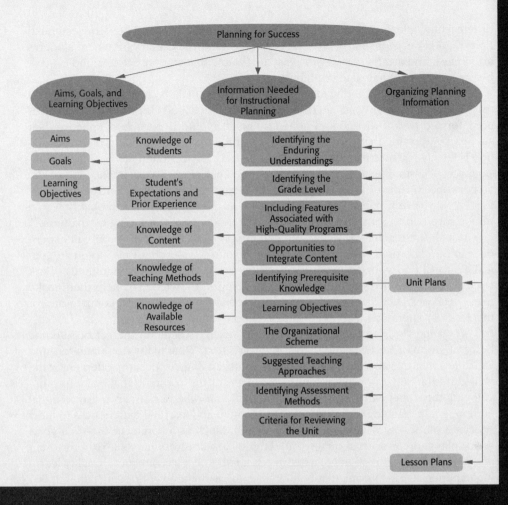

- Describe the function of *unit plans* in the planning process.
- Explain characteristics of *lesson plans*, and point out how lesson plans relate to unit plans.

Skilled professionals perform in ways that make their tasks seem effortless. An artist sitting at an easel creating a beautiful painting gives the appearance of doing something so easy that others may be tempted to pick up a brush and try. You may have personally experienced the frustration of attempting a task that poses few challenges for experts yet is demanding for a novice. The assumption that "this should be easy" reflects an inadequate appreciation for the knowledge this person has and for the years of practice spent perfecting the necessary skill.

This applies to skilled teachers as well. Skilled teachers make teaching look easy and fun. Many of the decisions they make are not noticed by the casual observer. For example, a casual observer does not note the information and non-verbal clues the teacher uses to make decisions about speeding up, slowing down, or reteaching a lesson. Similarly, many do not see or understand how an accumulation of good decisions has led to the current state of the classroom, where students are on task and are interested. It is easy to assume that student interest and on-task behavior is the natural state of affairs.

This has led many individuals, including policy makers, to the conclusion that teaching is easy and anyone can do it. This is not true. Good classroom performances are informed by knowledge and honed by practice. Effective teachers enhance their success by applying this knowledge and skill through careful planning. This preparation is largely invisible to a casual observer. Hence, novices often fail to grasp the importance of instructional planning because it is not seen. For example, one of the authors once overhead a new student teacher comment, "What is so hard about teaching? All you have to know is how to read the teacher's guide!" You probably would not be surprised to learn that this individual dropped student teaching by midterm.

At its heart, teaching is a decision-making process. The success you will experience in the classroom will tie directly to the quality of your decisions. If you are typical, you will find yourself making a decision about once every two minutes (Clark & Peterson, 1986). Experienced teachers have prior knowledge to help them make these decisions. As a novice teacher, your experience is limited. To compensate for this lack of experience, you need to invest more time in planning.

When individuals consider teaching, they usually focus on the act of standing before a group of students and delivering instruction. What many do not understand is that teachers are also designers. Using a sports analogy, spectators often enjoy the skilled performance of a team but are unaware of the planning that went into developing the strategy that provides the foundation for the performance. An essential component of teaching is the design of curriculum and learning experiences to meet specified purposes (Wiggins & McTighe, 1998). Much as a contractor needs a good set of plans to construct a quality building, or a seamstress needs a pattern to cut and sew a good garment, the teacher needs a good plan to construct a quality learning experience. This means that quality teaching is not an "off-the-cuff" affair. It is a planned experience designed to accomplish a specific purpose.

The complexity of the classroom setting adds to the difficulty of your role as a decision maker. Classrooms are public, multidimensional environments where many things occur at the same time (Doyle, 1986). This complexity adds pressures that, if not responded to appropriately, can cloud your judgment and interfere with your ability to make good decisions. Management theory informs us that one way to reduce the complexity and improve decision making is through careful planning. Because learning experiences should be designed to accomplish a purpose, it is important to consider the purposes of education and of the social studies.

AIMS, GOALS, AND LEARNING OBJECTIVES

The design process begins with consideration of purposes. This is what is commonly called *backward design*, which essentially means to begin planning with the end already in mind. The first step involves identifying the desired outcomes of an instructional sequence. Once you are clear about your desired outcomes, you consider the types of evidence or student performances that would indicate that the ends have been achieved, and finally, plan learning experiences will result in these types of evidence or performances (Wiggins & McTighe, 1998). This purposeful design is in contrast to the process used by some teachers of building their program around favorite activities or the content of the textbook.

Identifying desired outcomes is often more difficult than expected. It requires understanding that there are several different types of purpose statements, from very broad statements to those that are quite specific. If education is to accomplish the desired outcomes, these different purpose statements should be related.

At the broadest level, you will find that people have widely divergent views about the purposes of education. For example, as discussed previously, there are many who see the overall purpose of the social studies as transmitting our cultural heritage. Others see this broad purpose as preparing individuals to be reflective and concerned citizens. Varying views on these matters lead to different prescriptions for "good" planning and teaching. For example, if your priority is to help students develop a depth of knowledge of history and the social sciences, your lessons will look quite different from lessons you probably will develop if your highest priority is to develop reflective and concerned citizens.

In practice, your state curriculum standards will exert a strong influence on the priorities reflected in your social studies program. However, as a classroom teacher, you also will have an opportunity to bring your own professional expertise to bear on this issue. You will want to adopt a view that strikes a reasonable balance among accommodating mandated requirements and your understanding of the purposes of the social studies. Once you determine the purposes of your program, your challenge is to engage in planning activities that will enable you to develop day-to-day instructional practices that are consistent with those general purposes.

As you begin this process, you need to understand that purposes are explained in various ways. Individual purpose types vary in degrees of specificity (Moore, 2001). In casual conversation, people often use terms related to purposes, such as *aims*, *goals*, and *learning objectives*, interchangeably. For planning purposes, you will find it helpful to recognize important differences among these terms.

Aims

Aims are the broadest and least specific purpose statements. They are the types of purposes that are the subject of national debate about the overall direction of education and of specific subjects such as the social studies. *Aims* help establish a general orientation for the social studies and help individuals identify priorities for important policy actions such as program development and funding choices. Aims help you to understand what the public expects schools to accomplish. For example, people generally expect students who graduate from high school to be informed individuals who know what is required of citizens living in a democratic society. Because it is assumed that learners will acquire information related to citizenship responsibilities as they go through the entire school program, the "aim" of the social studies program to develop learners' citizenship capacity has implications for teachers at all levels.

The identification of aims prompts controversy. These debates often reflect a clash of philosophies. For example, some people think the primary mission of schools should be to prepare young individuals for life after school. They favor practical courses tied clearly to the world of work. Others feel that school's major mission is to prepare individuals for higher education. This means that students need to learn academic knowledge that may not necessarily have practical value in the workplace. You would expect quite different sets of aims to be favored by partisans of these two views.

Though there are variations from place to place, the following aims for social studies are among those supported in large numbers of American communities (adapted from *History-Social Science Framework for California Public Schools*, 1997):

- Understand the basic principles of democracy
- Understand what is required of citizens in a democracy
- Develop social skills and skills of political participation
- Solve problems and draw conclusions
- Recognize the sanctity of life and the dignity of the individual
- Recognize history as common memory
- Understand world regions and their historical, cultural, economic, and political characteristics
- Understand the basic economic problems facing all societies

Although you need to understand information about these broad aims the state and local school district may have for the elementary social studies programs, aims alone are too broad in scope to provide you much help in planning programs for the students in your own classroom. What is a first-grade teacher to do in contributing to the broad aim of understanding economic problems facing all societies? This is something that we expect graduates of the K–12 system to have, but it does not help a teacher at a specific grade level make decisions about what should be in their curriculum. Teachers need more specific information to decide on and engage in planning that will ultimately help the schools attain the aims that society has for education. This leads to the next level of purpose statements, goals.

Goals

Goals are narrower statements of purpose than are aims. They relate to aims but provide a more precise focus on a specific subject and specific grade level. For example, society has identified as an aim of education that of preparing informed citizens, but how do reading, mathematics, science, social studies, and other subjects contribute to that aim? How does the elementary school curriculum contribute? If, say, you are teaching third graders, the goals for third-grade social studies should identify the specific skills and content that you should teach that will contribute to learners' understanding of general aims such as producing good citizens or helping individuals understand enduring economic issues.

Individual school districts frequently establish goals for individual grade levels and subjects. School boards, curriculum committees, and textbook-selection committees may participate in the process of establishing them. They generally do this with reference to the "frameworks," "standards," or "essential elements" established by the state. Local officials translate these into specific programs for their local district. You will often find school district curriculum guides that list the goals for each grade level and each subject. The following are examples of goals that you might find in the social studies section of such a guide.

Students are expected to:

- Learn basic geographic features of the state
- Know the responsibilities of a citizen
- Understand that history is an interpretation of past events
- Grasp basic economic concepts, including *scarcity*, *specialization*, *trade*, and *economic interdependence*
- Explore the relationships of people in homes and schools
- Gather information from maps
- Compare lifestyles of people living in different regions
- Analyze contemporary events

Social studies goal statements help you to define your general responsibilities in teaching lessons directed at a particular group of learners (first graders, second graders, and so forth). In recent years, there has been a tendency for state and local school district officials to define goals in terms of learning outcomes as part of a general orientation that often is called *outcomes-based education* **(OBE).** This represents a shift from an emphasis on inputs, such as the types of material available or the experiences students have had, to a focus on outcomes that are defined in terms of what new knowledge or skill students have acquired as a consequence of their exposure to materials or learning experiences. Regrettably, in some cases OBE outcome goals have been defined narrowly in terms of changes in learners' standardized test scores. For example, a school district might establish as a goal that "the average scores on the annual fifth-grade assessment will increase by 5 percent." The flaw in this reasoning is that the test is not a goal. A valid test is only one indicator that the student has accomplished an important goal. Those who see the test scores as a goal are assuming that the standardized test is a valid indicator of the achievement of students in relationship to all important social studies goals. This may be an incorrect assumption. The test may have a very poor match with the actual goals of the curriculum and therefore be a flawed indicator of goal achievement.

In addition, there are several things that can be done to improve test scores that have little to do with helping students accomplish the aims that society has for the schools and for state and district goals. Thus, the scores may reflect skills in test taking rather than be valid indicators of the accomplishment of important outcomes.

Another issue related to this narrow interpretation of OBE is that it provides you as a teacher with little guidance related to how to design and deliver instruction that will result in improved standardized test scores. Goals associated with OBE are much more helpful when they identify particular topics lessons should address. To better grasp this point, consider the situations facing two fourth-grade teachers. Both are in school districts that, among other things, want fourth-grade teachers to help learners to develop an understanding of their state's geography. One of these teachers finds this as one of the outcome goals in the district's program guide:

At the end of the school year, on average, fourth graders will score at least 5% higher on a test over state geography than on a test given at the beginning of the school year.

The second teacher finds this outcome goal:

Fourth graders will identify similarities and differences among geographic features found in sections of the state that lie west of the Missouri River and east of the Missouri River and will suggest how these differences affect how people live in these two areas of our state.

Clearly, the teacher with the second outcome goal has a much better target for instructional planning. It suggests a need for lessons focusing on geographic features and on how different geographic features affect people's lives. The first teacher must guess about what kinds of content might be addressed on the standardized tests. As written, this outcome goal provides little practical guidance for teachers as they go about the business of planning units and lessons.

Even well-crafted goal statements describe distant learning achievements—kinds of understandings students typically will be expected to have at the end of the school year. As a teacher, you are faced with deciding where to start and how to sequence the material so that, in the end, your students will accomplish the specified goals. You are faced with the need to plan instruction for every day you meet your class. You need short-term targets for your daily lessons that provide guides for daily teaching much as goals provide guides for the yearlong program. This leads to the third level of purpose statements, learning objectives.

Learning Objectives

Goals provide important guidance to you as you plan units and lessons, but they are still quite broad in scope. They suggest general patterns of learning and abilities that your students will have at the end of a specific time frame such as an entire year of exposure to your teaching. Learning objectives provide you and your students with shorter-term targets. *Learning objectives* reference outcomes that comprise important parts of the learning goal to which they relate. To better appreciate this connection, let's look again at the second outcome goal introduced in the previous section:

Fourth graders will identify similarities and differences among geographic features found in sections of the state that lie west of the Missouri River and east of the Missouri River and will suggest how these differences affect how people live in these two areas of our state.

This goal references a broad range of content. For example, it obligates you to help your students understand general characteristics of different geographic features, locations of these features within your state, and possible influences that individual geographic features have on people's lives. In addition, the goal suggests that you need to help students develop thinking skills that will allow them to analyze and interpret data. Collectively, this goal imposes a set of obligations that will require many lessons and, probably, multiple units of work. You will need to develop numerous learning objectives to guide your development of instructional experiences related to this goal. Among others, you might develop objectives such as these:

Students in my class will:

- Recognize characteristics of physical features, including hills, mountains, plains, plateaus, valleys, rivers, and lakes
- Point out how physical features at a particular place influence how people make a living, the kinds of housing they occupy, and the kinds of recreational activities they pursue
- Describe differences in physical features in areas of the state that are located (1) west of the Missouri River and (2) east of the Missouri River
- Compare and contrast similarities and differences in how people make a living in areas of the state that are (1) west of the Missouri River and (2) east of the Missouri River
- Analyze differences in crops grown (1) west of the Missouri River and (2) east of the Missouri River

When you develop learning objectives, you need to remember that their focus should be on your students and their learning, not on the activities you plan or on the kinds of experiences learners will have as you teach your lessons. For example, "Read the chapter on the westward movement" is a student activity, not a learning objective. A learning objective addresses the question, "What should the student know or be able to do as a result of reading this chapter?"

Similarly, you want to avoid preparing learning objectives that focus on what you intend to do as you present your lesson. For example, the statement, "I will discuss the roles of community helpers," is a teacher activity, not a learner outcome. A learning objective would focus on what the students will learn as a result of the discussion. A basic question that can help you keep a clear focus on the purpose of learning objectives is, "How will I know students have learned what I want them to learn?"

You will find that your teacher colleagues vary in how they write learning objectives. Some are satisfied with quite general statements that suggest little beyond the general kinds of behaviors they expect students to demonstrate. Others prefer a format that not only specifies what students should be able to do as a result of their exposure to a given block of instruction but also describes conditions under which they will demonstrate the behavior and an acceptable proficiency level.

Learning objectives provide guidance for you as you go about the business of making instructional decisions. When written clearly with a focus on learning outcomes or the ends of instruction, they help you make decisions about the kinds of materials students need to encounter, the types of activity they should experience, and the amounts of time you should allocate for individual lessons. For example, if a learning objective requires students to demonstrate understanding by applying only low-level knowledge or comprehension thinking, you will need to (1) present learners with the information to be learned and (2) engage them in activities that, when completed, will provide you with evidence that they have accomplished this objective. Time allocation for a lesson of this type will be less than for lessons that require students to struggle with sophisticated analyses of complex information. When you design more intellectually challenging lessons, you will have to do more than merely provide time for members of your class to acquire and practice information. You also will need to provide them with instruction designed to teach them how to analyze the material. You will have to provide opportunities to practice these skills and, consequently, you will find it necessary to set aside more class time than for lessons that place fewer intellectual demands on your learners.

An important function of learning objectives is to communicate to learners what is expected of them. Providing students with written or verbal learning objectives at the beginning of a lesson helps maximize learning. This practice communicates to your learners what is important and helps them understand what they must do to be successful (Moore, 2001).

Learning objectives can also help you communicate with parents and others about your instructional intent. Much more is communicated about expectations when you are able to tell parents, "In social studies, members of the class will be expected to state economic differences between the North and South that contributed to the outbreak of the conflict," than when you simply advise them that "the class will be reading about the Civil War." The objective provides guidance to parents and others who are interested in helping members of your class succeed at school.

Learning objectives are especially useful to you when you design units of instruction and lessons for your own class. Understanding with clarity what students should be able to do allows you to explore alternative evidence that will indicate that individual students have learned. For example, you may well have students in your class who have limited proficiency in English. For these learners, you need to devise ways for them to demonstrate their learning that do not rely heavily on their ability to read or speak English (see Chapter 9). You might ask them to draw an illustration or state a concept orally instead of taking a more traditional test that would require them to write definitions or match a concept with an appropriate definition.

The following are examples of learning objectives for elementary social studies:

- Define the roles of different people in the community.
- Label the regions in the state and describe them.
- Explain the basic ideas in the Declaration of Independence.
- Demonstrate respect for the opinions of others.
- Describe steps in a procedure that will lead to the solution of a problem.
- Define some concepts associated with scarcity.
- Predict an outcome by applying generalizations to new problems.
- Write questions that can help lead to the solution of a problem.
- Distinguish between *fact* and *opinion*.
- On an essay test, identify at least three advantages and three disadvantages the British had at the time the Revolutionary War began.

You will find it easier to develop lesson objectives from some social studies goals than from others. For example, you will discover that you have to devote considerable time and thought when you prepare learning objectives for lessons that focus on inquiry or problem solving. In lessons you develop around these objectives, there may not be specific knowledge outcomes that can be easily identified. Rather, your focus is on how learners can use the processes of inquiry or problem solving. Verbs such as *compare, construct, apply*, and *explain* can be helpful as you develop learning objectives for these more complex goals.

It is important that you *do* take time to develop learning objectives that focus on developing students' more sophisticated learning abilities. You cannot let ease of development drive your preparation of learning objectives. If you do that, your program will provide few opportunities for learners to stretch their intellectual capacities. Because one important purpose of the social studies program is to prepare students for the challenges of citizenship by developing their thinking powers, instructional programs that fail to engage students in higher-level thinking do a disservice to young people.

INFORMATION NEEDED FOR INSTRUCTIONAL PLANNING

Researchers find that actions you will take as a teacher to design your instruction help you develop a mental picture of what you will emphasize in your lessons (Clark & Peterson, 1986). Planning aids you in identifying routines to be used in setting up and managing the classroom environment, selecting key points to be emphasized, determining the activity sequence you will follow, and thinking about probable student responses to various parts of the instructional experience. The more detailed and accurate the image you get from your planning, the higher the likelihood your instruction will yield learning.

Good planning takes into account information from several distinct categories (Savage et al., 2006):

- Students to be taught
- Students' expectations and experience
- Specific content to be introduced
- Alternative instructional approaches
- Available resource materials

Knowledge of Students

The contemporary student population includes young people who have diverse interests, motivations, and abilities. With increased mobility, diversity of student population can be found even in rural areas that were at one time fairly homogeneous. You will find a surprising range of differences even among students in a single classroom. These differences need to be taken into account when you engage in instructional planning. For example, you will want to develop lessons in ways that will allow as many of your learners as possible to achieve your learning objectives. This kind of success engenders self-confidence and is a powerful motivator.

Working with other teachers in sharing information about student resources and teaching approaches is invaluable.

Bob Daemmrich/PhotoEdit Inc.

Students' Expectations and Prior Experience

The personal expectations and prior experiences of your students influence their academic performance. Young people who are confident of their abilities and who believe that learning is important react differently to instruction than do students who lack these characteristics. This issue is particularly of concern in the social studies component of the elementary program. Many of your students, initially at least, may not think social studies content is interesting, important, or personally relevant.

Because of past experience, some of them expect social studies learning to be boring. These negative attitudes may have been shaped by the kinds of social studies instruction that they received in earlier grades. For example, some learners may have experienced frustration in dealing with lessons that failed to take into account their entry level of knowledge and were therefore unable to succeed. This possibility underscores the importance of taking time to determine what your students already know before you start planning new instructional experiences.

You may find that members of your class vary tremendously in their levels of social studies understanding. With the mobility of the population, it is likely that some youngsters in your class will have lived in various parts of the world. These young people may know far more about locations and characteristics of distant places than do other members of your class. At the same time, you may well have students in your room who have had very limited exposure to the world outside their own neighborhood. One of the authors once taught a group of students who had never seen an ocean. During a lesson, it became apparent that many in the class had the mistaken idea that a person could stand on a Pacific beach, look west, and clearly see the shores of Asia on the other side. Learners who start with misinformation of this magnitude are almost certain to experience difficulties grasping more sophisticated content—a situation with a high likelihood of producing failure, diminished levels of self-esteem, and low opinions of the social studies.

Diversity of students' backgrounds and differences in their initial attitudes toward the social studies should make attention to learner differences a priority in your instructional planning. Over time, instruction you plan and deliver that takes into account these differences will give members of your class real possibilities to succeed at tasks you embed within your social studies lessons. In time, the cumulative effect of well-designed and interesting instruction that leads to academic success acts to promote positive learner attitudes. If your lessons respond well to learner differences, you may find that members of your class who were indifferent (at best) to social studies lessons at the beginning of the year may rank the subject among their favorites by the end of the school year.

Knowledge of Content

Instructional planning requires you to identify specific elements of content that you want your students to learn. Listing general topics to be covered will not suffice. Careful plans deal with much more detailed information about key ideas and concepts that you will emphasize.

Knowledge of content to be taught requires more than identifying particular items of information. Lessons develop material in a sequential fashion. Therefore, you have to think about how new material can best be sequenced to promote learning. Sequencing decisions requires careful consideration of the characteristics of the students you will be teaching. The sequence of material provided in a textbook may or may not be appropriate for your objectives and for your students. A common barrier to effective lesson planning is the assumption that the textbook authors know best how their content should be organized. Remember that the text should be just a tool, not a prescription. As a professional, you have the responsibility to develop a plan that best responds to the needs of the young people who will be doing the learning.

Knowledge of Teaching Methods

Identifying the instructional approaches you will use is an important part of the planning process. This is the "fun" part of planning. Most teachers enjoy thinking of interesting activities they think will engage the students in the lesson. However, there is a danger here. You do not want to choose activities simply because you like them or think they would be well received by your learners. Although you do want to consider student motivation, you also want to make sure that the instructional approaches you select are appropriate given the purposes and the overall plan of your unit.

Usually, you will incorporate several techniques within a given instructional unit. Variety acts as an important student motivator. Also, certain learning objectives may be better served by some instructional techniques than by others. Your primary consideration in choosing a learning activity is how well it will help members of your class achieve the objectives.

In identifying specific techniques, consider the characteristics of the students, the potential of individual techniques to prompt their interest, the kinds of behaviors suggested by the learning objectives, and the specific nature of the content to be covered. For example, if you were considering developing an instructional sequence focusing on how a bill becomes law, your thinking might run along these lines:

> Well, I could have them just read about it in the text, but I don't think so. That's pretty dull. Besides, some of these students aren't good readers. Also, the text doesn't give them much feel for the drama of argument and debate that's part of the legislative process. So, there are three strikes against that idea: (1) boring; (2) some of them can't do it; and (3) it will give them an incomplete idea of the process.
>
> Okay, then, how about a simulation? They'll probably like it . . . more opportunities for them to talk. They always like to talk. It will also give the slower ones a chance to pick up on ideas from some of the more able kids. Finally, it will get them actively involved in debates . . . a pretty good stand-in for the kind of thing legislators do. I think we'll do the simulation.

Knowledge of Available Resources

The kinds of available instructional-support resources strongly influence what you choose to do. You need specific information about the availability of equipment (computers, projectors, televisions, videocassette players, etc.), appropriate instructional space (rooms with appropriate work spaces, rooms where specific equipment is located, etc.), learning-support resources for students (maps, globes, supplementary texts, library books, simulation games, etc.), and, as needed, human resources (special outside speakers, school librarians, etc.).

Planning resources that you may use while designing instructional experiences include district-level social studies curriculum guides and state social studies program frameworks and standards. These documents provide guidance regarding what content should be taught at each grade level and how it might be sequenced. Sometimes standards documents include lists of useful instructional-support materials and suggestions regarding teaching techniques.

ORGANIZING PLANNING INFORMATION

Once you have gathered information about learners, content, alternative instructional techniques, and available resources, you must organize it into a plan of action. Whether this plan is prepared in a careful, formal written form or drafted as a sketchy outline is largely a function of experience. In general, as a novice teacher, you will benefit from committing more time to the process of organizing planning decisions in a formal way. This process will help you to identify areas in which more specificity is needed. With experience, you will develop knowledge that will help you anticipate what needs to be included, and you will be able to use brief notations to remind you of what needs to be done.

Instructional planning goes forward at several levels of specificity. The first level of planning may be long-term planning focusing on the academic year. This may be a general outline of what is to be covered during the year. It is usually the result of reviewing district-level goals and textbooks and any associated state curriculum standards. At this point, a sequence of topics for the year is identified and time allocations are determined for each component of the yearlong plan. Your long-term plans must take into account special circumstances such as school holidays and testing schedules. A good yearlong outline will help ensure that you don't arrive at the end of the school year only halfway through the required curriculum.

The next level of long-term planning is the preparation of unit plans. Unit plans feature a more specific breakout of each of the components of the yearlong outline.

Unit Plans

Unit plans function as building blocks of your program. You will develop your individual lessons from unit plans. A **unit plan** is a set of related lessons organized around big ideas that can be applied to a variety of times and places. Units generally cover a time period of approximately two to four weeks of instruction. Your instructional unit describes the organizational scheme for the content to be taught and identifies teaching approaches you will use in introducing material to students. Therefore, you will need approximately 10 to 12 unit plans to cover the academic year.

Planning for units should prompt you to think about how content in the social studies might be integrated with information in other subject areas. For example, social studies unit topics may lead you to identify books members of your class can read as part of their reading lessons. Often you will find it possible to tie objectives from mathematics, science, music, and many other learning areas to content organized in your social studies units. These days, when more is expected of schools than there is time to fulfill the expectations, it is important to integrate your curriculum. The social studies is an excellent subject to use as an integrating core.

Instructional units must be planned in advance. Often, you will need to gather materials and make special arrangements. For example, you may have to order videotape titles, get approval for proposed field trips, and obtain commitments from speakers. As a rough guideline, it is a good idea to plan an instructional unit at least a month before you begin to teach it.

Unit planning typically begins with a consideration of content that state or local authorities require at a given grade level. After you identify this "must-be-included" information, you go on to select additional content.

However, this knowledge needs to translated into what Wiggins and McTighe (1998) call "enduring understandings." Enduring understandings are those big ideas or generalizations that connect the content. As the name implies, they are ideas that transcend time and space. They go beyond discrete facts and focus on concepts and the relationships among concepts that help us understand why things are the way they are and help us make predictions about the future. The enduring understandings ought to be broad enough to have transfer value; that is, they can be applied to situations and events other than the specific content or time being studied. For example, at a recent meeting an historian was lamenting that students in high school did not seem to understand the differences between the first and second battles of Manassas (Bull Run) during the Civil War. No doubt this is true. But one should ask the question, "Why is it important for individuals to know the difference?" There is so much specific information in history that it is unrealistic for any individual to have absolute command of facts about a given time period. The case could be made that understanding the differences between the two battles was important because this information was related to a larger, enduring understanding that everyone should know. In this particular case the differences between the two battles can be connected to the enduring understanding that people often romanticize war and see it as a glorious adventure until they actually view the death and destruction. In the first battle, people drove out in their carriages dressed in their best clothes to get a good vantage point to see the battle from much as they would an athletic event. They were soon fleeing back to Washington D.C. horrified and shaken by what they had seen. By the second battle, they had no such illusions. Throughout history we can find incidents of armies marching off to war full of optimism with flags flying only to be disenchanted when they actually viewed the tragedy up close. Perhaps we would have fewer wars if people could truly comprehend this enduring understanding.

By the end of the unit, you want members of your class to grasp the enduring understandings or generalizations and the embedded concepts. This is the beginning of the backward planning model. What are the enduring understandings or generalizations that you want students to know by the end of this particular unit?

Once you have identified enduring understandings or focus generalizations, you are in a position to ask these important questions when you design your individual lessons: "How will this particular lesson contribute to student learning of the enduring understanding?" "How should my lessons be sequenced so that they build in a logical manner to develop this understanding?"

Generalizations or enduring understandings help make the content meaningful to your students. If students believe that what they are learning relates to something useful and important, they are more likely to be motivated to learn the material. For example, learning the enduring understanding related to how individuals romanticize war may help them understand the attitudes of some individuals related to the war in Iraq.

Focusing on generalizations helps you avoid teaching unrelated facts for which students see no purpose. Too frequently, elementary students (and even college students) see social studies as a jumble of facts to be memorized and soon forgotten. One author once overhead a comment from a parent who had little use for the social studies program in the school: "I never saw the purpose of a subject that required kids to waste time memorizing names of Civil War generals." This parent's attitudes probably were shaped by a recollection of a social studies program that was excessively fact based and failed to develop any enduring understandings.

Good generalizations or enduring understandings also help you be creative as you think about accommodating students' interests and responding to their individual differences. Suppose you select an enduring understanding that focuses on factors that led to conflict in the Civil War. Some students may not have the reading skill or the prior knowledge to help them make sense out of the textbook. If you focus on the enduring understanding rather than the textbook chapter, you can creatively think of other examples, within their experiences, that can help them learn the important idea. For students with different learning styles, you can identify alternative ways for them to learn generalizations or enduring understandings and demonstrate their learning. Some members of your class may reach an understanding through reading, others through dramatic enactments, and still others through group investigations. Organizing your instruction around focus generalizations or enduring understandings opens the prospect for multiple ways of learning that go well beyond lessons that focus simply on "reading the text and answering the questions."

One of the basic questions you might be asking is, "Where do I find these enduring understandings?" There are several sources you can consult as you seek to identify enduring understandings or guiding generalizations for your unit plans. Some state curriculum documents and many locally developed units will identify the generalizations or main ideas that organize the content. You can also scan your text with the purpose of identifying the author's main points. These main points are often stated near the beginning of paragraphs. (The text's table of contents will also reveal the sequence of main ideas in outline form.) These points usually can be converted into generalizations or enduring idea statements that you can use as a focus for units and lessons.

Once you have identified the enduring ideas or generalizations, you need to identify the evidence that would indicate that students have learned them. This is the assessment component. It is important to consider assessment at the beginning of your planning so that you can purposely build learning activities and learning sequences that focus on how you will be assessing students. It is best to plan assessment when you plan the unit so that when you administer your assessment procedures, you will be evaluating the important content that you have taught. The assessment evidence can include informal assessment such as student work samples, as well as more formal ones such as teacher-made and standardized tests. Keep in mind, however, that many standardized tests do not assess understanding of enduring ideas. Therefore, when thinking about evidence that students have learned, you should consider multiple and alternative methods of assessment (see Stiggins, 2005, for examples).

Wiggins and McTighe (1998) suggest that several facets of assessment should be considered when gathering evidence that a person has learned. Among those facets, they state, is that someone who really knows material should be able to explain it, interpret it, apply it, and place it in perspective. When considering the types of evidence you would accept that someone has learned material you should consider these facets and provide opportunities for students to explain what they have learned, interpret what they have learned into a new context, apply it to a new situation, and explain the importance of what they have learned.

The next step is to identify the content and the sequence of activities that you predict will be beneficial in helping students learn the enduring understanding or focus generalization. In essence you are engaging in problem solving. You are starting with an end point—learning a generalization or enduring understanding—and predicting what sequence of activities will result in the desired outcome.

Guillaume (2000) suggests developing a planning web or a semantic map to facilitate this process. A *planning web* is a chart in which the focus generalization is identified in the middle of the page. The related concepts are identified and connected to the generalization. Examples of information that illustrate some of the concepts are identified and added to the web. Figure 10-1 presents an example of a planning web. Once you have completed a planning web, you can refer to it as you think about how to sequence information in your unit.

Wiggins and McTighe (1998) suggest using the acronym "WHERE" as a guide to planning a unit. The questions making up this acronym are as follows:

W—Where is the unit headed? What will be the criteria by which student learning will be evaluated?

H—How can students be *hooked* though engaging and provocative entry activities?

E—What activities will allow the students to *explore* the enduring understandings and essential questions?

R—Where will students *reflect, rethink* and *revise*?

E—How can students *exhibit* their learning?

Keeping questions like this in mind during planning can help you be creative as you think about the variety of activities that you will have in your unit. These questions serve as criteria for making sure that you include important elements of the unit.

FIGURE 10-1 • Example of a Planning Web for a Unit on "Families"

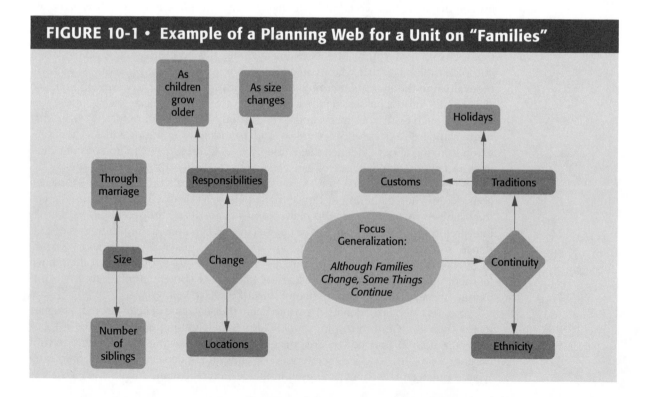

Sequence decisions require you to determine the order in which you will introduce content elements. In addition to considering the issue of sequence, you need to develop learning objectives for the unit and to suggest some activities that have potential to help students master the new content. You want to embed in the activities information about some social studies skills students will need to apply as they work with unit content (for example, skills associated with working with maps and globes and with conducting research). If there are ways to include content from other subjects, these cross-disciplinary ties need to be mentioned in your unit plan. You also need to consider how to associate values and affective outcomes with your unit.

At this point you will want to consider the instructional materials that you can use to teach the individual lessons. It is especially critical to do this so that you can obtain in advance any materials that you need to order.

Although we have presented this process as a linear one, in reality, unit planning is more of a start-stop-review-modify-start-again process. For example, you may identify an activity appropriate for teaching a given concept and then realize that there are some prerequisite activities needed before students can engage in the activity. You may need to go back and change the sequence. Or, you may discover that some of the material you planned to use is not available, and you may need to go back and develop a new activity. In other words, unit planning is not a nice, neat, step-by-step process. You need to be flexible and prepared to make adjustments.

Components of unit plans vary. Many of them include elements such as these:

- The enduring understandings to be learned
- The grade level for which the unit is intended
- Descriptions of features associated with high-quality programs
- Descriptions of opportunities to integrate content
- Identification of prerequisite knowledge
- Specification of learning objectives
- Unit organizational scheme
- Suggested teaching approaches
- Methods for assessing student learning of the content
- Criteria for reviewing the unit

You may format your units in various ways. Good formats make clear the relationships among learning objectives, teaching approaches, and needed materials.

Identifying the Enduring Understandings Identifying enduring understandings helps other interested parties identify what students are expected to achieve. It also serves as criteria for reviewing the activities included in the unit. Do they contribute to learning the enduring understandings?

Identifying the Grade Level Specification of the grade level gives important information about the target audience for the instructional program your unit is intended to serve. Identification of the intended grade level early in unit development helps you to keep a focus on the learners who will benefit from your instruction.

Including Features Associated with High-Quality Programs You want your unit to include elements that build students' understandings in the areas of social science and history, citizenship, global education, and problem solving. To ensure that attention is given to each of these four critical areas, you should think about questions such as these as you develop your units:

- What will be the citizenship outcomes? What knowledge, skills, values, and decision-making opportunities associated with citizenship will be included?
- What will be the history and/or social science outcomes? What generalizations, concepts, values, and skills associated with history and/or the social sciences will be emphasized? It is useful to remember the structure of knowledge presented earlier in the text (see Chapter 5). Generalizations that you want students to know as the result of the unit provide the basic organizing foundation.
- In what ways will unit contents help learners understand connections between our society and those in other parts of the world?
- What problem-solving opportunities will be provided? Having a good unit plan will allow you to identify those points at which students can be involved in problem solving and decision making.

Opportunities to Integrate Content   Social studies instruction provides you with good opportunities to integrate content from many school subjects. To take advantage of these possibilities, as you develop your units you need to think about how you can weave in content from reading, mathematics, science, language arts, music, art, and physical education.

Identifying Prerequisite Knowledge   When you begin to plan a unit, you start with certain assumptions about the learners to whom you will teach this new material. Because you may not be the only teacher who ultimately uses your unit as a basis for preparing lessons, you need to make clear your assumptions about your targeted group of learners. This information will help other teachers decide whether the unit content might be appropriate for their own students.

Learning Objectives   Recall that *learning objectives* are succinct statements that specify what students will be able to do as evidence that they have mastered unit content. Including learning objectives in unit plans helps you keep a clear focus on important instructional priorities.

You need to arrange learning objectives in an appropriate sequence. Those listed first should identify content introduced at the beginning of the unit. They may tie closely to initial learning activities that are designed to prompt students' interest in the general content of the unit. Your subsequent learning objectives will focus on the main body of content. The final learning objectives will be broader in scope and will normally relate to the higher levels of thinking that call on learners to synthesize, apply, and extend content introduced throughout the unit.

The Organizational Scheme   As stated earlier, there is no single way to organize a unit. The scheme you adopt should be one that you believe will work for you. However, there are some basic elements that you will want to consider as you decide on features of the organizational scheme you select.

First, units need to be organized so that relationships among their parts are clear. For example, it is most useful if the relationship between an objective and a learning activity is easily recognizable. You also want to be clear about which materials are needed for which part of the unit. Some unit developers choose to present all of the objectives, needed materials, and potential learning activities in separate lists. The problem with this approach is that it is easy to miss teaching some important learning objectives and overlook needed material until it is too late.

The organizational plan illustrated in Figure 10-2 is one that functions well. An outline or other general unit organizational plan need not be long. Often, you will find that three or four pages will suffice. You can keep in a file specific information you will need when teaching unit content (assignments, pictures, artifacts, outline maps, handouts, and so forth) and bring it out for use at appropriate times.

Suggested Teaching Approaches A unit is not just a collection of lesson plans. The goal of the unit is to provide a direction for you as you plan individual lessons.

FIGURE 10-2 • Unit Example

Unit Topic: We Live in Families

GRADE LEVEL: FIRST GRADE

Social Science Generalizations and Understandings:
The main focus generalization for the unit is *Although families change, some things continue*. It focuses on the history concepts of *change and continuity*.

Students will begin to develop the skills of *interviewing others* and *recording information*. Students will also acquire simple geographic knowledge related to *locating places* and *plotting information* on maps. The concepts of *movement* and *location* will be introduced. The anthropological concept of *ancestor* and the sociological concept of *norms, traditions, rules,* and *authority* will also be included.

Citizenship Opportunities:
Students will be helped to develop citizenship understanding by leaning how to work with others, the role of rules, and how authority operates in families.

Global Awareness:
Students will be introduced to family practices in selected other countries and will engage in simple discussions in which they will learn similarities and differences of those practices from those observed in their own families.

Content Integration:
The unit will integrate reading through the use of some children's literature. Learners will also apply their writing skills when they print vocabulary words and short simple sentences about their families. Music and art will be included in learning music from different eras and in drawing pictures of the family.

Problem-Solving Opportunities:
Students will learn problem solving and conflict resolution as they identify problems and issues that arise as change occurs in families.

Prerequisite Knowledge and Skills:
- Ability to write a simple sentence
- Basic understanding of a map of the world
- Simple understanding of time and chronology
- Knowledge of terms such as *family, grandparent,* and *parent*

(Continued)

FIGURE 10-2 • Continued

Learning Objectives	Teaching Approach	Materials
Unit Initiation: Helping learners identify similarities and differences found in individual families	• Read selections from children's books. • Have students identify questions that focus on information they would like to know about families. List and keep questions as a reference. • Ask students to identify how their families are similar to and different from those in the books.	• Garza, C. L. (1993). *Family Pictures.* (San Francisco: Children's Book Press) • Cole, C. K. and Kobayashi, K. (Eds.). (1996). *Shades of L.A.: Pictures from Ethnic Family Albums* (New York: New Press)
Unit Development: 1. Define a family	• Ask students, "What is a family?" • Introduce them to the concept of extended families. • Have them draw a diagram of their family.	Pictures that include families having different compositions (two parents and children; two adults, no children; single father and children; single mother and children; and so forth)
2. See examples of change in families	Have class members provide examples of ways their families have changed. These might include the birth of a new child, marriage of someone in the family, death, or divorce.	Chart paper to list examples of changes
3. Group and label items with common characteristics	• Do a concept-formation activity. • Begin with the opening question of "What are all of the things that change when a new baby comes home?" • List all responses. Have students group those that go together and give them a label.	A chart paper and marker for listing all of the student responses and stickers or symbols to place with items students group together
4. Explain the importance of taking responsibility	• Begin by noting that in most families different people have things they do to help the family.	Pictures of different people performing different tasks (i.e., mowing the lawn, cooking, etc.)

FIGURE 10-2 • Continued

Learning Objectives	Teaching Approach	Materials
	• Ask students to give examples. Tell them that this is what we call "taking responsibility." • Ask students to identify responsibilities of different family members. • Have students suggest what might happen if different people in the family did not fulfill their responsibilities. • Have students role play different family members doing jobs around the house.	Role-play cards with different family members listed on the cards
5. Predict how changes in the family change individuals' responsibilities	• Have students discuss how adding a new family member might change responsibilities for everyone in the family.	
6. Locate places on maps: Develop an understanding of how color can be used as a symbol on maps	Another way that families change is in where they live. • Ask if there are students in the class who have moved. • Have these students tell the class where they used to live. • On a master map, color your own state. Then use other colors to color in states from which members of the class have moved. • Give maps to students and organize them into groups. Ask them to color in the maps following the model that you have colored. • Explain that many U.S. maps features different colors so that outlines of the states are easy to see. Conclude by showing students a large map of the United States that is designed in this way.	Outline maps, crayons

(Continued)

FIGURE 10-2 • Continued

Learning Objectives	Teaching Approach	Materials
7. Identify how families have changed over time	• Ask students in what ways they think things may have been different when their parents were children. • After some discussion, go over the worksheet you want them to take home to complete with their parents. • Ask them to take these worksheets home and, with the help of their parents, fill them out to return the next day.	Handout with specific questions for parents
8. Identify how families have changed over the years	• Have students share the responses from parents. On a chart, list differences and similarities compared with today.	Chart with two lists, labeled "Similar to Today" and "Different from Today"
9. Identify how some things have remained unchanged	• Remind students that on the chart they completed there were some things that were the same for their parents and for them today. Ask students to think about some other things that may have remained the same (types of foods, traditions, etc). • Have students interview family members to identify traditions that have been passed down over the years. • Follow up by showing the CD-ROM and discussing similarities and differences that have occurred over the years in how certain traditions are observed.	CD-ROM: "Seasons and Holldays Around the World"
10. Identify family traditions	• Have class members share some family traditions.	Paper, art supplies

FIGURE 10-2 • Continued

Learning Objectives	Teaching Approach	Materials
	• Ask the class, "Why do you think some traditions continue? Why are they important?"	
Culminating Activities:		
1. Integrating what has been learned from the unit	• Ask each class member, working with members of the family, to start preparing a family album.	Materials for developing a family album
2. Formulation of generalizations	• Review what has been learned about families.	The list of questions developed at the beginning of the unit
	• Ask the class members, "What do you think we can say about things that change and things that stay the same in families over time?"	
	• Review the questions that were asked at the beginning of the unit.	

Evaluation Procedures:
• Keep a checklist of students' participation and their work on all assignments.
• Students will keep portfolios that include all information from interviews, pictures they have drawn, and so forth. Use the contents of the portfolios as a database for making judgments about individual student progress.

However, you also need to keep in mind that other teachers may also use units you develop. (Sometimes you will work with a group of teachers when developing units.) This means that the information you provide about teaching approaches needs to be general and flexible enough for several teachers to use the unit as a basis for preparing lessons for their own classes.

Because many teachers may use completed unit plans, most units do not include specific lesson plans. You and other unit users will develop these later and will prepare them in ways that are responsive to the needs and characteristics of your own learners. References to instruction in unit plans should be limited to brief ideas that will act as prompts to individual teachers as they begin thinking about how to apply units to their classroom. You are unlikely ever to teach the same unit in exactly the same way to successive groups of learners. Each group you teach will have different interests, motivations, and prior knowledge. You will need to alter the unit in light of these new circumstances.

The following example is at an appropriate level of specificity for use in an instructional unit. It provides a general suggestion to users, but it allows individual teachers to exercise their own judgments as they design lessons for use with their own learners:

Role play the decision to move west by assigning students to different roles such as a father, a mother, a sick child, and an elderly grandfather. Discuss the perspective of each of these people. As a class, discuss how each might feel if the family makes a final decision to move west.

This description of a learning activity indicates the general kind of teaching approach the unit developer has in mind. Yet, it leaves specific details regarding introducing the activity, assigning roles, specifying appropriate behavior standards, debriefing questions, and other details to teachers who will be planning lessons based on the unit.

Sometimes, suggestions for teaching approaches included in unit plans mention needed instructional materials. These might include such things as titles of specific books, names of films, descriptions of maps, and other support resources.

Identifying Assessment Methods In this part of the unit plan, you will include ideas about how to gather and evaluate information related to student learning. You may wish to include measurement and assessment tools such as checklists, rubrics, work samples, portfolios, quizzes, and formal testing techniques (see Chapter 12). These ideas are provided as suggestions. You and others who plan lessons associated with the unit will consider these ideas as you consider approaches that are well suited to the needs of the learners you will be teaching.

Criteria for Reviewing the Unit When you prepare an instructional unit, there are criteria that can help you enhance its quality. These can be used as a checklist when you develop the unit, and you can refer to these criteria again as you teach related material and think about improvements to the unit. Typical quality-check questions include the following:

- Is the whole range of social studies outcomes included?
- Is the material in the unit sequenced logically?
- Is the content appropriate for the students who will be asked to learn it?
- Are suggested teaching approaches the best that can be devised? Are these approaches consistent with behaviors referred to in the learning intentions?
- Are assessment procedures as good as they can be?

Lesson Plans

Instructional units are long-term plans. To implement them, you need to think about *short-term* instructional tasks that you must complete to acquaint learners with the general content described in the instructional unit you are teaching. The planning tool you use for this purpose is the *lesson plan*. Sometimes lesson plans describe what you and members of your class will do over the period of several days. Often, however, you will develop lesson plans that describe what you wish to accomplish during a single day.

Lesson plans serve some very important purposes. First, the process of developing a plan allows you to think through the lesson and anticipate difficulties. This can lead to the prevention of problems that can destroy a lesson. Second, lesson planning gives you sets of guidelines that give you confidence in what you are doing. They help diminish any anxiety you might have regarding what you should be doing and help you to appear more poised and secure in your role as a teacher. They also supply a readily available reminder you can consult if, as you are teaching, you forget something you intended to do. When you have a lesson plan available, it is easy to refer to it to get yourself back on track.

The level of detail in individual lesson plans varies. Inexperienced teachers often need to do more detailed planning than teachers who have had many years of successful classroom experience. As a rule of thumb, your lesson plan should include enough detail to enable a substitute teacher to implement your intended lesson without much difficulty. The trick is to establish lesson plans with enough detail to provide you (and, potentially, substitute teachers) with sufficient guidance without turning them into a word-for-word script.

Lesson plans often feature the following categories of information:

- Specific learning objectives
- Teaching approaches
- Ways to organize and manage learners
- Ideas to adapt instruction to meet the needs of special students

Lesson plans can be organized in various ways. The criterion to use when designing a lesson plan is, make sure that it is useful to you. Imagine that you are standing in front of a group of students and something occurs that takes your attention completely away from the lesson. What format would allow you to quickly refer to the lesson plan and get back on track? Figure 10-3 is an outline of a format for a lesson plan.

Lesson plans should be specific enough to allow someone else to conduct the lesson. The standard you might use for this is to imagine that you suddenly had to leave the classroom. If you gave your lesson plan to someone else, such as your principal, would they have enough detail to conduct the lesson in your absence?

Usually, student teachers complain about lesson plans because they may not see them in use by their supervising teacher. It is generally true that with experience, less detail is included in a lesson plan. However, in many places this is beginning to change.

Different schools and different school administrators have different requirements for lesson plans. In these days of accountability, more school administrators are requiring copies of lesson plans. They want to make sure that each teacher in the building is teaching the content standards required in that particular state. For example, one school principal requires all teachers to turn in their lesson plans for the following week on Friday before they leave the school.

Generally, most school administrators are not as demanding. However, they do want to make sure that you are teaching the required content. In addition, they often want something that can be used by a substitute teacher if you happen to be absent. Some require that you supply them with the content standards and your objectives for each day. Sometimes a well-developed unit plan will suffice.

FIGURE 10-3 • Lesson Plan Format Model

Lesson topic: _____   *Unit theme:* _____

Learning Objectives:

New concepts/vocabulary:

Time Allocation	Lesson Sequence	Materials
	Lesson Introduction:	
	Gain attention	
	Stimulate student interest	
	Establish a learning set	
	Inform students of objectives	
	Presentation of Material:	
	Logical sequence	
	Questions to be asked	
	Examples to be presented	
	Modeling	
	Checking for understanding	
	Adaptation for special-needs students	
	Lesson Extension/Application:	
	Extend the lesson to include global awareness and citizenship outcomes	
	Apply learning	
	Allow for practice of skills	
	Closure and Evaluation:	
	Review important learning	
	Get feedback from students on what they have learned	
	Reinforce what students have learned and reinforce good behavior	

In summary, planning is an important ingredient for success. As a novice teacher you will need to devote considerable time to your planning. However, the time you spend planning will pay off with fewer problems in the classroom and with more satisfying outcomes. The evidence indicates clearly that the amount and the quality of planning is an important ingredient in classroom success. Even experienced teachers spend considerable time planning, it is just that we often do not observe the tangible evidence of their planning because they do not write it all down on a lesson plan.

Our advice to those who are entering student teaching is, do not ignore the importance of planning. Those who do so are usually those who have problems and a less than satisfactory student teaching experience.

Web Check: There is an especially useful website maintained by the Curry School of Education at the University of Virginia. You will find resources here that can be useful in planning lessons, as well as a number of lesson plans on a variety of topics. There is also a link to Web resources that will take you to a variety of other sites with social studies resources and lesson plans. URL—http://www.teacherlink.org/content/social/instructional/

KEY IDEAS IN SUMMARY

- Competent instructional planning is a hallmark of a professional teacher. During the planning process, your obligations are to establish priorities for instruction, identify needed learning materials, consider organizational issues, and make decisions related to evaluating students and programs.
- Decision making is central to planning. As you discharge this responsibility, you will be challenged by the complexity of the classroom setting. Your learners represent a diverse group of individuals, and you operate in a public setting in a community that typically includes people who vary greatly in their beliefs about characteristics of high-quality school programs.
- You begin instructional planning by considering the aims and goals of your program. *Aims* are broad statements of purpose that describe what a society expects of the schools. *Goals* are much more specific statements that are derived from aims. Goals provide you with some general directions you can follow as you work to plan instruction for a particular subject and grade level.
- *Learning objectives* focus your attention on what students should be able to do as a consequence of their exposure to your teaching. Objectives help you to select instructional techniques and materials when you plan instructional units and lesson plans. They also often will help you to

convey to parents and other interested parties what you are doing when you teach certain kinds of content to your class.
- As you prepare to make instructional decisions, you need information related to (1) the general characteristics of the students to be taught, (2) the kinds of prior experiences learners have had that connect to proposed new content, (3) the content options from which you can choose, (4) alternative instructional methods, and (5) available resource materials.
- Long-term planning is planning that focuses on an academic year. Often your long-term preparation will include development of a number of instructional *unit plans*. A typical unit plan organizes instruction for a two- to four-week period of time. The unit plan should be organized around the teaching of enduring understandings or generalizations that help students organize specific information and make sense out of it.
- You will engage in short-term planning as you prepare to teach components of your long-term unit plans. Short-term planning often culminates in the development of *lesson plans*. Sometimes a lesson plan includes descriptions of what you and your students will do over a period lasting as long as several days. More frequently, lessons focus on a single day's instruction in a given subject.

that you need to consider carefully the characteristics of your learners when selecting instructional techniques and planning other aspects of your instructional program. What thoughts do you have about approaches you might take to match your teaching techniques to characteristics of students in your class? Why do you think these approaches will provide the information you need?

3. Suppose you are hired to teach social studies in a district with no social studies curriculum guides. How will you begin to plan your social studies program? (Who will you consult? What kinds of guidelines will you seek out, and where will you find them? How will you know "where to begin" at the start of the school year?)

4. Students in elementary classrooms have diverse needs. Which needs do you feel least capable of accommodating? What might you do to prepare yourself to respond to them more confidently?

ELEVEN

Interdisciplinary Dimensions

Scott Cunningham/Merrill

This chapter will help you to:

- Describe a rationale for integrating content from multiple subjects in social studies units.

- Explain steps you can follow to prepare an integrated curriculum.

- Point out how children's literature can be used as an integrating focus.

- Suggest ways to integrate content from the arts, music, mathematics, and science and technology into your social studies program.

- Explain how each of the seven language functions can be integrated into writing exercises embedded within your social studies lessons.

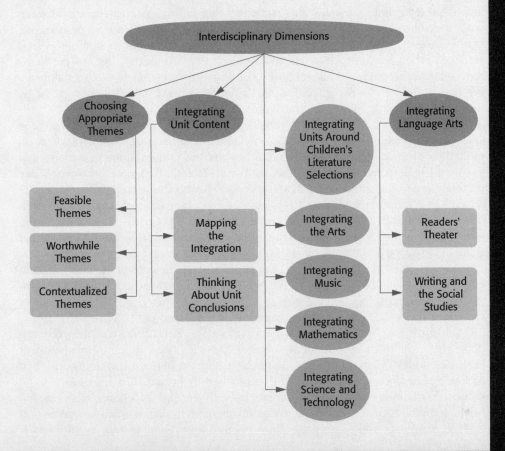

As we have noted, the major emphasis of the social studies is people. Developing an understanding of people and the human experience involves more than just learning history and the social sciences. Other subjects are also sources of important insights about people. For example, literature includes rich and varied explorations of diverse human experiences, including individuals' hopes, dreams, fears, and dilemmas. Music and art can provide us with insight into the human experience of feelings and emotions. The sciences include content relevant to understanding people and their relationship to the physical world. Science content can also help members of your class better understand technological changes that affect our lives. Content from mathematics and statistics can help learners develop more clarity and precision as they consider important issues. In short, many academic disciplines will serve you well as information resources when you work to develop lessons that will promote reflection and encourage development of your learners' sophisticated thinking abilities.

Experts who have studied consequences of lessons that focus narrowly on individual disciplines conclude that students often fail to see connections between what they have learned in school and the "real world" (Eisner, 1991). For example, mathematics educators have concluded that mastering facts and operations is best achieved when learners are taught in a context that "connects" them to problems they see as practical and real. Similarly, reading and language arts educators point out that reading and writing are best taught in the context of "real language" or by using topics that are interesting and significant to students.

Kellough (2003) states that interdisciplinary units are important in helping students avoid the idea that learning is unrelated and piecemeal. When you draw on multiple sources in planning social studies lessons, you communicate to students that the world is not composed of discrete subjects. Decisions people make each day require them to use information that does not respect content boundaries. For these reasons, it is important for you to emphasize interdisciplinary learning when you teach social studies lessons. If you restrict the range of your lesson planning to the traditional disciplines of history and the social sciences, you present a worldview that is limited in scope and that ill matches realities students encounter in their daily lives.

Reeves (2004) contends that the integration of subjects leads to the improvement of academic results for all students. He provides an example where students demonstrated great improvement on the state social studies test when dance, music, literature, vocabulary, history, and geography were integrated in a unit of study.

Developing an integrated curriculum is not easy. You cannot assume your students will profit from lessons simply because these lessons happen to involve them in singing songs, doing art projects, computing math problems, or writing stories that include social studies content. If you do not carefully prepare lessons that integrate content from diverse sources, you can end up with learning experiences that emphasize unimportant, even trivial content. Careful attention to planning is a key when you wish to plan units and lessons that draw content from multiple sources (Roberts & Kellough, 2007).

Planning worthwhile lessons that draw on multiple content sources often requires more of your time than will lessons that focus on a single subject. This is true because you have to know something about content from multiple disciplines, identify which aspects are important and relevant for your purpose, and then weave these elements into a lesson that is internally coherent and responsive to your students' needs.

As you proceed with this kind of planning, you need to develop a clear view of exactly what you wish students to learn from integrated-content lessons. Among other things, you have to consider how content from each subject area you choose to include relates both to your own social studies purposes and to the individual subjects from which you select individual content elements. For example, suppose you decide to choose some music from the Civil War era for inclusion in a social studies lesson. In addition to thinking about how this information will enrich learners' understanding of social studies content, you would also need to determine whether a music educator would consider the particular song you choose as an important and representative example of the music of the period. Failing to do this kind of thinking and simply selecting any Civil War song in a music lesson might result in your students learning neither significant music nor worthwhile social studies content.

The quality of the content you select and your skill in integrating it into coherent learning experiences for your students are the key variables. Suppose you are successful in developing outstanding social studies lessons that include content from multiple subjects. Does this, then, suggest that these subjects should be taught only as part of your social studies program and that you will no longer need to teach mathematics lessons, writing and reading lessons, art lessons, and so forth? It does not. Integrated lessons in the social studies merely provide opportunities for your students to enrich their understandings of these subjects in a context that helps them to better know the "real world" by putting their learning together in a unified way. You cannot stop teaching reading and writing skills, mathematical operations, or forms of artistic expression. It is folly to assume that all your students need to know about these subjects can be transmitted to them in interdisciplinary social studies units.

CHOOSING APPROPRIATE THEMES

How can you proceed if you decide to develop lessons that draw content from multiple sources? You can begin by identifying important themes or topics, and then identify content from various sources that can help students better understand these focus topics or themes (Beane, 1992). To implement this approach, you might choose these themes yourself or organize them around significant questions asked by your students. We believe that the concern of the social studies for the experiences and problems of people makes it ideally suited for interdisciplinary instruction. When you plan lessons that bring multiple subjects together, you act to extend learners' critical and creative thinking powers and increase the likelihood that they will see the content as interesting and important.

Any focus you select as an organizer for multidisciplinary social studies instruction should intrigue your students. If learners find your focus topic to be dull, you will have a hard time generating high levels of student interest in related lessons you develop. How should you go about finding out what kind of a focus might work with your class? Your students, themselves, are the best source of this information.

Suppose you are working with a group of fifth graders and wish to plan lessons that draw content from many subject areas. In grade 5, the focus of the social studies curriculum is usually U.S. history. You can begin your thinking by reviewing topics that are typical features of the fifth-grade program. These may include the following:

- Native American groups
- Colonization
- Forming a new government
- Growth of a new nation
- Westward expansion
- Sectional conflicts

Next, you can challenge your students to generate some questions related to these topics. For example, members of your class might develop questions such

An analysis of art about an historical event can stimulate inquiry into the event as well as demonstrate art elements.

© Bettmann/CORBIS

as these about how different kinds of people reacted to proposals for a new government:

- What kinds of people supported these proposals?
- What kinds of people did not?
- How might we explain differences in their feelings?

If students seem interested in these issues, this set of questions can serve as a focus for lessons you develop that draw content from a variety of subjects.

As an alternative, you can encourage your students to generate questions about present-day issues that interest them. One of the authors recently conducted a discussion with a group of fifth graders who had many important concerns and questions. Among other things, they wanted answers to these questions:

- Why can't people get along?
- Why do some people act as bullies?
- Why do some young people join gangs?
- Why do people pollute the environment?
- Why do companies go out of business and people lose jobs?
- Why do earthquakes happen, and how do people's lives change when they occur?

Some of these student-generated questions can easily be tied to required content of the fifth-grade social studies program. For example, you can adapt questions such as "Why can't people get along?" and "Why do some people act as bullies?" for use as focuses for lessons related to Native Americans ("What differences were there in ways of living of Native Americans and the colonists, and why did these lead to conflicts?" "Why did leaders of the colonists think they could impose their will on the Native Americans?") and colonization ("Why was there conflict between early colonists in England?" "What prompted some leaders in England to think the colonists were dangerous people?" "Why did some colonial leaders, once established in North America, try to impose their ideas on others?").

Successful planning of integrated lessons requires you to know your students and their concerns well. This is true because you want to design lessons that members of your class will find interesting. There are a few topics that seem to intrigue almost all students. For example, large numbers of primary-grade learners get excited about dinosaurs. Other topics may have less general appeal. Therefore, an interdisciplinary unit in the primary grades might be based on a dinosaur theme. Some interests of your students will be related to local conditions. For example, if you are teaching in western Nebraska, members of your class quite probably will have different questions, concerns, and interests than students living in inner-city Chicago neighborhoods.

Blumenfeld, Krajick, Marx, and Soloway (1994) offer guidelines you may find useful as you attempt to identify good focus themes for units. They suggest that focus themes, questions, or topics you select need to be:

- Feasible
- Worthwhile
- Contextualized

Feasible Themes

A *feasible* theme has a clear potential to lead to successful student learning. In considering the issue of feasibility, you need to determine whether members of your class have access to the resources they will need in their investigation. Do they have sufficient prerequisite skills and knowledge to successfully complete the task? If you organize your instruction around themes that are not feasible, you may undermine your students' self-confidence. If your pupils lose faith in their abilities to master the content you are teaching, they will quickly lose interest in your lessons. If this pattern persists, you may find members of your class increasingly resistant to subsequent thematic instruction activities you devise. To avoid this undesirable set of circumstances, you need to take particular care to (1) diagnose learners' interests, levels of prior knowledge about topics you wish to teach, and academic skill levels and (2) ascertain that materials your students will need to complete assigned tasks successfully are available.

Worthwhile Themes

Themes that are *worthwhile* meet the key "importance" test. Do the themes you wish to use have the potential to help members of your class understand complex content? Do these focus topics allow your students to think about information and situations that they will see as helping them better understand the realities they and their families encounter in the world beyond the school? Your purpose should not be to draw on multiple content sources as an end in itself. Rather, your objective should be to select themes that offer a real possibility of integrating a variety of subjects in ways that your students will see as relevant and that act to extend their intellectual, social, and personal development.

Contextualized Themes

Contextualized content includes information that responds to real and practical concerns of your students. For example, suppose you want to teach your learners about how conflict and controversy operate in a democratic society. If you choose to present this information in a lesson that focuses on debates in the General Assembly of the United Nations about environmental threats to Antarctica, many members of your class will wonder how such information ties to their own lives. On the other hand, if you begin by involving your learners in lessons that center on a local controversy whose outcome may touch their lives directly, your students will see the relevance of this material to themselves.

For example, suppose your community is facing a shortfall of funds to support public swimming pools. Some community members may want to reduce operational expenses by drastically reducing the hours that pools are open. Others may want to keep the pool hours unchanged but double the fees swimmers must pay. Either decision has a high probability of directly affecting the students. If you begin your study of how controversy and conflict operate in a democracy using a focus such as the swimming pool issue, then later you can build learners' interest in this topic in ways that will help them also see relevance in situations more distant from their personal experience, such as environmental threats to Antarctica.

INTEGRATING UNIT CONTENT

Once you have identified focus themes, the next step is to take action to integrate subjects that will be used to develop student understanding. In an integrated instructional program, you will spend most of the school day engaging learners in activities that revolve around the selected theme. For example, math problems, science investigations, reading and writing assignments, spelling lists, and music selections will all be tied to this common focus. This general pattern, however, does not mean that you try to draw content from every subject you teach. There may be some subjects that simply lack any reasonable relationship with the theme you select, and you do not want to force integration of content from these subjects when a logical connection to the selected theme is lacking (Shanahan, Robinson, & Schneider, 1995). If you try to do so, you may end up with content that distorts your learners' understanding of the subject and that has been inappropriately tied to your focus theme.

Mapping the Integration

One useful technique you can use to plan an integrated unit is to develop a graphic organizer that illustrates the connections among the various subjects. The organizer will help you to identify specific lessons you will need to develop. Figure 11-1 is an example of a graphic organizer for preparing a complete integrated unit for a fifth-grade classroom.

The bulleted points under each major heading in Figure 11-1 represent just a sampling of ideas you might draw from each subject in lessons you prepare that

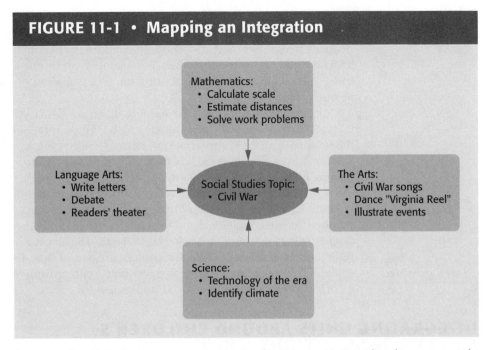

FIGURE 11-1 • Mapping an Integration

focus on the Civil War. For example, under the "Language Arts" heading, you might decide to add literary selections such as Judith Bentley's ***Harriet Tubman*** (1990) or Irene Hunt's ***Across Five Aprils*** (1966). Under "The Arts," you may wish to reference an intention to teach your students more about how art is used as a communication medium. You might also engage them in studying art prints and music as vehicles to convey more information about the emotional impact of the war.

Historians tell us that differences in levels of technological development in the North and South played an important role in determining the outcome of the war. For example, in the South there were fewer miles of rail lines than in the North, and existing lines tended to use different track widths or gauges. As a result, it was much more difficult to move troops and equipment in the South than in the North. Including lessons focusing on how technology affected the war efforts of each side in the conflict gives you an excellent opportunity for subsequent lessons focusing on how technological developments are changing our lives today.

There are abundant opportunities to apply math skills to content related to the War Between the States unit. Distances between places, calculations of amounts of food to supply armies, calibers of rifles used, and computations of sizes of different types of military units are just a few examples of how you might encourage members of your class to use content from mathematics.

Thinking About Unit Conclusions

A final dimension needs to be added to this pre-unit plan. This component requires you to think through some conclusions you would like learners to draw that go beyond their ability to recall specific information related to each of the subject areas from which you will be drawing content.

One approach is to involve students in a final unit project that has them integrate the information across different subject areas. When you do this you need to make sure that the enduring understandings are valid for the content areas outside of the social studies. For example, art or music understandings need to be valid so that you are furthering an understanding of these subjects as well as of the social studies.

An assignment of this kind requires them to "go beyond the givens" and to engage in more sophisticated thinking skills. These more sophisticated patterns of thinking enlarge their appreciation of issues and, at the same time, enhance their abilities to develop approaches they can use when confronting the sorts of challenging issues that will face them throughout their lives.

As you begin developing specific instructional activities for your integrated unit, you will be able to include numerous cooperative activities, whole-group activities, inquiry exercises, individualized learning exercises, and other active learning activities involving the use of technology and media. Developing integrated units requires basic understandings of different content areas and how they relate to the social studies. The following sections suggest how content from varying subjects can be incorporated into integrated social studies lessons.

INTEGRATING UNITS AROUND CHILDREN'S LITERATURE SELECTIONS

You will find good children's books to be an excellent source of materials for social studies lessons. In some cases, these books can also become the central focus for integrated units you prepare (Savage & Savage, 1993). For example, you could use Scott O'Dell's *Carlota* (1977), a story of early California, as a focal point for integrated instruction centering on such social studies topics as war, prejudice, and the roles of women.

If you use *Carlota* as a basic unit organizer, you can develop language arts skills by drawing students' attention to how the author uses words to develop the individual characters. The book also can promote some understanding of Spanish, as it features approximately 125 Spanish words. You can develop learners' computational proficiencies by developing mathematics-based word problems based on events in the book. Finally, you can draw content from science as you make reference to episodes in the book and ask members of your class to conduct experiments relating to weather prediction and adaptations to cold.

When considering children's books as major components of social studies units, your first thoughts may turn to historical fiction. Historical fiction has the capacity to tell compelling stories about people and events. Well-written fictional accounts stimulate students' imaginations and enhance their general interest in social studies. Often young people identify with the characters in the book and imagine themselves living in the depicted time period.

Though there are many attractive features to historical fiction, there are also limitations you need to know about when you use them as basic unit organizers. These books, although roughly based on real events, sometimes distort and change historical facts to fit the author's need to tell a story. You need to read books carefully to spot any historical inaccuracies. You can use information you gather from a careful reading of these books as a basis for helping learners distinguish between historically accurate and historically inaccurate content.

In some cases, you may wish to use works of nonfiction as unit organizers. Nonfiction titles embrace a huge range of content. In addition to traditional biographies of presidents, generals, scientists, and sports figures, you will find outstanding books focusing on experiences of people who have traveled to little-visited places, descriptions of wars and other important events, descriptions of how people in different world cultures go about their daily lives, and explanations of intriguing scientific and technological developments. You will find your learners respond well to well-written nonfiction titles. Many students are drawn to nonfiction because books of this kind deal with "real" events and people. The focus on reality can help your learners view events from different perspectives (Savage & Savage, 1996).

In preparing for a literature-based unit, you start by identifying the themes or questions for the integrated unit. Next, search for selections of children's literature that relate to the theme. Texts such as Norton's **Through the Eyes of a Child** (2003) identify good selections of literature related to a variety of themes and issues.

A good source for finding books that can be used as an integrating focus for social studies is the annual review of books in *Social Education*, an official journal of the National Council of the Social Studies (NCSS). The Carter Woodson Award, annually given by the NCSS, identifies exemplary multiethnic nonfiction books. Other sources include *Booklist, School Library Journal, Hornbook,* and *Publishers Weekly,* all of which provide good reviews of new books.

INTEGRATING THE ARTS

The objectives of the arts and the social studies are complementary in many ways. Eisner (1991) points out that what students learn about a culture is constrained by the forms of representation or the ways they learn about it. If the only means of learning about a culture is through textbooks, this places some limits on what students will learn. Therefore, lessons you develop that include content from art, music, and literature will enrich your learners' understanding and make your social studies instruction more vivid and interesting.

Including material from the arts in your social studies lessons helps students relate to the content in personal and meaningful ways (Selwyn, 1995). More specifically, content from the arts helps learners appreciate how the social studies connects to feelings, actions, and aspirations of real people. This understanding lends meaning to a subject that students otherwise might see as remote and disconnected from their lives. In planning units that center on content from the arts, you can use individual artistic works as artifacts that provide revealing glimpses into a culture (Collins & Chandler, 1993). Works of visual art can capture the mood, the color, the fears, and the joys of a group of people much better than can many written representations.

Lessons incorporating art can be useful as vehicles to help children make inferences. An acquaintance of the authors begins many of his social studies units with a collection of art prints and travel posters. Students investigate the prints in depth and

There are many opportunities to integrate social studies with art.

Scott Cunningham/Merrill

LESSON IDEA 11-1

TOPIC: Social Studies & Art

OBJECTIVES: As a result of the lesson students will (1) identify a social problem in their community, and (2) create an art piece to communicate their ideas about the problems.

ENGAGING THE STUDENTS: This lesson should follow lessons focused on the local community. Review with the class some of the issues they have discussed by saying, "As we have researched our local community we have found several things that we can identify as problems. These include litter, graffiti on walls, the loss of places to play as new buildings are built, and increased traffic. The problem *we* have is that *we* need to get others in the community to see these problems. How might we do this?"

DEVELOPING THE CONTENT: Say, "Pictures and artwork often get the attention of people. How might we use art to communicate our feelings about these problems to others?" Students then brainstorm how they might use art to communicate ideas. Help them remember principles of art that might make their pictures more effective. For example, they might decide that a collage could capture many dimensions of a problem. Color can be used to capture attention and communicate feelings and the use of line can draw the viewer's attention to the main point of the picture.

BRINGING CLOSURE: Review some of the student ideas and discuss with them the material that will be needed for them to complete their art project.

EXTENSION TO THE WEB: The EDSITEment website includes lessons plans and links to top humanities sites such as museums and cultural institutions.

URL—http://edsitement.neh.gov/

make inferences about the place and the time they are going to study. They write as many questions as they can. These learner-generated questions and inferences provide a focus for subsequent instruction. Students find this to be an exciting activity and this teacher has experienced great success over the years in generating student interest in his social studies units.

To gain information from a work of art, you need to have at least a modest degree of artistic literacy (Eisner, 1991). You have to know enough to be able to share basic information with your learners about art and art processes. Learners who know this contextual information can derive much more from their art lessons than those who do not. Good units that are built around content from the arts not only contribute to learners' understanding of social studies content, but also enrich their appreciation for the arts by helping them to place works of art in a particular social, cultural, or historical context.

INTEGRATING MUSIC

Much of what has been said about art can be said for music. Music also has the capacity to teach students about people. Music created by members of a particular group gives insight into their values, beliefs, hopes, and fears. It evokes the emotions and communicates aspects of a culture that cannot be communicated in any other way. For example, listening to the song, "God Save the South," popular in the South during the Civil War, gives us insight into the attitudes of many of the people who lived in the South. This perspective is one you cannot expect your learners to get by reading a textbook. Folk songs are particularly good sources of views of the common people. Regrettably, few elementary and middle school social studies textbooks devote much attention to this kind of information.

As with art, the goals of music and social studies are complementary. An understanding of culture and social conditions is important in developing a full appreciation of music. Music is created within specific contexts. When your learners know something about these contexts, they develop a more sophisticated understanding of music-related content. For example, armed with such insights, your students are better able to appreciate that messages and emotions are an integral part of the communication music delivers through skillful manipulation of melody, harmony, and rhythm.

For example, think about how the musical score of *Rodeo* by the American composer Aaron Copland captures the culture of the American West. The final movement, "Hoedown," depicts a tradition that promoted social interaction and unity for ranchers and their families who lived in the West. In addition, music from *Rodeo* includes elements you can use to help students learn how rhythmic changes can be used to identify different elements of a story and how tempo changes can be used to capture emotions.*

---

* Thanks to Jenna Hill, teacher, Gaver Elementary School, Anaheim City School District, Anaheim, California, for this idea.

Music and social studies can be easily integrated to the advantage of both subjects.

Anthony Magnacca/Merrill

LESSON IDEA 11-2

TOPIC: Communicating Through Music

OBJECTIVES: Students will (1) identify a theme or mood they want to communicate, (2) find a music selection that communicates that theme or mood, and (3) develop a multimedia presentation with the music and the social studies information they want to present.

ENGAGING THE STUDENTS: Say to students, "Usually when we see a movie, that movie has music as a background. Why do you think they do that? Let me give you some examples." At this point play some theme music, such as the theme from *Jaws* or *Star Wars*. Discuss how this music makes students feel, and what it communicates.

DEVELOPING THE CONTENT: Tell students, "In our social studies role-playing sessions, you have pretended you were a person who lived during a particular time in history and you have written letters to others about your experiences. What you are to do now is to select some music that you will use like the music in a movie. It should help communicate what your letters are all about. For example, if your letter is sad, what kind of music would you select? If it was funny, what kind of music would you want? When

you have found a good selection of music, we are going to record you reading your letter with the music playing in the background."

BRINGING CLOSURE: After students have had an opportunity to work together in selecting music to go with their letters, have them share what they have learned and found. In a later lesson, they can record their letters with the music.

EXTENSION TO THE WEB: Several websites present ideas for using music and the arts in the school curriculum. One site you may find useful for extending the ideas presented in this lesson is M.U.S.I.C. (Musicians United for Songs in the Classroom). The site has an extensive index of more than 3,000 songs that may be used at no charge (please note that fair use copyright clearance is for individual teachers for educational purposes only), and information on the stories behind many of the songs. The site also contains ideas for classroom activities and a page of useful educational links.

URL—http://www.learningfromlyrics.org/

You will have little difficulty finding sources of music to include in a social studies unit. Abundant tapes, records, and written music that reach far back in history and cross many cultures are readily available. Today, a variety of music also is available on the Web, in many cases as royalty-free downloads. In many parts of the nation, groups have preserved a part of their cultural identity through music and dance groups.

INTEGRATING MATHEMATICS

More and more, mathematical literacy is becoming an imperative of effective citizenship. The media bombards citizens daily with massive amounts of data and figures. Many public decisions result, at least in part, from interpretations of quantitative data. One example is the establishment of monetary policy that requires consideration of quantitative information that includes such variables as inflation indexes, interest rates, and unemployment rates. Many political campaigns include figures and claims that need to be verified by mathematical analysis. Similarly, consumers need to be prepared to protect themselves in a marketplace that requires a least some mathematical diligence. Daily advertising tries to take advantage of the limited mathematical sophistication of many potential buyers.

A society with a large percentage of mathematically illiterate individuals is in danger of its citizens making poor choices that can influence life in profound ways. The students you teach need to have mathematical knowledge to effectively discharge their future responsibilities as citizens. Mathematics educators are aware of this need, and they have been seeking ways of teaching mathematical operations in applied and meaningful contexts. The social studies component of the curriculum is a place where students' mathematics proficiencies can be developed in ways that learners will see as relevant to their own lives.

You will find numerous opportunities for teaching mathematical concepts in your social studies units. One of the more obvious examples is the teaching of graphs and map scale. Understanding the ratio of a map scale is important in order for your students to compute distances between points on a map.

Another important teaching area that ties naturally to mathematics is economics. Many economics and mathematics concepts are best taught together. Even in the primary grades, you can use the classroom store to teach concepts such as scarcity, addition, and subtraction. An interesting application in the middle grades features use of the Consumer Price Index (CPI). You can teach your students to use the CPI to determine how the value of a dollar has fluctuated over the years (Savage & Armstrong, 1992). The CPI can be useful to you as a tool for helping your students better understand meanings of prices in past years. Without a grasp of how the value of the dollar has changed over time, many of your learners, when they see that cars were priced well under $1,000 in the 1930s, may erroneously conclude that "cars were really cheap" in those days. Using some relatively simple mathematics students can learn to convert these old prices to modern equivalents. Here they learn that in contemporary dollars, these cars were really not that inexpensive.

LESSON IDEA 11-3

TOPIC: Where in the World Are We?

OBJECTIVES: As a result of the lesson students will (1) state the relationship between mathematics and navigation, and (2) calculate how many degrees east or west of the Prime Meridian a place is by comparing the time difference.

ENGAGING THE STUDENTS: Begin by saying, "Let's suppose that you are with the Pilgrims sailing to the new world. You sail out of the English Channel and into the Atlantic Ocean. The next day you wake up in the morning and look around. All you see is water. There are no road signs pointing to Plymouth Colony. How do you know where you are and which way to go?"

DEVELOPING THE CONTENT: Let the students suggest ways that could help them determine which way to sail. Then tell them that they already have some knowledge that would help them solve this problem. Ask them, "What is the shape of the earth?" (It is like a ball or a circle.) "What do we know about a ball or a circle from mathematics?" (Its circumference has 360 degrees.) "How long does it take for the sun to go from the highest point in the sky on one day to the highest point in the sky on the next day?" (It takes 24 hours.) "If we know that there are 360 degrees in a circle and it takes 24 hours for the earth to rotate so that the sun is back at the highest point in the sky, how many degrees per hour does the earth rotate?" (If 360 is divided by 24, the answer is 15 degrees per hour, or about 1,000 mph.) "Which direction does the sun cross the sky?" (It crosses from east to west.)

Tell students, "Now, if we know that the rotation of the earth is 15 degrees per hour and that the sun crosses the sky from east to west, we can use this information and two clocks or watches to help us determine where we are. Here is how we would do that. Since a circle or a ball doesn't have a starting or an ending point we have to choose one. Because England was a nation that depended on sea trade, they chose a beginning place that was near London for the starting point. That starting place is called the "Prime Meridian" or the Greenwich Meridian. Greenwich was a small village near London (it is now a suburb). A *meridian* is an imaginary line that runs from the north pole to the south pole. The Prime Meridian is labeled as 0 degrees. It can be found on any globe." (Point it out on a globe.) "Time there is called Greenwich Mean Time."

"As our sailing ship sails from London to Plymouth Colony, we would set both of our clocks based on the time along the Prime Meridian. As we sail away, we would post a guard on our clocks to make sure no one alters their settings. The next day we would use some other instruments to help us tell when the sun was at the highest point in the sky. What time would that be?" (It would be 12 o'clock or noon at that place.) "We would then set one of the clocks to 12 o'clock to represent our present location. Then we would compare the time at our present location to the clock that was set for the time along the Prime Meridian. For example, if it is noon where we are but our Prime Meridian clock says it is 2 o'clock in the afternoon along the Prime Meridian, where are we?" (We are 30 degrees west of the Prime Meridian.) "If our clock says it is noon where we are and it is 10 o'clock in the morning along the Prime Meridian, where are we?" (We are 30 degrees east of the Prime Meridian.)

Provide the students with a number of problems so that they need to figure out how many degrees east or west of the Prime Meridian they would be.

BRINGING CLOSURE: Ask, "What did we learn today? There are many ways that people have learned to use mathematics to solve very important problems. This is just one example, and it is still in use today. On National Public Radio (NPR), they often broadcast a news program from England. If you listen carefully you will hear the news commentator say, 'It is ___ o'clock GMT.' He is telling you the time of the broadcast according to Greenwich Mean Time."

Additionally, tell students, "Using this method tells us how far east or west we might be. It does not tell us how far north or south we might be. That is another mathematical application we will learn later."

EXTENSION TO THE WEB: The National Council of Teachers of Mathematics website contains content relevant to teaching mathematics in the schools. If you type "integrated content" into the search box you will get a listing of numerous articles and online discussions that relate to integrating content from mathematics into other curricular areas.

URL —http://www.nctm.org

INTEGRATING SCIENCE AND TECHNOLOGY

Science and technology are significant social forces. Any understanding of people and their actions in the past or present requires an understanding of prevailing levels of these important influences. Today's rapid scientific and technological changes have important, and often unforeseen, consequences for our society (Marker, 1992). The abilities of these forces to transform lives confront us with the need to make quick and frequent adaptations. Often these changes in how we go about our lives produce discomfort. As a result, concerns about science and technology today play important roles in debates about important public policy. These discussions bring into focus issues that are value laden. Citizens who are able to influence important policy decisions need to understand both values associated with individual positions and the technology and science that support recommendations for change. These conditions suggest a need for you to give a prominent place to content tied to science and technology in your social studies program.

LESSON IDEA 11-4

TOPIC: Understanding Precipitation

OBJECTIVES: Students will (1) define how rising air cools and forms precipitation, and (2) predict what would happen if mountain ranges were placed differently.

ENGAGING THE STUDENTS: Ask students, "What do you think happens when wind currents encounter mountain ranges?"

DEVELOPING THE CONTENT: Set up a science experiment demonstrating how warm moist air forms precipitation when it rises and cools. Many science textbooks include this experiment. It involves heating a beaker of water on a hotplate. The beaker has a pipette going from the stopper to another beaker. The air in the pipette can be cooled using ice. As the water heats, the moist air rises, cools, and then drops moisture in the other beaker. After completing the experiments, ask the students what happened.

Show students a map of the United States. Point out that the Rocky Mountains and the Sierra Nevada Mountains both run from the north to the south. The

prevailing wind currents blow from the west to the east from the Pacific Ocean. Ask the students what happens when the moist air comes to the mountain ranges. Then ask them how would things be different if the mountain ranges ran from west to east rather than from north to south. They can discuss in groups and try to identify as many things that they can that would be different.

BRINGING CLOSURE: Ask students, "What did we learn happens when air rises? How does that help us understand why there might be more precipitation in some places than others?"

EXTENSION TO THE WEB: At this site, you will find a collection of multidisciplinary lesson plans drawing on content from many disciplines including the sciences, reading, writing, music, drama, and social studies.

URL—http://www.eduref.org/cgi-bin/
lessons.cgi/interdisciplinary

Marker (1992) suggests several key points or generalizations related to science and technology that need to be taught to elementary youngsters. Among the ideas he suggests are the following:

- Technological changes seldom have an equal impact on all groups in society.
- Technology often changes more rapidly than social institutions.
- In a democratic society, citizens have a right and a responsibility to participate in the development of laws that control the uses of technology.

As a beginning point for teaching elementary school students about technology, you might engage your class in a discussion of ways that technology changes our lives. You might begin by asking such focus questions as, "How has the automobile changed the way people live? How has it made living easier? What problems have automobiles created that didn't exist before?"

You will have little difficulty uncovering opportunities to embed science-related ideas in your social studies units and lessons. In fact, you cannot teach some content in responsible ways without introducing some information from science. For example, if students are to understand climate patterns, they need to be familiar with some principles from physics (hot air rises, cold air falls, and so forth). Integration of science and social studies content is essential if you want your students to develop sophisticated understandings of some topics that commonly are featured in social studies programs. Fifth-grade social studies curricula often emphasize settlement of the American West. If students are to grasp the profound social and economic difficulties faced by settlers who attempted to establish themselves in locations west of the 100th meridian, they need to understand scientific principles governing climatic conditions in this part of our country.

INTEGRATING LANGUAGE ARTS

One of your obligations as an elementary school teacher is to develop your learners' abilities to communicate effectively. High rates of citizen literacy contribute to the stability of our democratic society. Work you do to promote the development of effective communication skills sometimes is referred to as instruction directed at developing learners' *communicative competence* (Tompkins & Hoskisson, 1991).

Communicative competence involves two major components: (1) transmitting meaning through speaking and writing and (2) comprehending meaning through listening and reading (Tompkins & Hoskisson, 1991). Because the ability to communicate clearly and effectively with others is so important, school subjects such as reading, spelling, writing, and oral language have been included in the elementary curriculum specifically for the purpose of transmitting these important skills to learners. In recent years, educators have realized that language and communications skills are best learned in contexts that tie directly to students' real-world lives and experiences.

This suggests that the social studies, with its emphasis on real people and how they live, is an area of the elementary curriculum that is especially well suited for lessons designed to enhance students' communicative competence. For example, as a social studies teacher, you require students frequently to work with print resources, including textbooks, encyclopedias, almanacs, magazines, and newspapers. Clearly, you want your students to develop good reading skills so they can benefit from information contained in the print materials you regularly use as part of your instructional program.

Readers' Theater

Readers' theater is an exciting language arts approach that you can easily incorporate into your social studies program. *Readers' theater* is an oral interpretation or a dramatic reading that involves two or more students reading from a script, using voice and gestures to portray a scene. These presentations are not plays; hence, a minimum of practice is required. Readers' theater has several benefits. It helps students learn to express themselves orally. This can be a benefit for all students. Some of the most fluent readers often read too rapidly and with little attention to expression (Norton, 2004). Those who have less developed reading ability often find it reinforcing as they are allowed to practice the material before reading in front of the group. Before sharing a readers' theater presentation, students need to read through a selection and make sure they comprehend what they have read. They should discuss as a group the mood, the style, and the plot. They should then discuss different ways of presenting the material to the class. They might use some creative writing to create a script or alter the selection they are reading to make it more dramatic and understandable. They need to develop an introduction to set the stage. Once they have performed these steps they should have time to rehearse until they are ready to present to the class (Norton, 2004).

A good way to begin is to have students work in cooperative learning groups. They can select an episode from a book they enjoy. The whole group should read the episode together and discuss what is happening. They might want to discuss the feeling of the characters and how they think the words would sound if spoken. Next they begin preparing a script by identifying the speaking parts of the different characters. They go on to decide who will play each character and practice reading through the script. Next they discuss what they can do to make the presentation interesting to the audience. When they are ready, they present their scene to the class. Historical fiction often has a great deal of dialogue and is especially well suited to readers' theater.

Writing and the Social Studies

In recent years, concerns about students' writing skills have paralleled worries about their reading abilities. As with reading, teachers have been encouraged to provide opportunities for students to write in all of their major elementary school subjects. Social studies lessons present excellent opportunities for members of your class to develop their writing skills.

Tompkins (2006) points out a number of ways that content area study can be combined with writing. Her suggestions include writing biographical sketches of a person being studied, creating data charts to compare information, writing "I am" poems about a person or topic, writing simulated letters and simulated journals, creating riddles about a topic, and writing song lyrics about a person or event. These are all approaches that help make both writing and the social studies active and meaningful parts of the curriculum.

Halliday (1973) identifies seven basic functions of language useful for writing activities:

- Instrumental function
- Regulatory function
- Interactional function
- Personal function
- Heuristic function
- Representational function
- Imaginative function

The *instrumental* function of language, sometimes referred to as the "I-want" function, concerns how people use language to meet their needs. For example, people write to apply for jobs, to place orders for goods and services, and to invite others to visit. You can involve your students in social studies–related instrumental writing by having them do such things as the following:

- Writing letters requesting information from government agencies
- Writing to invite special guests to the classroom
- Writing a class request to the principal
- Completing mock job applications or loan applications
- Writing captions to accompany collages of student-assembled pictures illustrating personal wants and needs

The *regulatory* function concerns tasks that control behavior or provide information about how a task should be performed. It is sometimes called the "do-as-I-tell-you" function. Road signs, directions for constructing or repairing something, and printed collections of traffic laws illustrate the regulatory function of written language. You can give students experience with regulatory writing through activities such as these:

- Writing to friends out of town inviting them to visit and giving them directions to the student's home
- Pretending that a trek over the Oregon Trail has just been completed, writing to friends in the East telling them what they should bring and providing them with other directions about "moving west"
- Writing rules for the classroom or the school, or for the care of pets or materials
- Writing suggestions to the principal about needed new rules
- Preparing written directions for such things as building a log cabin, making candies, or engaging in a traditional craft

The *interactional* function, sometimes called the "me-and-you" function, includes communications that seek to improve the quality of interpersonal relations. Social studies activities you assign that are consistent with this function include the following:

- Writing to a friend to visit the classroom
- Preparing and sending thank-you notes to special guests

- Creating personal holiday greeting cards to be sent to specific people
- Writing regularly to a pen pal in another state or country
- Playing the role of an explorer and writing an imaginary letter to a member of the explorer's immediate family back home

The *personal* function includes communications that seek to express personal feelings or ideas and to explore personal meanings. Letters to the editor, reaction statements, and poetry are examples of writing in this general category. The personal function is sometimes called the "here-I-come" function. The following examples illustrate ways you can involve students in personal writing:

- Writing letters to the editor in reaction to something printed in a news or editorial column
- Writing an account of a personally experienced event
- Preparing and sending a letter to a public official expressing a personal opinion about a controversial issue
- Writing a poem to express feelings about something studied in a social studies lesson
- Keeping a personal diary
- Preparing a time capsule that includes items of interest to class members along with explanations of some of their personal beliefs

The *heuristic* function of language, sometimes referred to as the "tell-me-why" function, has to do with seeking or gathering information. People exercise this function when they take notes or develop questions they want to have answered. The following examples suggest ways you can involve your students in heuristic writing as part of their social studies lessons:

- Writing down questions to be asked after study of a particular social studies topic, or to ask a guest speaker
- Keeping note cards with information about a topic that is being studied
- Taking notes while listening to a speaker
- Keeping minutes at a meeting
- Writing down hypotheses to explain a puzzling situation after considering relevant data

The *representational* function of language concerns the use of language to transmit information. It is sometimes referred to as the "I've-got-something-to-tell-you" function. The following examples suggest ways you can involve your students in representational writing in your social studies lessons:

- Maintaining an imaginary diary for someone who was present at an important historical event
- Writing a short history of the local community
- Preparing a classroom newspaper or newsletter
- Labeling items on a map and writing accompanying explanations
- Developing lists of major ideas to be included in oral reports
- Writing an account of a past event based on an oral history interview
- Writing a report of information learned on a field trip

The *imaginative* function is the creative, "let's-pretend" function of language. When people use this function, they allow their minds to wander in unpredictable ways. Possibilities for including imaginative writing in your social studies program include the following:

- Writing stories to complete a "what would happen if . . .?" question
- Writing a play or television script about something studied in a social studies lesson
- Writing song lyrics about a topic studied in a social studies lesson
- Inventing and writing novel solutions to important social problems such as drug abuse and air pollution
- Preparing a written account describing what life might be like 50 years from now
- Preparing political cartoons referring to current topics and issues

These seven functions are all part of a comprehensive writing program. Teachers too often restrict social studies writing activities to those related to the representational function. You need to encourage other kinds of writing. Over time, this kind of training will improve the sophistication of your students' writing skills. These skills make them more effective communicators, not only in their social studies classes but in other settings as well.

This chapter has made a case for integrating social studies with other subjects in the curriculum. Not only does integration help students see connections between various subjects and improve learning in all of the subjects, it can also lead to increased interest and motivation. For you, as an elementary teacher, seeking connections between subjects also will stimulate creativity and increase the enjoyment of teaching.

Furthermore, in an age when more information is being added to the curriculum, it just makes sense to find ways of including this information without increasing the amount of time students spend in the classroom. Integration across subjects is important to keep valuable social studies content from being cut.

KEY IDEAS IN SUMMARY

- When you plan units and lessons in ways that integrate content from multiple subject areas around important topics or themes, you help your students understand the relatedness of subjects and present them in content that often appears to them highly relevant to the realities they confront in their daily lives.
- Planning good integrated units and lessons demands a heavy investment of your time. You must identify valid information about several subjects, identify content from each that relates to your focus theme, and weave all elements together in ways that are internally coherent and responsive to your learners' needs.

- Several options are open to you as you seek to identify organizing themes for integrated units. Two of these approaches require you either to (1) identify themes that are embedded within topics normally taught at your grade level or (2) survey your students to identify their interests and concerns and follow by using these issues as a focus for thematic instruction. The themes you select need to be feasible, worthwhile, and contextualized.
- A useful device you can use as you plan to integrate content from multiple sources is the *graphic organizer*. A graphic organizer illustrates the relationships among different topics.

When you complete a graphic organizer, you have a visual picture of major content divisions and suggestions for activities to include in the complete unit plan.

- Part of your preliminary thinking about an integrated unit should focus on kinds of conclusions you hope learners will draw as a result of their exposure to the content you have selected. One approach you may wish to take is to develop some general questions you expect students to be able to answer when they have completed their study of the new unit.

- Children's literature selections are excellent sources you can use as focuses for integrated lessons and units. After reviewing social studies topics and identifying themes you have selected, you can identify high-quality works of children's literature with content that relates to the topics or themes you have chosen.

- Objectives of the social studies curriculum and the arts curriculum are complementary in many ways. Artistic representations communicate much about the cultures that produce them. Content from the arts represents a valid addition to kinds of information your students get when they work with prose materials.

- Music has much to teach us about the people and cultures that produce it. Interdisciplinary lessons and units that embed musical content communicate some aspects of culture that cannot be effectively transmitted using prose alone. Content from music is particularly appropriate when you have an interest in transmitting content that focuses on feelings and emotions.

- Your students are coming of age in a society that increasingly requires effective citizens to have high degrees of mathematical literacy. The media today assaults the senses with huge volumes of quantitative data. Many policy decisions use quantitative information to support alternative decisions. To help your students grow in their abilities to analyze information that includes a quantitative dimension, you need to include content from mathematics in your interdisciplinary lessons and units.

- Science and technology are important social forces. Among other things, rapid scientific and technological changes affect how we live. All evidence points to accelerating rates of change in future years. Hence, as you work to give your students insights about issues facing our society, you need to embed information that will help them to appreciate the roles science and technology now play in our lives.

- Content from language arts can be included in multidisciplinary lessons and units in several ways. One approach you may wish to take will involve your students in *readers' theater.* When you use this approach, your learners identify selected incidents from the social studies or from children's literature. They then write a script of the incident and present it to the class. This involves the four main language processes: reading, writing, speaking, and listening.

- When you integrate content from language arts, you are concerned with developing students' writing, as well as reading, skills. Writing activities can be organized under seven major functions of language: (1) instrumental, (2) regulatory, (3) interactional, (4) personal, (5) heuristic, (6) representational, and (7) imaginative.

CHAPTER REFLECTIONS

Now that you have read the chapter, think about these questions.

1. How do you feel about the idea that some themes for interdisciplinary instruction might be developed from questions your students develop? Are they mature enough to do this? What advantages or disadvantages do you see in using learner-generated questions as a basis for identifying organizing themes for interdisciplinary lessons or units?

2. How do you differentiate among characteristics of (1) feasible themes, (2) worthwhile themes, and (3) contextualized themes?

3. Suppose you decided to build an integrated social studies unit that incorporates a number of selections from children's literature. How would you identify the focus for the unit, and which specific literary selections would you choose? Why do you believe these titles would serve your purposes well?

4. How comfortable are you in using art and music to learn about the social studies? What do you know about art? What do you know about music? Where could you get more information to help you use these subjects to teach social studies content?

5. Some have called the social studies the "integrating core" around which the content of other subjects could be organized. Take a social studies topic that interests you. What math and science content can you logically relate to the topic? How would you create a lesson integrating this content?

TWELVE

Assessing Social Studies Outcomes

Mike Medici/Silver Burdett Ginn

This chapter will help you to:

- Define basic terms associated with assessment
- Describe types of assessment.
- Compare norm-referenced evaluation and criterion-referenced evaluation.
- Describe differences between selected response and constructed response assessment.
- Explain the features of an assessment blueprint.
- Design an evaluation and grading plan.

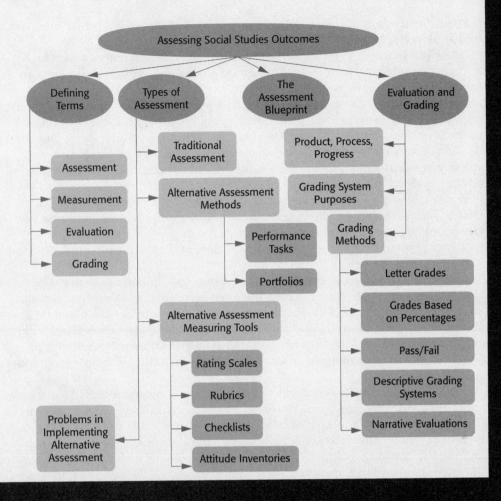

Accountability is a major emphasis in education. Parents, politicians, and policy makers will no longer accept teacher assurances that all is well and students are learning. Contemporary teachers are being called on to present evidence that students are learning and making satisfactory progress. Frequent testing is a centerpiece of the "No Child Left Behind" legislation and any criticism of this testing is dismissed as "making excuses" for education failure. In addition, many states have adopted state standards that students are expected to achieve (see Chapter 1). Assessments have been developed to determine how well students achieve these standards and are used as the basis for holding teachers accountable. Assessment has become an important part of the educational landscape.

Unfortunately, there is a large degree of "assessment illiteracy" in education (Popham, 2001). Many teachers and administrators do not understand basic assessment principles and therefore unsound assessment programs and procedures have been implemented that have the potential to harm teaching and learning. Teachers must understand assessment as a means of self-preservation as well as a necessary tool for promoting quality social studies (Savage, 2003).

Assessment needs to be viewed as an important and vital part of teaching. As a teacher, you have a professional obligation to determine whether students are learning. Knowing how well your students are performing is vital in order to determine allocations of time and resources. You need information that informs you regarding the effectiveness of your teaching. As a teacher, you cannot improve unless you have accurate information about the impact of your teaching on your students. You need to know who has mastered the content, who needs assistance, where you need to allocate your time, and how fast to pace the curriculum. In addition, you must have information about individual student achievement to deliver accurate and honest information to parents about the progress of their child. Finally, the public has a right to know how well the schools are performing and how wisely they are using the resources provided to them. This is true whether it is a tax-supported public school or a voucher- and tuition-supported private school.

However, as with most things, there are sound and unsound assessment practices. Just because assessment occurs does not mean that valid and worthwhile information is being collected. The basic question is not whether there will be an assessment of student learning, the question is whether the assessment will be a valid one that provides useful information. Unsound assessment does little more than provide useless and misleading information that ends up wasting valuable time and scarce resources.

To draw valid conclusions about student learning, assessment should focus on important educational outcomes. However, it must be remembered that schools are expected to address a variety of educational goals that reach beyond the scope of knowledge about traditional academic subjects. These goals include problem solving, creative thinking, interpersonal relationships, attitudes and values, and self-discipline. Because these important goals cannot be assessed the same way, multiple assessments are required. Making decisions about the quality of school programs based on narrow assessments of limited educational outcomes is misleading at best.

In this chapter we will provide some basic principles and ideas that will help you to move toward a sound assessment program that will be a valuable part of your teaching.

DEFINING TERMS

The first step in moving toward a sound assessment program is that of understanding basic terms. If terms are not clearly defined, misunderstanding can occur and important issues can be overlooked.

Assessment

The first term that needs to be defined is assessment. *Assessment* is a broad term referring to everything that is done to gather, analyze, and use information about student learning in order to make intelligent decisions (Tanner, 2001). One function of assessment is that of program evaluation. This purpose helps those concerned reflect on the performance of all students to determine if instruction is effective and helps educators make sound decisions about overall teaching and the curriculum. Another function of assessment is to provide teachers with information about student learning and progress. A third function is to provide similar information to students and other interested individuals, such as parents. These functions help teachers make decisions about individual students and their needs. When developing an assessment plan, it is important to keep all of these functions in mind. In this chapter we restrict our discussion to how teachers receive, interpret, and make use of student achievement information.

There are several things you need to know when making decisions about individual students that can be gathered though assessment. It is useful to know (1) how much students know before beginning a unit of study (diagnostic assessment), (2) what progress are students making during a unit of study (formative assessment), and (3) how much students have learned as a result of their engagement in the unit of instruction (summative assessment).

Diagnostic and formative assessment are best viewed as methods that provide information about student progress rather than information about goal attainment. *Diagnostic* assessment provides information before starting a learning sequence to make sure students have the prerequisites for success. *Formative* assessment provides information during a learning sequence so that adjustments can be made to maximize the probability of success. *Summative* assessment determines whether goals are achieved.

The particular assessment tools you use should be related to the type of information you want to gather and the purpose of the assessment (McMillan, 2001). For example, in diagnostic assessment, quick and informal procedures, such as interviews or responses to oral questions, provide insight into what a student already knows about a subject. Likewise, formative assessment might use a combination of short samples of student performance and teacher observations as indicators of how well students are progressing.

Summative assessment, on the other hand, should be a more rigorous process focusing on clearly defined objectives, valid procedures for gathering the data with the least probability of error, and criteria by which the data will be evaluated. One of the most common abuses of assessment is that data are gathered through the use of a test that has very little relationship to important instructional goals. Therefore, the data are invalid for making important decisions. For this reason, it is best to consider assessment when you define your instructional objectives. This helps you make sure that you do assess important objectives and that your assessment data is valid. (See Stiggins, 2005, for a thorough discussion of the types of assessment and their uses.)

Measurement

A second term that should be understood is measurement. *Measurement* describes the process by which the amount of something is indicated. In education, we are usually trying to measure knowledge, skills, and attitudes. Data in these areas can be gathered using a variety of measurement tools. Traditional measurement tools include true-false tests; student work samples; multiple-choice, matching, and fill-in-the-blank tests; and short answer and essay tests. Other, less traditional ways of gathering data include portfolios, rubrics, checklists, competency demonstrations, performance tests, and observations. The basic point is that there are numerous ways of gathering data in addition to what we think of as a traditional "test."

Measurement tools might be classified into two types, selected response and constructed response (McMillan, 2001). *Selected response* tools are those where the individual being assessed chooses a response from alternatives proved by the assessor. *Constructed response* types are those where the individual being assessed constructs rather than chooses a response. Both types have advantages and disadvantages.

The measurement tool used needs to be consistent with the nature of the goal being assessed. For example, if we wish to determine how heavy something is, we weigh it. If we wish to determine distance, we use a ruler or tape measure. We certainly wouldn't try to determine the weight of an object using a ruler or tape measure. While there might be some rough correlation between something like our girth and our weight, it would be at best a very inaccurate measurement. However, such a practice frequently occurs in education. If you want to determine how well a student can perform a particular skill, a multiple-choice test is unlikely to provide you with valid data. You need to have them perform the task in a way that satisfies the basic criteria for success. As Stiggins (2005) writes, "the artistry of classroom assessment emerges when teachers orchestrate a careful alignment among user information needs, achievement targets, and assessment methods" (p. 64).

Evaluation

A third term that is often used interchangeably with assessment is evaluation. *Evaluation* is making a judgment about the adequacy or the quality of something. Once you gather data through measurement, you need to ask what the data mean. Evaluation is the process of comparing the performance of an individual to criteria that helps make sense out of the data.

Normally there are two ways that evaluation criteria are determined. One is through what is termed *norm-referenced* evaluation. When using norm-referenced evaluation, the performance of an individual is compared to a reference group. On a teacher-constructed measurement tool, the performance of an individual might be compared to the performance of the rest of the class. This is what is commonly called "curving." A distribution of student scores is constructed and those at the top are identified as superior and those at the bottom are identified as failures. A conceptual problem related to this common practice is that the success of any one individual is determined by the performance of the group. If the class has a great number of high-achieving students, an individual might be identified as unsuccessful, whereas if they were in another group composed of lower-achieving students they might be identified as above average.

In addition, there are numerous situations where the standing of a person relative to a normative standard is irrelevant. For example, when we get on an airplane, we don't care how the pilot scored in terms of a normative group, we want to know if the pilot has mastered all the competencies required to get the plane off the ground, navigate it to the appropriate destination, and safely land it. We certainly do not want a pilot who has a high ranking in a reference group of incompetents!

For standardized tests, test developers usually administer the test to a sample of individuals and establish norms based on their performance. For this process to be valid, the sample needs to be representative of the total population. The performance of a given individual is then compared to the norm. There are some instances where norms are appropriate. For example, in child growth and development it is useful to know how the development of a given child compares to the norm. A wide variance from the norm might indicate a problem that needs to be investigated. Similarly, it is useful to know how students compare to a national norm in order to make informed decisions about the curriculum and our priorities. If students are regularly scoring below the norm, it also might signal the existence of a problem.

A second method for establishing evaluation criteria is ***criterion-referenced*** evaluation. This does not focus on a reference group but focuses on identified levels of acceptable performance. For example, in our previous pilot example, all pilots would be expected to reach a minimum level of performance required to fly an airplane regardless of how well the rest of the group performed. If none of the pilots in a group were able to meet the standards, none of them would pass.

In the classroom, using the criterion-referenced approach means that any students, or all, or none, may achieve success. Success is based on the level of performance as measured against a standard established as an indicator of acceptable performance. One major problem is that this standard may vary from teacher to teacher. One teacher might have very high standards so that few students reach acceptable levels and another teacher might have such low standards that all students achieve them with little effort.

In some subjects, such as mathematics, it can be relatively easy to establish indicators of required competence. For example, everyone needs to learn how to do addition problems almost flawlessly if they are to be successful in mathematics. However, does citing a given number of facts about the home state indicate that a student is competent in state history? It is not as easy to define the minimum criteria levels for many social studies objectives.

Grading

A final term is grading. A ***grade*** is how an evaluation is communicated to other interested parties. It is basically a communication system, and the effectiveness of a grading system ought to be based on the clarity with which it communicates the evaluation to others. The traditional system is the "A," "B," "C," system. However, if interested individuals, such as parents and students, do not understand the basis for a letter grade, then the communication is broken and the grading system is of questionable value. (See Arter & Chappuis, 2006, for an in-depth discussion of this issue.)

It is especially important for students to understand the basis for grading. If they believe that grades are arbitrary and based on chance or subjective criteria, there is little motivation for them to put forth additional effort.

TYPES OF ASSESSMENT

Whether you are focusing on information related to the overall effectiveness of your social studies program or on individual student performance, you want to adopt assessment procedures that allow you to answer "yes" to this question: "Are my assessments requiring students to demonstrate behaviors that are well matched to my learning goals and the demands they will face in the real world?"

In recent years, two general categories or philosophies of assessment have been popular. One of these categories is usually called "traditional assessment." Traditional assessment is generally comprised of those types of assessment where data regarding the presence of a given trait or attribute are gathered under controlled, standardized conditions. These are what most of us would refer to as "tests." They are usually paper-and-pencil–driven assessments containing multiple-choice or essay items where all individuals in a given testing situation are expected to respond to the same stimuli. There are generally "correct" and "incorrect" responses and student responses can be measured using a "key" of correct answers.

However, in recent years, some assessment experts contend that this "artificial" testing environment creates conditions that distort the assessment process and leads to erroneous conclusions about whether students have learned or acquired the necessary traits or attributes. They state that assessment ought to be a "natural" component of the teaching–learning process. Assessment should be "natural" or "authentic" by measuring student performance on real or authentic tasks. The assessment task should not be some sort of an "add-on" that intrudes and distorts teaching and learning (Smith, Smith, & De Lisi, 2001). This approach is consistent with the constructivist approach to learning and involves students more directly in making decisions about the assessment process. This approach is often called *authentic*, *natural*, or *alternative* assessment. In this chapter we view *alternative assessment* as the broader definition and will generally use this term.

Basic questions to ask regarding the type of assessment to use are, "What is the goal I am assessing?" and "What type of evidence is needed to indicate success?" The answer to these questions will provide guidance in selecting traditional or alternative assessment approaches.

Traditional Assessment

There are several selected response measurement tools that are generally used in traditional assessment, including true-false, multiple-choice, and matching items or tests. These types of measurement tools have the advantage of being easy to score. They have clear right and wrong answers and can be scored quickly. In some instances, machine scoring can be used to significantly reduce the time spent identifying correct responses. These measurement tools also have the advantage of measuring a wide selection of content. For example, a student can respond to numerous multiple-choice items covering a range of content in less time than that required to write a response to an essay item.

However, these measurement tools also have potential disadvantages. First, constructing good, valuable items that distinguish between those who know and those who don't know can take a lot of time. It is relatively difficult and time consuming to write good items. Too often, teachers wait until the last minute and end up writing poor items. Thus, student scores are based more on chance than on the attainment of important objectives. In addition, selected response items often do not measure important or complex objectives. Well-constructed multiple-choice items do have this potential, but considerable skill and effort is required to construct good items.

In the elementary grades there is often a temptation to use true-false items. Some teachers simply take content out of the textbook and change the wording around to make some of the items false. The data gathered through this measurement procedure are of questionable validity and value. At best, they measure low-level rote learning. True-false items are also subject to guessing. Every student has a 50 percent chance of getting an item right regardless of what they know. Therefore, it is difficult to discriminate between those students who have learned and those who have not.

The most common type of constructed response measurement used in traditional assessment is the essay item. Other constructed response types are short answer or sentence completion items. One of the advantages cited for an essay item is that it can measure complex outcomes. While this is true, teachers who give essay items often look for specific information when scoring so the item becomes little more than an inefficient measure of low-level learning. Essay items can also be influenced by factors such as handwriting and writing skill. Individuals with good writing skills can often "bluff" their way to a higher score.

Because essay items tend to focus on a very narrow content selection, it may be difficult to determine whether a student has learned all of the objectives. For this reason, short answer items are often a better choice. In addition, short answer items are more appropriate for upper-elementary and middle school students who have not mastered writing skills. Constructed response items such as sentence completion are a lot like true-false items. They tend to measure recall and rote learning and are of questionable value in determining whether a student has learned complex concepts.

Supporters of the traditional assessment approach argue that these measurement tools provide more objective data, are fair because they require all students to do the same tasks under the same conditions, and that the results are more readily accepted by other interested parties. In addition, traditional assessment is the approach most often used by large-scale, high-stakes accountability (standardized) tests and it only makes sense to prepare students to take these types of tests.

However, additional concerns must be considered. Although standardized test scores themselves are criterion referenced, as percent correct, to the national or state standards the test relates to, student outcomes are often *reported* using a norm-referenced basis such as averages or percentiles. This identifies how well each student has performed compared to the sample of students used to norm the test. It does not allow useful conclusions to be drawn concerning how well a given student has mastered a particular objective.

When test results are reported using a criterion-referenced basis, such as percent correct, it is important to identify if multiple items focused on the important concepts or content. How a student responds to any one item is a poor indicator of their overall knowledge of the concept or the content.

Alternative Assessment Methods

You have probably heard someone say that "teachers shouldn't teach to the test." The logic behind this view is that most tests sample too narrow a range of what students need to know. What is the real problem here? Is it the act of teaching to the test, or is it the test itself? Today, many educators argue that poorly designed tests pose the greater difficulty.

Their concerns result from an appreciation that students' performances on many traditional test types are poor indicators of their levels of expertise. For example, if your purpose is to test students' abilities to write clear, coherent paragraphs, a true-false test requiring them to recognize appropriate and inappropriate usages of "who" and "whom" will give you a poor measure of your learners' writing abilities. You cannot presume that students receiving even high scores on such a test are better writers than students with lower scores. What you need are assessment procedures that tie more clearly to your instructional purpose: developing learners' writing skills. This means that the assessment procedures you adopt should require students, to the extent possible, to engage in behaviors that have a clear, logical relationship to what you have been teaching. If your intent has been to improve the writing skills of members of your class, then your assessment should require them to write.

You probably can think of many examples where assessment is directly related to what proficient people are expected to do in the "real world." For example, at some time in your life you may have tried out for a part in a play. Tryouts typically require people to become familiar with the play, read the lines of one of the characters, use appropriate vocal expression, and employ appropriate gestures. The person selecting the cast wants to choose actors who will play their roles credibly. The selection process, logically, requires people seeking parts to speak lines and do other things that, if selected, they will do when the play is presented. It simply

Teacher observation of student interaction is a form of informal, alternative assessment.

Mike Medici/Silver Burdett Ginn

would make no sense to base cast selection on scores on a multiple-choice test given over the content of the play. In short, the kind of assessment that typically is used to select people for roles in a play is ***authentic***; that is, the process requires a prospective actor to engage in and be judged on behaviors that are relevant to what this person will be expected to do if chosen to play a part.

This is an example of "authentic assessment" because the assessment has a clear relationship to the real task the individual will be expected to demonstrate. ***Authentic*** or ***natural*** assessment seeks opportunities to measure student learning in the content of a natural or authentic task. This type of assessment is based on what students are able to demonstrate in a setting that replicates many features of the world beyond school.

Most of us have also participated in situations where there is a mix of traditional and alternative, authentic assessment. For example, obtaining a driver's license generally requires a traditional assessment relating to knowledge of the "rules of the road" followed by actually driving a car and following the commands of the examiner.

Supporters of authentic/natural assessment argue against educators making summary judgments using only data drawn from tests that require students to recall isolated bits of information in an artificial situation. Instead, they argue that teachers should first assess students to determine their mastery of the necessary factual underpinnings to the targeted learning, and then, as Herman (1997, p. 9) suggests, emphasize "how and whether students organize, structure, and use that information in context to solve complex problems." Supporters of natural assessment point out that the assessment task itself becomes a learning opportunity and is therefore more consistent with the overall purposes of education (Spady, 1994).

Performance Tasks   An important part of alternative assessment is the construction of the performance task. This requires you to define a task where students will apply and demonstrate the skills and knowledge consistent with the learning objectives. For example, if you are interested in whether students have learned a problem-solving skill, they need to be presented with a task that requires them to solve a problem. If you want to assess their ability to work cooperatively with others, then they need to be given a performance task that requires them to do this.

Examples of performance tasks include performing a dramatization or a role play, participating in a simulation, conducting an interview, giving a skit, writing a poem, preparing a report, developing a collage, making a model, preparing a slide show, creating a data display, creating a diorama, and conducting a mock trial. Performance tasks have long been a part of some aspects of the school curriculum. For example, science fairs ask students to develop something that demonstrates knowledge of science and art programs require students to assemble samples of their work in a portfolio. The same sort of requirements can be applied to assessing social studies outcomes.

When defining a performance task for students, you need to clearly define the learning target, and use that definition to clearly present the nature of the task. For example, if your learning target is, "Students will learn at least three events in our state's history, and know how these events relate to one another," you could then tell students that their task is to create a museum display on some aspect of state history. The display is to include written material, a diorama, graphs, maps, and pictures and murals. The clearer learning target and the nature of the task are defined, the higher the potential quality of the performance.

Your ideas on performance tasks are limited only by your creativity, within the constraints of the defined learning target. They can become assignments that both motivate students as well as provide you for an opportunity to assess important social studies outcomes.

Portfolios One of the common approaches to alternative assessment is the use of portfolios. A *portfolio* is a collection of student work that covers a specific period of time. Student portfolios are analagous to an artist's portfolio. The artist puts together a selection of their work to demonstrate their abilities to others. Similarly, portfolios in social studies provide students with opportunities to organize and present samples of their work, often together with personal reflections that indicate what they have learned (Stiggins, 2005). If portfolios are kept and built over time, they provide a developmental profile of students in your class from the beginning to the end of the school year. Some schools pass them from teacher to teacher. This process allows for a cumulative growth record that spans many years of an individual learner's development.

You can configure portfolios in many ways. You might choose to include any of the following features:

- Assignments students have finished
- Written comments by students about content they have learned (or about other relevant issues)
- Written comments by students that include their thoughts about and reactions to discussions, speakers, and other instructional events
- Prompt questions for the student that you write in the portfolio
- Written responses by the student to your prompt questions
- Pasted-in materials such as photos, sketches, short articles, drawings, and maps
- Summary statements regarding what has been learned
- Self-evaluation statements regarding those parts of the content students now think they know well and those parts they continue to find difficult to understand

You need to adjust these guidelines so they make sense given the age and sophistication levels of your students. For example, if you are working with very young children, you might develop a format that includes samples of work, anecdotal records, checklists or inventories of important behaviors, responses of students to questions and requests, and results of screening tests (Grace, 1992). This approach provides you with an age-appropriate vehicle for gathering and monitoring information about the development of each person in your class.

Properly speaking, a portfolio is primarily a communications tool; teachers and the students themselves use the portfolio's contents to demonstrate to others the extent of their achievement. Portfolios also may be used as assessment tools when students collect their contents specifically for teacher evaluation. However, portfolio assessment takes time. One recent study found that teachers were committing about 17 hours a month to work with learner portfolios (Herman, 1997). This number would seem high if the only function of the portfolio were to evaluate students. However, remember that portfolios function not only as a database for making judgments about your learners' progress, but also as an integral part of your instructional program. Hence, you may find the time required to use portfolios is justified given the learning benefits that come to your class members as a result of portfolio-connected work they do.

Alternative Assessment Measurement Tools

For the most part, selected response measurement tools do not fit well with alternative assessment. The basic philosophy of alternative assessment focuses on making the assessment task more authentic and realistic and selected response tools do not fit well with this philosophy.

Selected response in alternative assessment is best viewed as allowing students to select the items they wish to include in a portfolio. While the included items are those actually constructed by the student, the requirements for a portfolio often indicate a list of items to include. Thus, the student must select items from those you prescribe.

Alternative assessment fits more naturally with constructed response as a type of measurement. Generally the assessment is based on student performances, assignments, projects, demonstrations, exhibitions, collections, student response papers, reaction papers, and self-evaluations.

These types of items require the creation of some different measurement tools and evaluation procedures. Measurement tools often used in connection with alternative assessment include rating scales, rubrics, checklists, and attitude inventories.

Rating Scales Most of us are familiar with the rating scale. It is a commonly used assessment or measurement tool when observing a performance. Generally, rating scales involve some sort of a hierarchy indicating the quality of the thing observed, usually consisting of 3 to 5 points along a scale. These points are often identified with qualitative terms such as *excellent, above average, good, adequate,* and *unacceptable*. Other rating scales use a strictly numerical scale, such as 1 to 5, with one end of the scale labeled as *best* and the other as *worst*.

Rating scales are developed by identifying a set of focus characteristics such as "clarity of presentation," "accuracy," or "neatness." A rating scale might then be created for each important characteristic. Products or presentations are then assessed by indicating the quality along the points on the scale.

In some instances there is common understanding of what is meant by "excellent" or "good." For example, judges for Olympic events such as gymnastics or skating may have such clear understanding of gradations of performance that they can award ratings with a high degree of consistency across judges. Some veteran teachers claim that they have so much experience that they can easily discern differences in products and performances. However, for many educational performances there is not a clear understanding of what is meant by these evaluative terms. As a result, two raters who observed a given student might award the learner quite different ratings. In the language of test-design specialists, this rating scale lacks *reliability* (the ability to produce consistent results when applied to similar situations). For this reason, rating scales, although relatively easy to construct and score, are often viewed as limited when measuring authentic or natural performance tasks. Figure 12-1 shows a sample rating scale.

Rubrics A common measurement tool often used for alternative assessment purposes is what is called a rubric. A *rubric* is a mechanism that "defines the features of work that constitute quality" (Arter & Chappuis, 2006, p. 3). Many rubrics are simply behaviorally anchored rating scales. What this means is that for every point on a rating scale a behavioral descriptor is provided so that the evaluator will

FIGURE 12-1 • Example of a Rating Scale for Cooperative Learning

Always		Usually		Never
Always		**Usually**		**Never**

Accepts responsibility for achieving group goal.

5	4	3	2	1

Performs assigned role.

5	4	3	2	1

Listens to the contributions of others.

5	4	3	2	1

Contributes to the group discussion.

5	4	3	2	1

Works cooperatively with others.

5	4	3	2	1

know whether the portfolio or the performance merits the score of a 1, 2, 3, and so forth. Good rubrics have clear descriptors so that there is a high degree of observer agreement concerning the score. This means that two or more people who view the same product or performance will award similar scores. Rubrics can go a long way in removing a lot of the subjectivity that is often present in alternative assessment techniques. However, good rubrics are difficult to construct and often require considerable time to test and revise so that they truly capture different levels of performance.

There are some other advantages to rubrics that can benefit instruction. Clear rubrics help you define your instruction. If you have defined different levels of performance, those definitions help you make sure your instruction is consistent with the expected performance (Arter & McTighe, 2001). This relationship is not as clear in other measurement tools, such as checklists. Another advantage of quality rubrics is that when provided to students, they give them a clearer understanding of what they need to do to be successful. Most students are interested in getting the best grade or the top rating. However, often they do not know what they have to do to get that grade and view the whole grading scheme as a game of chance. A good rubric gives them constructive guidance in reaching the higher scores and allows them to engage in self-evaluation.

One critic once complained that if students knew what was expected, they would be able to do it! This is certainly the case. As Stiggins (2005) puts it, "students can hit any target that they see and that holds still for them" (p. 34). After all, aren't we interested in trying to get all of our students to perform at the highest possible

FIGURE 12-2 • Rubric for an Oral Presentation

5 Problem questions is clearly stated, with important aspects emphasized
Presentation is smooth and flowing
Eye contact established and maintained
Notes used but not read from directly
Sufficient data and facts incorporated
Conclusions logically flow from data

4 Problem question is clearly stated, but important aspects may not
be emphasized
Presentation is generally logical with a couple lapses
Moderate eye contact
Notes used, with some reading from notes
Some facts and data included
Conclusions not fully supported by information

3 Problem question is stated with little or no emphasis on important
aspects
The presentation does not have a smooth flow
Very little eye contact
Most of the presentation read from notes
A few bits of information included
Conclusions minimally supported by data

2 Problem question read with little enthusiasm
Presentation not logical, skips around
Very little eye contact
Whole presentation read from notes
Minimal information included
Conclusions minimally supported by data

1 Problem question not clearly stated or not stated at all
No logical flow to the presentation
No eye contact
No notes written or used
No meaningful information presented
No conclusion or conclusion unsupported by data

level? This critic's concern was that norm-referenced grading on a curve would not work in evaluating performances. Rubrics offer criterion-referenced alternatives, and are especially suited to authentic assessment contexts. Figure 12-2 shows a sample rubric.

Checklists Another type of measurement tool often used in alternative assessment is a checklist. A *checklist* identifies important components that must be present in a product or a performance. The difference between checklists and rubrics is that rubrics allow you to make qualitative distinctions in a performance whereas a checklist identifies only whether certain components are present or absent. A checklist might be useful in assessing exhibitions, demonstrations, student reports, and student performances. Checklists can be used in combination with more traditional assessment approaches; for example, a checklist might be useful when scoring an essay question. The checklist directs attention to the significant things that should be contained in the item. Then comments or a rubric might be added to indicate the quality of the essay.

Because checklists have a simple "yes-no" dimension, making an evaluation based on the data gathered from a checklist can be problematic. There are a couple of variations that can be added to make them more useful in the evaluation process. One technique is to base the evaluation on the number of items on the checklist that are included in the performance. For example, 8 out of 10 is good, 6 out of 10 acceptable, 4 out of 10 unacceptable. Another technique is to award different point values to the items on the checklist. Those that are identified as the most important might be worth more points that those that are of minor importance.

Checklists are especially useful in measuring behaviors in authentic or natural settings. For example, the examiner for the driver's license test cited earlier uses a checklist to determine whether the candidate has passed the driving performance part of the examination. On the checklist, some items are considered so important that if not present, the candidate immediately fails. Other items lead to lesser deductions.

Measurement specialists Gronlund and Linn (1990) identify characteristics of good checklists. The following list draws on their work:

- Identify and describe each desired student behavior as specifically as possible.
- Add to this list the most common incorrect, or error, behaviors.
- Arrange the list of desired behaviors and incorrect, or error, behaviors in the approximate order one might expect to see them.
- Develop a simple procedure for checking each action as it occurs.

A complete set of checklists on each class member not only provides you with information about each child but also can indicate problems shared by a significant number of students. If you find that large numbers of students are confused, you can remedy this situation by addressing relevant content during subsequent classroom discussions and lessons. Figure 12-3 presents a sample checklist.

Attitude Inventories Not all assessment is directed at obtaining measures of students' cognitive achievement. There are times when you may be interested in knowing something about your learners' attitudes. This is especially true in alternative assessment where there is an interest in measuring outcomes other than knowledge acquistion. Attitude inventories are useful for collecting information about student attitudes and feelings.

Attitude inventories call on students to rate their relative interest in subjects or topics. One approach is to present members of your class with a list of alternatives. Tell them to indicate their preferences in rank order. If there are six items, they will indicate their first- through sixth-place preferences.

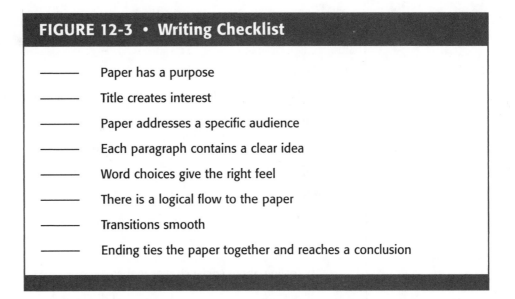

FIGURE 12-3 • Writing Checklist

——— Paper has a purpose

——— Title creates interest

——— Paper addresses a specific audience

——— Each paragraph contains a clear idea

——— Word choices give the right feel

——— There is a logical flow to the paper

——— Transitions smooth

——— Ending ties the paper together and reaches a conclusion

Suppose at the beginning of the school year you found that members of your class ranked social studies as low in importance and low in their interest level. A significant part of your effort during the year might be directed toward stimulating an interest and helping students see the importance of social studies in their lives. To determine the success of your efforts, you could administer an attitude inventory several times during the school year. You would first administer the inventory at the beginning of the year. Students could then complete the inventory again at various times later in the year after they had been exposed to lessons designed to enhance their interest. Your hope would be that later administrations of the attitude inventory would reveal that your social studies lessons had resulted in improved student interest in the subject. Figure 12-4 presents a sample attitude inventory.

Problems in Implementing Alternative Assessment

Although there is solid logic to support the idea of alternative assessment, implementing it often poses difficulties. In a nutshell, although many people agree that students should be expected to demonstrate in sophisticated ways what they have learned, there is by no means widespread agreement about what form these demonstrations should take or the criteria to apply for evaluating them. In addition, natural or authentic assessments that can be applied to large populations are difficult to design and costly to implement and evaluate. Therefore, they may not be a practical alternative to traditonal assessment procedures that are used for accountabilty purposes. For example, one state attempted to apply natural assessment to the certification process for new teachers. The state decided that all certification applicants would provide a video of their teaching along with their application for the teaching credential. The idea was quickly dropped when they confronted complex issues such as identifying a set of criteria that could be applied to all teaching episodes

FIGURE 12-4 • Social Studies Attitude Inventory

Instructions:

Place an X on the spot along the line that best indicates how you feel.

1. I think social studies is

   Interesting ____|___|___|___|___|___ Boring

   Important ___|___|___|___|___|___ Unimportant

2. When I think of social studies I usually think of

   Facts ___|___|___|___|___|___ People

   Long ago |___|___|___|___|___|___ Today

3. My feeling about social studies is that

   I like it ___|___|___|___|___|___ I dislike it

across all subjects and grade levels, training observers to view the videos fairly and consistenly, and the tremendous amount of time (and cost) required to view the thousands of videos that would be submitted in a given year.

Long-standing tradition also represents a challenge to those favoring more use of alternative assessment procedures. Parents and other community members have memories of school days featuring essays, short-answer quizzes, and lots of tests with true-false and multiple-choice items. They also are used to seeing grades awarded according to students' performances on these kinds of exams. Alternative assessment represents a departure from these familiar procedures. Because even some of its supporters admit that debate remains about what should go into a high-quality authentic assessment program, some educators, administrators, parents, and others in the community may be reluctant to support efforts to move away from more traditional evaluation practices.

Another issue has to do with the cost of authentic assessment. Estimates vary widely, but some work has been done that compares costs of traditional multiple-choice testing of learners with authentic assessments. It has been reported that the cost of preparing, administering, and grading hands-on authentic assessment tests is 400 to 500 percent higher than preparing, administering, and grading more traditional multiple-choice tests (Herman, 1997). This cost differential probably ensures that many schools will opt for a middle ground that encourages teachers to use a mix of alternative assessment and traditional assessment in their instructional programs.

In summary, it is fair to say that interest in alternative assessment is high. Support for the idea of requiring learners to engage in sophisticated demonstrations of learning continues to grow. Researchers are hard at work on issues associated with establishing quality standards for a variety of alternative assessment approaches.

THE ASSESSMENT BLUEPRINT

One of the basic principles of assessment is that important and worthwhile objectives should be its focus. Unfortunately, many teachers assess what is easiest to measure or base their evaluations on subjective feelings. Therefore, some important objectives may not be assessed at all and the data gathered may inaccurately indicate what students have learned. This relates to the issue of fairness. A *fair* assessment is generally defined as one that is not unduly influenced by factors unrelated to the learning objectives (McMillan, 2001). Most of us can probably point to a time in our education when we felt we were not assessed fairly.

One way of addressing the fairness issue is to develop an assessment blueprint. An *assessment blueprint* outlines what will be assessed and how it will be assessed. This helps you focus your instruction on important objectives and helps you avoid last-minute decisions based on questionable data. It is best to outline the assessment blueprint when you are planning the unit of study.

The blueprint should identify the objective for the unit of instruction, assessment procedure for each objective, and the weight given to each assessment. For example, suppose you are teaching a unit in the upper elementary grades on weather and climate. Your objectives might be as follows:

1. Knows basic terms such as thermometer, barometer, rain gauge, wind current, precipitation, humidity, high pressure, low pressure.
2. Understands influences of bodies of water and wind currents on the climate of a given place.
3. Interprets weather maps.

The next step would be to identify an assessment procedure for each objective. The types of assessments you choose should be based on the nature of the objective and the characteristics of the students you are teaching. For example, in early elementary grades, you will probably use very few formal measurement tools. Rather, you would rely more on daily work, observations of participation, and student projects. However, in upper grades, more formal tests and measurement tools are likely to be introduced.

The assessment blueprint should identify important objectives and the method you will use to assess each of the objectives. Table 12-1 is an example of a blueprint for this weather and climate unit.

In this unit there are three major objectives. The first objective, knowing basic terms, lends itself to traditional assessment measures such as a quiz. It can also be assessed through daily work assignments or student observation. There are clear definitions to the terms and a simple quiz would be an efficient way to measure this type of knowledge.

The second objective requires students to know the influence of various factors on climate and how the climate of a place is related to where that place is located in relationship to those factors. While parts of this objective could also be assessed using traditional measurement tools such as multiple-choice items, this teacher felt a performance task asking student to make predictions based on the location of various influences would be a better indicator of student learning.

TABLE 12-1
Assessment Blueprint for Weather and Climate

OBJECTIVES	ASSESSMENT TYPE	TOTAL VALUE
Knows basic terms	Daily assignments, traditional assessment quiz using matching, multiple-choice items	20 points
Influences of wind currents, bodies of water, mountain ranges on climate	Performance Task: Provide the student with a map of a place showing oceans and prevailing winds, mountain ranges. The student predicts the climate.	40 points
Interprets weather maps	Performance Task: Students are provided with simple weather maps taken off of the Internet. They work in a group with others to present a weathercast to the rest of the class.	40 points

The third objective was also measured using a performance task. This time, students would have to work in a cooperative learning group with others to present a mock weather broadcast. This would allow the teacher to assess other important objectives such as cooperation and ability to work with others.

The teacher also decided that knowledge of terms was less important than the other two objectives and so assigned it only 20 points. The other two objectives were viewed as central to the unit and were therefore given more points toward the total.

EVALUATION AND GRADING

Once data have been gathered and recorded for each learner, you need to evaluate student performance. Evaluation and grading are among the more difficult tasks for teachers and many do not like to do them. There are several reasons for their reluctance. First, there are several sources of data and lots of information that need to be considered. This information might include homework assignments, daily work, portfolios, classroom observations, group projects, quizzes or examinations, student notebooks, and journals. How much weight should be given to each data source in arriving at a final evaluation? This is really a matter of professional judgment, but your decision should be based on the assessment of how well students achieved your important learning objectives.

Secondly, there are many other variables that are often considered when evaluating a student. The evaluation might consider attitude, attendance, effort, class participation, work habits, and progress. How should these be factored into the evaluation? The general feeling among educators is, do not factor anything into an evaluation as a grade that does not *directly* relate to communicating a student's level of achievement of the specific learning objective or objectives (Stiggins, 2005). In some schools separate evaluations are made for content attainment, attitudes, and work habits.

Product, Process, Progress

Basically, three dimensions are typically considered in an evaluation—the product, the process, and the progress. *Product* refers to the summative performance of the student. It addresses the question, what was the outcome of the learning sequence? *Process* refers to how the student arrived at the outcome. The process might take into account effort, creativity, work habits, cooperation, and attitude. *Progress* refers to student growth and how much the student progressed over the course of a unit or the grading period.

Of these three, it is generally easiest to assess the product. The product is something concrete that can be evaluated against state or school district standards or compared to the work of others. Although there are those who argue that all that is important is the final product or the outcome, there is evidence to the contrary. Process can be at least as important. For example, a major reason people are dismissed from their job is not because they lack skill but because they are unable to work with others. Therefore, if we are preparing students for the world outside the classroom, the process is at least as important as the product. In addition, because of rapid change and innovation, our students will be facing a world that we can barely imagine. This requires that they are able to adapt to new situations and be creative. Once again, process variables seem to be critical.

Consider this scenario. Suppose one student begins a unit with a great deal of knowledge about the subject and scores high in the initial assessments. However, the student puts forth little effort and shows little growth. Another student enters the unit with little prior knowledge and scores poorly on initial assessments. However, this student puts forth a great deal of effort and demonstrates considerable growth. At the end of the unit both students are at about the same place. Should they both be given the same grade?

One of the authors once worked in a school district where grades were to be given according to whether the student was functioning on grade level. For example,

Conferences with individual students is a good method to use when assessing process.

Scott Cunningham/Merrill

a student in the third grade who was reading on the third-grade level was to get a grade of "C." A student reading on the fourth-grade level was to be given a "B" and one reading at the fifth-grade level or above was to get an "A." In this particular school all the students were from low socioeconomic backgrounds and most were from Spanish-speaking homes. The learning deficits of students from such socioeconomic backgrounds are well documented. Many start school one or two years behind their middle-class counterparts. In other words, they start school as "D" or "F" students and must work twice as hard as their middle-class counterparts to even get a "C." Was this a fair evaluation process that communicated important information to others? Probably not.

Grading System Purposes

The beginning point for making decisions about the grading system you will use is to identify the purpose of the system. There are several important purposes for grades.

1. *Communicating the evaluation to parents and other interested parties.* Evaluation is making judgments about the quality of the work, and grading is communicating the evaluation to other interested parties. This is an important purpose because parents want to know how well their child is doing in school. In later years the grades students receive take on increased importance as they seek admission to higher education and employment. Communicating the results of the evaluation to others is an important purpose and needs to be done thoughtfully.

2. *Incentives for students to learn.* This is often a major concern of elementary teachers. All students want to be successful and they often view grades as indicators of their success. There is evidence that the amount of effort that students put forth is related to the grades they have received (Guskey & Bailey, 2001). This is just common sense. Would you continue to put forth effort in a job where that effort was never recognized? How would you feel about going to work every day when you perceived little or no possibility of success? How do you react when you believe your chances for success are slim? Put yourself in the role of students who come to your class every day with these expectations. How highly motivated do you think they will be?

   Students often see grades as the "paycheck" for their school efforts and as reinforcement for their actions. Grades can be especially powerful in the elementary school. Students are just forming their self-concepts and low grades can establish an image of failure that can follow them for the rest of their life. Students who put forth considerable effort and do not see it reflected in their grades are likely to decrease their effort or give up entirely.

   On the other hand, when grades are given too freely, students feel little incentive to put forth effort. In other words, grades have value when they are perceived both as being related to effort and ability and as just and fair. Most of us who have been in classes in higher education have experienced satisfaction in a grade lower than the highest when we know that the course was difficult, we put forth good effort, and the grade was a fair indication of our performance.

3. *To select and identify students for special programs.* Grades are often used as indicators of special needs. For example, students who consistently do well in some part of the curriculum are chosen to participate in gifted and talented programs and for special enrichment opportunities. Teachers often encourage students with special talents to seek opportunities to develop those talents. Similarly, low grades are often used as indicators for students who need special help in some area.

In general, teachers generally spend considerable time trying to determine whether a grade is a fair indication of student performance and how it is likely to impact the student. Often the grade given is the result of balancing those purposes.

Grading Methods

Once the purpose of the grading system is identified, then you can move on to deciding the method that best matches your purpose. Remember, you want a grading system that most clearly communicates your evaluation to other interested parties. One choice might be a narrative system that provides a lengthy description of student performance. However, this is time consuming. At the opposite end of the spectrum is the traditional letter grade. This is where one symbol is used to summarize student performance. However, using one symbol to represent a variety of assessments and objectives doesn't convey much information and can be very misleading.

One decision you need to make is to determine if you are going to use a norm-referenced system or a criterion-referenced system. Remember, a *norm-referenced* system compares the performance of an individual to a reference group and a *criterion-referenced* system compares performance to a standard.

We generally prefer a criterion-referenced system. One reason for our choice is that we think norm-referenced systems set up needless competition between students. Because growth and development rates can vary greatly in elementary-aged students, we think it is better to judge student progress against a standard as opposed to against each other. In addition, our philosophy is that we want all students to achieve competency and a norm-referenced system may not readily indicate this.

There are several grading methods that can be used with either norm-referenced or criterion-referenced systems. Often the specific method used will be determined by the school or the school district. They seek to have some uniformity in the grading system so that parents will not be confused.

Letter Grades Letter grades are the most common grading method. They have a long history in American education and therefore are readily accepted by others outside of education. However, an important concern is identifying what a letter grade actually means.

Most report cards have a key that gives a brief descriptor for each grade. Many of the letter grade systems seem to be keyed to a norm-referenced evaluation system. A common key is as follows:

A = Excellent
B = Above Average

C = Average
D = Below Average
F = Failing

This key is centered around "average." This is clearly a normative term. A problem with this norm-referenced system is that we don't know the reference group against which the student is evaluated. Is it average for this class? The average for this school? The average for all students at this grade level? *Average* is usually defined subjectively by the teacher and the definition varies greatly from teacher to teacher.

The letter grading system can be keyed to a criterion-referenced system by changing the descriptors. A key that would define a letter grading system in terms of a criterion-referenced system might be as follows:

A = Exceptional Performance
B = Good Performance
C = Acceptable Performance
D = Poor Performance
F = Unacceptable Performance

These descriptors have no indication that the student is being compared to others. It might be possible for all students to reach the good or exceptional levels. Or, it might be that no one reaches these levels.

As with norm-referenced definitions, there is a potential problem. How is *acceptable* defined? What is required are specific indicators or a rubric for each of these levels so that the teacher, parents, and all other concerned parties have clear understanding of what is defined as exceptional, good, and so forth. Doing this task well can eliminate many disagreements and has the advantage of telling both student and parents exactly what needs to be done to receive a higher grade.

Grades Based on Percentages Another method for assigning grades is to base the grade on the percentage of points accumulated or percentage of objectives achieved. This is also a popular grading system.

One of the most common approaches is to decide on the amount of points that are to be given for particular assignments and examinations. At the end of the grading period these points are totaled and grades are then given based on the percentage of total points the student has received. The following grading scale is often used:

90% + = A
80–89% = B
70–79% = C
60–69% = D
< 59% = F

An issue that needs to be addressed when using a percentage system is to decide the relative weights given to various assessments. For example, how many total points should be given for daily work? How many points of the total should be given to the portfolio? Should work habits, attitude, and so on be given points that are a part of the total?

Another important task when using a percentage system is to have a scoring rubric for each assessment that provides guidance for deciding how to allocate the points. If, for example, a particular assignment were to be worth 10 points, you need to define what a 9 or a 10 would require, what a 7 or an 8 would require, and so on. This would be a matter of professional judgment and different teachers might award points differently.

One difficulty associated with using a point system for grading is that parents still assume a norm-referenced system when interpreting grades. They interpret a grade of "C" as meaning average and "B" as above average. Care needs to be taken to make sure that parents understand the basis for the grading system.

Pass/Fail This is one of the simplest grading methods and one that some teachers prefer. This eliminates making fine distinctions. Pass/fail could be useful in early elementary grades for discouraging competition and the negative self-image problems that might result when learners receive low letter grades. The pass/fail system would appear to be an appropriate one in an age of standards-based instruction. Each student demonstrates they either have reached a minimum level of competence for each standard or they have not.

An important consideration in a pass/fail system is defining a minimum level of competency or the criteria for a "pass." In some instances, teachers might argue that a pass requires "mastery" of the material while others might set the standard at a level that would be equivalent to "average" in a norm-referenced system. Once again, this is a matter of professional judgment. Many social studies standards are vague enough to leave lots of room for judgment. Therefore, pass/fail decisions would vary from teacher to teacher.

Another issue relating to pass/fail relates to how students who go beyond the minimum are reinforced or rewarded. Some argue that in a pass/fail system, students are reinforced to only put forth the minimum amount effort needed to pass. There is no incentive for excellence. While this can certainly be the case in higher grades, most elementary students are not simply working for a grade and reinforcement can be provided on individual projects and assignments.

One variation often found in elementary schools is a three-level grading system. This might be categories designated as E, S, and N, defined as "excellent," "satisfactory" and "needs improvement." This allows for some recognition for those who are going beyond the minimum and changing "failing" to "needs improvement" softens the negative impact of the term *fail*. However, this can be misinterpreted by parents to mean that everything is generally fine except for a little needed improvement.

Descriptive Grading Systems In an age of standards-based instruction, the ambiguity often associated with letter grades has led some schools and even some states to develop more descriptive categories for grading. For example, in Kentucky many elementary schools have adopted the categories of the statewide assessment system. These categories are "Novice," "Apprentice," "Proficient," and "Distinguished." These categories identify points along a proficiency continuum and attempt to avoid pejorative labels such as "failing" or "poor." Other terms that are commonly used in descriptive systems are "beginning," "progressing," "acquiring," "extending," and "advanced." These terms combine the evaluation of a product and progress. For example, "proficient" and "advanced" certainly indicate that the product is acceptable. Terms such as "beginning," "progressing," "acquiring," are progress terms.

This type of grading system is more aligned with standards-based instruction. The standard is identified and then the continuum used to indicate the student progress toward meeting the standard.

While these terms are more descriptive than the traditional letter grade system, the question of whether they communicate more information to parents and others is open to debate. Once again, the terms need to have definitions or indicators attached to them. For example, exactly what is meant by the terms *apprentice* or *proficient?* Shouldn't we always be expecting students to be progressing? When should a student cease to be a novice and be expected to be proficient? These definitions, by themselves, offer little guidance to a parent or students.

Whether these systems are successful in eliminating the negative connotations associated with letter grades is also questionable. Some parents and older students just convert them to letter grades and state, "Oh, that's the same as a 'C.'"

Narrative Evaluations *Narratives* are written descriptions of student achievement. They have most often been used in early elementary grades and are often used in combination with parent conferences. However, a few universities also have developed narrative evaluations. The contention is that they can provide a much more detailed and specific indication of the strengths and weaknesses of a given student. They point out that the narrative can address a number of important variables.

However, narrative systems are only as good as those writing them. Because it takes considerable time to write narratives, (just think of how much time would be required to write narratives for 30 students in all the subjects taught in an elementary classroom!) they tend to be relatively brief and often very general. In many cases, the same phrases are used over and over as the teacher writes the narrative. In fact, some places offer a computerized menu of comments that can be used when developing a narrative. Therefore, narratives may not be much more personalized than other grading systems.

In summary, a number of grading system options is available to you as a teacher. The specific system may be designated by the school or the school district where you are employed. However, you will still have many decisions to make. The bottom line is that grading is still largely a matter of professional judgment. You need to make sure that you have assessment data to support the judgments you make.

KEY IDEAS IN SUMMARY

- Your assessment responsibilities go well beyond developing and administering procedures related to what your students learn. Today, you also need to consider what you can do to document the overall effectiveness of your instructional programs and to assess how well your learners are meeting the expectations contained in state curriculum standards.

- Authentic/natural assessment involves the use of procedures that encourage your learners to master and demonstrate content in ways that are highly similar to how this content is used by proficient adults. The idea is to get away from traditional testing techniques that reward behaviors that, sometimes, have little relevance for the world beyond school. In using alternative assessment, you are challenged both to identify appropriate ways for students to demonstrate what they have learned and to establish appropriate standards to use in judging the adequacy of students' performance.

- *Portfolios* increasingly are used in alternative assessment programs, both as communications tools and as a means to gather student work for teacher evaluation. One of their advantages is that they make evaluation an integral part of your instructional process. You can design portfolios in many ways. Among features you may wish to include are (1) samples of assignments students have completed, (2) written comments by students about what they have learned, (3) written comments by students about their reactions to instructional events they have experienced, (4) prompt questions that you write yourself, (5) student responses to your prompt questions, (6) visual materials pasted in by your students, (7) summary statements regarding what has been learned, and (8) self-evaluations written by your students about their mastery of various elements of content.

- *Rating scales* and *checklists* provide information about specific student behaviors. You can also use rating scales to make judgments about several levels of performance. Most checklists indicate only whether a student can or cannot do something.
- *Rubrics* are mechanisms for defining quality in student work. They define specific behavioral indicators at each step of the rating scale so that the evaluator has a guide for evaluating the work.
- You can use *attitude inventories* to obtain information about learners' reactions to various school subjects and to various parts of your social studies program. They require students to rate their relative interest in alternative selections.
- You need to remember that you can use results of student assessment to provide general information about the effectiveness of your program as well as information about how well each person in your class is doing. By examining these test results, you can learn which aspects of your lessons were well understood and which parts confused your learners. You can use this information to modify your instruction in ways that will help learners better grasp sections that, initially, many may not have well understood.
- Grading is one task that most teachers dislike. This is because there is usually a number of variables that must be considered when giving a grade. These variables include the product of the learning, the process of learning, and the progress of the students. Most grades reflect a compromise that includes two or more of these variables.
- There are a number of grading systems currently in use in elementary schools. The search continues as educators try to find grading systems that communicate clearly to others the performance of the student. Common approaches include letter grades, percentages, pass/fail, descriptive, and narrative systems. All systems have some element of subjectivity and require professional judgment to apply.

CHAPTER REFLECTIONS

Now that you have read the chapter, think about these questions.

1. As a teacher today, your assessment obligations go well beyond evaluating students and using results to award grades and communicate progress to parents. You also need to consider ways to gather assessment data to provide evidence regarding (1) the overall effectiveness of your social studies program and (2) how well members of your class are living up to performance expectations embedded within state-level standards. As you think about these tasks, what are some actions you can take to prepare for these important assessment responsibilities?

2. You now are familiar with some arguments by people who either (1) strongly support or (2) strongly oppose authentic assessment. How do you feel about authentic assessment, and on what do you base your position?

3. Do you think that process and progress as well as the final product should be included when evaluating students? How will you consider process and progress in your evaluations of students?

4. What is your position on norm-referenced and criterion-referenced grading systems? What do you see as the advantages and the disadvantages of each?

5. What grading method do you prefer? Why do you prefer that system? What types of records will you need to keep to support that method?

6. Suppose you looked carefully at the results of a test you had given to members of your class and found that students had failed to respond correctly to large numbers of items related to two areas of content your exam covered. It is clear that you could revise lessons related to this content so that subsequent groups of students might grasp it more adequately than your present group of learners. But what about members of your present class? What might you do to help them better master material that your test scores suggest they failed to learn well?

REFERENCES

Altenbaugh, R. J. (2003). *The American people and their education: A social history.* Upper Saddle River, NJ: Merrill/Prentice Hall.

Armstrong, D. G. (2003). *Curriculum today.* Upper Saddle River, NJ: Merrill/Prentice Hall.

Arter, J., & Chappuis, J. (2006). *Creating & recognizing quality rubrics.* Portland, OR: Educational Testing Service.

Arter, J., & McTighe, J. (2001). *Scoring rubrics in the classroom: Using performance criteria for assessing and improving student performance.* Thousand Oaks, CA: Corwin.

Au, K., & Kawakami, A. (1994). Cultural congruence in instruction. In E. Hollins, J. King, & W. Hayman (Eds.), *Teaching diverse populations: Formulating a knowledge base* (pp. 5–23). Albany, NY: State University of New York Press.

Baer, J. (1993–1994). Why you shouldn't trust creativity tests. *Educational Leadership, 51*(4), 80–83.

Baker, C. (1996). *Foundations of bilingual education and bilingualism* (2nd ed.). Philadelphia: Multilingual Matters.

Beane, J. A. (1992). The middle school: The natural home of integrated curriculum. *Educational Leadership, 95,* 9–13.

Beard, C. A. (1934). *A charter for the social studies.* New York: Scribner's.

Bednarz, S. W., Bettis, N. C., Boehm, R. G., DeSousa, A. R., Downs, R. M., Marran, J. F., et al. (1994). *Geography for life: National geography standards.* Washington, DC: National Geographic Research & Exploration.

Bentley, J. (1990). *Harriet Tubman.* Danbury, CT: Franklin Watts.

Berman, S., & La Farge, P. (Eds.). (1993). *Promising practices in teaching social responsibility.* Albany, NY: State University of New York Press.

Beyer, B. K. (1988). *Developing a thinking skills program.* Boston: Allyn & Bacon.

Bigge, M. L., & Shermis, S. S. (1999). *Learning theories for teachers.* New York: Longman.

Blumenfeld, P., Krajick, J., Marx, R., & Soloway, E. (1994). Lessons learned: How collaboration helped middle grade science teachers learn project-based instruction. *Elementary School Journal, 94*(5), 539–551.

Bower, B., Lodbell, J., & Owens, S. (2006). *TCI brings learning alive!* Palo Alto, CA: Teachers' Curriculum Institute. Retrieved from http://www.teachtci.com/

Branson, M. S. (2001, February 5). Making the case for civic education: Educating young people for responsible citizenship. Manhattan Beach, CA: Conference for Professional Development for Program Trainers. Retrieved from http://www.civiced.org/articles_mb2001.html

Bruner, J. (1960). *The process of education.* Cambridge, MA: Harvard University Press.

Carin, A. A., & Bass, J. E. (2001). *Methods for teaching science as inquiry* (9th ed.). Upper Saddle River, NJ: Merrill/Prentice-Hall.

Center for Civic Education. (1994). *National standards for civics and government.* Calabasas, CA: Author.

Chapin, J. R., & Messick, R. G. (1999). *Elementary social studies: A practical guide* (4th ed.). New York: Longman.

Checkly, K. (2006). Social studies jockeys for position in a narrowing curriculum. *Education Update, 45*(5), 1–2, 8.

Cheney, L. V. (1987). *American memory: A report on the humanities in the nation's public schools.* Washington, DC: National Endowment for the Humanities.

Cheney, L. V. (1997, Nov. 11). "Fuzzy math"?: Once again, basic skills fall prey to a fad. *New York Times,* p. A15.

Cherry, L. (1990). *The great kapok tree: a tale of the Amazon rain forest.* San Diego: Harcourt Brace Jovanovich.

Clark, C., & Peterson, P. (1986). Teachers' thought processes. In M. Wittrock (Ed.), *Handbook of research on teaching,* (3rd ed., pp. 255–296). Upper Saddle River, NJ: Merrill/Prentice Hall.

Collins, E., & Chandler, S. (1993). Beyond art as product: Using artistic perspective to understand classroom life. *Theory into Practice, 32*(4), 199–203.

Commager, H. S. (1965). *The nature and study of history.* Upper Saddle River, NJ: Merrill/Prentice Hall.

Cornbleth, C. (2002). What constrains meaningful social studies teaching? *Social Education, 66*(3), 186–190.

Cummins, J. (1981). The role of primary language development in promoting educational success for language minority students. In California State Department of Education (Ed.), *Schooling and language minority students: A theoretical framework* (p. 12). Los Angeles: California State University, Los Angeles Evaluation & Assessment Center.

DePaola, T. (1983). *The legend of the bluebonnet: An old tale of Texas.* New York: Putnam.

Dewey, J. (1910). *How we think.* Boston: D.C. Heath.

Doyle, W. (1986). Classroom organization and management. In M. Wittrock (Ed.), *Handbook of research on teaching* (3rd ed., pp. 392–431). Upper Saddle River, NJ: Merrill/Prentice Hall.

Drake, F. N., & Nelson, L. R. (2005). *Engagement in teaching history: Theory and practices for middle school and secondary teachers.* Upper Saddle River, NJ: Merrill/Prentice Hall.

Dunn, R., & Dunn, K. (1972). *Practical approaches to individualizing instruction.* New York: Parker.

Dynneson, T. L., & Gross, R. E. (1999). *Designing effective instruction for secondary social studies* (2nd ed.). Upper Saddle River, NJ: Merrill/Prentice Hall.

Echevarria, J., & Graves, A. (2003). *Sheltered content instruction: Teaching English-language learners with diverse abilities* (2nd ed.). Boston: Allyn & Bacon.

Edwards, C. H. (2005). *Teaching and learning in middle and secondary schools.* Upper Saddle River, NJ: Merrill/Prentice-Hall.

Eisner, E. (1991). Art, music, and literature within social studies. In J. Shaver (Ed.), *Handbook of research on social studies teaching and learning* (pp. 551–558). Upper Saddle River, NJ: Merrill/ Prentice Hall.

Elkind, D. (1981a). Child development and the social science curriculum of the elementary school. *Social Education, 45,* 435–437.

Elkind, D. (1981b). *Children and adolescents: Interpretive essays on Jean Piaget* (3rd ed.). New York: Oxford University Press.

Erikson, E. H. (1982). *The life cycle completed: A review.* New York: Norton.

Federal Reserve Bank of Minneapolis. (1998). *Economic literacy survey.* Minneapolis, MN: Author. Retrieved from http://minneapolisfed.org/ pubs/region/98-12/survey.html

Foxfire Fund. (2002). The Foxfire approach to teaching & learning. Retrieved from http://www.foxfire.org/teachi.htm

Freeman, D., & Freeman, Y. (2001). *Between worlds: Access to second language acquisition* (2nd ed.). Portsmouth, NH: Heinemann.

Freiberg, H. J., & Driscoll, A. (2000). *Universal teaching strategies* (3rd ed.). Boston: Allyn & Bacon.

Garcia, E. (2002). *Student cultural diversity: Understanding and meeting the challenge* (3rd ed.). Boston: Houghton Mifflin.

Gardner, H. (1991). *The unschooled mind.* New York: Basic Books.

Gardner, H. (1993). *Frames of mind: The theory of multiple intelligences* (10th anniversary ed.). New York: Basic Books.

Geiger, E. (n.d.). *Service learning toolbox: Work pages and checklists to help you get started and keep you going.* Portland, OR: Northwest Regional Educational Laboratory.

Gerwin, D., & Zevin, J. (2003). *Teaching U.S. history as mystery.* Portsmouth, NH: Heinemann.

Goble, P. (1978). *The girl who loved wild horses.* New York: Bradbury.

Good, T. L., & Brophy, J. E. (2003). *Looking in classrooms* (9th ed.). Boston: Allyn & Bacon.

Grace, C. (1992). *The portfolio and its use: Developmentally appropriate assessment of young children.* Urbana, IL: ERIC Clearinghouse on Elementary and Early Childhood Education. (ERIC Document Reproduction Service No. Ed 351 150)

Greenspan, A. (2005). The importance of financial education today. *Social Education, 69*(2), 64–66.

Gronlund, N. E., & Linn, R. L. (1990). *Measurement and evaluation in teaching* (6th ed.). Upper Saddle River, NJ: Merrill/Prentice Hall.

Guillaume, A. (2000). *Classroom teaching: A primer for new professionals.* Upper Saddle River, NJ: Merrill/Prentice Hall.

Guskey, T. R., & Bailey, J. M. (2001). *Developing grading and reporting systems for student learning.* Thousand Oaks, CA: Corwin.

Halliday, M. A. K. (1973). *Explorations in the functions of language.* London: Edward Arnold.

Herman, J. L. (1997). *Large-scale assessment in support of school reform: Lessons in the search for alternative measures.* CSE Technical Report 446. Los Angeles: University of California, Los Angeles, Center for the Study of Evaluation.

Hirsch, E. D., Jr. (1987). *Cultural literacy: What every American needs to know.* Boston: Houghton Mifflin.

History–social science framework for California public schools: Kindergarten through grade twelve. (1997). Sacramento, CA: California State Department of Education.

Hunt, I. (1966). *Across five Aprils.* New York: Tempo.

Hunter, M. (1976). *Prescription for improved teaching.* El Segundo, CA: TIP Publications.

Kashatus, W. (2002). *Past, present and personal.* Portsmouth, NH: Heinemann.

Kellough, R. D. (2003). *A resource guide for teaching K–12* (4th ed.). Upper Saddle River, NJ: Merrill/Prentice Hall.

King, M., Fagan, B., Bratt, T., & Baer, R. (1992). Social studies instruction. In P. Richard-Amato & M. Snow (Eds.), *The multicultural classroom* (pp. 287–299). White Plains, NY: Longman.

Lasley, T. J., Matczynski, T. J., & Rowley, J. (2002). *Instructional models: Strategies for teaching in a diverse society* (2nd ed.). Belmont, CA: Wadsworth.

Leming, J. S. (1989). The two cultures of social studies education. *Social Education, 53*(6), 404–408.

Lipman, M. (1988). Critical thinking—What can it be? *Educational Leadership, 46*(1), 38–39.

Lutkus, A. D., Weiss, A. R., Campbell, J. R., Mazzeo, J., & Lazar, S. (1999). *The NAEP 1998 civics report card for the nation.* Washington, DC: U.S. Department of Education, Office of Educational Research and Improvement, National Center for Education Statistics.

Marker, G. (1992). Integrating science-technology-society into social studies education. *Theory into Practice, 31*(1), 20–26.

Martorella, P. H., Beal, C. M., & Bolick, C. M. (2005). *Teaching social studies in middle and secondary schools* (4th ed). Upper Saddle River, NJ: Merrill/Prentice Hall.

Marzano, R. (1992). *A different kind of classroom: Teaching with dimensions of learning.* Alexandria, VA: Association for Supervision & Curriculum Development.

McGuire, M. E. (2005). *The Oregon trail.* Fort Atkinson, WI: Highsmith.

McMillan, J. (2001). *Essential assessment concepts for teachers and administrators.* Thousand Oaks, CA: Corwin.

McTighe, J., & Lyman, F. T., Jr. (1988). Cueing thinking in the classroom: The promise of theory-imbedded tools. *Educational Leadership, 45*(7), 18–24.

Miles, M. (1971). *Annie and the old one.* Boston: Little, Brown.

Mohan, B. (1986). *Language and content.* Reading, MA: Addison-Wesley.

Moore, K. (2001). *Classroom teaching skills* (5th ed.), New York: McGraw-Hill.

Morton, J. S. (2005). The interdependence of economic and personal finance education. *Social Education, 69*(2), 66–69.

National Center for History in the Schools. (1996). *National standards for history.* Los Angeles, CA: Author.

National Commission on Civic Renewal. (1999). *A nation of spectators: How civic disengagement weakens America and what we can do about it.* Washington, DC: Author.

National Commission on Excellence in Education. (1983). *A nation at risk: The imperative for educational reform.* Washington, DC: U.S. Department of Education.

National Council for the Social Studies Board of Directors. (2000). Service learning: An essential component of citizenship education. *Social Education, 65*(4), 240–241.

National Council for the Social Studies Task Force on Curriculum Standards for the Social Studies. (1994). *Expectations of excellence: Curriculum standards for social studies: Bulletin 89.* Washington, DC: National Council for the Social Studies.

National Council for the Social Studies Task Force on Scope and Sequence. (1989). In search of a scope and sequence for social studies: Report of the National Council for Social Studies Task Force on Scope and Sequence. *Social Education, 53*(6), 376–385.

National Council on Economics Education. (1996). *Voluntary national content standards in economics.* New York: Author.

National Council on Economics Education. (1999). *Standards in economics survey.* New York: Author.

National Education Association. (1911). *Address and proceedings.* Washington, DC: Author.

National Service-Learning Clearinghouse. (2005). Service learning is . . . Retrieved from http://www.servicelearning.org

Nelson, C., & Harper, V. (2006). A pedagogy of difficulty: Preparing teachers to understand and integrate complexity in teaching and learning. *Teacher Education Quarterly, 33*(2), 7–21.

North Central Regional Educational Laboratory. (2005). 21st century skills: Global awareness. Retrieved from http://www.ncrel.org/engauge/skills/global.htm

Norton, D. (2003). *Through the eyes of a child: An introduction to children's literature* (6th ed.). Upper Saddle River, NJ: Merrill/Prentice Hall.

Norton, D. (2004). *The effective teaching of language arts* (6th ed.). Upper Saddle River, NJ: Merrill/Prentice Hall.

O'Dell, S. (1977). *Carlota.* New York: Dell.

Passe, J. (2002). Like it or not: Social educators must keep up with popular culture. *Social Education, 66*(3), 234.

Peregoy, S. F., & Boyle, O. F. (1997). *Reading, writing, and learning in ESL.* New York: Longman.

Perkins, D. (1993–1994). Thinking-centered learning. *Educational Leadership, 51*(4), 84–85.

Popham, W. J. (2001). *The truth about testing.* Alexandria, VA: Association for Supervision & Curriculum Development.

Powell, R. R., McLaughlin, H. J., Savage, T. V., & Zehm, S. (2001). *Classroom management: Perspectives on the social curriculum.* Upper Saddle River, NJ: Merrill/Prentice Hall.

Public Law 107-110. (2002, January 8). No Child Left Behind Act of 2001. *Statutes at Large* (115 Stat. 1425).

Quigley, C. (2003). What needs to be done to ensure a proper civic education? First Annual Congressional Congress on Civic Education, Washington, DC: United States Senate. Retrieved from http://www.civiced.org/articles.php

Ravitch, D. (1985). *The schools we deserve.* New York: Basic Books.

Reeves, D. B. (2004). *Accountability for learning: How teachers and school leaders can take charge.* Alexandria, VA: Association for Supervision & Curriculum Development.

Renzulli, J. (1978). What makes giftedness: Re-examining a definition. *Phi Delta Kappan, 60*(3), 180–184, 261.

Reyes, M., & Molner, L. (1991). Instructional strategies for second-language learners in the content areas. *Journal of Reading, 35*(2), 96–103.

Risinger, C. F. (1992). *Current directions in social studies.* Boston: Houghton Mifflin.

Risinger, C. F. (2002). Two different worlds: The dilemma facing social studies teachers. *Social Education, 66*(3), 231–233.

Risinger, C. F. (2003). Encouraging students to participate in the political process. *Social Education, 67*(6), 338–339.

Roberts, P. L., & Kellough, R. D. (Eds.). (2007). *A guide for developing interdisciplinary thematic units* (3rd ed.). Upper Saddle River, NJ: Merrill/Prentice Hall.

Rosenshine, B. (1983). Teaching functions in instructional programs. *Elementary School Journal, 83*(4), 335–352.

Rosenshine, B. (1986). Synthesis of research on direct instruction. *Educational Leadership, 43*, 60–69.

Ruggiero, V. R. (1988). *Thinking across the curriculum.* New York: Harper & Row.

Sanders, W. (2001). *Measurement and analysis to facilitate academic growth of student populations.* Presentation to American Association for Colleges of Teacher Education, Dallas, TX.

Savage, M. K., & Savage, T. V. (1993). Children's literature in middle school social studies. *The Social Studies, 84*(1), 32–36.

Savage, M. K., & Savage, T. V. (1996, Fall). Achieving multicultural goals through children's nonfiction. *Journal of Educational Issues of Language Minority Students, 17*, 25–37.

Savage, T. V. (1999). *Teaching self-control through management and discipline.* Boston: Allyn & Bacon.

Savage, T. V. (2003). Assessment and quality social studies. *The Social Studies, 94*(5), 201–206.

Savage, T. V., & Armstrong, D. G. (1992). Were things really so cheap in the "good old days"? *The Social Studies, 83*(4), 155–159.

Savage, T. V., Savage, M. K., & Armstrong, D. G. (2006). *Teaching in the secondary school* (6th ed.). Upper Saddle River, NJ: Merrill/Prentice Hall.

Scheid, K. (1993). *Helping students become strategic learners*. Cambridge, MA: Brookline.

Schmidley, A. D. (2001). *Profile of the foreign-born population of the United States: 2000*. U.S. Census Bureau, Current Population Reports, Series P23–206, Washington, DC: U.S. Government Printing Office.

Seefeldt, C. (2005). *Social studies for the preschool/primary child* (7th ed.). Upper Saddle River, NJ: Merrill/Prentice Hall.

Selby, D. E., Pike, G., Myteberi, F., Llambiri, S., Dautaj, A., Gjokutaj, M., & Rexha, B. (2000). *Global education: Preparation of children to face up to the challenges of the 21st century*. Tirana, Albania: UNICEF.

Selwyn, D. (1995). *Arts and humanities in the social studies, Bulletin 90*. Washington, DC: National Council for the Social Studies.

Shanahan, T., Robinson, B., & Schneider, M. (1995). Integrating curriculum: Avoiding some of the pitfalls of thematic units. *Reading Teacher, 48,* 718–719.

Shanks, T. (1998). *The reflection model*. Santa Clara, CA: Bannan Institute, Santa Clara University.

Short, P. (1994). The challenge of social studies for limited-English-proficient students. *Social Education, 58*(1), 36–38.

Slabbert, J. A. (1994). Creativity revisited in education: Reflection in aid of progression. *Journal of Creative Behavior, 28*(1), 60–69.

Slavin, R. E. (1980). *Using student team learning*. Baltimore: Johns Hopkins University, Center for Social Organization of the Schools, Johns Hopkins Team Learning Project.

Smith, J., Smith L., & De Lisi, R. (2001). *Natural classroom assessment: Designing seamless instruction and assessment*. Thousand Oaks, CA: Corwin.

Sousa, D. A. (2001). *How the brain learns* (2nd ed.). Thousand Oaks, CA: Corwin.

Spady, W. G. (1994). Choosing outcomes of significance. *Educational Leadership, 51*(6), 18–22.

Steinbrink, J. E., & Bliss, D. (1988). Using political cartoons to teach thinking skills. *The Social Studies, 79,* 217–220.

Stiggins, R. J. (2005). *Student-involved assessment for learning* (4th ed.). Upper Saddle River, NJ: Merrill/Prentice Hall.

Suchman, J. R. (1962). *The elementary school training program in scientific inquiry*. Report to the U.S. Office of Education, Title VII, Project 216. Urbana, IL: University of Illinois Press.

Taba, H. (1962). *Curriculum development: Theory and practice*. New York: Harcourt, Brace & World.

Tanner, D. E. (2001). *Assessing academic achievement*. Boston: Allyn & Bacon.

Terrell, T (1981). The natural approach in bilingual education. In California State Department of Education (Ed.), *Schooling and language minority students: A theoretical framework* (pp. 117–146). Los Angeles: California State University, Los Angeles Evaluation & Assessment Center.

Tompkins, G. (2006). *Literacy for the 21st century: A balanced approach* (4th ed.). Upper Saddle River, NJ: Merrill/Prentice Hall.

Tompkins, G., & Hoskisson, K. (1991). *Language arts: Content and teaching strategies*. Upper Saddle River, NJ: Merrill/Prentice Hall.

U.S. Bureau of Education. (1916). *Report of the committee on social studies*. Washington, DC: U.S. Government Printing Office.

U.S. Code (annotated). Vol. 10401-12700, Title 42, Section 12511, Chapter 23 (1995).

U.S. Department of Education. (2000). *Twenty-second annual report to Congress on the implementation of the Individuals with Disabilities Act*. Washington, DC: U.S. Government Printing Office.

Vaught, S., Bos, C., & Schumm, J. (2003). *Teaching exceptional, diverse, and at-risk students in the general education classroom*. Boston: Allyn & Bacon.

Wade, R. C. (2000). Community service learning in the social studies. In R. C. Wade (Ed.), *Building bridges: Connecting classroom and community through service-learning in the social studies* (Bulletin 97). Washington, DC: National Council of Social Studies.

WEEA Equity Resource Center. (2000). Equity facts. Retrieved from http://www.edc.org/WomensEquity

Wentworth, D. R., & Schug, M. C. (1994). How to use an economic mystery in your history course. *Social Education, 58*(1), 10–12.

Wiggins, G., & McTighe, J. (1998). *Understanding by design.* Alexandria, VA: Association for Supervision & Curriculum Development.

Winebrenner, S., & Berger, S. (1994). Providing curriculum alternatives to motivate gifted students. *ERIC EC Digest 524.* Alexandria, VA: ERIC Clearinghouse on Disabilities & Gifted Children.

Wink, J. (1997). *Critical pedagogy: Notes for the real world.* New York: Longman.

Woolfolk, A. (2004). *Educational psychology* (9th ed.). Boston: Allyn & Bacon.

INDEX